Self-Determination

Self-Determination

THE OTHER PATH FOR
NATIVE AMERICANS

EDITED BY

Terry L. Anderson,
Bruce L. Benson, and
Thomas E. Flanagan

STANFORD UNIVERSITY PRESS
STANFORD, CALIFORNIA
2006

Stanford University Press
Stanford, California

Printed in the United States of America
on acid-free, archival-quality paper

Library of Congress Cataloging-in-Publication Data

Self-determination : the other path for Native Americans / edited by Terry L. Anderson,
    Bruce L. Benson, and Thomas E. Flanagan.
        p.   cm.
    Includes bibliographical references and index.
    ISBN-13: 978-0-8047-5441-5 (cloth : alk. paper)
    1. Indians of North America—Economic conditions.   2. Indians of North
America—Land tenure.   3. Indian business enterprises—North America.   4. Land
tenure—Government policy—North America.   5. Right of property—North America.
6. Self-determination, National—North America.   I. Anderson, Terry Lee, 1946–
II. Benson, Bruce L. (Bruce Lowell), 1949–   III. Flanagan, Thomas, 1944–

E98.E2S45 2006
333.2–dc22   2006006595

Typeset by TechBooks, New Delhi, in 11/14 Adobe Garamond.

Contents

Tables, Figures, and Maps

TABLES

FIGURES

MAPS

Foreword

In many ways, this book has been inspired by the work of Hernando de Soto. In *The Other Path* (1989) and *The Mystery of Capital* (2000), he showed the importance of individual property rights in the Third World. The absence of well-defined and enforceable rights to land not only jeopardizes the security of ordinary people in their homes, farms, and businesses, but it also deprives them of investment capital by which they could improve their lives.

Similar observations can be made about the native people of North America. Their reserve lands and reservations are encumbered with a complicated variety of collective and suboptimal individual property rights that often get in the way of productivity and investment. Their efforts at entrepreneurship have to run a gauntlet of administrative and regulatory authorities. And, perhaps worst of all, their rich history of entrepreneurship has been revised to fit a view that individual property rights are alien to Native American heritage, rather than an essential part of it.

This book tries to illuminate "the other path" that Native Americans could take—the path of self-determination, individual ownership, investment in human and physical capital, and competitive achievement in the market economy. The authors in this collection argue that self-determination and sovereignty, essential as they are, will be fruitless if they only mean the transfer of political control from Washington and Ottawa to band and tribal authorities without limits on the sovereign. Self-determination must become economic as well as political.

The chapters are, more or less, ordered according to their chronological coverage of Native American property rights and sovereignty. Chapters One and Two debunk the myth that property rights were inimical to prereservation Indian economies. Chapters Two, Three, and Four emphasize the importance of customary property rights for modern policy. Chapter Five introduces the issue of sovereignty to the mix, and Chapter Six provides empirical estimates of the importance of property rights, the rule of law, and sovereignty to economic performance on US reservations. Chapter Seven brings the focus squarely onto sovereignty and discusses the "paradox" that sovereign powers create for reservation governments. Chapter Eight shows how sovereignty plays a major role in the success or failure of gaming and how other sovereigns, especially states, compete for gaming profits. Chapter Nine provides a case-study of a Canadian tribe that has achieved real self-determination and used its sovereign status to promote diversified economic progress. Finally, Chapter Ten summarizes and draws implications regarding property rights and sovereignty for modern tribal policy.

We are honored to have Nobel Laureate Douglass North write the introduction to this volume. Without his pioneering work in institutional economics, our application of the property rights theory to the problems of Native Americans would scarcely have been possible.

As the editors of this volume, we owe a great deal to Michelle Johnson who kept us on track, communicated with the authors and the press, proofread better than we did, and yet all the while kept her good humor. Thanks Michelle!

We are also grateful to the Donner Canadian Foundation, which funded the research and production of this volume from the beginning. Its philanthropic efforts illustrate how fortunes created under a regime of individual property and economic freedom contribute to nonmaterial values of free inquiry and open discussion.

About the Contributors

Christopher Alcantara is a doctoral candidate in the Department of Political Science at the University of Toronto. He has published articles in the *Canadian Journal of Law and Society*, *Queens Law Journal*, *Alberta Law Review*, *Canadian Journal of Native Studies*, and *Journal of Canadian Studies*. His current project looks at the division of matrimonial real property on Canadian Indian Reserves. His Ph.D. dissertation seeks to explain why some aboriginal groups have been able to complete comprehensive land claim agreements with the Canadian government, and why some groups have not been able to complete such agreements.

Terry L. Anderson is the Executive Director of the Property and Environment Research Center (PERC); Senior Fellow at the Hoover Institution, Stanford University; and Professor Emeritus at Montana State University. His work helped launch the idea of "free market environmentalism" with the publication of his book, coauthored with Donald Leal, by that title. Anderson is the author or editor of thirty books, including the most recent, *The Not So Wild, Wild West*, coauthored with P. J. Hill. He has published widely in both professional journals and the popular press, including the *Wall Street Journal*, the *Christian Science Monitor*, and *Fly Fisherman*.

Bruce L. Benson is the DeVoe Moore Distinguished Research Professor in Economics at Florida State University. He has published over 110 academic journal articles, four books, and over forty book chapters on the economics of law and crime, property rights, public choice, and spatial pricing, including several focused on Native Americans. In recognition of this body of work, he was the recipient of the 2001 "Distinguished Scholar Award" given to a member of the Association of Private Enterprise Education "who has, over a sustained period of years, made a significant contribution to the research and literature of free market economics."

Ann M. Carlos is Professor of Economics at the University of Colorado at Boulder, Boulder, Colorado. She has published broadly in a number of areas. In addition to her work with Frank Lewis on Native American history and Canadian economic development, she is currently engaged in a NSF-funded project on the microfoundations of the development of early capital markets.

Thomas E. Flanagan is Professor of Political Science at the University of Calgary and a Fellow of the Royal Society of Canada. His books on aboriginal issues include *Louis 'David' Riel: 'Prophet of the New World'*; *Riel and the Rebellion: 1885 Reconsidered*; and *First Nations? Second Thoughts*. He managed the national campaign of the Conservative Party in the 2004 federal election and remains an adviser to Stephen Harper, the Leader of the Opposition in the Parliament of Canada.

Craig S. Galbraith is the GlaxoSmithKline faculty fellow in economic development, and Professor of Entrepreneurship and Technology Management at the Cameron School of Business, University of North Carolina Wilmington. He received his doctorate from Purdue University. His research interests include ethnic economies, developmental entrepreneurship, technology transfer within entrepreneurial enterprises, and developmental and technology history.

David D. Haddock has been Professor of Law and Economics at Northwestern University since 1989, and a Senior Fellow of PERC since 1997. He teaches law and economics in both the economics department and the law school, with special emphasis on the application of property rights economics to legal questions, which he has applied to environmental questions, and comparative industrial structures across nations, with particular emphasis on broadcast, transportation, automobile production, and professional sports. Haddock has published articles that apply economic tools to the study of several legal areas in addition to Indian law, such as antitrust, torts, corporations, family law, and extraordinary legal sanctions.

James L. Huffman is a graduate of Montana State University, the Fletcher School of Law and Diplomacy, and the University of Chicago Law School. He has been on the faculty of Lewis & Clark Law School since 1973 and has served as Dean since 1993. Huffman has written extensively on the subjects of natural resources, property rights, and constitutional law.

D. Bruce Johnsen is Professor of Law at George Mason University, a leading center for Law and Economics scholarship. He holds a B.A., an M.A., and a Ph.D., all in economics, from the University of Washington, as well as a J.D. from Emory University. His scholarship focuses on the economics of property rights, which allows him to address topics as diverse as antitrust, competitive federalism, principal-agent relations, Native American institutions, corporate finance and financial institutions, securities regulation, and business ethics. Johnsen has published widely in both peer-reviewed social science journals and law reviews and in the popular press.

Ronald N. Johnson received his Ph.D. in Economics from the University of Washington in 1977 and joined the faculty at the University of New Mexico as an Assistant Professor. He moved to Montana State University in 1981 and retired as full Professor in 2001. Throughout his academic career, Johnson's research has focused on natural resource and property rights issues, industrial organization, and political economy. His articles have appeared in the *American Economic Review, Journal of Political Economy, Review of Economics and Statistics, Journal of Law and Economics, Economic Inquiry,* and numerous other journals.

Frank D. Lewis is Professor of Economics at Queen's University in Kingston, Canada. He has published broadly in the area of Canadian economic development, but his research has also included the economic histories of the United States, Australia, and Israel. He and Ann Carlos have done wide-ranging work that includes railway financing, but most of their joint research have dealt with Native American History.

Robert J. Miller is an Associate Professor of Law at Lewis and Clark Law School in Portland, Oregon. He teaches Indian Law, Cultural Resources Protection, and Civil Procedure, and has taught Indian law courses since 1993. He also serves as a tribal judge for various Northwest tribes and is the Chief Justice of the Court of Appeals for the Confederated Tribes of the Grand Ronde Community of Oregon. He serves on the boards of the Oregon Native American Business & Entrepreneurial Network and the Tribal Leaders Forum; he has also served on the board of the National Indian Child Welfare Association for nine years, and is a past Chair and organizer of the Oregon

State Bar Indian Law Section. Miller has published numerous articles on Indian Law issues and has spoken at dozens of federal, state, and private conferences across the country. He is enrolled citizen for the Eastern Shawnee Tribe of Oklahoma.

Douglass North is the Spencer T. Olin Professor in Arts and Sciences at Washington University in St. Louis. In 1992, he became the first economic historian ever to win one of the economics profession's most prestigious honors, the John R. Commons Award, which was established by the International Honors Society in Economics in 1965. North is corecipient of the 1993 Nobel Memorial Prize in Economic Sciences and founder of Washington University's Center for New Institutional Social Sciences. His current research includes property rights, transaction costs, and economic organization in history, as well as economic development in developing countries.

Dominic P. Parker is a Senior Research Fellow with PERC and is also an NSF Fellow and Ph.D. student studying environmental economics and science at the University of California, Santa Barbara. In addition to studying economic development on American Indian reservations, Parker has written articles and directed seminars on the topics of private land conservation and the political economy of fish and wildlife management. Parker holds a M.S. in applied economics from Montana State University.

Carlos L. Rodriguez is on the faculty of the Cameron School of Business, University of North Carolina, Wilmington, where he teaches international management and strategy. His research interests are factors of firm performance and innovation diffusion in emerging economies, and ethnic and indigenous entrepreneurship.

Jacquelyn Thayer Scott O.C., Ph.D., LL.D. (Hons.) is Professor of Organizational Management and Public Administration at Cape Breton University (CBU), in Sydney, Nova Scotia, and Deputy Chair (Operating Head) of the Prime Minister's Advisory Council on Science & Technology for the Government of Canada. From 1993–2002, she was President and Vice-Chancellor of CBU (formerly known as the University College of Cape Breton). She has also served as Director of the School of Continuing Studies at the University of Toronto, been on the faculty at the University of Manitoba, operated her own public relations and management consulting firm, and has been employed as a journalist by the Canadian Press and the Columbian Newspapers.

Curt H. Stiles is a professor of corporate strategy and international management at the Cameron School of Business, University of North Carolina Wilmington. He received his Ph.D. from Northwestern University. Professor Stiles' research interests are structural determinants of business and entrepreneurial performance, business and enterprise history, and ethnic economies.

Self-Determination

Introduction

DOUGLASS C. NORTH

The history of Native Americans has been fundamentally colored by the perceptions—or the belief systems if you will—of the writers. This is true of all history, but is particularly so in this case. Whether written as a story of conquest, exploitation, paternalism, or greed, it deserves a better story—one that tries to comprehend the complex evolution of Native Americans from their lifestyles before the advent of European occupation, through the era of disruption that occurred in the conflict with the conquerors, to the reservation system and, finally, to the variety of efforts to confront the consequences of that system. It requires a far richer understanding of the complex nature of human cultures, and equally, of the fundamentals of economic and societal change than we have possessed.

The enormous variety of human cultures that has evolved has reflected the experiences of humans in different physical settings—experiences that crystallized into different understandings of the human condition. The beliefs that humans possess as a result are the essential determinants of the choices that humans make. Although economists have correctly understood

I

economics to be a theory of choice, they have neglected to understand the complex nature of the human mind and its intimate interplay with the environment that produces those choices.

Societal change is a consequence of demographic change, change in the stock of knowledge that underlies the human command over nature, and change in the institutional structure that is the underlying source of human interaction, and that therefore, defines the incentive structure of a society. Although a complete analysis would entail a theory of all three components and their interaction, no such integration exists; nor indeed, do we have complete theories of the individual components. However, in the past several decades we have made a great deal of progress on each of the components, and as a consequence, can tell a much better story than heretofore. The essays that follow do just that.

I wish to set the scene for what follows by putting the chapters in a historical context and highlighting some of the implications for a better comprehension of that overall history than we have had heretofore.

The interplay between human comprehension and the environment is most strikingly apparent when a fundamental change in the environment occurs. The introduction of the horse into the life of the plains Indians and, to a lesser degree, the introduction of the fur trade in the Hudson Bay area, were exogenous sources of change that induced alteration in many dimensions of the societies. The basic institutional structure responded to the consequent changes in relative prices. The alteration in property rights that resulted, however, can be properly understood only in the context of the overall structure of the affected societies. We need to take into account both the demographic and stock of knowledge interactions. We can then have a far richer story than we can get by a narrow focus on property rights changes alone.

Such a qualification in no way detracts from the major theme running through all the essays, which is that the institutional structure, and specifically property rights, are essential and fundamental determinants of economic and societal performance. In particular, the interplay between exogenously imposed rules and culturally derived tribal rules and norms has resulted in a fundamental but still incompletely understood aspect of societal performance. In the light of our still far-from-understood characterizations of economic development in third world countries, this is not a surprising finding, but it does illustrate the importance of this collection of essays that goes beyond its illuminating features of Native American history and contributes to a deeper comprehension of overall economic development issues.

One other feature of this collection of essays deserves special attention. Although property rights are a necessary condition for understanding performance, they are not a sufficient condition. They must be supplemented by leadership and investment in knowledge in order for Native Americans to escape the tragic consequences of the reservation system. The introduction of casinos has received much publicity and, in some instances, has dramatically increased tribal income. However, there are a number of other proposals put forward in the essays that offer more positive long-run prospects.

ONE

False Myths and Indigenous Entrepreneurial Strategies

CRAIG S. GALBRAITH, CARLOS L. RODRIGUEZ, AND CURT H. STILES

It is easy to find popular opinions regarding the historical context of Native American economics and trade. The *Encyclopedia of Native American Economic History*, for example, states that Indian culture was "fundamentally a set of collectivist social and economic systems" (Johansen 1999, p. xv). In the early 1960s, Stewart L. Udall, Secretary of the Interior under President Kennedy's administration, was fond of lecturing Americans that "the Indians were, in truth, the pioneer ecologists of this country" (Wilson 1992, para. 14). And Winona LaDuke, the Native American running mate in Ralph Nader's 1996 presidential bid, argued that the "concept of private land ownership was foreign to us. We have traditionally had collective landownership, with individual and family use rights" (LaDuke 1999, para. 4).

What are the common threads in these statements? First, they are historically inaccurate, and second, they are fundamentally misleading in describing the entrepreneurial potential of the indigenous cultures of North America. While tracing how these false myths became so ingrained in the modern perception of Native American culture is, in itself, an interesting exercise, in this chapter we argue that these beliefs have become so potent that they now influence the way modern researchers and policy makers treat economic behavior among indigenous populations.

Over the past decade, much has been spoken and written about the nature of indigenous economic development in both the popular and academic literatures. Within this context, indigenous entrepreneurial activities are often cited as the "second wave" of economic development, with the first wave of economic development being direct governmental support and wealth transfer policies (Stevens 2001). As entrepreneurial behavior plays an increasingly important role in the economic development of indigenous populations, business and management theorists are more carefully investigating the nature and theoretical foundations of indigenous entrepreneurship.[1]

Most, albeit not all, modern treatises on indigenous economic and entrepreneurial development assume, or at least argue, that there are several inherent characteristics of these native populations that make them unique and at odds with the European-based cultures that ultimately dominated the landscape. The most often cited characteristics suggest that indigenous populations are fundamentally more collective in their societal activities, they historically have a different sense of private property ownership, and their desire to enjoy economic development is essentially subordinated to a more "harmonious" relationship with nature.

The purpose of this chapter is to directly challenge these critical assumptions and argue that, in fact, many of these often cited economic characteristics are the result of an artificial nineteenth-century "collective" land tenure system and a twentieth-century "romantic" image. As such, we argue that these historical distortions are inconsistent with economic theory, and that they cloud not only our ability to properly understand the well-documented low incidence of self-employment and entrepreneurial activity among modern indigenous populations, but also our societal efforts to create the mechanisms capable of remedying this situation. It is our belief that once a more accurate historical context regarding indigenous economic and entrepreneurial behavior is understood, then policy makers, tribal leaders, and researchers can start formulating well-thought-out entrepreneurial strategies for a sustainable "second wave" of economic development.

Although our arguments focus on the historical economic culture of indigenous populations in the United States and, to a certain extent, Canada, similar challenges can be made for other indigenous communities, such as those in Brazil (Garfield 2001, 2004) that have also labored under forced land tenure and property right systems since the nineteenth century. We recognize that most of the world's indigenous populations, such as those in Mexico, South America, Asia, and Africa, have, at best, only weak land and property rights systems at the present time. And as de Soto (2000) argues, for these populations, new and better-designed property rights and land tenure systems certainly need to be created. We suggest that, in addition, these new property right regimes need to be free of the distortions introduced by the nineteenth-century legal anachronisms and false assumptions.

Property rights, in fact, are one of the most important instruments of societal and economic development. To Demsetz (1967, p. 347), they are mechanisms that assist people to "form those expectations which (they) can reasonably hold in their dealings with others." There is solid evidence relating efficient property rights systems with long-term economic growth.[2] When such systems are properly developed, they become capable not only of lowering the various costs of both organization and market transactions, but also of creating the right links between effort and reward—thus fueling value-added entrepreneurial activity. This evidence provides a robust basis for the main arguments of this chapter.

The next sections examine three commonly referenced "myths," and discuss them within the context of institutions and property rights. We then comment on the effects that these distorted views had on the creation of nineteenth-century land tenure systems and the implication of these static economic regimes for the development of entrepreneurial activity among the indigenous populations of North America.

THE ECONOMIC CONTEXT OF FALSE MYTHS

False Myth One: Indigenous Populations Historically had Either a "Different" or More Communal Sense of Property Ownership

One of the most commonly repeated false myths, often put into the context of landownership, is that indigenous populations historically did not view property as private, or that they shared communally the various factors of economic development (Mika 1995; Johansen 1999). There is little historical basis for this myth. Instead, there is ample historical and anthropological research to indicate that precolonial indigenous populations had a highly developed sense of individual private property, including that of land (Anderson 1995; Miller 2001; Bangs 2002), and that the forces for the cooperative collection or ownership of these rights were primarily economic, and not cultural, in nature.

In truth, many of the well-known early European settlements in North America were far more communal in nature than the surrounding precolonial indigenous settlements. For example, in 1620 the Mayflower pilgrims established the Plymouth colony in Massachusetts as a communist collective. The settlers immediately began to experience free rider problems and the colony declined. Using the surrounding indigenous people as a model for individual land rights and economic sustainability, Governor William Bradford finally privatized much of Plymouth's property, and the young colony subsequently prospered (Bethell 1998). Massachusetts land deeds from the 1620s and afterward clearly show that the local indigenous people not only understood and defined their individual-based land rights prior to and during their early contact with Europeans, but also that colonial courts consistently pursued policies intended to protect the property rights of these local individual Indians during land transactions (Wright 1906; Bangs 2002). As Bangs (2002, para. 13) notes: "Communal land ownership is a concept that cannot be derived from the documented information."

A similar philosophical difference occurred between the eighteenth-century Spanish Catholic missionaries and the local farming bands in the southwestern regions of the United States. Building upon the monastic notions of communal behavior and support, the early Franciscan and Dominican padres founded the missions in the Southwest under the ideal of a native-owned communal economy,[3] an economic system that proved somewhat at conflict with the local indigenous population's sense of private property and landownership rights (Margolin 1978). For various reasons, the missionary system broke down; and, after the 1834 secularization proclamation of Governor José Figueroa, half the property of the California missions was to be redistributed to the former mission Indians as individual private property, something that was never fully accomplished (Hudson 1901).

Even the free-range livestock grazing strategy of both the early eighteenth-century rancheros in Texas and the large pioneer nineteenth-century cattle ranchers of Wyoming and Oklahoma had at its foundation a broader communal notion of land and water rights. These rights were often seen as more family-specific and, on occasion, even individual-specific by local native horticulturists, who relied on irrigated croplands (Morriss 2001; Miller 2001).

From where does the myth of broad communal property ownership come? As with any pre-twentieth-century diversified culture, there was no standardized system of property rights among the local indigenous people. Instead, the key to appreciating the importance of property rights and ownership among indigenous North American communities is understanding the critical factors of production and economic activity for a particular tribe, how those factors of production and their related assets evolved over time, and how the economics of institutional and organizational frameworks used to organize, manage, and police property rights are tied to these productive and technological activities. Simply put, property right systems develop when assets are valuable and scarce, and societal gains from internalizing the potential externalities associated with the use of these assets are greater than costs of internalization (Demsetz 1967).

For the static farming-based tribes, landownership and related property rights were highly developed. Among the farming bands in southern California, a family member would gain private ownership over land by a classic homesteading process of required improvement for purposes of farming. This land could then be protected against trespassers and squatters, and it could also be sold, leased, and inherited. Included in these property rights were the instruments for land development such as plows (Shipek 1982, 1986, 1987). Less valuable land might be collectively managed for temporary grazing, with strong controls over any "free rider" problems. Similar systems were evident throughout California during precolonial times (Margolin 1978).

This finely tuned concept of individual or family landownership is repeated for almost every precolonial indigenous farming-based community, particularly those with significant population pressures and scarce arable land (Debo 1970). In fact, among almost all North American farming tribes, land was considered private and either individually or family owned as long as improvements were made and the land used (Copper 1949). Different tribes used different methods such as rocks or sticks to mark property boundaries, and the recording and transfer of these property rights differed from tribe to tribe, usually by a combination of written and oral traditions (Herskovits 1940).

Not surprisingly, in fishing-based communities, individual private ownership focused on fishing-related assets (Rogers and Taylor, 1981; McMillan
1999). Pacific Northwest Indians had well-defined salmon rights. Individuals and families even owned parts of lakes, inland seas, and rivers that had
valuable seafood deposits (Collings 1997). Among the Eastern James Bay
Cree, fishers had to obtain permission to access land "owned" by the tally-
man, or beaver boss (Collings 1997). The Lummi tribe of the northern Puget
Sound and southwestern British Columbia allowed individual property to
be inherited (Higgs 1982).

Similarly, once pelts became an important trade item, the fur-trapping
natives of Canada and the northern regions of the United States quickly
established small family ownership over prime trapping territories and beaver
houses,[4] and both inter- and intratribal trade of pelts became largely an
individual effort (Trigger 1978; Ewers 1997). Fur-trapping territories were
carefully marked and defended. The Inuit of northern Canada, in spite of
a stated generosity regarding the use of their lands, had definite concepts
about the territorial rights and limits of the tribe and band, as well as systems
of tenure and allocation within these groups (Usher 1992, p.46). In some
other cases, even passes for travel into another family's trapping and hunting
areas were privately owned (Oberg 1973), and punishment of trespassers was
strictly enforced (Speck 1915). Property rights were so well developed that a
starving native could legally kill a beaver to eat, but he had to leave the fur
and tail for the rightful owner (Leacock 1954).

In the more nomadic hunting and extortionist raiding tribes, the horse,
once acquired from the Spanish, gradually became the most valuable and
therefore, privately owned asset of an individual (Ewers 1969). Horses were
individually marked, and they were regularly sold, traded, or leased. A stolen
horse, if recovered in a retaliatory raid, would be returned to the original
owner (see also Roe 1955). Firearms, another important factor of production
for these tribes, were also valued, clearly marked, and individually owned.
Ownership of land, however, although important for farming tribes, was irrelevant as a factor of production for these nomadic tribes and thus culturally
and economically immaterial (Llewellyn and Hoebel, 1973).

Individual slave ownership and trade were also prevalent among precolonial indigenous tribes throughout North America, extending to the end of
the nineteenth century (Bailey 1966). By the early nineteenth century, for

example, intertribal slave markets, particularly in Canada, were well defined, with transaction prices indexed in terms of either blankets or copper plates (Herskovits 1940). Similarly, the plains Indians considered slaves and, in some cases, wives, as private property that could be bartered for horses and other commodities.

It is interesting to note that because certain valuable assets such as horses, firearms, wives, and slaves were more portable, and thus with individual property rights more easily monitored and enforced than with farming land, fishing areas, and fur-trapping regions, the recording of these rights among the nomadic tribes was naturally less sophisticated. There is also evidence that some types of privately owned, portable assets could be used as a primitive form of venture capital, where the returns would be shared between the asset owner and the entrepreneur.

Property rights also extended to other products of individual effort. Before the introduction of firearms, members of a buffalo hunt would mark their arrows, thus claiming ownership over a kill (Steward 1938). In early Cheyenne tribal law, a private property system was well established, covering a variety of different assets including productive activities and constituting a basic component of Cheyenne organization. Property rights over blankets, jewelry, pottery, and other manufactured trade items were strictly enforced (Llewellyn and Hoebel, 1973).

In addition, Native Americans extended property rights to whole classes of intangible assets such as songs, stories, body markings, and ceremonial rituals (Densmore 1939). These intangibles were also privately owned, inheritable, and could be sold in a manner that was often more sophisticated than in many contemporaneous European systems (Laird 1976; Greaves 1996).

We argue that property-related difficulties between Native Americans and immigrant Europeans in the seventeenth to nineteenth centuries were rarely caused by any cultural or philosophical differences regarding the fundamental notions of property rights and ownership. Instead, these issues and disagreements primarily arose when the local economies of Native Americans and Europeans differed in their productive activities and thus in their perceptions about the *types* of local assets and factors that were valuable and scarce and therefore subject to private ownership and legal trade.

However, when Native Americans and Europeans shared similar local economies such as small-plot farming, typically the two cultures had a clearly understood and agreed-upon set of mechanisms to support the contractual sale of the relevant asset such as cropland or water rights. For example, in their relations with the static farming-based Mahican Indians of the Northeast, the colonizing Europeans recognized the fee-simple rights of cropland ownership by the Mahican owner and always approached the lineage leader for purchase in order to start their own farms (Brasser 1974). This conclusion is repeated by many other researchers who have examined actual deed transactions in early colonial times (Wright 1906; Bangs 2002).

Several authors have suggested that because European and indigenous farming or hunting methods were historically different, it is inappropriate to apply European property theory to cultures with non-European economies (see Tully 1995; Bishop 1997). We argue that this position ignores the role technology plays in developing the factors of production and the group ownership over these factors among precolonial indigenous populations. It also ignores how organizational solutions to manage the resulting economic externalities are established. Thus, although extended family or clan owner-ship of farming and hunting tracts appeared, on the surface, common among some North American indigenous populations, we believe the true explana-tion is more an economically driven issue of cooperative strategies to access social capital while managing economic externalities, which has little to do with fundamental differences between the two cultures regarding property rights.

For example, in his analysis of precolonial Iroquois farming, Bishop (1997) acknowledges that clearing forests with fire and stone axes encouraged shared labor and group ownership. Or, to use our terminology, the more primitive technology used by the precolonial Iroquois demanded cooperative strate-gies to achieve some level of economic efficiency. However, due to a lack of an institutional framework to effectively organize these cooperative strate-gies among unrelated entities, the Iroquois, like the highland Scottish clans, had to access the social capital derived from related parties in the form of clans and families. Because of network complexity, however, social capital typically has substantial diminishing returns to scale or, in other words, the larger the radius of the network that is required to access social capital, the weaker the ties among its members. This naturally results in relatively small and fragile cooperative organizations that rapidly dissolve and are replaced as technology or demand/supply conditions change—as they did when the entrepreneurially inclined Iroquois adopted the European trapping, farming, and trade technologies. In these situations, weak property right regimes are easily abandoned and new ones quickly established as productive technologies become more efficient.

Thus, the issue is not a cultural difference between the European and indigenous views of property as proposed by Tully (1995) and Bishop (1997, 1999), but rather how different cultures solve the fundamental and difficult calculus between technology, factors of production, institutional frameworks, and social capital. Nor does this complicated calculus allow for ill-defined and broad culturally based definitions that suggest: "most or all of North America was private property (of Native Americans) at the time of (European) contact" (Bishop 1999, p. 43).[5]

False Myth Two: Indigenous Populations Historically had a More Collective Attitude Toward Economic Issues

Similar to the myth of property rights, historical evidence points to a virtual absence of broad collective involvement of early Native Americans in economic initiatives other than in community-organized trading events and in the enforcement of certain externalities such as overgrazing.[6] In fact, with the exception of piracy and raiding, which for obvious reasons, were more of a tribal band initiative, the vast majority of Native American business enterprises were either individual or family based and, in these aspects, did not differ from the vast majority of their contemporaneous European counterparts. The Kolchan of Alaska, for example, substituted family property rights for band ownership in trapping areas as soon as the fur trade became an important economic activity and source of wealth (Hosley 1981).

However, due to specific cultural and institutional characteristics of pre-colonial Native Americans, the problem of economic organization was never adequately solved; that is, the efficient mechanisms that make the costs of business transactions competitive were not fully developed. This prevented these populations from actually finding an ideal configuration of economic institutions and, without these, the engines that fuel economic and societal development—the entrepreneurial initiatives of individuals and economic units—are curtailed.[7]

The whole body of institutional economics literature[8] argues that the basis for economic institutions must be found in those enforceable formal and informal contractual systems that ultimately make the costs of transacting within organizations competitive with market transaction costs.

Nevertheless, a structured legal system sophisticated enough to allow efficient economic organization among nonrelated members (such as employees, owners, customers, suppliers, and financiers) is not easily developed. The problem becomes even more difficult as the tradable assets become less product- or region-specific (Galbraith and Kay, 1986; Kay 1997). Without the advantages offered by these tight structural and language-related institutional mechanisms, the boundaries of the economic organization will remain limited, ill-defined, and economically inefficient. Western civilization struggled with this concept for a long time, and it was not until the early seventeenth century, when the earliest settlers landed in Jamestown, Virginia, that a crude but workable construct of Royal Charters came into common practice.

In fact, while the foundations of contractual rights were broadly understood in the United States by the early nineteenth century, the European-based economic frontier in North America still lacked a completely systematic and standardized framework for recording and enforcing property rights. In some territories, each frontier town or county had its own system, and property rights were often poorly defined at best. English, Scottish, Scandinavian, French, and Spanish legal concepts were in direct competition throughout the nation. Not surprisingly, enforcement was often at the point of a gun or at the hands of a lynch mob. Thus, the bloody Johnston County war in Wyoming, the infamous lynching of the female cattle rustler, "Cattle Kate" and, perhaps even the gunfight at the OK corral, were not so much about right and wrong, but rather represented an evolutionary process of developing a uniform and enforceable system of economic values, commerce, and property rights during the nineteenth century (Morriss 2001).

Although the economic costs of complex European-based frontier business were relatively high by modern twenty-first century standards, the contemporaneous Native American family-oriented economic organization was at an even greater disadvantage regarding transaction costs. Native Americans, lacking a universal, systematic, and standardized contractual model to organize unrelated economic stakeholders, combined with the inherent transaction costs associated with nonuniformity of language[9] and an oral-based legal tradition, simply could not act collectively as economic units in sizes much larger than the family or subclan. In some tribes, the rights over physical property such as farmland and hunting areas were even defined by ownership of songs in which the words actually defined the parameters of the rights (Laird 1976). Although the songs and, therefore, the rights could be inherited or traded within a small tribal band, a broader-based commerce in these types of assets was almost impossible. By the late nineteenth century, as the European-based economic frontier consolidated into a more uniform legal and contractual system, Native American populations simply could not compete, no matter how entrepreneurially inclined some of their members were. In essence, although there were incentives for Native Americans to internalize many of their economic transactions, the organization costs of doing so were prohibitive. On a broad global level, this historical relationship between economic development and economic and legal institutions is empirically seen to be crucial, or as Acemoglu, Johnson, and Robinson (2001, p. 1369) conclude, "it is obvious that institutions matter."

It is also well recognized that communal property inevitably results in large economic externalities, most notably, the free rider problem. Among precolonial Native Americans, in instances where there appeared to be some type of collective tribal ownership of assets, it almost always involved ceremonial buildings (Oberg 1973), a type of asset where externalities can be easily managed. And even then, individual users would pay rent for using the collective structures, similar to the system in a modern community-owned recreation center or church building. In addition, ceremonies performed by *shamans* would be negotiated and paid for (Miller 2001).

War was also a collective effort, often with economic overtones. However, without efficient economies of organization, centralized control was relatively weak, as evidenced by the competition between multiple spiritual *shamans* and war chiefs, the generally disorganized line of battle, and the fact that many tribal members would act as free riders by electing not to participate, but still benefit from a victory (Mishkin 1940; Secoy 1953).

In some cases, collective seasonal trading markets, similar to the European medieval fair or the modern farmers' market, would be established where individual entrepreneurs would work within an agreed-upon location and time frame, oftentimes under the auspices of the local spiritual institutions. One of the often studied and largest precolonial trading markets that appeared to follow this model was Chaco Canyon in New Mexico. In general, however, and contrary to the "myth," until the reservation system was fully implemented in the late nineteenth century, business enterprise and economic activity among indigenous people of North America remained almost always at the individual or small family level of organization.

False Myth Three: Indigenous People Historically Practiced a Philosophy of Environmental Protectionism and Were Less Concerned About Productive, Innovative, or Entrepreneurial Activity

The myth that somehow indigenous people were more attuned to nature and less inclined to maximize their personal or tribal wealth is one of the most persistent and perplexing legends of the modern era, and one that has obtained almost religious proportions in modern times. The introduction of a popular Native American web site, for example, attempts to argue:

> ...the arriving Europeans seemed attuned to another world, and they appeared to be oblivious to the rhythms and spirit of nature. Nature to the Europeans—and the Indians detected this—was something of an obstacle, even an enemy. It was also a commodity: A forest was so many board feet of timber, a beaver colony so many pelts, a herd of buffalo so many robes and tongues.[10]

The economic history of precolonial indigenous people is actually far better described as a history of utilizing technology and innovation to maximize the yield from the land and other productive assets.[11] It is well documented that, throughout North America, indigenous cropland was cleared by classic cut-and-burn methods, rivers and streams were diverted and dammed for irrigation, and fishing tribes used fish wheels and other artificial devices to channel fish to shoal water for the catch (Netboy 1958). Hunting tribes burned forest undergrowth to facilitate game development and hunting access.

In Southern California, for example, where the precolonial population density was high and arable land scarce, successful agriculture inevitably involved irrigation of some sort. Carrico (1986, p. 9) argues that "Indian people . . . were actively controlling and enhancing their environment and were not the passive foragers often portrayed as 'Digger Indians'." And Margolin's (1978) apt description of the Central California bay area before the arrival of Europeans as "a deeply inhabited environment, [whose] landscape bore the cultural imprint of its people as surely as did the farmlands of Europe or New England"[12] could be equally applied to all precolonial North American people, particularly those with static population centers.

Native American people were also remarkable in their rapid adoption and consumption of modern technologies, a classic Schumpeterian requirement for successful entrepreneurship and economic development (Schumpeter 1934). The adoption of the French trap, the European gun, and the Spanish horse completely altered both the economic and institutional frameworks for many tribes (Harvey 1996). As a consequence, by the eighteenth century, some of the agricultural and gathering tribes of the Northeast started to aggressively compete with the French in the fur trade (Speck and Eisley, 1942; Leacock 1954; McManus 1972); and, by the nineteenth century, many of the seasonal gathering and herding tribes of the Great Plains evolved into the great horse-based hunting and raiding tribes (Foreman 1934; Holder 1970). However, as Anderson (1997b, p. 47) correctly points out:

> . . . (environmental) shaping doesn't have to mean despoiling. Whether this shaping encouraged conservation depended, for Indians as for humans every-where, on the incentives created by the extant system of property rights. The historical American Indians did not practice a sort of environmental com-munism in tune with the Earth; yesterday, as today, they recognized property rights.

Thus, when assets were considered valuable, private ownership rights became explicit and the precolonial indigenous people were careful to manage these assets, just as Europeans of the same time did. Under these circumstances, sophisticated environmental management techniques such as crop rotation and fishery releases were evident. In other words, the "externalities were internalized" (Demsetz 1967). For example, among subarctic tribes, Nelson (1973) documents extensively the efficient and responsible environmental management practices of the Kutchin under conditions of scarcity.

However, for assets that were perceived as plentiful and naturally replace-able or imitable, the behaviors of indigenous people were quite different and, in a sense, perfectly coherent with economic rationality principles. Evidence suggests that when assets such as buffalo and timber were considered plenti-ful and replaceable, indigenous people tended to aggressively and wastefully harvest them, possibly to extinction in some cases. Fur traders in the seven-teenth and eighteenth centuries recorded how Canadian tribes slaughtered large numbers of caribou and musk ox, eating only a few tongues and leaving the rest to rot (Hearne 1969). During the eighteenth and early nineteenth centuries, the hunting tribes of the American plains organized large buffalo hunts that forced hundreds of animals over steep cliffs, but then used only a small fraction of the meat and skin from the dead (Haines 1970; Anderson

1997a). In spite of modern myths, the indigenous people of North America never viewed buffalo herds as an asset to be maintained and renewed, and by 1840, these large-scale Native American hunts had driven buffalo from significant portions of its original habitat (Baden, Stroup, and Thurman 1980). Other game would be hunted using similar means; for example, desert jackrabbits were driven into nets, often with the majority of the carcasses left rotting and wasted (Downs 1966). The severity of this problem of hunting overkills was such that some wildlife biologists and anthropologists have attributed the extinction of several species in North America to overharvesting by early precolonial indigenous people (Martin and Klein, 1984).

The "overkill" mentality of nonscarce assets also contributed to a serious free rider problem among precolonial indigenous communities. Hunters were regularly accompanied by a poor class of beggars and scavengers hoping to benefit from surplus kill. After the adoption of the horse and firearm, hunts became less of a collective effort, with individuals who hunted claiming complete ownership of the kill. And with the advent of individual buffalo hunts, free rider problems among the indigenous settlements were reduced, as tribal free rider classes turned toward the neighboring European settlements for assistance in the form of charity,[13] petty theft, and engagement in more aggressive small gang activity such as raiding isolated and poorly defended European homesteads and small Native American and Mexican farming villages.

Even among the static farming and horticulturist tribes, if land was seen as plentiful, there was little or no crop management. The indigenous farmer would typically overfarm the land until nutrients were depleted, erosion became prevalent, and yields were reduced, then simply move on to another nearby site. Similarly to what was happening in many locations in Europe about the same time, timber in some areas of North America was also overharvested for fuel and building. One of the most probable explanations for the mysterious disappearance of the cliff-dwelling Anasazi of Colorado and New Mexico during the thirteenth century was the mismanagement of timber and agricultural resources in a time of climate changes (Lekson 2002).

Anderson (1997b) reports that this tradition of indigenous overkill continues into modern times on reservation land where tribal members are not restricted by state environmental laws regarding the number or size of animals that can be hunted. Many reports have been filed by wildlife experts that document massively destructive hunting by tribal members using ATVs, motorcycles, and semiautomatic rifles to the point where, on some reservations, sport game has all but disappeared.

This is not to suggest that indigenous people were more or less environmentally destructive than other cultures, only that they tended to be influenced by the same incentives of economic scarcity or abundance and by the same entrepreneurial desire to innovate and improve. But differences in the way economically important assets were owned and managed also impacted the basic societal and entrepreneurial fabric of these tribes. The horticulturists were governed by an extreme class stratification that was unshakably rigid and that drew all wealth upward into the hands of the upper class. Labor was sedentary, and warfare was low-status, avoided by the upper class and left for the commoners, and not a guaranteed route to success (Holder 1970).

In contrast, the nomadic hunters had a leadership system that rewarded individual initiative and provided substantial status mobility for those in the lower economic strata who were willing to be entrepreneurial. Wealth acquisition was encouraged, rewarded, and pursued with aggression. There were few territorial ties, and land tenure was loose with no tradition of viewing land as a capital asset. For these tribes, privately owned assets such as horses, guns, and slaves were more mobile, had lower transaction costs, and were favored as mechanisms of wealth accumulation (Foreman 1934). For example, in early Blackfoot society the adoption of the horse led to the emergence of distinct classes, with the entrepreneurial and innovatively successful class enjoying horses, brilliantly painted *tipis*, fine clothing richly adorned with bead embroidery or quillwork, multiple wives, ownership of medicine bundles, and greater participation in religious ceremonies. Yet Blackfoot society continued to promote reminders of "equal opportunity" in ceremonial events such as staged hunts (Ewers 1969). Holder (1970), in the conclusion of his comparative study of the two basic cultures, stated that the horticulturists did not adapt because there was no personal advantage for leaders of these tribes to introduce a nomadic lifestyle.

Source of the False Myths

It is quite clear that early historians and eyewitness chroniclers suggest that when assets were scarce and valuable, most, if not all, North American indigenous peoples had a strong belief in individual property rights and ownership. There are also indications that indigenous people had a vigorous entrepreneurial interest in maximizing the productivity of these assets, including land, through the use of available technology and societal innovation. Hodge (1910) notes that individual private ownership was "the norm" for North American tribes. Likewise, Steward (1938) asserts that among Native Americans, property held communally was limited. Similarly, Densmore (1939) concludes that the Makah tribe in the Pacific Northwest had property rights similar to Europeans. These early twentieth-century historians and anthropologists had the advantage of actually interviewing tribal members who had lived in prereservation Indian society.

By the late 1940s, however, these original and first-hand sources of information had died, and, in spite of the overwhelming historical evidence to the contrary and of their fundamental inconsistency with the economic theories of externalities, transaction costs, and property rights, these false myths and historical distortions began to take dominant shape. In particular, by the mid-1960s, the tone in many college history books, history-inspired films and novels, and even speeches within influential political circles had completely changed (Mika 1995). A typical historical distortion, for example, is found in Baldwin and Kelley's best-selling 1965 college textbook, *The Stream of American History*, where they write, "Indians had little comprehension of the value of money, the ownership of land . . . and so land sharks and grog sellers found it easy to mulct them of their property" (p. 208). These myths were further fueled by popular books such as Jacobs' (1972) *Dispossessing the American Indian*, which suggested that Native Americans felt that land (and other property) was "a gift from the gods" and as such not subject to private ownership. Not surprisingly, gradually more and more people started to honestly believe that the indigenous people of North America had been historically communal, nonproperty oriented, and romantic followers of an economic system more harmonious with nature.

Although the root causes behind this deviation from historical fact are, in and of themselves, both interesting to investigate and open to debate, it is also important to understand the meaning of this shift as it relates to the topic of modern indigenous entrepreneurship. As often seen in the popular press (Selden 2001), tribal leaders in both the United States and Canada often repeat these myths as facts when discussing business, economics, and entrepreneurship during tribal conferences and congressional hearings. Does this modernist deviation from history actually signal a fundamental change in modern Native American thought and culture, or does it simply originate from a series of misunderstandings and structural artifacts?

Anderson (1995) attributes the beginning of the myth to settlers who, when looking for farm land in the Great Plains, interacted only with the nomadic tribes that did not view land as an important asset. These settlers then mistakenly generalized the lack of interest in land assets among the nomadic tribes to infer a lack of property rights among all tribes. We argue that this fiction was further propagated in the nineteenth century by a virtual army of East Coast newspaper journalists, dime novelists, and Washington politicians, many of whom never ventured further than the cozy confines of a St. Louis hotel. Reported, retold, and unchallenged in the cities of the East Coast and in the congressional halls of Washington D.C., these incorrect perceptions of property rights and individual enterprise ended up as the basis for later laws and institutional codification. Considering that most of the contractual economic laws and property rights systems of Native American peoples were both oral and nonuniform, it was impossible at the time to accurately present a more truthful alternative to the "noble savage" stories of the East Coast newspapers.

However, although the well-documented two-way confusion regarding property rights and other cultural symbols between the local indigenous population and the European newcomers was perhaps the source of these legends (see Miller and Hamell, 1986), it is the nature of the land tenure system of the modern reservation that began to institutionalize and codify the legends, with dramatic consequences for indigenous entrepreneurship and the subsequent economic development of Native Americans.

INSTITUTIONALIZING THE MYTH: THE RESERVATION AND LAND TENURE SYSTEM

In the United States, the modern relationship between land tenure and the reservation system was formally established with the General Allotment Act of 1887, known as the Dawes Act, and later with the 1934 Indian Reorganization Act.[14] In effect, these governmental actions created two serious problems. First, they institutionalized a land tenure and property rights system that was fundamentally collective in nature, forcing a culturally alien legal system upon the indigenous populations that, in fact, carried a strong belief in individual property rights, were highly entrepreneurial and innovative, and had little experience or interest in collective organization. Second, making naught the Native American struggles to develop an economic organization efficient enough to compete with the neighboring nineteenth-century European settlers, the reservation system actually further increased the costs of transacting within that framework and then made it into law.

Congressional actions, as well as various other judicial decisions, created in US reservations a system of four types of land tenure: fee simple (privately owned land), individual trust, tribal trust, and federal trust. Modern reservation land tenures are, for the most part, a combination of individual and tribal trust land. Land that was used individually for a homestead or for subsistence farming was typically granted as personal property and constituted individual trust land. These assets could be improved, leased, or inherited among tribal family members. Tribal trust land, however, was considered tribal land for the common good and, as such, managed by the elected tribal council.

Although individual trust lands have some characteristics of privately owned property, they are nevertheless still within the Indian trust and the rules and regulations established by the various laws. As a result, there are substantial costs associated with the form in which this important asset is held, and these costs ultimately affect the nature of entrepreneurial behavior within the reservation system. Title, for example, cannot be transferred. Hence, while individual trust land can be mortgaged, it cannot be used as collateral and the income derived from the asset, rather than the asset itself, becomes the collateral for the loan. There are also jurisdictional issues associated with loan defaults or other claims on individual trust land, and successive generations of inheritance create situations of fractional ownership of property among distantly related tribal members, which may in turn prevent reaching consensus regarding the use of the asset as collateral.

Civil and tribal litigation over much of the individual trust land is another limitation. As an increasing number of cases related to individual property rights, inheritance, and divorce are filed these assets become virtually useless as forms of collateral. Finally, considering that much of the individual trust land was originally designated for small family farming, these properties are now considered suboptimal in size for modern agricultural development. These increased transaction costs inevitably lead to a greater cost of capital being associated with these assets, thus creating inherent inefficiencies in the system and rendering real estate, usually the most important source of capital for entrepreneurial initiatives, virtually inaccessible (de Soto 2000).

Implications for Indigenous Entrepreneurship

There is abundant research to suggest that access to and liquidity of individual and family specific capital are critical to entrepreneurial activity.[15] However, at least for the North American indigenous people, the potential for accumulating family or individual specific equity capital is severely limited by the modern reservation land tenure structure. As a result, much of reservation land sits underutilized as a capital resource for individual entrepreneurs. The increased cost of capital of individual land clearly inhibits individual initiatives and shifts the focus to tribal trust land, which, by definition, is a collective process of both ownership and decision making. As a result, the second, third, and fourth generation tribal members over the last century were driven to adopt a more collective perspective in property ownership. This happened because the existing land tenure system does not allow for individual entrepreneurial options, even if those options are more attuned with the traditional notions of private ownership, individual property rights, and the innovative application of technology to enhance individual capital that were common among precolonial native populations (Miller 2001).

Another largely ignored issue has been the continuous migration of the more entrepreneurially inclined tribal members off the reservation. It is well documented that much of the migration off North American reservations occurred during the 1940s to the 1970s when small-acreage farming became nonviable and the dramatic growth of urban cities created greater employment opportunities elsewhere. In their study of entrepreneurial spin-offs from casino gaming on US reservations, Galbraith and Stiles (2003) reported that many senior tribal members indicated that the more entrepreneurial indigenous individuals and families had moved off the reservations to start businesses in the cities, while those remaining on the reservations suffered from chronic poverty, alleviated only by a collective welfare system (Robbins 2000).

Regardless of the reasons, the fact remains that there has been a dramatic evolution in the past several decades to a more collective orientation among indigenous people in the United States. However, we believe that this trend has been driven by an institutional artifact of collective land tenure systems that is counter to both the historical context and culture of the indigenous communities. Within this framework, we believe that a modern theory of indigenous entrepreneurship must lie in a combination of examining both the institutional imperatives and the cultural orientation of modern indigenous people.

The above discussion of the mythical notions of historical Native American economic culture is not simply an academic challenge to a commonly cited stream of revisionist modern history, instead, it has a deep impact on our notion of indigenous entrepreneurship and its ability to affect the economic welfare of indigenous populations. Although much of the world's economic development has been at best uneven, resulting in disparate levels of development in various societies, economic historians have begun to uncover the fundamental engines of economic development. Most economists and developmental entrepreneurship researchers examining the historical roots of sustainable economic development agree that a continually improving system of property rights and institutional frameworks is critical to economic growth.[16]

De Soto (1989, 2000) has made the forceful argument that economic development requires the establishment of institutions that protect property rights and the creation of a sophisticated legal system that allows the efficient transfer and development of these rights, as well as the ability to extract full benefit from them. To de Soto, as well as to other notable economists, commonly cited values such as trust between market exchangers reside primarily in the descriptive knowledge obtained from a system of property rights and the codification of these rights of property and market exchange through the legal system. In his discussion of the economic problems confronting the poor of South America, for example, de Soto (2000) argues that the entrepreneurial initiatives of these groups are severely restricted by their inability to access the most basic and important source of capital, i.e., their land. Due to the institutional void of nonexistent deeds and property recordings, a weak civil and contractual legal system, and the corruption of the ruling classes, this land-based capital sits unused and unproductive.

The path to economic development of the North American native populations under the reservation system was set off in a direction opposite to the traditional values of these peoples. Development became dependent upon this artificial nineteenth-century collective codification that creates not only excessively high transaction costs, but also the historical myths that further the inability of indigenous North American populations to prosper in the larger, more efficient system of broader society. Rather than the "institutional voids" found in other parts of the world (Khanna and Palepu, 1997; de Soto 2000), for North American native populations, the entrepreneurial problem is grounded in the "frozen capital" of the reservation system, a land tenure arrangement that forces a collective ownership regime upon cultures that are historically noncollective, possess well-defined property rights and personal ownership of productive assets and, as such, are highly entrepreneurial. On top of this institutionalized cultural disharmony, the collective nineteenth-century reservation system creates legal barriers, which increase both organization and transaction costs relative to modern economic institutions, thus artificially altering the efficient boundaries of Native American enterprises.

Not surprisingly, individual entrepreneurial activity among tribal members has been an abysmal failure. Galbraith and Stiles (2003), for example, investigated gaming and nongaming Native American tribes in the southwestern United States and found mean average business startups for nongaming tribes of typically less than 0.15 per 100 adult tribal members (see Table 1.1),

Table 1.1. Business Births.

(A) Mean Annual Business Births per 100 Tribal Members, 1998–2001

	Southern California		Arizona	
	Gaming Tribes	Nongaming Tribes	Gaming Tribes	Nongaming Tribes[a]
	0.13	0.04	0.43	0.15

(B) Estimated Total Employment per 100 Tribal Members from Business Births, 2002

	Southern California		Arizona	
	Gaming Tribes	Nongaming Tribes	Gaming Tribes	Nongaming Tribes[a]
	0.95	0.16	2.97	NA

NOTE:
[a]The relatively large Tohono O'odham community of numerous Apache bands.
SOURCE: Data from interviews with nine Southern California tribal bands and four Arizona tribal bands.

a business birth rate significantly lower than most developed economies (about 0.37/ 100 adults in the United Kingdom and estimated over 1.00 in the United States) (Levie and Steele, 2000; Fraser of Allander Institute, 2001).

When examining employment from business startups, the picture is even bleaker. The vast majority of the tribal startups were microenterprises or hobby businesses, generating employment several levels below typical employment generated from business births in developed economies. This is particularly worrisome because research has indicated that a region's business birth rate is highly correlated with both job growth and economic development in that region (Ashcroft and Love, 1995).

These empirical results are completely consistent with our arguments. Due to the individual property right barriers created by the reservation system, nongaming-related entrepreneurial firms simply cannot access their individual or family specific capital, and thus need to compete at the low microlevel of entrepreneurial activity. However, gaming-related individual enterprises, which tend to be somewhat larger, are mostly protected monopolies providing inputs to a tribal-owned casino, and thus shielded from the higher organization and transactions costs associated with the reservation system.

CONCLUSION

This chapter discusses the theme of indigenous entrepreneurship by exploring the historical attitudes of Native Americans regarding property rights, collectivism, and the productive use of environmental and productive resources. Many commonly cited opinions and assumptions are, in fact, simply historical distortions or even outright myths. Indigenous people, like any population, are subject to the basic economic forces of externalities, scarcity, and transaction costs that ultimately ground notions of property rights, encourage entrepreneurial behavior and technological adoption, and define the boundaries of economic organization. Indigenous people were both highly entrepreneurial and acutely aware of the economic forces around them, but labored under a regime of high transaction costs associated with a nonuniform and nonstandardized system of laws, contracts, and language. These economic disadvantages were then institutionalized by a nineteenth-century collective land tenure system that was alien to the cultural, economic and entrepreneurial context of most indigenous tribes of North America.

Historical distortions have engendered the development of misdirected public policies that prevent indigenous populations from exploring the full potential of entrepreneurial initiatives to overcome the conditions of poverty, unemployment, and low economic growth. Indigenous populations and cultures are unique, however (Peredo et al. 2004). For them, or any cultural group for that matter, we argue that it is not only the codification of property and market rights that is important for economic and entrepreneurial development but also, in a broader sense, the codification of culture. This includes not only property and market rights, with emphasis on the right to organize into efficient institutions, but also the codification of art, music, literature, language, and intellectual know-how—those elements that we often use to define "culture." In addition, the rights emanating from this cultural codification framework must also be protected, understood, and allowed to exchange in a manner that reduces both market transaction costs and the internal costs of organizing.

In spite of the debacle of a forced collective land tenure system, within the last two decades several forces are at play that now create an opportunity, at least for some tribal communities, to engage in entrepreneurial activities that have the potential to contribute to their economic development. These opportunities have come under the form of: (a) government-sanctioned monopolies, such as casino gaming, which have created substantial income for some localized reservation economies, and (b) the environmental economies, particularly in the area of game hunting and fishing on reservations, which have resulted in large tracts of naturally preserved land, and (c) the sale of natural resources, such as minerals, timber, and oil that are best accessed and managed by large estate holdings. For tribes with access to these types of opportunities, the gains can be substantial.

Successful entrepreneurial behavior that maximizes value creation within tribal regions must also balance three competing forces: (a) the scale efficiencies inherent in the opportunities stemming from economies based upon environmental activities and natural resource management, and (b) the individual entrepreneurial need to access the "frozen capital" locked up in an anachronistic nineteenth-century collective land tenure system, and (c) the current social pressures and policies created by the historical distortions regarding indigenous attitudes toward property rights, collective economic organization, and the productive use of environmental resources. This is the challenge taken on by this volume.

NOTES

1. See, for example, Brosnan (1996); Vinje (1996); Anderson (2002); Galbraith and Stiles (2003); Frederick and Henry (2004); Anderson and Giberson (2004); Peredo et al. (2004).

2. See, for example, Keefer and Knack (1997); Acemoglu, Robinson, Johnson (2004); World Bank (2005).

3. Under the Spanish missionary system, the local Indians technically owned all assets, and the missionaries were to stay at one location for not more than ten years, then turn the mission land, building, livestock, and other productive assets over to the indigenous community. Although this was accomplished in several Latin American countries, the missionary system in North America was never fully developed to this point (Bolton 1917; Archibald 1978).

4. See Speck (1915); Speck and Eisley (1942); Lips (1947); Leacock (1954).

5. It is interesting to note that almost all of the treatises that argue for broad and ill-defined standards of precolonial Native American property rights (Bishop 1999) usually ignore the economic issues of abandonment, how property definitions and organizational boundary solutions rapidly changed with the entrepreneurial adoption of new productive technologies, the historical role of property appropriation and enslavement through the common intertribal warfare of precolonial Native American populations, and the implicit and explicit definitions of property in the earliest land deeds and property sales between Europeans and indigenous people.

6. See Herskovits (1940); Holder (1970); Shipek (1987); Salisbury (1996); Anderson (1997a, 1997b); Rubin (1999).

7. See Schumpeter (1934); Demsetz (1967); North (1990); de Soto (1989, 2000).

8. See, for example, Williamson (1975); Teece (1982); North (1990).

9. Between 300 and 500 distinct languages were spoken by North American indigenous people (Krauss 1998; Mithun 1999).

10. Quoted from http://www.nativeamericans.com, para. 4. Cited: September 9, 2004.

11. See Huffman (1992); Anderson (1995, 1997a); Anderson and McChesney (1994, 2003).

12. Cited in Wollenberg (2002), ch. 1, para. 4.

13. There is also some evidence that the nonlanded class of the indigenous populations comprised the majority of the Catholic mission converts in the southwestern United States, because the eighteenth-century Mission communal system offered work, food, and shelter for spiritual conversion, and that the land-owning class typically resisted the more communal system (Hudson 1901). For example, Jackson and

Castillo (1996) report a disproportionately high number of young males within the Mission system.

14. Canada followed a somewhat similar process of establishing a reservation system for its indigenous people during the nineteenth and twentieth centuries.

15. See, for example, Evans and Leighton (1989); Black, De Meza, and Jeffreys (1996); Bates (1997); Burke, FitzRoy, and Nolan (2000).

16. See, for example, De Alessi (1980); North (1990); Clague et al. (1997).

TWO

Property Rights and the Buffalo Economy of the Great Plains[1]

BRUCE L. BENSON

Despite a tremendous amount of anthropological, historical, and ecological evidence to the contrary, many policy advocates and a surprising number of academics apparently continue to believe that prior to European conquest, North Americans were environmental stewards who lived in peaceful communal societies characterized by common access property. Such views also appear to be widely held by the general public, including many Native Americans. The purpose of this chapter is to challenge these persistent myths because they continue to be raised as barriers to the kinds of policy reforms that can lead to dramatic improvements in the living standards of today's Native Americans.

The chapter does not simply rehash historical, anthropological, and ecological evidence regarding such myths; rather, it explains why this evidence actually makes sense in the context of the economic theory of property rights and illustrates why the selective evidence cited in support of the persistent myths is being misinterpreted. This theory predicts that property rights

evolve when the benefits of creating rights (the internalization of externalities due to conflicting claims over and uses of a resource) are expected to
exceed the costs (e.g., transaction costs of negotiating to voluntary solutions of a dispute over property, or the cost arising from the use or threat of
force to assert and/or protect claims). Specifically, this chapter demonstrates
that the economy of the preconquest Plains Indians, as well as much of
the interaction between individuals, bands, and tribes in the Plains region,
is explained by the drive to create property rights in buffalo (and inputs
to buffalo hunting such as horses and buffalo range), in the rich agricultural lands of the Plains river valleys, and in goods and resources that could
be traded for the products of or inputs to the hunt, the products of horticulture, or the inputs to or products of warfare (e.g., captives traded as
slaves).[2]

The focus on the buffalo economy of the Great Plains is chosen because the
persistence of beliefs about communal life and property, rather than a dominant belief in individual autonomy and a desire for private property, may
result in a generalization to other Native American cultures of widespread
misunderstandings about the nomadic equestrians of the Great Plains. After
all, a large fictional literature, along with movies and television, seems to
stress strong chiefs making decisions for the community as a whole regarding the use of the "tribe's" (rather than the individual's) resources. Although
much of this fictional literature also describes Plains Indians as extremely
warlike, relatively recent contributions depict them as peaceful unless they
were attacked by others (particularly whites), and as protecting the environment. In particular, they allegedly preserved the buffalo (e.g., by using
all parts of the bison they killed) at sustainable levels until white buffalo
hunters arrived to slaughter the herds.[3] As explained below, however, Plains
Indians were engaged in virtually continuous intertribal wars, well before
the arrival of European-American settlers and soldiers, in an effort to control
access to (create property rights in) resources such as buffalo and agricultural
land in the river valleys. Where they were successful, as in some of the river
valleys, private use rights were established, but where they were unable to
establish and maintain limits on the consumption of a resource, they chose
to consume rather than conserve. In particular, they dramatically reduced
the buffalo stocks long before the notorious white hide hunters entered the
picture.

However, the theoretical and historical analysis should not be seen as a criticism of Native Americans. If anything, it is a criticism of those who perpetuate myths about Native American history and culture in order to facilitate their pursuit of political objectives. The objective is not to criticize but to inform, by showing that Native Americans are like all other humans in that they respond to incentives and constraints within their institutional environment, and change those institutions when it is beneficial to do so. The second section offers specific examples of the kinds of myths propagated by some policy advocates and academics, while the third (and accompanying Appendix) provides a nontechnical overview of the economic theory of property rights. Key economic resources (land, buffalo, and later, horses) and activities (hunting, agriculture, trading, and warfare) on the Great Plains prior to imposition of the reservation system on Plains Indians are then discussed, followed by an explanation of the changing patterns in hunting, agriculture, trading, and warfare on the Plains during this prereservation period in the context of the economic theory of property rights.

PERSISTENT MYTHS

Prominent Standing Rock Sioux scholar and former executive director of the National Congress of American Indians, Vine Deloria, Jr. (1970, p. 175) maintains that Indians prefer a "tribal-communal way of life, devoid of economic competition." In addition, precontact/preconquest Native American societies allegedly did not recognize private property rights and would rather not do so today either: "While the rest of America is devoted to private property, Indians prefer to hold their lands in tribal estate, sharing the resources in common" (Deloria 1970, p. 170). Similarly, Bruce Johansen (1999, pp. xiv–xv) writes in *The Encyclopedia of Native American Economic History*, "Viewing economics from a native American perspective is in many ways a mirror image of the dominant capitalistic economy of our time.... After compiling several dozen tribal and national profiles, I began to notice that certain patterns were emerging, all of them related to the imposition of capitalism on what is fundamentally a set of collectivist social and economic systems." Outspoken advocate Ward Churchill (1996, p. 203; 2003, p. 150) also makes such arguments, describing the 1887 General Allotment Act as "a measure designed to destroy what was left of the basic indigenous socioeconomic cohesion by eradicating traditional systems of collective land holding." He goes on to contend that "the nature of the indigenist impulse is essentially socialist, insofar as socialism—or what Karl Marx described as 'primitive communism'—was and remains the primary mode of indigenous social organization in the Americas" (Churchill 1996, p. 514; 2003, p. 279). In another recent example, Mika (1995, p. 31) contends that there is a "distinctive social nature of the Native American tribe—a culture that has been historically nonproperty oriented . . . "[4] Even if the claims cited above were true and communal property rights did characterize many Native American economies, it would not follow that communal rights are the "preferred" arrangement of rights under any and all circumstances. Property rights must be specified and recognized either through agreement or as a result of force, and both processes can be quite costly, so the actual rights arrangements that exist at any point in time do not simply reflect preferences. They also reflect the costs and benefits of establishing and/or altering the rights structure, as emphasized below.

Property rights can be established through force, but in this context, Deloria (1970, p. 197) also contends: "it was much safer and more humane when Indians controlled the whole continent." Churchill (1996, p. 524; 2003, p. 286) similarly suggests that warfare among Native Americans was little more than a rough game as it was a:

> . . . more or less firm principle of indigenous warfare not to kill, the object being to demonstrate personal bravery, something that could be done only against a live opponent. . . . This is not to say that nobody ever died or was seriously injured in the fighting. They were, just as they are in full contact contemporary sports like football and boxing. Actually, these kinds of Euroamerican games are what I would take to be the closest modern parallels to traditional inter-Indian warfare. For Indians, it was a way of burning excess testosterone out of young males, and not much more.

Although some confrontations between Native Americans did involve the kinds of nonlethal demonstrations to which Churchill alludes (e.g., the taking of coups), this behavior does not generalize to all or even most intertribal warfare. As explained below, Plains warfare also involved massacres of entire communities, for instance, often through torture and mutilation.[5]

And once again, even if characterizations of Native American warfare such as Churchill's were completely accurate, it would not follow that this reflected the beliefs ("principles") of the indigenous population, because the approach to warfare is not just determined by preferences. The technology of warfare, and, therefore, the cost of alternative types of confrontations, as well as the expected benefits of warfare, should also determine warring practices.

Native Americans were also supposed to be the first environmentalists in the Americas, at least according to former Secretary of the Interior, Stewart Udall (Wilson 1992, p. 17). An important source of such contentions is the belief system attributed to Native Americans regarding the environment. Their concept of "mother earth" (Johansen 1999, pp. 167–69) presumably included a respect toward land and animals that prevented destructive overuse. In this context, Deloria (2004, p. 37) contends that "self-discipline became the cornerstone of Indian philosophy—what was enough, was enough," suggesting that Native Americans were stewards of nature, "attuned to their" environment (Deloria (1995, p. 57). Similarly, according to Churchill (1996, p. 464; 2003, p. 249), "Far from engendering some sense of 'natural' human dominion over other relations, the indigenous view virtually requires a human behavior geared to keeping humanity within nature, maintaining relational balance and integrity (often called 'harmony'), rather than attempting to harness and subordinate the universe." Historian Angie Debo (1970, p. 3) also writes: "While the white man sought to dominate and change the natural setting, the Indian subordinated himself to it."[6]

Although many Native Americans may have held religious beliefs or philosophies such as those suggested by these authors, the conclusion reached by many of them does not necessarily follow. As Bishop (1981, p. 55) notes, "Just as it is possible to practice conservation without 'respecting' game, so it is possible to respect animals and simultaneously and perhaps unawaredly hunt them into extinction if the motives and means for obtaining them are present." Again, behavior is a function of beliefs, but it also depends on incentives and constraints. Thus, as Brightman (1987, p. 125) notes, it is clear that some Native American communities did practice conservation while others did not. Indeed, "If hunters are unaware that animals can be managed, they may also be unaware that they can be hunted to depletion" (p. 132). Similarly, if hunters do not have the capacity to manage access and use, they may be unable to prevent depletion. And of course, management requires limitations on access.

It may well be that some and perhaps many precontact and preconquest Native Americans held some and even many of the beliefs attributed to them by Deloria, Churchill, Johansen, and others, but beliefs are not the sole determinants of behavior, as stressed above. Beyond that, a strong case can actually be made that the current view that precontact Native Americans held such beliefs is a result of arguments propagated by Europeans in order to justify the taking of land belonging to Indians. The idea that Native Americans did not develop property rights clearly was proposed by the European monarchs who claimed first discovery rights in order to justify the claims that kings were immediate owners of all colonized lands with the power to dispose of it as they saw fit (Egleston 1886, p. 4). Indeed, the European version of international law held that Indians only had a right to occupancy (Snow 1921, p. 25), and that they were incapable of alienating such land because they did not own it (Chandler 1945, p. 36). Naturally, colonial settlers who were given royal land grants readily accepted this perspective on native property rights. As a result, no land title examined in colonial courts (or early state courts) was ever considered to depend on any transfer of claims from Indians (Snow 1921, p. 121).

The depiction of preconquest Native Americans as environmentalists who preserved nature also has roots in the political validation process in support of taking land from Indians. By "constructing an image of the Indians as nomadic hunters who did not change the landscape," Europeans could claim: 1) Indians had no "natural right" to the land[7] because they had not mixed their labor with it; and 2) Europeans would put native-owned lands to higher valued uses, so from a utilitarian perspective, European occupation was justified (Wilson 1992, p. 17). The characterization of Native American socioeconomic relationships as socialist or communist was also promoted by the Indian policy reformers of the 1880s and their opponents, as: "Both were prone to use the word 'communism' in a loose sense to describe Indian enterprise" (Otis 1973, p. 11) in their political efforts to impose institutional changes on reservation populations (and in the process, make more Indian lands available to non-Indian settlers). Such politically motivated contentions probably continue to be propagated, at least in part because they provide rhetorical justifications for various socialist/communist and environmental ideologies and political actions by Indians and non-Indians alike.[8] They also serve as justification for widespread limitations on individual ownership of land on many reservations (i.e., so-called individual- and tribal-trust lands that are inalienable and under the oversight of the Bureau of Indian Affairs as trustee).

THE ECONOMIC THEORY OF PROPERTY RIGHTS

A lack of specified property rights to a resource (e.g., a buffalo herd) implies a right of access for everyone; and given the economic assumptions of rational behavior in pursuit of personal well being, each individual has incentives to use as much of the "common pool" resource as possible before other users consume it. Therefore, the commons becomes crowded (e.g., with hunters) and the resource (buffalo herd) is depleted as the result of overuse (Hardin 1968).

Rapid depletion of such a resource is not an inevitable outcome, however. As Demsetz (1967) emphasizes, property rights are defined when externalities become so significant that the benefits of internalization exceed the costs of property rights development.[9] Therefore, where a common pool actually persists, it implies that the cost of creating and/or enforcing property rights exceed the benefits. Johnson and Libecap (1982) point to three types of costs that can be relevant: 1) exclusion costs; 2) internal governance costs when exclusive right are shared by a group; and 3) imposition of punishment for violating an open-access constraint imposed by a strong coercive authority (e.g., the state). Costs of defining and enforcing property rights may be very high with a migratory species such as buffalo. High governance costs, the second point, are also relevant with migratory animals if the species travels across the territorial claims of groups that do not have close linkages and the low costs of cooperation that accompany such linkages. Transaction costs may also be high for many other reasons such as asymmetric information and lack of credibility in commitments. Exclusion costs and governance costs are key to understanding behavior among Indians on the Plains prior to their subjugation on reservations.

Property rights, whether individual or communal, require that ownership claims be recognized and respected by others. Such recognition can arise through the effective use of violence (e.g., deterrence or forceful expulsion) or through cooperation (e.g., negotiation resulting in an agreement to define boundaries and respect each other's claims). Umbeck (1981a) explains that the decision to negotiate or fight depends on the cost and benefits of the alternatives.[10] Where no one has a comparative advantage in violence and the costs of negotiation are low, individuals can agree to recognize a relatively equal initial distribution of exclusive property rights. Given the option of employing violence, however, an "agreement . . . must ration to each individual as much wealth as he could [expect to] have through the use of his own force" (Umbeck 1981a, p. 40).

Anderson and McChesney (1994) develop a "raid or trade" model to explain the trends in cooperation (trade, treaties) and conflict that characterize the history of Indian-white relations. Their model (developed more fully in the Appendix) also helps explain inter tribal relations on the Great Plains. In short, inter tribal relations depend on each tribe's perception of the marginal benefits of acquiring territory for hunting or agriculture and the marginal costs of defending territory. Given that the marginal benefits of acquiring incremental amounts of land decline as the marginal costs of defending that land rise, there are limits to the amount of land that any tribe will try to acquire or defend.

Anything that changes the marginal benefits or costs will disrupt the equilibrium and lead to more or less land acquisition or defense. For example, suppose that tribe A acquires horses, thus increasing the value of controlling additional buffalo lands and increasing the cost to tribe B of defending land it now controls. In this circumstance, tribe A will take some land from tribe B. Alternatively, suppose that tribe B becomes more efficient at horticulture thus increasing the benefits of acquiring more land for farming. In this case, tribe B will acquire land previously controlled by tribe A.

Whether the acquisition occurs by trading or raiding will depend on each tribe's perception of the expected costs and benefits associated with war and negotiation.[11] Therefore, a change in the pattern of intertribal relations (e.g., from nonconfrontational to violent or vice versa) and in property rights can occur if some change in technology (for the productive uses of the resource, for fighting or for negotiation), institutions (e.g., of governance), relative values (e.g., the trade value of a productive output), ecological conditions (e.g., sustained drought in some but not all areas), or degree of uncertainty occurs that changes at least one group's expected surplus from negotiation.

ECONOMIC RESOURCES AND ACTIVITY
ON THE GREAT PLAINS PRIOR TO
THE EURO-AMERICAN CONQUEST

The Great Plains are cut by a series of rivers draining from the western mountains to the east. These rivers cut down through the uplands creating wide alluvium-covered bottoms, and the resulting valleys constitute about seven percent of the land area in the region. Because this region is semiarid, "The river bottoms, in effect, form a completely different ecological zone from that of the surrounding Great Plains.... The river systems with their rich alluvium and constant water supply form wooded extensions of the central valley ecological zone which finger westward far out into the Plains proper" (Holder 1970, p. 3). Plains Indians adapted to the environment by developing horticultural activities in river valleys that were suitable for agriculture. Outside the river valleys, short grasses and mixed grasses dominated, as precipitation is insufficient to support trees or the tall grasses of the Iowa and Illinois prairies. These short grasses were ideally suited for bison, which Plains Indians hunted for thousands of years (Isenberg 2000, pp. 21–24). Hunting buffalo focused on the Plains during summer and fall seasons, and on the valleys and other areas with sheltered forage during the winter. Thus, access to land was valuable for two reasons: Indians practiced agriculture in the valleys and hunted buffalo on the plains (and in the valleys during the winter), either by doing both at different times of the year, or by specializing in one activity and trading and/or raiding for the products of the other.

Buffalo Hunting[12]

Recent ecologically based estimates suggest a maximum carrying capacity for the Plains of something less than 30 million head of bison (Flores 1991; Isenberg 2000, pp. 23–30). Despite such apparent abundance, however, bison populations periodically declined due to drought and other natural occurrences (Isenberg 2000, pp. 11–27). Furthermore, although there were large numbers of buffalo on the Plains, they were far from ubiquitous. As spring began, insects and the attraction of new grass moved bison from the sheltered river valleys, foothills, and parklands to the prairie. Calves were born between early March and late June in different parts of the Plains, depending upon climate conditions. The bison population tended to be widely dispersed during this period, in small and highly mobile herds. When the bison came into rut in midsummer, the mature bulls, which traveled alone or in small male-only herds for most of the year, joined the cows, forming a much smaller number of much larger herds. The bulls' activities, along with the biting insects, warm weather, and increasingly scant water and forage kept these large herds constantly moving. In late summer, herds gravitated toward increasingly scarce water in the foothills, parklands, and river valleys where forage also tended to be relatively plentiful. The timing of all such movements depended on weather conditions.

In addition, humans played an important role in bison movement and numbers.

> In the last 10,000 years, the Great Plains have never been without human influences; the very dominance of the bison . . . owed itself, in part, to the hunters who, at the end of the last Ice Age, helped to kill off giant herbivores and thereby opened a niche for the bison. . . . [And] To assume an unchanging harmonious relationship between Indians and the Great Plains environment classes both Indian culture and nature as static. (*Isenberg 2000, p. 12*)

Humans were in the Plains when it became grassland about 10,000 years ago but they "did not, and could not, live in timeless harmony with their surroundings and their neighbors. They repeatedly seized opportunities and overcame challenges presented by the environment and their human neighbors" (Binnema 2001, p. 54).

Mishkin (1940, p. 121) explains that "Buffalo provided the Plains Indians with virtually everything they needed: food; tepee skins, robes, and clothing; weapons, tools, utensils, and glue made from horns, bones, and hooves; bags and buckets made from beef paunches or the membranes around the heart; bowstrings made from buffalo gut. . . . The buffalo herds were the source of Plains Indians' independence and prosperity."

During the pedestrian period, hunting by individuals and families occurred during the winter and spring, but large-scale hunts in the summer and fall required several small groups to come together as "bands." Large numbers of participants, with an optimal size of between 100 and 300, depending on terrain and forage, were required because a herd had to be driven toward a natural trap or jump, and the buffalo could move much faster than humans on foot. Therefore, as the buffalo neared the trap or jump, people lined the route that the buffalo were to follow.[13] The Indians also frequently set grass fires to help drive and steer the animals toward the jump or trap. Large scale was also required to butcher the number of animals that were killed in a successful hunt and to preserve the meat. Bands dispersed when they were not engaged in drives.

Horses changed the way Plains Indians hunted. Large numbers of individuals were no longer required for drives because individual hunters could kill buffalo with relative ease: "The favorite method . . . was the band chase on horseback. . . . The [band chase] . . . was not dependent on special topographical features which were necessary for impounding the buffalo from cliffs" (Mishkin 1940, p. 21). A small group of hunters on fast horses rode upon running buffalo, selected animals to kill, and fired arrows into them until they went down. In addition, search costs fell as hunting communities did not have to wait for the buffalo to come into the relatively small area that they could cover on foot.[14] With horses, the distance that a whole camp roamed during the year increased from about 50 miles in the preequestrian period to over 500 miles, and the area around the camp that hunters and scouts explored also expanded dramatically. A small group of hunters could cover a hundred miles in a day or two. In fact, the horse made finding and hunting buffalo so much easier and more certain that new tribes (e.g., the Apache, Shoshoni, Comanche, Pawnee, Sioux, etc.) invaded the Plains as they obtained horses.

The lifestyle and well being of Plains Indians improved dramatically, as Mishkin (1940, p. 19) explains in his discussion of the Kiowa:

> The tempo of life was drastically accelerated, values completely revised. . . . Longer tepee poles and more skin covers could be carried which permitted the Indians to live in larger tepees. Preserved food could be transported in sizable quantities . . . to the previously impoverished . . . real wealth had been given in the shape of food surpluses, stores of buffalo robes, tepee covers and other objects of value which could for the first time be accumulated in quantities since it could be transported. More than that, the horse became the object of highest value in the culture. The horse industry involving the acquisition of horses, herding, training, lending, and trading became a major industry for the Kiowa.

Many other tribes enjoyed similar increases in their standard of living, and the potential to capture such wealth as equestrian buffalo hunters was what attracted invaders from every direction.

One individual could easily kill enough buffalo in a few minutes to supply his family for months, so Indians became much more selective in their hunts. For example, cows were much better to eat than bulls (Binnema 2001, p. 51), and cows with calf were particularly attractive in the spring because the fetus was a source of fat needed to prevent protein poisoning. Buffalo became so easy to hunt, at least during some periods of the year, that the Indians also began using the individual animals much less intensively. They often took only the choice cuts of meat, leaving the rest for the wolves, bears, and buzzards. So hunting evolved from relatively infrequent but mass nonselective kills by pedestrians to relatively frequent selective kills by equestrians, and from consuming as much of the buffalo as possible to consuming only selected parts of the buffalo.[15] Furthermore, entry of new equestrian bands meant: "Greater numbers of animals were slaughtered each year and more hunters were involved" (Holder 1970, p. 112). When Euro-Americans began trading for buffalo robes, Indians responded by killing even more buffalo, often taking only a small amount of very select cuts of meat, along with large numbers of robes for trading. Indeed, in contrast to many claims, increased hunting by Indians began to significantly reduce the size of buffalo herds long before white hide hunters arrived on the Plains (Isenberg 2000; Flores 1991). Because buffalo were migratory, it was difficult to establish even band or tribal property rights to them (although attempts were made, as explained below). The dramatic increase in mobility and hunting capacity that arose with the horse, along with the rapid growth in the Plains Indian population, both through invasion by previously non-Plains tribes and through better health,[16] in conjunction with the high cost of negotiations discussed below, intensified the common pool nature of buffalo resources. Intertribal warfare often resulted in restricted access to hunting territories, but within those territories, Indians were not able to limit hunting practices sufficiently in order to maintain herds at a sustainable level (in large part because of internal governance costs, as explained below). Before turning to these issues, however, consider agriculture, another important economic activity in the region.

River Valley Agriculture

Archeological evidence suggests that some horticulture was practiced in Plains' river valleys at least 1500 years ago, and substantial horticultural communities were in the Nebraska- and Kansas-river valleys around AD 1000 (Bamforth 1994, p. 102). These horticulturalists grew varieties of beans, squash, tobacco, and sunflowers, but corn tended to be the dominant crop.[17] At about the same time, horticultural villages were developed in the middle Missouri basin near the Knife and Heart rivers by Siouan language ancestors of the Mandan and Hidatsa. Agricultural land was divided into individualized family plots with private usufruct rights associated with each plot (Carlson 1992, p. 68).[18] Linton (1942, p. 50) explains that a family would live in the center of its fields (unless and until significant military threats existed, as discussed below), and other members of their community recognized their property rights to both the land that they worked on and to nearby land that they expected to cultivate later.

By the sixteenth century, scattered horticultural groups were combining so that "by the eighteenth century large, stable villages appeared. . . . The transition was essentially one leading from small, scattered clusters of farmsteads to large, compact, often fortified villages . . . throughout the area" (Holder 1970, p. 27). Many factors influenced this change, including growing threats from outside groups, as discussed below, and ultimately, acquisition of horses, which allowed horticulturalists to increase their hunting and agricultural production range from a village, as well as extending the potential for and range of trade. Individualized usufruct rights for families still held for the farming plots scattered around such villages, however.

The middle Missouri villages were at the agricultural margin for much of the period under consideration (Binnema 2001, p. 68).[19] These Indians, therefore, always devoted substantial time to buffalo hunting, maintaining clan and tribal claims to wide expanses of the uplands Plains for that purpose (Holder 1970, pp. 29–30).

Trade

Long before Europeans arrived, active trading relationships existed throughout most of North America.[20] Furthermore, after the arrival of the horse, nomads could focus on buffalo hunting (and raiding), in part because they could then trade surpluses from the hunt (and raid) for agricultural products. Indeed, as Steckel and Prince (2001, p. 292) explain, Plains Indians probably had the most nutritious diet in the world at the time, as they were the tallest population in the world. They note that this advantageous diet arose because the Indians were able to consume substantial amounts of protein from buffalo, but "less well known is the dietary diversity that provided vitamins, minerals, and other micronutrients. This rich diet was supplemented by an extensive network of trade in foodstuffs among tribes and by exploitation of extensive native plant resources" (Steckel and Prince 2001, p. 291). Thus, agriculture remained an attractive pursuit where conditions for growing crops were conducive, both to supplement the dietary requirements of the horticulturalists themselves and to trade with the nomadic hunters. In fact, horticulturalists, such as the Mandan and Hidatsa on the middle Missouri, developed market-like institutions for trading their produce for the produce of the hunting tribes. Annual gatherings including trade fairs were held in or near their villages, often in June or early July before the buffalo rut: "They were considerable affairs at which horses and products of the chase were exchanged for garden produce and European trade goods" (Holder 1970, p. 90–97). Thousands of members of different tribes attended these gatherings.[21]

Cooperation for Conflict

Voluntary exchange of goods was not the only form of intertribal cooperation. Large-scale war parties were also launched from the summer gatherings, often consisting of members of multiple bands and/or tribes. Beyond that, "Tribes survived, maintained their identity, and strengthened their own war effort by forming alliances with one or more neighboring tribes. The allied tribes had common enemies" (Ewers 1997, p. 175). In this regard, however, "The term 'alliance,' with its connotations of established protocol, permanence, and formality, inaccurately describes relationships on the ... plains. ... Terms such as 'coalition,' 'affiliation,' and 'association' better capture the essence of these relationships. ... They were expedient combinations in which distinct and autonomous groups worked toward specific aims, but which did not necessarily entail reciprocity" (Binnema 2001, p. 15).

In order to understand the changing patterns of warfare and coalitions, the myth of "Indian Nations" led by authoritarian "chiefs" must be addressed. A much more accurate picture is given, for instance, by Holder (1970, pp. 101–02), in discussing the Sioux, when he states that these groups "have been characterized as 'anarchistic' by some observers. ... There was no Sioux Nation, although Europeans tried assiduously to so characterize these groups. They were little better than loose aggregates of more or less closely related family groups." Similarly, Lowie (1954, p. 113), in writing about the Crow, notes that, although certain "titles" (i.e., "chiefs," given European translations) existed, they were "honorific and implied little authority for the bearer, though an exceptionally powerful personality could exert great influence."[22] These chiefs did not have the authority to order warriors into war or to accept peace. Rather, they attempted to persuade the parties to follow their lead (Lowie 1954, p. 113).[23] As a result, military coalitions were largely temporary spontaneous arrangements between individuals who were loosely linked by kinship and/or ethnic relationships.[24]

Coalitions could also be fragile as individual autonomy was very important within bands, and band autonomy was similarly important within tribes. As Holder (1970, p. 106) emphasizes, it is clear that "the individual [was] . . . supreme." In fact, if a warrior decided to raid a tribe that was on friendly terms with a chief, the chief did not consider himself to be responsible for the actions of his fellow band or tribe member. This means that negotiation costs for different groups of Indians tended to be very high, because no individual "chief" could credibly commit other members of his band or tribe to live up to any agreement.

Warfare

After observing intertribal relations on the Plains, Cox (1832, vol. 1, pp. 216–19; vol. 2, p. 133) emphasized: "The only cause assigned by the natives of whom I write, for their perpetual warfare, is their love of the buffalo." The objective of such warfare was a desire to create fear in enemies in hopes of expanding a band's or tribe's hunting territory and/or inducing others not to pursue buffalo into claimed territory (i.e., establish exclusive band or tribal property rights to territory and the buffalo in it, rather than common property for members of all tribes). If members of a group were capable of destroying their enemies or driving them from the area, they could control it, at least for a while. In fact, "the entire conception of 'territorial grounds' among the nomads of the Plains rests very much upon the claims of the stronger" (Roe 1955, p. 95). Such claims could be quite widely respected. For instance, Father Marquette, commenting on the Illinois about 1670, noted: "These people . . . dare not go and hunt wild cattle [buffalo], on account of their enemies" (Thwaites 1896–1901, vol. 59, p. 157). In general, however, the relatively small populations of most tribes, given the amount of hunting territory required for effective control of migratory buffalo, meant that claimed territories could not be fully occupied or even fully patrolled. As Steckel and Prince (2001, p. 288) report, the collective population of all the Plains tribes was "well under 100,000 at the beginning of the nineteenth century," so population density in the Plains was very low. Nonetheless, even if an enemy was not to be completely deprived of hunting opportunities in a claimed territory, military harassment could raise the costs of hunting in the contested buffalo range. Ewers (1997, p. 12) explains that "Plains Indian warfare most commonly was prosecuted by numerous small war parties. . . . Their purpose was not to destroy the enemy but to . . . harry them, keep them off balance and at a distance, and weaken them by stealing their horses." This "purpose" and approach reflect the scarcity of warriors relative to the large areas that tribal groups attempted to control, however. In fact, once horses populated the Plains, a focus of the vast majority of all raids was to capture horses.

Different reasons have been proposed to explain the horse-raiding focus. Grinnell (1923, vol. 2, p. 2) contends: "There were many brave and successful warriors of the Cheyenne . . . who on their war journeys tried to avoid coming into close contact with enemies, and had no wish to kill enemies. Such men went to war for the sole purpose of increasing their possessions by capturing horses; that is, they carried on war as a business—for profit." In contrast, Lowie (1927, p. 356) asked, "Why did a Crow risk his neck to cut loose a picketed horse in the midst of the hostile camp when he could easily have driven off a whole herd from the outskirts?" inferring that the reason was a desire for prestige rather than profit.[25] Mishkin (1940, p. 61, note 11) answers Lowie by citing Grinnell (1923, vol. 2, p. 15), however, and noting that "Undoubtedly, this was a more daring deed but at the same time a more profitable one" as the best horses were those picketed inside the camp. There is yet another factor to consider: an effective horse raid also reduced the ability of an enemy to hunt and fight. Because horses varied in quality and function, most (probably seventy-five percent) were used for transport, others were ridden by family members, and only a select few were "buffalo horses" fast enough to be used for the buffalo chase, military actions, and racing. A successful raid that captured buffalo horses, which were the horses picketed near their owners' teepees, significantly limited the enemy's ability to compete for buffalo, both through hunting and through warfare to control access.

Other characteristics of intertribal relations were also consistent with the objective of limiting access by other tribes to buffalo. For instance, "First hand accounts of intertribal actions repeatedly referred to mutilation of the dead or dying—the taking of arms as well as scalps as trophies, even the dismembering of the privates, and, particularly in Texas, cannibalism. . . . Make no mistake about it; the horrors of Indian warfare were not especially dreamed up for revenge on whites" (Ewers 1997, p. 14). Similarly, a successful surprise raid against an enemy camp or a battle between war parties of significantly different sizes often resulted in a massacre. Fear of such brutality clearly could deter potential rivals from venturing too close to a band or tribe's territorial claims. On the other hand, if a raid was discovered and the raiders confronted by similar numbers of armed defenders, large-scale casualties were rare (Smith 1938, p. 431). When two equally powerful groups or individuals faced off, the incentives were to "cooperate" (i.e., retreat) rather than fight. However, backing down could result in loss of prestige and earning capacity (see the discussion below regarding the correlation between prestige and wealth), so both sides tended to tacitly agree to the norms of warfare (e.g., counting coup rather than killing an enemy) when the risks of a violent confrontation were high for both sides. Many of these tactics were seen by whites as "cowardice" (stealth or retreat in the face of resistance—see Roe [1955, p. 225]), but they were quite sensible given the relatively small number of warriors a band or tribe had, and their focus on limiting access by others to the buffalo herds they wanted to control.

The plentiful bison herds of the region repeatedly attracted invaders from outside the Plains, particularly as new methods of hunting and/or warfare developed. Each change shifted the costs of fighting or negotiations or the benefits of controlling buffalo range, and led to new raid-or-trade decisions in the never-ending battle for exclusive property rights. Other resources were also valuable, as explained above. In particular, changes in agricultural productivity and in the technology of warfare also led to changes in the allocation of property rights to agricultural land.

THE DYNAMICS OF SHIFTING PROPERTY RIGHTS IN THE RAID-AND-TRADE ECONOMY OF THE GREAT PLAINS

Warfare on the Plains has a long history. Archaeological evidence suggests that in the late 1200s, Caddoan groups began moving up the Missouri into South Dakota, for instance, where they found themselves in conflict with the previously established Siouan horticulturalists. The agricultural communities in the middle Missouri changed in response. Scattered families began moving into villages, which gradually got larger and were fortified (Bamforth 1994, p. 104). These fortifications, created by both ethnic groups, consisted of ditches, often ten feet deep and twenty feet wide, as well as wooden palisade defensive works around all parts of the village, with bastions giving defenders an ability to set up a cross-fire against attackers. The villages also were typically located in relatively inaccessible sites on steep ridges overlooking the river. Despite such defenses, warfare persisted and apparently intensified as drier and colder conditions induced the Siouan villagers to move southward and attack Caddoan strongholds. At one site, Crow Creek, Siouan apparently mutilated and killed about 500 Caddoan villagers around 1325 (Binnema 2001, p. 68). Archeological evidence, including burned houses and palisades, and a ditch with the remains of a minimum of 486 bodies (evidence of up to another fifty skeletons also was present) suggests that the people were killed in a single massacre. About forty percent of the skulls have at least one and often several fractures, about twenty-five percent have broken teeth and gum lines, ninety percent show cut lines consistent with scalping, and evidence demonstrates that many of the bodies were cut and mutilated in various ways (missing body parts including hands, feet, and heads, slit noses and throats, etc.). As Bamforth concludes, "The demographic profile of the remains recovered from Crow Creek is consistent with that expected for the slaughter of an entire village, with the exception of an under representation of young women" presumably taken as captives (a finding that is consistent with other sites as well). The warfare waged between the Siouan ancestors of the Hidatsa/Mandan and the Caddoan ancestors of the Arikara over control of agricultural land was clearly fierce and deadly when conditions changed the marginal valuation of land for one of the tribal groups. After all, this warfare was over property rights to agricultural land, because "corn comprised from 78 to 90 percent of the total diet of the bodies found at Crow Creek, implying that horticulture was essential to their survival," and such battles occurred as the northernmost horticulturalists attempted to move "south, into areas which [because of climatic change were] more favorable for farming" (Bamforth 1994, p. 110).

Radiocarbon dating indicates that the Caddoan and Siouan villages "shifted back and forth somewhat between AD 1300 and 1500" (Bamforth 1994, p. 105), but the Caddoan eventually thwarted the Siouan efforts to move southward. As a result, the Siouan had to supplement their horticultural efforts with hunting and gathering, and with trade (Binnema 2001, p. 68). Thus, even these agricultural communities sought access to the buffalo. A series of environmental and technological changes also altered the relative value of access to buffalo and/or the relative cost of raiding. Although the entire history of Plains warfare over control of access to buffalo cannot be told, a few examples will be provided to illustrate the results of changes in the costs and benefits of fighting and negotiating.[26]

The Apache Expansion

Because the horse spread slowly, it gave some Indian groups significant comparative advantages over their neighbors in both hunting and warfare, at least for a while. The Apache who occupied the extreme southwestern Plains in the seventeenth century were apparently among the first to obtain horses, along with the Pueblos, and soon after, the Utes who were located west of the Rocky Mountains (Secoy 1953, p. 6).[27] Once they had horses, the Apache developed a new military technique and invaded the plains to their north and east.

Emulating the Spanish, mounted Apache protected themselves and their horses from enemy arrows using tanned layers (about six) of buffalo leather as "armor" (Secoy 1953, p. 14). They also obtained iron from the Spanish to tip arrows and lances. Spanish-style saddles were required for using lances to prevent the rider from being unseated from the shock of impact with an enemy foot soldier (Secoy 1953, p. 61). As a result, Secoy (1953, p. 23) explains:

> In the early phase of Apache expansion the impact of armored horse men upon unarmored footmen was apparently nearly as devastatingly effective as the Spanish cavalry of Coronado and De Soto had been. Thus, the Apache were able to expand eastward into central Texas, central and western Oklahoma, Kansas, and western Nebraska, as well as to occupy all of eastern New Mexico and Colorado. In the process of displacing their enemies from desirable lands the Apache discovered an additional motive for war. This was the taking of captives for sale to the Spaniards.

The Apache advanced north along the east side of the Rockies because this area was "excellent open buffalo country" and only sparsely populated by people who could easily be eliminated or captured for sale as slaves. As they gained control of sections of the southern Plains, individuals claimed family sized agricultural plots in the river valleys of eastern New Mexico and Colorado, and western Nebraska, Kansas, and Oklahoma, and adopted a mixed horticulture and hunting lifestyle. From the spring through August, they practiced individualized sedentary agriculture, while nomadic buffalo hunting was pursued in the fall and winter. "This new combination of maize, buffalo, and the horse furnished a basis for the subsistence of an enlarged population. . . . This increase, in turn, stimulated a drive toward expansion" (Secoy 1953, p. 8). As the Apache moved beyond the High Plains, however, to the northeast and southeast, they came into conflict with relatively dense populations of Caddoan. These sedentary horticulturalists (and seasonal pedestrian buffalo hunters) occupied river valleys, and were organized for military purposes into loosely united confederations that slowed the Apache advance because they had relatively large numbers of warriors compared to the Plains bands that the Apache had easily overrun. Furthermore, by 1690 the Caddoan of eastern Oklahoma were using horses for war and hunting. They also equipped themselves with the riding gear and armor that the Apache used. Although they had fewer horses and less metal for arrowheads and lances than the Apache, they had more warriors. Thus, these tribes (e.g., the Pawnee) were able to halt the Apache advance to the east. Apache dominance of the southern High Plains was not threatened, however, until they were attacked from the north.

Shoshoni and Comanche Invasions

The Numic-speaking peoples (e.g., Utes, Comanche, Shoshoni) were, at one time, restricted to the southwestern Great Basin, but by around 1500 they had occupied the northern limits of the Basin and the margins of the northwestern Plains. By 1600, these Numic-language groups were linked from the southern Rockies to the upper Yellowstone. When the southernmost Numic bands (Utes) acquired horses, this extensive territorial linkage quickly became a horse-trading network, allowing the Shoshoni to be the first bands with territory extending into the northwestern Plains to have horses. The Shoshoni on both sides of the Rockies were mounted hunters by 1700. Although the upper Snake River region and the Columbia Basin west of the Rockies supported large herds of bison when it was occupied by these Numic bands, those herds quickly disappeared with the onslaught of equestrian hunters (Binnema 2001, p. 52; Butler 1978, pp. 106–12; Secoy 1953, p. 33). As Secoy (1953, p. 33) explains:

> Shoshoneans then, like the Apache, apparently expanded explosively in all favorable directions . . . for buffalo hunters. Hence, the Shoshoneans probably first advanced directly eastward onto the High Plains through the gap in the Rocky Mountains at South Pass in southwestern Wyoming. From this point on the Plains Shoshonean groups appear to have radiated out to the south, east, and north.

The Comanche, one of the Numic (Shoshonean) groups, moved south when they entered the High Plains, passing "through excellent buffalo territory, toward the source of horses in New Mexico," while other Shoshoni moved in other directions "driving out or exterminating the then inhabitants" (Secoy 1953, p. 33).

The Comanche (and Shoshonean, in general) employed Apache-like cavalry tactics, so they met little effective resistance as they moved southward along the eastern front of the Rockies until they confronted the Apache. Unlike the Apache, however, the Comanche adopted a year-round nomadic buffalo-hunting lifestyle. This meant: "The sedentary spring and summer phase of Apache life proved to be a great military liability when they were pitted against a foe always on the move" (Secoy 1953, p. 31). The Comanche attacked the isolated Apache rancherias one at a time, using overwhelming force and surprise. The Apache attempted to retaliate by gathering forces from various bands but they were generally unable to find the Comanche who were constantly and erratically moving to avoid detection. Thus, during the first quarter of the eighteenth century, the Comanche were able to sweep the Apache from the northern parts of the territory they had so recently occupied. They were in control of a large land area extending well into Texas before the middle of that century.

Note some of the implications of this Comanche success for the institutions and economy of the Plains. Indians such as the Apache, who developed a mix of hunting and agriculture, may have had an advantage in generating a sustainable healthy diet, but that required them to be sedentary for part of the year, making them vulnerable to attack by pure nomadic hunters. That is, although the benefits of claiming individualized property rights in plots of agricultural land were high, the Comanche tactics made the cost of doing so much higher. Therefore, survival on the Plains required that Indians either adopt nomadic buffalo hunting, à la the Comanche, or move into large fortified villages. Thus, at least some who adopted a nomadic existence did not necessarily do so because "Indians prefer to hold their lands in tribal estate, sharing the resources in common," as Deloria (1970, p. 170) contends. Many may have preferred the Apache practice of horticultural production on privatized agricultural property (as evidenced by such practices in most of North America), while hunting for only part of the year, but they had little choice if agricultural land was not sufficiently concentrated to support a large fortified village. The Apache were unable to defend their claims to dispersed agricultural lands, so they died or were forced to abandon them. Where geographically concentrated productive land was available (e.g., for the Mandan, Hidatsa, as well as for some of the Pawnee, Omaha, Arikara, Osage, Wichita, and other Caddoan), however, fortified villages were able to survive and even prosper by practicing horticulture on privately held parcels of land and trading with various nomadic tribes. After all, nomads specialized in hunting (and raiding), and in order to obtain sufficient variety in their diets for a healthy existence, they had to obtain agricultural produce (Steckel and Prince, 2001). Some gathering of berries, nuts, roots, and other foods was practiced, but generally not enough to survive on. They either had to raid or trade to obtain such goods. Nomads did both.

There was another valuable commodity for trading that could be obtained through raiding: captives to sell as slaves. Consider the Shoshoni who moved east and north rather than south. Horses allowed formation of larger war parties than their enemies. Their supply of horses came, in part, from the same Numic-speaking trading network that originally channeled horses up the west side of the Rockies. The Shoshoni also developed trade relations with the Comanche on the east side of the mountains, who served as middlemen, trading horses and metal obtained from the Spanish for war captives. These captives were sold as slaves to the Spanish, and many were transported to the Caribbean Islands. Thus, the Shoshoni "raided for captives continuously and on a large scale, in order to exchange them for goods and horses in the south" (Secoy 1953, p. 38).

The Shoshoni domination of and advancement into the northern Plains continued for about a generation (1735 to 1765). By the 1730s, they had accumulated enough horses to trade with members of other tribes that they chose to cooperate with. The Shoshoni remained on relatively good terms with the Crow, for instance, in part because they valued the Crows' trade contacts with the horticultural Hidatsa on the Missouri. The Crow could trade horses from the Shoshoni for agricultural produce and for European goods that reached the Hidatsa through the developing fur trade network, so the Hidatsa also valued the Shoshoni-Crow trade connection (Binnema 2001, p. 92). The Shoshoni and Crow (who were also friendly with the Flathead and Kutenai who had invaded the western margins of the northern Plains) clashed with the Blackfeet, Sarsi, and Gros Ventre in the north, as well as with Mandan and Arikara on the Missouri and the Apache in western Nebraska and northeastern Colorado. Although they dominated the northwestern Plains well into the eighteenth century, they "simply did not have a large enough population to occupy or even patrol the territory they dominated. Their rivals continued to hunt in a broad contested zone, although always at the risk of Shoshoni attack, especially during the summers, when small pedestrian hunting parties were no match for the large, mobile mounted war parties" (Binnema 2001, p. 92).

The Blackfeet, Sarsi, and Gros Ventre also suffered incursions into the northern Plains by the Cree and Assiniboine from the northeast. However, the Shoshoni were so strong and aggressive that a loose coalition of these five tribes formed for defense against this common enemy. After all, the Shoshoni had many more horses than any of these northern tribes, so the incentives for members of all five tribes was to raid the Shoshoni in pursuit of horses rather than raiding each other (Secoy 1953, p. 47). Furthermore, the Shoshoni attacked the five tribes indiscriminately in their effort to take captives that they could trade southward, and "This reinforced the polarization of all surrounding tribes toward the Snake [Shoshoni] as the enemy. Since the hostility of this functionally defined group of tribes was focused on the Snake, the opportunities that existed for intertribal aggression were ignored" (Secoy 1953, p. 41). The Blackfeet coalition could not be destroyed, and they (particularly, the Blackfeet and Gros Ventre) continually made forays against the Shoshoni. They began to obtain horses through such raiding, and through trading. They probably traded with the Flathead (Ewers 1968, pp. 12–13), although perhaps some Shoshoni also traded with Piegan bands of the Blackfeet during periods of relatively peaceful relationships (Binnema 2001, p. 211, note 26). Indeed, Piegans were probably the first of the Blackfeet bands to have a substantial supply of horses sometime in the 1730s, and they spread to the Blood and Siksika bands, as well as the Gros Ventre soon thereafter. The Cree and Assiniboine had reasonable numbers of horses on the northeastern plains by 1750, although they did not have as many as their neighbors to the west and south.

Guns, Horses, and Changing Coalitions

The Cree and Assiniboine approached the Plains from the forests to the north and east. These woodland tribes were heavily involved in the fur trade, exchanging beaver pelts for manufactured goods, including guns, and they used their guns to advance westward and gain control of more areas rich in beaver. The Plains did not have abundant beaver supplies, so most Cree and Assiniboine moving westward did so to the north of the true Plains, ultimately occupying the transitional belt between the Plains and the northern forest, all the way to the Rockies. Some Cree and Assiniboine bands moved into the northern Plains, however, quickly choosing to adopt the nomadic buffalo-hunting lifestyle. Guns, at least in small numbers, were much less useful for Plains warfare against equestrian enemies than they were in the woodlands against pedestrians. They required too much time to load and fire in the face of attack by mounted warriors. Therefore, as the Plains Cree acquired guns from their woodland relatives, they quickly traded them to the Assiniboine for horses that the Assiniboine obtained from further south.

Guns could be effective in Plains warfare if a sufficiently large number of warriors were armed, perhaps with multiple weapons per warrior, so long reloading pauses could be avoided by rotating fire. Euro-American fur traders were moving further west during this period,[28] and transportation of furs and hides improved dramatically (e.g., large boats could travel from St. Louis up the Missouri as far as the middle of present-day Montana), allowing the traders to profitably ship buffalo robes as well as small furs. Trade in buffalo robes (and pemmican) allowed the northern Plains tribes to obtain large quantities of guns, as well as ammunition and other goods.

With the influx of both guns and horses in quantity, warfare tactics changed again. Although leather armor stopped arrows, it did not stop bullets, and it was both heavy and cumbersome. Thus, it was abandoned, as was the lance, and this meant that the specialized heavy saddles were no longer needed. Warrior-hunters armed with guns replaced their Spanish-style saddles with stuffed leather pads, which were much less restrictive and allowed for much more mobility on the horse. The first tribes to adopt this new tactic in the northern Plains had a new comparative advantage in warfare. Other tactics also changed as equestrian nomads obtained guns. For instance, while guns initially tended to require larger military units for effectiveness, their increasing abundance meant that all warriors could carry multiple weapons. Thus, the size of military units once again declined. Individual warriors' power to kill was increased and killing could be carried out from a much greater distance, so large-scale confrontations practically disappeared.

The Blackfeet coalition had much better access to guns and other goods from the fur traders than the Shoshoni, who had to obtain such goods indirectly through the Hidatsa-Crow trade linkage, or from the Numic-speaking tribes to their south and west (but the Spanish were much more reluctant to provide guns to Indians than were the Euro-American fur traders). As more guns were obtained by the Blackfeet-coalition tribes over time, increasing numbers of horses also reached members of the coalition. The combination of horses and guns in quantity, along with new military tactics, ultimately allowed the coalition to turn the tide against the Shoshoni, and when this occurred the coalition tribes went on the offensive. The Blackfeet were the most active, in part because they occupied most of the area between the Shoshoni and the other tribes, and during the 1770–1800 period they advanced west and southwest to the Rocky Mountains and the upper Missouri river, evicting the Kutenai, Flathead, and Shoshoni. The growing superiority of the coalition tribes also dramatically limited the ability of the Shoshoni to take captives, which reduced their opportunities to trade southward and reduced the flow of European goods to them, further increasing the advantage that the coalition tribes were gaining. The Blackfeet and other coalition tribes did not have large quantities of valuable furs to trade for guns, ammunition, and other goods (although as a market for buffalo robes developed they were in a position to supply substantial quantities of this product), but they were able to "produce" another "tradable product" through raiding: captives (particularly females) who were sold to the Canadian traders and transported into eastern Canada as slaves (Secoy 1953, p. 56). In this way, the Blackfeet coalition obtained more guns as well as iron arrowheads, metal knives, and axes, while the Shoshoni had few guns and found their access to iron diminishing.

The growing advantage of the coalition tribes further increased their success in horse raiding, so they increased their horse herds at the expense of the Shoshoni. As a result, these tribes were able to push the Shoshoni south and west, gaining control "of vast new bison hunting grounds" (Secoy 1953, p. 57). However, the Blackfeet gained most of the horses captured in warfare and most of the captives to trade for guns and other goods, so a gap grew between them and the other tribes in the coalition. As the Blackfeet gained an advantage in warfare relative to the Shoshoni and its own coalition supporters, their incentives to cooperate with other coalition members declined, making raiding against former supporters more attractive than cooperating: "As a consequence, the former allies began to separate into two increasingly hostile and warring groups, comprising the Blackfoot and their satellite tribes, the Sarsi and sometimes the Atsina [Gros Ventres], on one side, and the Plains Cree-Assiniboine combination, on the other" (Secoy 1953, p. 58).

The spread of the gun and horse ultimately tended to equalize power among the contending tribes, so each of the northern Plains groups was able to hold a section of the bison range, at least seasonally. As long as buffalo were sufficiently plentiful in the areas under control, additional territorial expansion was not desirable, given the small numbers of warriors each tribe actually had. A decline in the market for slaves also made raiding for captives less profitable, further reducing the incentives to engage in warfare. Secoy (1953, p. 65) suggests that "The only remaining economic motivation was the continuing pressing demand for horses . . . a secondary motive that developed out of these raids was the need to avenge the deaths of relatives, which often occurred on such expeditions." This view of the motivation for raiding is incomplete, however. The tactics adopted by competing groups of Indians still reflected the economic motivation of establishing relatively secure property rights to buffalo by deterring rivals who might attempt to hunt in the same area. When these tactics worked, they had significant impacts on buffalo herds. The various groups would hunt in the areas they controlled, but as La Salle reports, "The Indians do not hunt in . . . debatable ground between five or six nations who are at war, and being afraid of each other, do not venture into these parts except to surprise each other, and always with the greatest precaution and all possible secrecy" (quoted in Parkman 1910, p. 194). The tendency to avoid hunting in the boundary areas between the competing groups meant that buffalo populations would stabilize or even expand in the so-called "boundary zones" (Flores 1991, p. 483), or "war zones" (Martin and Szuter 1999), or "war grounds" (White 1978, p. 334). On the other hand, the intensive hunting in territories under reasonably secure control of individual tribes meant that buffalo populations declined significantly in these areas, as the individual tribes failed to solve the commons problem within their hunting territories.

Some of the tribes may have attempted to limit access to the tribal commons by their own members. Johansen (1999, p. 36) contends, for instance, that strict cultural sanctions were established against overhunting (although sanctions should not be required if the beliefs allegedly underlying his Indian-as-environmental-stewards argument cited above actually determine behavior). Whether such cultural beliefs and potential sanctions existed or not, they were not successful. Overhunting clearly occurred (Butler 1978; Flores 1991; Isenberg 2000), as explained in more detail below, so the individual hunters and bands within these tribal societies apparently did not have sufficient incentives to restrain themselves. This probably reflects the relative insecurity of the territorial claims, as well as the migratory nature of the buffalo, which could not be constrained within the territory of an individual tribe. Hunters recognized that if they did not kill buffalo when they were available, the animals would probably move out of their range and into the territory of a rival tribe. It also probably resulted from the large territorial areas relative to the small populations of each tribe, which made monitoring of any cultural or "contractual" agreement to limit hunting very costly (i.e., high internal governance costs), particularly with so many of the potential "monitoring resources" (warrior hunters[29]) occupied in protecting the territories from outsiders and in hunting. Thus, implicit promises to limit hunting were not likely to be credible, even within a tribe. Without trust, some sort of recourse is required to enforce rules, and the highly individualistic nature of the culture and lack of any institution with enforcement power (e.g., the lack of authoritarian chiefs) also meant that no centralized coercive power was able to enforce any agreed-upon hunting quotas (let alone enforce them). Thus, as Johnson and Libecap's (1982) analysis suggests, high exclusion costs due to the migratory nature of the buffalo, the limited numbers of warriors relative to the territory needed to contain such animals, and high internal governance costs, produced a free-access commons problem within tribal territories. Buffalo herds, therefore, tended to be depleted within the territories controlled by each tribe.

The depletion of buffalo within relatively secure tribal hunting ranges also meant that the boundary zones became increasingly attractive. Therefore,

> Borders dividing contending tribes were never firm . . . [a] loss of game in a large part of one tribe's territory could prompt an invasion of these neutral grounds. . . . In the contest for these rich disputed areas lay the key . . . to many . . . aboriginal wars. . . . These areas were, of course, never static. They shifted as tribes were able to wrest total control of them from other contending peoples, and so often created, in turn, a new disputed area beyond. (*White 1978, pp. 334–35*)

Pursuit of the dwindling numbers of buffalo meant that stable territorial claims tended to be short-lived, and while warfare varied in intensity, it did not end until the buffalo were gone.

Continuing Decimation of the Buffalo Population

Any contention that the Plains Indians were peaceful environmental stewards is obviously false. Although white hide hunters clearly were responsible for the final decimation of the bison population between 1867 and 1883 (Mishkin 1940, p. 12), those who blame the eradication entirely on these hide hunters (e.g., Roe [1955, p. 192]; Johansen [1999, pp. 36–37]) fail to ask several key questions. For example, "If the bison herds were so vast in the years before the commercial hide hunters [who first arrived on the southern Plains in 1867 and did not move north until several years later], why were there so many reports of starving Indians on the Plains by 1850? And . . . given our standard estimates of bison numbers, why is it that the hide hunters are credited with bringing to market only some 10 million hides . . . ?" (Flores 1991, p. 446). The answer is that the buffalo population was already being systematically overhunted. Indeed, the Shoshoni and other equestrian Numic hunters exterminated the buffalo population in the Columbia and Snake River areas west of the Rocky Mountains before the end of the first quarter of the eighteenth century (Butler 1978), and Sioux destroyed the buffalo populations east of the Missouri by the end of that century (White 1978, p. 324). Both tribes then moved further into the Plains in pursuit of the herds that existed there. Continued highly effective hunting by growing numbers of nomads eliminated bison from large parts of the Plains before white hide hunters arrived. As Map 2.1 suggests, the end of the 1850s saw the shrinking herds, all located on the far western Plains, under continual pressure. The Blackfoot controlled access to and hunted the remaining herds on the tributaries of the upper Missouri; the Teton Sioux, northern Cheyenne, northern Arapaho, and Crow competed for the Powder River herds; and the Comanche, southern Cheyenne, southern Arapaho, and Kiowa were able to subsist on the herds in the Upper Arkansas and Red River valleys. Outside these regions, nomads were impoverished (Isenberg 2000, p. 112). The Assiniboine were starving in 1846, and the Sioux that remained east of the Missouri were destitute by the mid 1850s: "In the spring of 1855 those bands, as well as the Assiniboine and Cree, subsisted solely on wild berries, roots, and the occasional putrefying carcass of a drowned bison

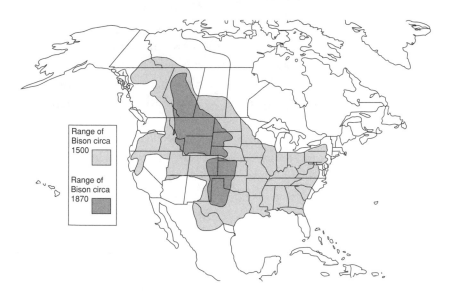

Map 2.1.   Shrinking Buffalo Range, 1500–1870.

SOURCE: Information used to draw this map came from several sources, including Secoy (1953), Butler (1978), Lehman (1997), and Canadian Geographic Exploration and Discovery (2005).

that washed downriver" (Isenberg 2000, p. 113). The Gros Ventre were in a similar condition in the late 1850s. The fact is that the Plains Indians had been unable to solve the commons problem, despite decades of warfare in an attempt to secure property rights, and they apparently knew it. Mishkin (1940, p. 122) quotes Cheyenne Chief Yellow Wolf, who stated in 1846: "We have long since noticed the decrease of the buffalo, and we are well aware it cannot last much longer."[30] Therefore, long before hide hunters invaded the southern Plains in 1867 (and the northern Plains several years later), the buffalo population, and the wealth of the nomadic equestrians of the Plains, had declined dramatically.

CONCLUSIONS: MORE BUFFALO WARS

The shifting patterns of raiding and trading, and of the control of property rights to hunting territories and agricultural lands that occurred in the Great Plains prior to Euro-American conquest have only been hinted at in this chapter. Perhaps the most dramatic invasion of the Plains was the Sioux expansion from the east, and one of the most powerful coalitions on the Plains would ultimately be the one between the Sioux, the Cheyenne, and the Arapaho. This coalition significantly altered property rights to both agricultural lands and buffalo territory. Furthermore, another extremely important determinant of the relative capacities for warfare and the relative value of land was the spread of European diseases. Mortality rates of between fifty and ninety percent were common whenever smallpox, measles, cholera, and other new diseases struck Plains bands (Calloway 1996, p. 40); but importantly from the perspective of the economic theory of property rights, diseases often affected some tribes much more significantly than others, thereby changing the balance of power on the Plains. Epidemics were particularly deadly for the sedentary horticultural villages, while the Sioux were relatively untouched.

Although the full story has not been told, the point that Plains Indian life revolved around efforts to create and enforce property rights in agricultural land and in buffalo should be clear.[31] More importantly, this chapter illustrates that Plains Indians were not primitive communists who adopted communal property and preserved their environment. Even if they did have fundamental different religious or cultural beliefs than Europeans, they responded to the incentives they faced. Thus, prereservation Plains Indians had a long history of: 1) adapting rapidly to changing circumstances; 2) cooperating (negotiating) and/or fighting in an effort to establish exclusive property rights to scarce resources; 3) using natural resources in the pursuit of their objectives (and doing so excessively when they were unable to establish exclusive rights to those resources); 4) engaging in economic competition and trade; and 5) emphasizing individual autonomy rather than communal life.

APPENDIX

The Anderson-McChesney (1994) model is adopted here to consider intertribal relations on the Great Plains. Some of its implications can be illustrated by considering Figure 2.1 (but see Haddock (2003) for an excellent discussion of this model and related literature). Suppose that two Indian communities are located at points A and B and that the group at A currently claims the

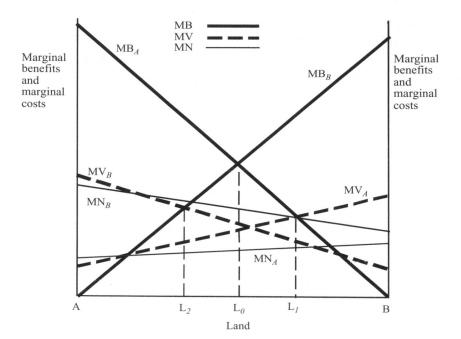

Figure 2.1. Raid or Trade.

territory between A and B. The two groups may place different values on such land (e.g., because of locational convenience, or perhaps one group has better agricultural or hunting technology, or the other has access to good agricultural or hunting lands in another direction), but both would like to control the territory (perhaps to privatize it for horticulture, or because it is prime buffalo habitat). For the Indians at B, the diminishing value of each additional unit of land is represented by the marginal benefit curve MB_B. Similarly, suppose that the Indians at A have marginal valuation curve MB_A. These values have to be denominated in something, of course, so imagine that they are the prices that each group would be willing to pay (e.g., in horses, buffalo robes, dollars) for each additional unit of land, assuming that the use of force is ruled out. This suggests that if transaction costs are zero, the group at B will purchase BL_0 units of land, making both better off. However, negotiation costs are not zero and both parties have an alternative: violence.

Let MV_A be the expected marginal cost of using violence to defend each additional and more distant unit of land through force for the Indians at

A. MV_A increases with distance from A (e.g., supplies and support from the village are costly to transport but they are important inputs for defense). The expected marginal cost of using violence in conquest for the Indians at B (MV_B) also presumably rises with distance from B for similar reasons. Given the MV_i and MB_i curves in Figure 2.1, the marginal cost for A of protecting the land between B and L_1 is greater than the marginal benefits of keeping it. Similarly, the potential invaders from B will consider the land between L_2 and A not to be worth trying to take. However, there is a "zone of controversy" between L_1 and L_2 within which the Indians at A have incentives to resist an invasion (their marginal valuations exceed their expected marginal defense costs) and invaders from B are inclined to invade (their marginal valuations exceed their expected costs of conquest), all else equal. Importantly, however, it does not follow that there will be violent conflict over the land in this zone, because negotiation and exchange, although costly, is still possible.

Assume for now that the parties can calculate their expected costs of negotiation and of fighting, and that they know their subjective valuations of land. Therefore, the expected gain or surplus from negotiating over a particular parcel of land for the tribe at A equals their expected total cost of fighting for that land, minus their expected total cost of negotiating to a mutually acceptable allocation of the land, plus the expected total value of the portion of the parcel regained (or retained) from the invaders through fighting (a value that can be negative or positive). If this surplus is positive, then the tribe at A would rather negotiate than fight. MN_A, the marginal cost of negotiating over each unit of land (which might also rise with distance, e.g., perhaps because the cost of monitoring the agreement is greater for land further from the village) is drawn in Figure 2.1 to suggest this possible relationship for land in the zone of controversy. The Indians from B have similar options, so their expected gain from negotiation is equal to their expected total cost of fighting, minus their expected total cost of negotiating, plus the anticipated total value of land that they have taken but that is then lost through fighting (which can be negative or positive). MN_B represents a hypothetical marginal cost of negotiation for Indians at B.

The total surplus that can be gained through negotiation is the sum of the surplus for each tribe, and if this total is positive, then there are potential gains from trade. In other words, even if one side has a negative expected surplus from negotiation, as B apparently does in Figure 2.1, the total surplus could be positive if A generates a sufficient negotiation surplus to compensate for B's negative surplus. Therefore, the parties could negotiate to a mutually beneficial exchange as A transfers land to B at a price that is low enough to compensate B for their relatively high negotiation costs (i.e., compensates them for not fighting). Fighting (or invasion from B and retreat by the Indians at A) is likely if the total surplus for negotiation is negative, however. Finally, note that the size and sign of the surplus can change. For instance, the potential surplus from negotiation falls if either A's or B's cost of fighting (MV_i) falls, either of their costs of negotiation (MN_i) increase, the value of land A gains by fighting (MB_A) increases (e.g., due to a technological change in production, an increase in the trade value of their product, etc.), or the value of land for B lost through fighting (MB_B) decreases.

NOTES

1. This chapter draws from a larger project on "Buffalo Wars: An Economic Analysis of Inter-Tribal Relations on the Great Plains" supported by the Earhart Foundation. I thank David Wishart, David Haddock, P. J. Hill, Ronald Johnson, D. Bruce Johnsen, and other participants in sessions at the Southern Economic Association (2002, 2003) and Association of Private Enterprise Education (2004) meetings for very helpful comments on various drafts of this and a related paper.

2. Note that this chapter spans a long time period and large geographic area, and therefore, it deals with a very large number of Native American tribal groups (e.g., Apache, Comanche, Kiowa, Shoshoni, Pawnee and other Caddoan societies, Hidatsa, Mandan, Arikara, various Blackfeet groups, Gros Ventre, Sarsi, Kutenai, Flathead, Nez Perce, Cree, Assiniboine, Crow, various divisions of the Sioux, Cheyenne, Arapaho). Furthermore, many of these groups were not on the Plains at the beginning of the period of analysis, entering only later, after they obtained horses and/or guns. Therefore, in the introductory and theoretical sections, where general principles and predictions are established, terms like Native American, American Indian, or Indian will be used interchangeably, essentially as shorthand for the large number of different tribal groups. This should not imply that these diverse communities were identical in any cultural or social sense. All it implies is that their incentives and the methods available (e.g., negotiation, warfare) to control access to (establish property rights in) various resources were similar. Of course, the historical material refers to the relevant tribal groups.

3. This belief also characterizes a fair amount of scholarly literature. For instance, Roe (1955, p. 192) claims: "There is not a fragment of evidence that I have been able to discover to suggest that the Indians would ever have exterminated the buffalo herds." Similarly, Johansen (1999, pp. 36–37) contends that "strict cultural sanctions

came into play against killing such animals [buffalo] in numbers that would exceed their natural replacement rates.... Native people on the Plains used nearly every part of the buffalo in their everyday economy.... [Thus,] The slaughter of the vast buffalo herd that had once roamed the plains and prairies began in the 1840s" when "competition with European-Americans, including deliberate slaughter, reduced the buffalo population..." Innovative Indians certainly did find ways to use virtually every part of the buffalo, but that does not mean that they used every part of every buffalo that they killed, as explained below. They also may have attempted to enforce cultural sanctions regarding the hunt, but the cost of enforcement was too high to prevent overhunting.

4. Numerous similar claims can be cited despite widespread evidence of recognized individual, household, family, and clan (which Deloria [1988, pp. 232–33] correctly suggests is analogous in many ways to a corporation) rights in agricultural lands, in fisheries, and in hunting territories (Anderson 1995, pp. 31–43; also see Anderson 1992), and extensive trading networks (Johansen 1999, pp. 247–49).

5. There is a very large historical and anthropological literature on intertribal warfare on the Great Plains, drawing upon historical records kept by European explorers, traders, and missionaries, as well as prehistoric archaeological evidence and verbal histories gathered through interviews with and observations of postcontact Native Americans. A number of apparently conflicting explanations of this warfare appear in this literature. Some of these explanations are consistent with Churchill's arguments, as they focus on custom or culture (e.g., war described as a "game" motivated by desires for prestige in light of cultural characteristics, war as a characteristic of primitive culture, tribes have traditional enemies). Other explanations of intertribal warfare center on (blame) Euro-Americans (e.g., Indians from the East were pushed into the Plains causing conflict, horses were introduced, capitalists introduced trade in consumer goods and guns), while still others stress economic motivations (but not in the context of an economic model of decision making). It should be emphasized that many anthropological and historical studies describe events or observations without explicitly offering *a priori* theoretical hypotheses about what is being described. Some of these descriptions clearly draw on *a priori* assumptions, however, at least implicitly, and/or reach conclusions about motivations or causes based on implicit hypotheses. In a few cases, the implicit assumptions and hypotheses and/or explicit conclusions are largely consistent with some, and occasionally most, of the theoretically derived hypotheses presented below. In fact, many of the apparently conflicting explanations that have been offered, often in an effort to rebut other explanations, are actually not conflicting. Instead, they each focus on part of the overall picture, but fail to see the connections between the part they focus on and the parts that others emphasize. This chapter is motivated by the various explanations of intertribal war that exist (some of which recognize a relationship between warfare and trade). Space limitations prevent presentation of these explanations, but a critical review is offered in Benson (2005).

6. For a small sampling of many similar statements of this kind, see Tully (1994, p. 190); Mika (1995, p. 30); Bishop (1997, pp. 319, 330); and Johansen (1999, pp. 167–69).

7. For a related discussion, see Wilson (1992); Bishop (1997); Tully (1994); and William (1990).

8. Starna (1982, p. 468) attributes the resurrection of the argument that Indians have a unique environmental ethic (which they call a "pan-Indian mythology") to non Indian environmentalists of the 1960s.

9. Part of the cost of each use decision in a commons is external to the decision maker, so all individuals overuse, causing congestion and depletion. Furthermore, benefits of investing in maintenance are external to the decision maker as others cannot be excluded from consuming them, so underinvestment in such activities results.

10. These basic ideas are not unique to economists. In writing about Plains Indians, for instance, Bamforth (1994, p. 112) notes: "cultural-ecological research in anthropology makes it clear that humans rarely engage in extremely expensive patterns of behavior without very good reason." See also Binnema (2001, pp. 58–59)

11. The actual costs of fighting and negotiating are uncertain, a priori, in part because they each depend on the uncertain strategies of the rival tribe. Consideration of some of these kinds of issues in a game-theoretic model is provided by Skaperdas (1992), Rider (1993), and others, but the objective here is simply to make predictions in a "comparative-statics" sense, and the preceding discussion is sufficient for that purpose.

12. The terms "bison" and "buffalo" will be used interchangeably in reference to the American Bison of the Great Plains. Varieties of buffalo species actually inhabited virtually all of North America at one time. Most became extinct in prehistory due to both climatic changes and human hunting (Isenberg 2000, p. 12, p. 63; Smith 1975). However, the species that adapted to the Plains survived and thrived in great numbers because they were smaller and faster than the other species, and they reproduced faster (Isenberg 2000, pp. 63–64), so they required less forage, were less vulnerable to pedestrian hunters, and replaced their losses to hunters at a sustainable rate.

13. An alternative was the "surround." Men drove buffalo into a semicircle arrangement where the women were dispersed along fences and barricades. As the animals entered, they slowed and began to mill around. Men moved in to kill them with bows and arrows. This also was not a small-scale operation because the drive had to be long enough to exhaust the buffalo.

14. Smaller groups became much more independent as a result, and this had a significant impact on intertribal relations, as explained below.

15. When they had to hunt on foot, the uncertainty of successful hunts created incentives to take as much meat as possible from a kill, drying, and preserving a good deal of it for future use. Nonconsumption of meat occurred only when a drive

was so successful that too many buffalo were killed for a band to be willing or able to butcher and preserve the meat.

16. See Steckel and Prince (2001) regarding the health conditions of Plains Indians.

17. Corn was apparently first cultivated in the Tehuacán Valley (Mexico City) about 5000 years ago, and then gradually spread through large parts of North America.

18. Fee-simple ownership was not common in the Plains, probably in part because Indians did not have written language, so the recording and transferring of titles was costly relative to the benefits. See, for example, Ellickson (1993). Something close to fee simple did arise in some Indian agricultural systems, however (Copper 1949, p. 1), where large investments were required to prepare the land (e.g., in parts of the southwest where irrigation canals were dug) or harvest the product (e.g., peach and *piñon* groves) (Anderson 1995, p. 36; Kennard 1979, pp. 554–57).

19. Between 1150 and 1200, horticulture was introduced in the Souris, Assiniboine, and Red River valleys. However, these communities abandoned horticultural activities during the drier climate episode that began around 1250 and agriculture was not reestablished in these areas after that.

20. For details about trade, see Reeves (1990), Ewers (1997), Holder (1970), and Binnema (2001).

21. Trade, particularly within tribes, tended to be ritualistic, in the form of gift exchanges. If someone's gift was not considered to be adequate, however, they would be subject to social sanctions. Through generosity individuals gained social stature and prestige. The fur trade was carried out in the same way. Manufactured goods were given to Indians who reciprocated by giving furs and other products to white traders. "Much has been written about the profits whites made from the fur trade. It would be difficult to believe that Indians did not profit from that trade, also. . . . They offered furs, buffalo hides, and pemmican from animals which were abundant in their country in exchange for manufactured goods which they wanted" (Ewers 1997, p. 33).

22. Holder (1970, pp. 123–24) explains:

> . . . ideal was individualistic in the extreme. . . . After a lucky raid a family might suddenly find itself rich with an abundance of horses. True, this . . . fortunate family might raise its status to the highest in the group by the mere fact of making itself poor in giving. Shortly, there would be gifts from others. . . . There was no hereditary group to whom wealth was funneled before it found its way unevenly back down to the others. . . . Even the 'simplest soldier' could climb to the top of the ladder, and even he could defy the chief. Although the position of hereditary chief is reported by some observers, this post . . . carried less prestige and . . . authority than it was possible to achieve through individual effort.

23. The lack of formal institutions of government does not imply that these "band societies" were disorganized mobs (Binnema 2001, pp. 11–12):

> [B]and societies achieve through informal means exactly what state societies accomplish in other ways. Indeed, the flexibility, fluidity, and informality of band societies enable them to respond quickly and effectively to the rapidly changing circumstances they typically face.... This fluidity did not threaten but enhanced the communities' stability.... Dissenters, for instance, were encouraged to acquiesce rather than to agitate when they disagreed with the majority of band members. If they did not accept the decision of the majority, they could vote with their feet by joining another band either temporarily or permanently.... Despite apparent individualism,... Individuals knew that they could not survive long unless they were members of a supporting community. No community wanted troublemakers.

24. Spontaneous associations were quite common, however. When different bands spoke the same language, shared similar beliefs and customs, and/or a common history, it was clearly easier for them to cooperate. Perhaps more importantly, members of most bands in a particular tribal group had brothers, sisters, parents, children, aunts, or uncles in most other bands in an area and they were also linked through marriage to individuals in other bands. In this regard, "kinship entailed reciprocal obligations. When one band was unsuccessful in the hunt or feared attack by enemies, it could count on the assistance of neighboring kin.... Kinship ties also crossed ethnic lines, however. By focusing on a single group ... we risk overlooking the important network of relationships that existed between ethnic groups" (Binnema 2001, p. 13). Indeed, while some writers such as Simmel (1955, pp. 33–34) contend that the only type of social interaction between tribal groups is warfare, this simply is not the case (Murphy 1957). There was a great deal of friendly contact, and of "mixing, merging, and amalgamation" of bands from different ethnic backgrounds; it was common for a camp to include members of several local bands from several tribes (Binnema 2001, p. 13).

25. The apparently extreme interest of warriors in acquiring prestige led a number of anthropologists and historians to conclude that warfare was a game played in order to gain social recognition (e.g., see Turney-High [1949]). Warfare was an individual choice, however, in which prestige and economic well being were intertwined (Mishkin 1940, p. 34). For instance, war leaders were entitled to all of the booty from a successful raid. They "generously" gave these gains to their followers in order to establish reciprocal obligations, and in anticipation of even greater gifts being given back to them in the future (Lowie 1954, pp. 105–06, pp. 115–16). In other words, prestige and profit were not mutually exclusive motives. They were actually highly correlated.

Economic incentives have also been downplayed to stress cultural determinism: "From infancy a Plains Indian boy had it dinned into his ears that bravery was the path to distinction, that old age was an evil, while it was a fine thing to die young in battle. He would hear famous warriors reciting and perhaps enacting their exploits on public occasions; he would see such men honored and likewise drawing material rewards . . . Thus, every lad was conditioned to emulate the example of eminent warriors" (Lowie 1954, p. 106; also see Hoig 1993, pp. 22–24). Such arguments fail to ask why Indian males were indoctrinated in this way, however. As Hoig (1993, p. 17) notes: "The very desire for security and peace fostered the need for a protective military body within the tribe," but the strength of individual autonomy meant that members of bands and tribes had strong incentives to instill such beliefs in their young males. Thus, the successful warrior was honored, but he also received all sorts of personal rewards.

26. Important technological advances occurred. As an example, archeological evidence indicates that Indians began producing pemmican (a mixture of a large amount of bison fat and grease together with dried berries that could be stored for considerable time) at least 4,800 years ago (Reeves 1990, p. 170). Bison that survived through harsh winters drew on fat reserves, but the resulting protein-rich meat actually increases caloric requirements and hastens starvation if eaten in-discriminately, due to an accumulation of nitrogenous end products that poison the body. Therefore, "To avoid protein poisoning Plains Indians had to main-tain their intake of fat and carbohydrates during late winter and early spring" (Binnema 2001, p. 51). By killing bison cows in the early autumn and processing them into pemmican, Indians dramatically increased their chances of survival on the plains.

Another important technological advance was the bow and arrow, which appeared on the northwestern plains between AD 150 and 250; "a turning point that ushered in the era of the classic pedestrian Plains Indian way of life" (Binnema 2001, p. 61). The ability to rapidly fire multiple projectiles, relative to the atlatl, allowed more intensive use of large bison drives (Kehoe 1978, p. 79). The benefits of controlling hunting territory increased, and not surprisingly, substantial invasion of the Plains occurred (Binnema 2001, p. 61).

27. Secoy (1953) is the "classic" work on intertribal warfare, although some of his details have been challenged (Ewers 1992).

28. As European traders moved further west, they began trading guns and am-munition to the Kutenai, Flathead, and Nez Perce, who then won "back a section of the buffalo Plains for the summer hunt" (Secoy 1953, p. 59). Furthermore, their coalition with the Shoshoni was broken.

29. Johansen (1999, p. 36) further contends that the military organizations within the Cheyenne, Sioux, and some other Plains tribes enforced cultural rules and im-posed sanctions against hunting buffalo during certain parts of the year and against harvesting more animals than an individual could use, although specific references to evidence of such enforcement are not provided. In this same context, he correctly notes that these warrior organizations policed band hunts to prevent individuals from hunting early, before the band as a whole was ready, but this would tend to

increase the number of animals killed, as it prevented the potential stampede of a herd before the full force of the band's hunters could be brought to bear.

30. Euro-American observers also recognized that the Indians were destroying the buffalo population long before hide hunters entered the Plains.

> "Edwin James, . . . a naturalist, wrote in 1823: 'It would be highly desirable that some law for the preservation of game might be extended to, and rigidly enforced in the country where the bison is still met with.' . . . In 1841 . . . George Catlin, in a widely read book, advocated that the entire plains region be set aside as a national park to preserve both the buffalo and the Indians who depended on it for their livelihood. . . . Five years later Father De Smet accurately predicted that the plains from the Saskatchewan to the Yellowstone would be the 'last resort' of the buffalo." (*Ewers 1997, pp. 57–58*)

31. Other implications can also be seen. For instance, the intertribal relations on the Plains and their inability to establish secure property rights in buffalo were both important determinants of the relationships that developed with the final invader of the Plains: the Euro-Americans. Ewers (1997, p. 197) points out that most historians view the Indian-white wars on the Plains from an "ethnocentric viewpoint." He cites Dee Brown's *Bury My Heart at Wounded Knee* (1970), which is subtitled "An Indian History of the American West," as an example, pointing out that "Brown ignored the fact that Indians of different tribes had very different views of that history. He sought to interpret the Indian wars of the northern Great Plains only as Indian-white wars, and described them only from the viewpoint of the Sioux hostiles. Brown brushed off as 'mercenaries' those tribes that became allies of the whites against the Sioux." But the fact is that the Crow, Arikara, and other tribes that fought with the Whites against the Sioux had suffered and were still suffering as a consequence of Sioux aggression during the 1860s and 1870s. Indeed, the Euro-American invasion of the Plains was simply the last in a long series of invasions by "outside tribes" in the ongoing buffalo wars, and like earlier invaders, they found some groups on the Plains who were willing to cooperate with them against common enemies, and other groups that chose to fight their advances.

THREE

Native American Property Rights in the Hudson Bay Region: A Case Study of the Eighteenth-Century Cree

ANN M. CARLOS AND FRANK D. LEWIS[1]

With the emergence of a commercial fur trade in Canada, animals that had been a source of food and clothing exclusively now attained value in exchange for European goods. Harold Demsetz (1967) argued that, in response to the new opportunities, it was in the interest of some native groups to establish formal property rights to the animals that were the basis of this trade; but, as he rightly pointed out, the outcome depended to a large degree on the costs and the benefits of any new structure.[2]

Eleanor Leacock (1954), whose examples Demsetz cited, discovered that some Indian groups did indeed establish well-defined property rights after the advent of a commercial fur trade, and the institutional arrangement helped them control the harvesting of some fur-bearing animals. Leacock's focus was on the Naskapi and Montagnais tribes of Newfoundland and Labrador, who were among the first of the natives to participate in the trade.

At issue in this chapter are the arrangements of other groups who came to dominate fur-trading activity as it moved to the interior of the continent. In the lands adjacent to the St. Lawrence and Ottawa rivers, the Hurons were the major players in the early years, acting as middlemen to the interior tribes until they were dispersed by the Iroquois. Farther to the west, in the hinterland of Hudson Bay, Cree groups, of which there were several, became the main participants. The Cree hunted the animals, prepared the pelts, and transported and traded the furs either to the Hudson's Bay Company, which by the late seventeenth century had established posts along the bay, or to French traders who traveled from the east using the interior water routes.

The Cree and other Native Americans involved in the fur trade established the rate of extraction of the fur resource and, as the correspondence of the Europeans makes clear, had a central role in determining the quality and type of goods offered to them in exchange.[3] Yet, despite their influence and long-term interests, many native groups, among them the Cree, depleted the stock of animals upon which the commercial fur trade was based.

Why did Native Americans not conserve the beaver and other fur-bearing animals, which had become such an important determinant of their living standards? Demsetz argued that the property rights that might have protected the fur resources would emerge only if the benefits of establishing such rights exceeded the costs. Although much was to be gained from secure property rights to fur-bearing animals, Indians also faced the more compelling interest of meeting subsistence food requirements primarily through the hunting of large game. As explored below, the rules that developed to help assure subsistence were inimical to a property rights regime appropriate to the fur trade; and this tension goes some distance in explaining the failure to protect the furbearers. Conflict among native groups, which increased in intensity as a result of the fur trade, also weakened those property rights that might have promoted conservation of the animal stocks.[4]

The literature on Native American economic behavior suggests a clear distinction between the property rights to animals that were a direct source of food and other subsistence goods, and those furbearing species more associated with European trade. Resources such as game were essentially common property. Even though native groups, often to the level of the family unit, could have well-defined hunting territories, the rights to these territories were severely curtailed. Outsiders were prohibited from trapping animals specifically for the fur trade, but they were permitted onto a territory to hunt for food. Thus, although beaver and some other non-migratory furbearing animals were, nominally, private property resources, whereas larger migratory game was common property, there is little indication that game was

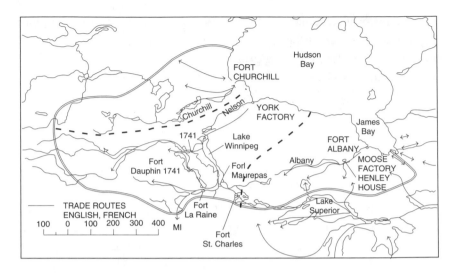

Map 3.1. Hudson's Bay Company Hinterlands.
SOURCE: Map was created based partly on information in Harris (1987), Plate 60 by Arthur Ray.

in seriously short supply until the nineteenth century. Another distinction between beaver and large game is that, whereas the demand for game was limited by the food requirements of native households, the demand for the European goods that could be purchased with beaver furs was much more price- and income-elastic. It is this distinction that may account for much of the difference in harvesting intensities.

This chapter focuses on the Western Woodland Cree, who inhabited the hinterland of York Factory, an area that includes northern Ontario and parts of Manitoba and Saskatchewan (see Map 3.1). A commercial fur trade was introduced into this region decades in advance of any European settlement.[5] Thus, in comparison to many other parts of colonial North America, the response of the Western Cree to the introduction of the commercial trade allows us to examine the impact of that trade within a largely isolated traditional society. Cree political, cultural, and societal interactions played a key role in many aspects of tribal behavior, including their approach to conservation. These social and cultural norms included what has been described in literature as the "Good Samaritan" constraint and, related to that social norm, as an ethic of generosity.[6] Both these norms, which involved a restrictive view of trespass, reduced the benefit to conservation. Further complicating the establishment of rights to beaver and other non-migratory furbearing animals was an environment where nomadic groups traveled over relatively large territories hunting migratory game and where the introduction of guns changed power relationships, further contributing to the movement of native groups. These features of Cree society had an influence both on their harvesting strategies and on their choices over the broad range of European producer and consumer goods that became available.

The next section begins with a brief account of the early commercial fur trade in Canada and moves to a discussion of Western Woodland Cree society during the traditional contact phase. This is followed by a discussion of the nature and extent of depletion of the beaver stock in the hinterland of Hudson Bay during the eighteenth century and an examination of the forces that led to this outcome, including the nature of the property rights to the beaver resource. Of special interest are the social norms of the Cree and other Indians involved in the trade, including their views on trespass, hunting boundaries, and security of property. Finally, the chapter considers the native treatment of property rights to large game animals and explores why the communal arrangement that characterized these resources not only provided insurance against starvation, but may also have helped conserve these resources.

THE COMMERCIAL FUR TRADE IN CANADA

The commercial fur trade originated in the sixteenth century as an adjunct to cod fishery, as English fishermen in the Gaspé and along the St. Lawrence River began receiving furs, mainly beaver, in exchange for a limited range of European goods. Later, under French rule, the trade became more formalized and spread inland, facilitated by the St. Lawrence and Ottawa River systems. However, actual contact between Europeans and most Indians was constrained. Indian middlemen, especially the Huron, who entered the trade in 1611, dominated the trade routes. Until 1648, when they were crushingly defeated and dispersed by the Iroquois, the Huron were able to protect their position by obstructing French exploration and restricting passage of other tribes through the major waterways.[7] After 1648, although faced with other middleman traders, the French became increasingly successful at bypassing Indian attempts to control access to the trade.

It was into this environment of an expanding French presence that the Hudson's Bay Company was formed. After receiving its charter in 1670, the Hudson's Bay Company quickly established several posts around James Bay and further west along the coast, initiating a rivalry with the French and later English and Scottish merchants operating out of Quebec that lasted for a century and a half (see Map 3.1).

The focus of much of the literature on the fur trade has tended to be on the operation and organization of the French and English traders and companies.[8] The Europeans certainly mattered and indeed were central to the operation of the fur trade and to the evolution of beaver stocks throughout the lands of the Cree. Focusing exclusively on the actions of the Europeans, however, can obscure the fact that they did not come to an empty land. Rather, European operations were superimposed on an already well-developed and complex Indian trading structure. For many years, native goods from the Canadian shield—furs, copper, dried berries, moose skins, antlers, and fish—had been moving south to be exchanged for tobacco, corn, gourds, fishnets, wampum, raccoon, and squirrel skins (Harris 1987, plate 35). So even though Native Americans had technologies primitive in comparison to those of the Europeans, trade was not new to America, and the notion of exchange had already been well established. What commercial trade did, however, was change the relative value of the indigenous trade goods. The return from pelts, in particular, increased dramatically.

Trade in furs was based on European demand. Beaver pelts, by far the most important of the furs, were shipped from Hudson Bay or down the St. Lawrence and across the Atlantic, eventually to be transformed into the high-fashion felt hats that remained popular in Europe for almost two centuries. Prior to Canada's entry into the industry, Russia had been the main source of furs, and the technology for felting beaver and other furs was already well established.[9] What Canada had to offer the market was a top-quality product whose characteristics were ideally suited to that technology and to the economic arrangements that developed between Europeans and Native Americans.[10]

Beaver was the best of the staple furs, namely those furs whose wool could be transformed into felt for use primarily in the hatting industry.[11] Because only the short interior hair could be felted, it was necessary to separate those hairs from the outer covering of guard hairs. Guard hair could be removed by shaving or combing the pelt, but separation also occurred when the Indians wore the beaver pelts as clothing. Over the course of a year, the pelt would become greasier and more pliable and eventually the guard hairs would fall out, producing what was known as *castor gras* or coat beaver. Thus, for some Native Americans, beaver pelts became a joint product, directly providing clothing as before trade, but thereafter supplying a trade good as well. Differentiated from the *castor gras* and ultimately more important in terms of number of pelts traded was the *castor sec* or parchment beaver, the pelt of a freshly killed animal. Felt for the hatting industry was produced using a combination of coat and parchment beaver, with the proportions depending on the extant technology.

In the 1720s, the technology changed in a way that shifted the proportions in favor of parchment beaver, and native traders responded to Hudson's Bay Company incentives by altering the supply of the two types of beaver pelts. In addition to these technological advances was a dramatic rise in European demand for beaver hats. The increase played back into the market for the primary product, raising the price per skin paid to the Indians by the Hudson's Bay Company and by the French traders with whom the company competed.[12]

NATIVE SOCIAL NORMS IN THE HUDSON BAY HINTERLAND

This chapter focuses on the native groups that participated in the Hudson Bay trade, especially the Western Woodland Cree and others in the hinterland of the largest trading post, York Factory. Anthropological and early historical records are sparse as few Europeans ventured into the interior to record Indian life,[13] but trading records from the York Factory post have been preserved. These provide a detailed picture of some aspects of native affairs, both in quantitative and qualitative terms. The post's account books document the volume of furs arriving at the post and the commodities purchased by native traders; and diaries and journals kept by the factors give a description of activities in the hinterland at a time when there were no European explorers.

Although the French were trading in the York Factory hinterland by the 1740s (Fort Dauphine was built in 1741), it was not until the last quarter of the eighteenth century that there was a significant European presence across the western Canadian interior and, hence, a more detailed record of conditions in the region. These observations, however, reflect life among the Cree well after they had begun participating in the commercial trade. Thus, our descriptions of the early years of contact must be treated more as speculation, but speculation that is informed by economic analysis of the fur trade data, by evidence related to the cultural and social life of the Cree, by archeological remains, and by reports of European observers.

Throughout the historical period, the area of central and southern Manitoba and Saskatchewan was inhabited by the Algonquian-speaking Western Woodland Cree and the Siouan-speaking Assiniboine. These were seminomadic groups who moved across the region with the seasons, mainly in response to the annual migrations of the large game. The archeological remains indicate that, just prior to contact, the Assiniboine occupied the boundary-waters area between Minnesota and Ontario as well as a large portion of south-central Manitoba, with the Cree living to the north and east. Later, the geographical distribution of these groups changed, and by the end of the eighteenth century those tribes comprising the Western Woodland Cree occupied the full boreal forest west of Hudson and James Bays, including the northern portions of Ontario, Manitoba, Saskatchewan, and Alberta (Helm 1981, p. 256). At the same time, the Plains Cree had split off and were living in the parkland and plains in southern Saskatchewan.[14] In essence, the territorial divisions by the end of the eighteenth century were the result of movement and migration by the Cree and Assiniboine. Frank Secoy (1971) discusses the importance of guns to the increased movement of tribal groups, but his concern is mainly with the Plains Indians. Nevertheless, power shifts in the boreal forest region may also have been affected by the introduction of firearms. Ray (1974, pp. 3–23) outlines how the Cree's, and, to a lesser degree, the Assiniboine's greater access to guns from the Hudson's Bay Company contributed to a considerable increase in their territory during the late seventeenth and early eighteenth centuries.[15]

The full boreal forest, which by the end of the eighteenth century had become the home of the Western Woodland Cree, is densely forested with white and black spruce and broad-leaved trees such as white birch and trembling aspen. To the north, the boreal forest transitions into tundra and to the southwest into parkland and plains. In the forest, the main food animals were woodland caribou, moose, elk, wood bison, and white-tailed deer. Of these, moose and woodland caribou were the more important. Smaller mammals that could be a source of food included beaver, hare, muskrat, woodchuck, porcupine, and squirrel.[16] The main furbearing animals were beaver, mink, marten, otter, lynx, fox, and muskrat.[17] Also traded, but of much less importance, were squirrel, wolverine, grey wolf, and fisher (Helm 1981, p. 257). Although caribou and moose were the primary food sources, Native Americans also consumed fish, waterfowl, and berries when available. The Plains Cree occupied the grasslands, which were well stocked with game such as pronghorn antelope, mule deer, red deer, and bison. Of these, bison was the most important, with bison hunts taking place during the summer. In the autumn, for protection from the elements, these Cree groups moved into the parkland, which was rich in a variety of resources including the big game animals that wintered over.[18]

Although information on the socioterritorial organization of the Cree is fragmentary, it appears consistent with what is known from the late contact-traditional period. The smallest unit was the nuclear or polygynous family. Local bands consisted of several families.

The annual cycle of hunting food and trapping furbearing animals for trade is important in explaining the institutions that governed exploitation of the animals. In summer, these bands came together to form a regional group that would camp in their summer grounds. At the same time, families were free to leave one group and move to another on the basis of kinship (Helm 1981, p. 259). The largest gatherings occurred in the summer when food sources allowed for greater congregations. In the late summer, the bands broke up as each family group traveled to its wintering territory. Autumn was the hunting season for moose, elk, and caribou. The main time for hunting beaver and other small mammals was late November and December, after the animals had grown winter pelts, and again in March when temperatures rose. Activities were limited in January and February.

DEPLETION OF THE BEAVER STOCK

Once Europeans began offering goods in exchange for furs, Native Americans were faced with the choice of participating in the trade or pursuing their traditional ways. The choice of trade had social and ecological consequences. One was a decline in the beaver and some of the other animal populations upon which this trade was based.[19] That the beaver were depleted has been widely accepted in historical descriptions of the fur trade. Carlos and Lewis

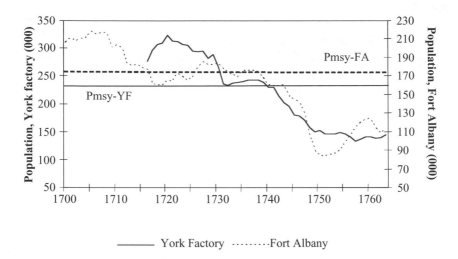

Figure 3.1. Simulated Beaver Populations: York Factory and Fort Albany Hinterlands, 1700–1763.

SOURCE: Carlos and Lewis (1993).

(1993), for example, show that in much of the region served by the Hudson's Bay Company, the underlying stocks had diminished significantly by the 1750s. The York Factory hinterland was by far the largest both in area and in the number of beaver harvested; and the hinterland served by Fort Albany and Moose Factory was second in importance (see Map 3.1). For the areas served by these trading posts, Carlos and Lewis (1993) simulated beaver populations that dropped to levels well below those consistent with maximum-sustained-yield harvesting (see Figure 3.1). In the York Factory hinterland, the beaver population is estimated to have declined to 130,000, or about 60 percent of the biological optimum of 231,000 (the level consistent with maximum sustained yield). In the Fort Albany hinterland, the beaver population fell to half the optimum level of 172,000.

Decreasing beaver populations were related to the prices native traders received at the posts. Beginning in the late 1730s, in response to higher prices in London and competition from French traders in the interior, fur prices at the York Factory trading post started to increase, and it was after several years of higher prices that the beaver populations began falling (see Figure 3.2). Carlos and Lewis (1993, 1999a, 1999b) concluded that higher prices for furs induced greater harvesting effort on the part of Indians, and the increased effort depleted the stocks.[20]

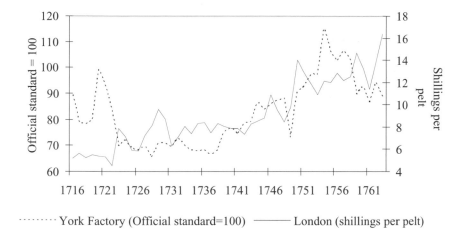

Figure 3.2. Price of Beaver Pelts in London and at York Factory, 1716–1763. SOURCE: Carlos and Lewis (1999a).

By analyzing the composition of the European goods purchased and how that composition changed over time, Carlos and Lewis (2001) showed that Indians responded positively to the incentive of higher compensation. This positive labor supply response to increasing prices and wages was common to other groups of the time, among them European consumers and American colonists, who, as Jan de Vries and others have argued, were part of what they describe as the "industrious" revolution of the eighteenth century.[21]

Table 3.1 provides a description of the pattern of trade at York Factory in 1740.[22] Values are given in *Made Beaver* (MB), which was the unit of account used at all Hudson's Bay Company trading posts.[23] For example, 250 guns were traded to the Indians at a price of 14 MB, giving a total value of 3,500 MB. Rather than listing the commodities traded in alphabetical order, we have broken them into categories of producer, household, and luxury goods.[24] Many of the items which are listed in the table as producer goods were used to help the Indians acquire food and other products necessary for subsistence, but there was an even greater range of luxury goods. Tobacco and alcohol were important components, but the group included a wide variety of luxuries, among them cloth of various kinds, beads, jewelry, and vermillion. In nonnative societies, luxuries tend to have high price and income elasticities of demand, implying that as the price of these goods falls and incomes rise, total expenditure on these goods goes up. Trading at Hudson's

Table 3.1. Value of Goods Received at York Factory in Trade, 1740.
("*Made Beaver*")

	MB/UNIT	MB		MB/UNIT	MB
PRODUCER GOODS			**OTHER LUXURIES**		
Files	I	308	Baize (yd)	1.5	II
Fishhooks	0.071		Bayonets	I	150
Flints	0.083	193	Beads (lb)	2	319
Guns	14	3,500	Buttons	0.25	10
Gun worms	0.25	85	Cloth (yd)	3.5	3,455
Hatchets	I	762	Collars brass	2	60
Ice chizzles	I	472	Combs	I	346
Knives	0.25	828	Duffel (yd)	2	14
Mocotaggans	0.5		Earrings	0.25	
Net lines	I	218	Egg boxes	0.333	47
Powder horns	I	181	Flannel (yd)	1.5	29
Powder (lb)	I	3,360	Gartering (yd)	0.667	244
Scrapers	2	108	Glasses burning	2	16
Shot (lb)	0.25	1,847	Handkerchiefs	2	18
Twine (skein)	I	114	Hats	4	140
			Hawkbells (pair)	0.083	42
Guns and		9,165	Lace (yd)	0.667	123
related goods			Looking glasses	I	108
OTHER		2,810	Medals	0.167	
TOTAL		11,975	Needles	0.083	34
			Pistols	7	182
			Pumps	2	
HOUSEHOLD GOODS			Razors	0.5	
Awls	0.125	105	Rings – seal	0.333	
Blankets	7	1,323	Rings – bath	0.167	
Fire steels	0.25	94	Rings – plain	0.125	106
Kettles	1.5	1,018	Sashes	1.5	72
TOTAL		2,540	Scissors	0.5	28
			Shirts	2.5	226
			Shoes (pair)	3	
TOBACCO AND ALCOHOL			Spoons	0.5	13
Brandy (gal)	4	1,514	Stockings	2.5	64
Water strong (gal)	4	132	Sword blades	I	5
Rundlets	I	350	Thimbles, thread		I

Table 3.1. (Continued)

Tobacco (lb)	2	4,543	Trunks	4	148
Tobacco boxes	1	162	Vermillion (lb)	16	296
Tobacco tongs	0.5		Worsted binding (yd)	0.667	59
			Worsted knit (yd)	0.5	
Alcohol and related goods		1,864			
Tobacco and related goods		4,705	TOTAL		6,364
TOTAL		6,701	Producer Goods		11,975
			Household Goods		2,540
			Alcohol and Tobacco		6,701
			Other Luxuries		6,364
			GRAND TOTAL		27,579

SOURCE: Carlos and Lewis (2001).

Bay Company posts indicates that Indian demands followed this pattern. During the eighteenth century, as fur prices at York Factory increased, the share of native expenditure on producer goods fell markedly from 60 to 40 percent. Because producer goods were important for native survival and their quantities could hardly have fallen, the declining producer goods share implies much greater purchases of luxuries. Indeed, expenditures on luxury items, in particular cloth, increased. Such consumption patterns would have required greater labor input by Indians. Thus, as the price of furs rose, Native Americans put more effort into the commercial sector with the result that beaver stocks were depleted below the biological optimum.

PROPERTY RIGHTS AND DEPLETION

Native Americans responded to higher fur prices as industrious consumers by raising their level of harvesting effort, a consequence of which, as noted above, was a significant decline in beaver stocks. Depletion, though, was an outcome that depended to a large degree on the property rights structures that natives had developed. Before considering the actual structure of Indian property rights, it is useful to consider various categories of resource ownership. Among the general forms are open access, communally based property rights with controls over access by outsiders, and private property with exclusive use rights to the owner. There are then subclassifications within each of these general categories (Feeny et al. 1990, p. 5). Discussions of depletion are often framed starkly in terms of open access versus private property, where typically open access is said to lead to the tragedy of the commons and private property to optimal management. What must be explicitly recognized is not just the ownership structure *per se*, but also the degree to which access can be controlled. A common property environment can lead to a tragedy of the commons since it will be in no one person's interest to conserve. It is important to recognize, however, that whatever the property rights arrangement, the environment in which that arrangement applies can have an important bearing on how a resource is exploited.[25] In a communal framework, for example, the benefits of a resource are distributed to the members of the community based on agreed-upon rules. For such a property rights structure to function, these rules that affect the rights of individuals within that community must be specified and enforced. Individual rights will depend on a variety of factors, such as the social and cultural institutions in place and changing ecological and market conditions.

For Native Americans, fur pelts were the means of accessing iron technology and a range of luxury goods previously unavailable. Given that beaver was at the core of these options, the natives' decision to deplete, whether conscious or not, was a serious one. In what has been described as the "naive" theory of property rights (Eggertsson 1990, p. 250), Demsetz (1967) argued for the emergence of secure rights when the benefits of establishing such rights exceeded the costs, but he did so independent of any discussion of the cultural or social construction of the society. To the extent that cultural factors mattered, Demsetz's essential message does not change, but it does require that we broaden the interpretation of the costs and benefits.

A key to the nature of property rights to beaver and other resources was the Indians' notion of territoriality.[26] Of particular interest to anthropologists has been the question of whether territoriality was an aboriginal construct or whether it came about in response to the commercial trade. In the precontact period, did individuals or groups within the community have the right to restrict access to a resource or hunting ground, that is, to prevent trespass? To the extent that territoriality is aboriginal, it suggests that, even prior to the emergence of European trade, there were benefits to establishing a property right to some resources or territory. At issue here is the extent to which property rights structures, which may have been aboriginal in origin, could be used to promote conservation.

In his examination of territoriality among northeastern Algonquian, Bishop (1986) documents that a concept of trespass existed. Using Father LeJeune's description (taken from the Jesuit Relations) of an attempt of some Abenaki to reach Trois-Rivières in 1637 and the reaction of the Montagnais, Bishop (1986, p. 47) concludes:

> These Barbarians have a very remarkable custom. When other nations arrive in their country, they would not dare pass beyond without permission from the Captain of the place; if they did, their canoes would be broken to pieces. This permission to pass on is asked for with presents in hand; if these presents are not accepted by the Chief, not being minded to let them pass, he tells them he has stopped the way, and that they can go no further. At these words they have to turn back, or run the risks of war.

Toby Morantz (1986), in her work on the eastern James Bay Cree, also concludes that Indian property systems included components of territoriality or trespass. Contemporaries, moreover, recognized group territories, referring to "the land of" the Montagnais, of the Cree, of the Huron, of the Iroquois, and of subgroups among these. In fact, there were nearly twenty to twenty-five identifiable groups exploiting the resources on or near the main water route between Québec and Sault Ste. Marie (Bishop 1986, p. 46).

Exclusive hunting territories also existed. Citing Le Clercq, Bishop (1986, p. 57) provides a seventeenth-century example of hunting territories among the Attikamek, who were boreal Algonquians: "It is the right of the head of the nation . . . to distribute the places of hunting to each individual. It is not permitted to any Indian to overstep the bounds and limits of the region, which shall have been assigned to him in the assemblies of the elders. These are held in autumn and in spring expressly to make this assignment." And fur trader Joseph Chadwick in 1764 noted that in Maine Indians divided their land into heritable family hunting territories: "hunting ground and streams were parceled out to certain families" including the right to heritability (quoted by Cronon 1983, p. 105). Thus, within the historical record, there are examples of territoriality and a concept of trespass, both institutional arrangements that could have led to conservation by native groups.

Certainly for the eastern James Bay Cree, on whom there has been considerable anthropological work, family hunting territories existed by the beginning of the nineteenth century and likely earlier. Morantz (1986, p. 74) cites the district chief at Rupert's House who wrote in 1823: "It appears to me that the Coast Indians and the majority of the inland Indians who visit Ruperts [sic] House are tenacious of their property in their lands and are not pleased when other Indians encroach on them." In an 1827 letter to London about western Indian tribes, Governor Simpson wrote: "we are endeavoring to confine the natives throughout the country now by families to separate and distinct hunting grounds, this system seems to take among them by degrees and in a few years, I hope, it will become general but it is a very difficult matter to change the habits of Indians" (Morantz 1986, p. 74). It is not clear whether Simpson's proposed changes involved a reassignment of land rights or the introduction of a new system but, in either case, it seems that Canadian Indians were not hostile to family hunting territories. Although the habits of the Western Cree appear not to have supported such a system during the eighteenth century, Milloy (1991, p. 59) clearly documents that those who became Plains Cree had "modified those rules, rituals, and practices" which had governed their woodland life. Thus, questions pertaining to the lack of development of family hunting territories must lie within the social and cultural framework of the Western Woodland Cree themselves, as well as with the economic constraints that they faced.

As a hunter-gatherer society, the fundamental concern was the provision of an adequate supply of food, with each society evolving to optimize food-gathering capacity. One result was that families or groups moved with the seasons in order to be in the most productive location for that time of year.[27] Migration *per se* did not prevent the establishment of family property rights because a family could go back to the same winter hunting grounds year after year and because beaver are nonmigratory. However, the lack of a continuous presence in an area mitigated against enforcing rights to beaver territories.

Related to the annual cycle of migration was the changing pattern of Cree territory over the seventeenth and eighteenth centuries. From the end of the seventeenth until well into the eighteenth century, the Western Woodland Cree moved west and north, and the Plains Cree broke off and moved west and south. At the same time, the Chipewyan tribes who lived to the north of Cree territory shifted southeasterly, and the Ojibwa moved into land on the northern edge of Lake Superior.[28] Such movements, perhaps related to the introduction of guns to the region, attenuated the ability of any group to establish secure family-based property rights. In particular, with each move westward, new information had to be gathered and processed thus slowing the development of well-defined property rights. Contributing to the migration, especially westward migration, may also have been the depletion of the beaver in the East.[29]

The ability to conserve was further confounded by war. Certainly during the seventeenth century, war, with its attendant population shifts, reduced the incentive to conserve.[30] It is important to recognize, however, that the tribes and groups from the St. Lawrence river basin west were changing territory even prior to the introduction of the commercial trade: "Indian country had its own historical dynamics, its own patterns of population movements, conquests, and political and cultural change that had being going on for centuries" (Richter 2001, p. 39). A commercial trade was, therefore, superimposed on these already existing patterns of movement. Of course, a commercial trade may also have contributed to migration by exacerbating existing tensions between tribes, making future conflict more likely. But interestingly, while war, due in part to the introduction of firearms, was the primary force for migration in the seventeenth and early eighteenth centuries, after 1720 further population shifts in Cree and Assiniboine territory tended to be more peaceful.[31] Why migration continued to occur is a matter of speculation. Perhaps disease changed the locations of more southerly groups with a concomitant shift of other populations, or perhaps changing weather patterns caused a shift in animal migrations. Another possibility is that the Cree's and Assiniboine's greater access to guns and the consequent shift of power relationships allowed these groups to expand their territory simply through the threat of force.

Migration attenuated the ability to conserve. Also, other forces worked against secure rights to the beaver resource. Families could grow or shrink and, depending on the influence of a chief, kin members could move from one family grouping to another.[32] Indeed, if a chief died, family members might disperse to other family groups (Helm 1981, p. 259). The result would be a transfer of rights to those beaver left unharvested in the previous cycle. As Williams (1969, pp. 169–70) and Ray and Freeman (1978, pp. 67–68) note, more northerly groups did not have corporate patrilinear clans and were less able to transmit high status attributes to their heirs. In such circumstances, personal abilities would determine the new chief.

European-introduced disease would have contributed to the lack of property rights by raising the price of labor relative to natural resources, including beaver, and thus decreasing the return to establishing property rights. In addition, there was the potential that those tribes who were especially hard-hit by disease would be vulnerable to groups that were relatively unscathed, the result being a shift in the balance of power and a reassignment of property rights to resources. There is no evidence that the epidemics reached the St. Lawrence–Great Lakes region until after 1634, but once in the area, mortality rates, although certainly lower than those further south, may have reached fifty percent (Harris 1987, plate 35). These epidemics were devastating not only because of the mortality, but also because of the social dislocation resulting in a reordering of groups, bands, and families. Both the change in the relative price of resources and labor and the shift in power among groups contributed to a weakening of the previously existing property rights assignments and of the ability to establish new secure relationships.

Another contributing factor to the lack of property rights was the insurance value associated with open access to the food source. Following on the seminal work of Richard Posner (1980), Thráinn Eggertsson (1990, p. 303) posits: "A whole range of social institutions in primitive societies helps to provide this vital insurance service. The sharing of surplus harvests, gift giving, reciprocal exchange, norms specifying the size of kinship groups, . . . the assignment of respectability and prestige to giving rather than to accumulation, . . . can be analyzed in terms of the insurance principle." As noted earlier, for all hunter-gatherer societies in the Hudson Bay region, food provisioning was paramount and hunting was unpredictable due to the variability in large game.[33] In response, the Cree and other native societies developed rules and behaviors that helped insure against hunger, and possibly starvation. Fikret Berkes (1986, p. 153) notes that the "family hunting territory is merely a small part of a larger resource use system with rules, practices, and ethics. Focusing only on territoriality and on one species (beaver) gives a distorted picture of the overall resource use system." He emphasizes: "All resources are subject to the overriding principle that no one can prevent a person from obtaining what he needs for his family's survival" (p. 153).

This characteristic of property institutions has been referred to by John McManus (1972) as the "Good Samaritan" principle. McManus pointed out that it limited the range of privilege of native groups to their land and ultimately affected, not just the ownership of the animal resources, but also their exploitation. The principle, which applied to any potential food source animal, allowed an outsider to kill a beaver for food and personal use, but he was not permitted to sell the pelt.[34] The Good Samaritan principle, therefore, affected the ability of any one group or family to conserve. In a bad hunting season, anyone's beaver became a source of food and clothing for others. In the event of a number of consecutive poor seasons, it might well have been possible that the conservation efforts of one family would be offered up to the greater necessity of the tribe. Clearly, in the rigorous subarctic environment this was as it should be.[35]

Another feature of aboriginal society that affected the ability of families or groups to conserve the beaver resource was the "ethic of generosity." Again, the basis for this ethic was the unpredictable natural environment. Under this social norm, any visitor to someone's encampment was to be supplied with food and shelter. Such actions were reciprocal and, in the subarctic world, were an insurance mechanism against the elements. Insurance and property rights are not incompatible, but the informal nature of this aboriginal form of insurance led to a serious moral hazard problem. Those who chose to conserve in the long run would be providing more insurance than those who did not. The result was, as is typical of markets with moral hazard, less conservation, and ultimately less insurance than would have been optimal.

The ethic of generosity was also a source of prestige. As elucidated by Bishop (1986, p. 52), "chiefly offices also required validation." In order for captains or chiefs to take office as a result of lineage and kin relations, they had to show themselves worthy of that office. This worthiness was demonstrated through generosity demonstrated by giving away output, often at a mortuary feast or possibly at a potlatch.[36] Anthropologists have documented how the commercial trade changed the scale, if not the nature, of Indian relations in regard to the ethic of generosity. Again quoting Bishop (1986, pp. 51–52), "For at least a short period, the feast grew greatly in magnitude and scale to include many different groups and huge expenditures of food and other goods. Like mid-nineteenth-century potlatches, these early contact feasts contained demonstrations of power by the chiefs." Writing as early as 1641 of a feast hosted by the Nipissing, the Jesuit Relations[37] note:

> When the Nations are assembled, and divided, each in his own seats, Beaver Robes, skins of Otter, of Caribou, of wild Cats, and of Moose; Hatchets, Kettles, Porcelain Beads, and all things that are precious in this Country, are exhibited. Each Chief of a Nation presents his own gift to those who hold the Feast, giving to each present some name that seems best suited to it. (*Quoted in Bishop 1986, p. 22*)

Generosity in itself was not inimical to private property. Indeed, as Johnsen (1986a) persuasively argues, the potlatch among the Kwakiutl Indians allowed for a stable allocation of rights over differentially productive fishing sites. The beaver resource, however, was much more broadly and equally dispersed so that variations in output were more a reflection of differences in labor input than variations in beaver density. Feasts were a means of equalizing consumption, but especially once a commercial fur trade was introduced, they created incentive problems with regard to how the beaver resource was to be exploited. As well, the introduction of a commercial trade provided "new opportunities to circumvent chiefs . . . to aspiring individuals" (Bishop 1986, p. 56). In such periods of competition, there was the incentive on the part of Indian trading captains, particularly, to increase the beaver harvest despite the long-term effect on the stocks.

PROPERTY RIGHTS AND THE PRESERVATION OF LARGE GAME

The literature on Native American economic behavior suggests a clear distinction between the property rights to inputs that were a direct source of subsistence goods such as food, clothing, and shelter, and inputs associated with the luxuries obtained through the trade with the Europeans. Resources such as game were essentially common property. And while a native group, often to the level of the family unit, might have a well-defined right to a hunting territory, the rights to this land were curtailed as outsiders were permitted onto the territory to hunt for food. Thus, beaver and other non-migratory furbearing animals were private property resources to the degree that their use was limited to the European fur trade and the private rights could be secured, whereas large game was common property. As outlined earlier, beaver were depleted in many areas both because beaver had uses other than in the fur trade and because natives had limited success in enforcing whatever rights did nominally exist. Property rights to large game were even weaker, but there is little indication that game was in serious shortage until the early nineteenth century.

The Indians in the trading hinterlands of Hudson Bay had, and continue to have, a diet consisting mainly of meat and fish. During the eighteenth century, the meat component included beaver and waterfowl, but by far the larger part of meat consumption was provided by large game, mainly moose and caribou. Although there are references in the literature to the importance of beaver in the native diet (Ray 1974, p. 27; Innis 1956, p. 13), an analysis of the returns from York Factory indicates that even in this highly productive beaver region, beaver flesh could have accounted for no more than a small part of meat and fish consumption, perhaps five percent.[38] Instead moose and caribou, which were plentiful, supplied much of the native food requirement.

Why large game remained plentiful long after the introduction of guns and other producer goods is a question for which there are several possible explanations. Perhaps big game was so abundant that even the improved hunting technology had little effect on the stock, but this hypothesis implies that something other than a resource constraint was limiting the native population.[39] Alternatively, when guns became available, perhaps they did not sufficiently improve the Indians' ability to hunt large game animals.[40] Finally, Indians, both before and after European contact, might have limited their hunting activity so as to promote conservation, or at least prevent severe depletion. Bishop (1986, p. 54) is skeptical of such deliberate attempts by Indians to control the animal stocks, arguing that "given a lack of understanding of biomass systematics [Indians] could not have known that their hunting strategies were either reducing or increasing the overall game population." Adrian Tanner (1979, p. 44), on the other hand, argues that the Mastassini hunters in the region of James Bay learned the natural habits of the animal species in the region and were sensitive to population changes. Their hunting strategy included avoiding areas where the stocks appeared to be threatened.[41]

It remains an open question whether Indians preserved the game in the region of Hudson Bay through deliberate calculation or whether the moose and caribou remained numerous despite unrestrained hunting practices. Nevertheless, a case can be made that such social norms as the Good Samaritan rule and the ethic of generosity, which may have been inimical to the protection of beaver stocks, actually helped create an environment that encouraged conservation of the moose, caribou, and other large game animals. As distinguished from the beaver resource, which through trade could provide a variety of luxury goods, large game provided for subsistence consumption, almost exclusively.[42] The demand by a household for large game was thus highly inelastic and, as a consequence, insensitive to the (implicit) price of the resource. Variations in the overall hunt depended, instead, on the size of the native population in the region. Carlos and Lewis (2004, pp. 331–34) illustrate formally that where two native groups, each with the objective of maximizing their own population, compete for the same animals, the long-run stock of animals is smaller and hunting more intense relative to a regime in which a single native group has exclusive rights to the resource.[43] Because all had access to large game, which, unlike beaver, migrated long distances, it was in the interest of individual tribes to harvest at rates consistent with such overall sole ownership. The Good Samaritan rule was a social norm that had the effect of shifting property rights to game in such a direction. The result was a closer to optimal game population, a somewhat larger harvest, and a much-reduced level of hunting effort than would have been the case if the various groups had competed for the animals.

CONCLUSION

Given the nature of the anthropological and historical records, there is little doubt that native societies in eighteenth-century Canada and even earlier understood aspects of territoriality, trespass, and property ownership. Once European trade was introduced, Native Americans made, in regard to property rights, a clear delineation between animals that had a commercial value, especially beaver, and those that provided exclusively for subsistence. Despite the expected response of establishing stronger property rights in the commercial area, rights that might have protected the beaver and other species involved in the commercial trade, many of the animal stocks were depleted. Important to the failure of a secure property rights regime was tribal migration, disease, and social dislocation caused by the arrival of Europeans. The newly formed Hudson's Bay Company made guns available to native groups, especially the Cree. During the late seventeenth and early eighteenth centuries, the Cree and Assiniboine expanded their territory and, although the expansion was largely complete by 1720, the dislocation continued to affect the security of tenure to beaver in much of the fur-trading hinterland. Also overriding the attempts to establish property rights that would have fostered conservation were the social norms of the Western Woodland Cree and other native groups who traded in the hinterland of Hudson Bay. The Good Samaritan rule and the ethic of generosity helped ensure native survival, but their emphasis on equality and wealth redistribution hindered property accumulation and reduced the incentive to conserve. The result was that Native Americans in the region of Hudson Bay were unable to protect the beaver stocks.

The survival and subsistence of the subarctic Indians underlay their approach to property, conservation, and resource extraction. Questions surrounding the introduction of a commercial trade tend to dominate discussions of aboriginal society, certainly in the case of the Cree and Assiniboine. The reality, however, is that commercial trade was a relatively small part of aboriginal economic activity. In the eighteenth century, the fur trade constituted at most thirty percent of the native economy (Carlos and Lewis 2001, p. 1057). Traditional work was paramount and, among traditional activities, acquiring sufficient food was the first order of importance. Conserving the beaver was subsidiary to that objective. Because it was the large ungulates that provided the bulk of the fat and protein, it was essential to have rules in place that promoted use of these resources in the most effective way possible for all the groups involved. Thus, the aboriginal structures that provided insurance against hunger impeded the attempts to protect the beaver.

NOTES

1. The authors thank Bruce Benson for helpful comments. Support for this project was provided by the Social Sciences and Humanities Research Council of Canada.

2. Ellickson's (1993) wide-ranging discussion of property rights in land takes Demsetz as its point of departure. Numerous illustrations are given including some drawn from the Native American experience. Barzel's (1997) classic statement of the property rights model includes contemporary as well as historical examples of Demsetz's argument (see especially Chapter 6).

3. For an account of some of this correspondence and its relation to the type and quality of goods supplied by the Hudson's Bay Company, see Carlos and Lewis (2002).

4. Our discussion, which takes Demsetz's "naive" view as a starting point, belongs to a literature that explicitly defines the costs and benefits of particular property rights regimes within the social, cultural, and political environment in which trade is taking place. For a review of this literature, see Eggertsson (1990).

5. The Hudson's Bay Company presence was essentially limited to the trading posts along the bay coast.

6. On the Good Samaritan rule, see McManus (1972), and on the ethic of generosity see, for example, Bishop (1986).

7. River systems provided focal points that were amenable to control.

8. There is an extensive literature. A good bibliographic reference is Rea (1991), *A Guide to Canadian Economic History.* The classic references on fur trade institutions and organization would probably be Innis (1956), *The Fur Trade in Canada,* and Rich (1958), *The Hudson's Bay Company.* Only starting with the work of Ray (1974), *Indians in the Fur Trade,* and Ray and Freeman (1978), *"Give us Good Measure",* does the focus shift to the role of the Indians in the trade.

9. The Russians had perfected a technology of combing the pelt to remove the interior hairs. They managed to keep this technology secret until the beginning of the eighteenth century when it spread to England and France.

10. In fact, the Hudson's Bay Company was formed at a time when European supplies of beaver had disappeared and the Russian stock had become severely depleted.

11. Only certain pelts were suitable for felting. The most important were beaver, coney, rabbit, and muskrat. These pelts have a double coating of hair: short, soft, barbed hair close to the skin, protected by longer, stiffer, smoother hair called guard hair. It is the barbed nature of the interior coat that allows the wool to be felted.

12. For an expanded discussion of these issues, see Carlos and Lewis (1999a, 1999b).

13. Two examples, from the first half of the eighteenth century, of direct observations by Europeans are Joseph Robson's (1752) account of his life at York Factory and Andrew Graham's Observations (Williams 1969).

14. The boreal parkland border formed the dividing line between these two groups. For the Plains Cree, the western boundary, established as an outcome of conflict between a coalition of Blackfoot and Cree and the Shoshoni, ran from Edmonton through the elbow of the South Saskatchewan River to the Yellowstone and Missouri rivers (Milloy 1991, p. 63). Assiniboine territory lay to the south, both north and south of what would become the United States–Canada border.

15. A theory of the relation between violence (or the threat of violence) and control of resources has been developed by Umbeck (1981a) and illustrated in the case of the California gold rush of the mid-nineteenth century (Umbeck 1981b). Umbeck's analysis has also been applied to Indian–White relations (Anderson and McChesney 1994).

16. A subspecies of hare, the varying hare, also known as the snowshoe hare, was the most important of these smaller mammals. They ranged over much of the northern half of North America.

17. Beaver was by far the most important pelt traded by number and value.

18. On the importance of bison in parkland areas during the winter months, see Isenberg (2000).

19. Marten was another furbearer whose numbers declined. See Carlos and Lewis (1993).

20. Some historians have argued against the positive labor supply response by native hunters assumed by Carlos and Lewis. See, for example, Heidenreich and Ray (1976) and Krech (1999). The traditional view expressed by Heidenreich, Ray, and others is that the Indians involved in the fur trade were "satisficers." Their objective was a given quantity of European trade goods; thus, increases in the price of furs were offset by reductions in the number of furs brought to the trading posts.

21. See, for instance, Ray and Freeman (1978) or Krech (1999) on the question of Indian labor supply and de Vries (1993) on industrious consumers.

22. Indian traders also received gifts from the Hudson's Bay Company, listed as "Expenses." In 1740, Expenses were seven percent of the value of goods received in trade.

23. All furs and all European trade goods were denominated in the company's unit of account, the "*Made Beaver*," which was equal to the price of one prime beaver skin.

24. Price and income elasticities of the goods natives consumed cannot be determined and, in that sense, the division of consumer goods into the household and luxury categories is somewhat arbitrary. Blankets and kettles, the main "household" goods, served essentially the same functions as had skins and native-produced pots in allowing the aboriginals to achieve subsistence. These goods are distinguished from the colored cloth, jewelry, alcohol, fine Brazil tobacco, and other items that were not needed for subsistence and whose consumption was likely more sensitive to income and price.

25. In fact, as Demsetz suggests, a change in the trading environment that increases the possibility of depletion can itself affect the property rights arrangements.

26. See the special issue of *Anthropologica* (1986), published by the Canadian Anthropology Society, on this subject.

27. The inability to store surpluses reinforced the migratory nature of these groups. Native groups in the eighteenth century did not buy or trade for food either from the Hudson's Bay Company or the French. Indeed, some native traders supplied fresh meat to the European trading posts.

28. The Cree were the first in the region to get good access to guns, and this undoubtedly played a role in the expansion of their territory in the late seventeenth and early eighteenth centuries. By 1720, though, "the bulk of that expansion appears to have been completed and a somewhat more peaceful period began as intertribal trading patterns became well established" (Ray 1974, p. 23).

29. The suggestion here is that depletion in one region contributed to migration and weakened property rights in another; the result being depletion in both regions. See Ray (1974, ch. 10).

30. To the extent that one tribal group became dominant, as did the Cree, war could lead to more secure property rights. Ray (1974, pp. 12–23) suggests that by 1720 the Cree had consolidated their territory, but only after that date do we see serious beaver depletion. This suggests that, even in the Cree sphere of influence, property rights to beaver were not secure. Another possibility is that outside that

sphere, but within the Hudson's Bay trading hinterland, the property rights of other tribes, such as the Assiniboine, Ojibwa, and Sioux, were weak.

31. See Ray (1974, ch. 10). The Hudson's Bay Company records note that the main area of Cree aggression was towards the Chipewyan to the north. To help reduce these tensions, the company opened Fort Churchill in the early eighteenth century so that Cree and Chipewyan were not trading together at York Factory. In Secoy's (1971) terms, these actions helped equilibrate the balance of military power.

32. Discussion of changes in family size in a variety of tribal groups is included throughout Helm (1981).

33. Outbreaks of epizootics among the animal population would reduce the harvest. Independently of these types of problems, a winter with either too much snow or too little snow would lead to very poor hunting conditions and so reduce the food harvest.

34. Beaver pelts had long been worn by natives, and only with the arrival of the Europeans did they become a trade good as well.

35. Because of the variability of large game, the threat of starvation was rarely far off (Rich 1960, vol. 1, pp. 383, 439, 495, 505, 598, 603, 633). Large game was the foundation of the native diet and, although in typical years, beaver comprised a small part—perhaps five percent—the share of beaver and other small game increased during periods of shortage. And satisfying just five percent of the diet required killing substantial numbers of beaver (Carlos and Lewis, 2004, p. 331).

36. As argued by Johnsen (1986a), the potlatch could also be used to reduce the tension over unequal division of property rights. Using the example of the Kwakiutl Indians in the Pacific Northwest, whose salmon fishing sites were differentially productive, Johnsen points out that the potlatch allowed groups to maintain property rights over the better sites by reallocating a share of their catch.

37. Jesuit Relations (1632–1773) were the annual communications of the Jesuit mission in Quebec to the superior in Paris. They are made up of various written reports and letters that reflect the work in the field and contain information about the missionaries' travels, studies of the peoples they met, and geographical details of the terrain covered. They provide an extraordinary resource for any study of French Canada and Native Americans in the seventeenth century. See Thwaites (1896–1901).

38. The calculation applies estimates of native food requirements based on caloric needs and recent practice, estimates of the per capita harvest of beaver in the eighteenth century, and the quantity of meat that could have been provided by those beaver. Details are available on request. As noted above (Note 35), despite the relatively small share of beaver in food consumption, hunting beaver for food had the potential of seriously affecting the stocks.

39. Of course, in much of the Americas the aboriginal population was devastated by European diseases. In the northern part of the North American continent, however, epidemics seem to have been less severe.

40. Eighteenth-century guns were not accurate and took some time to reload. Unless a hunter downed an animal or seriously wounded it with the first shot, he

usually did not get another attempt. See also Isenberg (2000) on the hunting of bison by the Plains Indians.

41. Alchian and Allen (1969, 19–29) point out that you do not have to understand the system to act as if you do, and Johnsen (1986a) in his work on salmon shows that northwest coast Indians let larger salmon pass upstream to spawn as if they understood fisheries biology.

42. Moose skins were occasionally traded, but the number was small.

43. Given that large game migrated long distances, assigning tribes exclusive property rights to more narrowly defined hunting territories was not only ineffective, it would have encouraged the kind of destructive competition outlined.

FOUR

A Culturally Correct Proposal to Privatize the British Columbia Salmon Fishery

D. BRUCE JOHNSEN[1]

"[I]ndividual permanent catch quotas of a regulator-determined [total allowable catch may be] only a stage in the development of management from licensing to private rights."
  —*Anthony Scott* (1989)

"[A]boriginal rights . . . must be permitted to maintain contemporary relevance in relation to the needs of the holders of the rights as those needs change along with the changes in overall society."
  —*Lamer, C. J. paraphrasing Lambert, J.A. in Delgamuukw* (1997)

Canada now faces two looming policy crises that have come to a head in British Columbia. The first is long-term depletion of the Pacific salmon fishery by mobile commercial ocean fishermen racing to intercept salmon under the rule of capture (Brubaker 1997). Despite over a century of licensing requirements, gear restrictions, season limitations, and other traditional regulatory restrictions aimed at conservation, the race to intercept salmon persists, and political gridlock leaves little hope for a traditional regulatory solution. The second crisis results from Canadian Supreme Court case law recognizing and affirming "the *existing* aboriginal and treaty rights of the aboriginal peoples of Canada" under s. 35(1) of the Constitution Act, 1982. These decisions give the aboriginal "subsistence fishery" a fixed priority claim to the seasonal salmon catch over incumbent commercial fishermen and reduce the evidentiary burden on the tribes in perfecting title to traditional tribal lands. The result has been at least one large land settlement and a destabilizing wave of further claims to land and fishing rights throughout British Columbia (Walker 2001).[2] With British Columbia's salmon fishery on the decline, tensions run high between native and commercial fishermen.

Much of the legal instability over aboriginal rights can be attributed to the Canadian courts' misplaced reliance on cultural anthropology to frame the legal discourse. Cultural anthropologists have traditionally regarded the northwest coast tribes as "hunter-gatherers" who had the good fortune to reside in an environment naturally "superabundant" with salmon, which they were content to "exploit" to meet their "material subsistence needs." This view is clearly contrary to any plausible economic interpretation of the historical evidence, and the ethnocentric Marxist terminology used to describe it is ill suited to reconciling aboriginal rights with Crown sovereignty in a way that promotes the Canadian Commonwealth.

In contrast to cultural anthropology, the property rights approach to economic theory emphasizes man's universal search for growth opportunities. When Europeans made first contact on the coast, the tribes had established relatively sophisticated economic institutions—primarily the pervasive potlatch system—to define and enforce exclusive tribal property rights to salmon streams (Johnsen 1986a, 2001).[3] Given that Pacific salmon return to their natal streams to spawn and were beyond the tribes' ability to intercept prior to that time, tribal ownership of streams effectively included secure ownership of native salmon stocks, including the real option to take advantage of newly discovered growth opportunities. This gave the tribes the incentive to accumulate the stream-specific knowledge to husband these stocks. Rather than being the fortunate beneficiaries of a naturally rich environment, the compelling conclusion is that the northwest coast tribes created the observed superabundance of salmon through centuries of purposeful husbandry and active management of other resources. By any reasonable standard, they were not hunter-gatherers content to meet material subsistence needs; they were institutionally sophisticated salmon ranchers who actively sought and proudly achieved prosperity. This view is entirely consistent with the weight of the historical evidence and with the vast body of literature on the economics of property rights.

This chapter relies on the property rights approach to economic theory to identify a joint solution to British Columbia's looming policy crises that would reassign aboriginal fishing rights in a common wealth enhancing way. This would involve a two-party privatization auction in which the Crown recognizes those with vested interests in the mobile ocean fishery as an "incumbent" class of claimants and British Columbia's First Nations as a "rival" class. The Crown would then auction exclusive ownership of the salmon fishery to the highest bidder in a modern variant of the tribes' traditional cultural practice for resolving title disputes known as the "rivalry potlatch." As a precondition of the auction, if the tribes were to win they would pay the incumbents their losing bid and then abolish the mobile ocean fishery by assigning exclusive stream-based tribal rights to salmon stocks in accordance with each tribe's traditional lands and subsequent intertribal negotiations. Because this institutional structure is a far more efficient form of organization than mobile ocean fishing under the rule of capture, a privatization auction could reestablish the distinctive "core" of aboriginal rights in a culturally correct way that promotes the Canadian Commonwealth, while compensating incumbent fishermen for relinquishing their claims.

To lay a proper foundation, the second section describes the crisis facing the British Columbia salmon fishery under the rule of capture. The third section provides a brief historical and cultural background on the northwest coast tribes. The fourth section examines the current law regarding aboriginal rights, beginning with a brief legal history of the tribes followed by a summary of three important Canadian Supreme Court cases that attempt to reconcile aboriginal rights with Crown sovereignty. The fifth section reviews earlier work that demonstrates the role played by potlatching and other tribal institutions in enforcing property rights to salmon streams, diversifying stream-specific risk, and encouraging the accumulation of stream-specific knowledge of salmon husbandry, and shows how judicial reliance on the discourse of cultural anthropology has distorted the case outcomes in favor of land rights over fishing rights. This is followed by a section describing how the British Columbia salmon fishery could be privatized. The possibilities for wealth creation from a negotiated settlement, as opposed to pure wealth transfer from further litigation, are truly promising and consistent with the Canadian courts' emphasis on the tribes' distinctive aboriginal rights. The principles of corporate finance help explain how the tribes could recreate a modern version of the potlatch system to achieve tribal prosperity, while restoring the British Columbia salmon fishery to its once prolific state.

REGULATION OF BRITISH COLUMBIA SALMON FISHERY

British Columbia supports five species of Pacific salmon, with each species exhibiting obvious differences in average size, color, markings, life history, and spawning habits and habitat, with these characteristics varying considerably even within species. From the ocean, mature salmon enter their natal streams to spawn every two to six years in what marine biologists call a "run." In the trunk sections of larger rivers, a run might consist of many different populations of a given species destined for different tributaries within the drainage. In smaller rivers with a relatively uniform spawning habitat, the species' run and population tend to be identical. Larger rivers contain more separate species and more distinct populations within each species. The term "stock" represents the current and future generations of successive populations of a given species, and ownership of a salmon stock can therefore be regarded as a capital asset.

Stream-specific environmental factors influence the number of fish in a run, including cycles of predation, cannibalism, variations in freshwater food supply, parasites, water temperature, stream flow, salinity, and siltation during runoff. Depending on the topography, soil content, vegetation, and other influences within the stream drainage, environmental shocks from extreme weather and other natural influences can affect local conditions quite differently, which, in turn, affect the survival of fertilized eggs and already hatched smolts. Human factors also affect the number of fish in a run. Through low ranges of fishing effort, an increase in effort applied to a population increases returns, but past some point it decreases returns.

After enjoying centuries of stream-based tribal property rights, tribes in British Columbia quickly lost exclusive ownership of their salmon stocks with the arrival of commercial canneries, first at the mouth of the Fraser River in 1871, and then gradually northward up the coast. It appears that the canneries began by purchasing substantial quantities of salmon from the natives, but they soon vertically integrated or contracted with boat operators to intercept salmon in tidal waters (Harris 2001, pp. 26, 47). The race was on to intercept salmon in a mixed-stock open-access fishery subject to the rule of capture. The result has been a long downward trend in salmon stocks and social waste on a staggering scale that continues to this day.

The traditional response to declining stocks by government regulators at the Canadian Department of Fisheries and Oceans (DFO) has been licensing requirements, license buy-backs, shortened seasons, and increasingly draconian gear restrictions on remaining licensees in an effort to achieve "maximum sustained yield," a conservation objective that neglects the opportunity cost of fishing effort in its calculus. As a result, strategic industry participants have invariably stayed one or two steps ahead of the DFO, overfishing various salmon stocks in spite of an ever-tightening web of regulations. Between 1950 and 1997, nearly fifty percent of the salmon populations in British Columbia were wiped out due to overfishing and other intrusions on the fishery. Fishermen routinely put themselves in danger to win the race to intercept salmon, leading to needless accidents and even loss of life (Jones 1997, pp. 4–5).

In 1992, Canada, the United States, Japan, and the Russian Federation signed the North Pacific Salmon Treaty, establishing a complete ban on salmon fishing outside the signatories' 200-mile exclusive economic zones north of 33 degrees latitude. Industry experts, including DFO regulators, believed that by eliminating Japanese and Russian fishing of Canadian salmon stocks, the looming crisis would be resolved. They were mistaken. By 1994, the salmon fishery was so overcapitalized in relation to available stocks that the British Columbia government was forced to pay out $63.7 million to idle fishermen in unemployment insurance (Jones 1997). This says nothing of the management subsidy implicit in the DFO's 1994–95 annual budget of $49 million, $45.6 million in excess of the $3.4 million it collected in licensing fees. Yet, in the same year the Fraser River sockeye fishery reached a crisis when roughly two million expected escapements failed to arrive at their spawning grounds. Prompted in part by a 1994 report that the Fraser sockeye fishery had come within twelve hours of being wiped out entirely, Canada's fisheries minister closed it entirely in August 1995. The response from command-and-control regulators was yet another wave of draconian gear and licensing restrictions and massive license buy-backs at further expense to taxpayers.

Next to overfishing, degradation of spawning habitat may be the most pressing problem facing Pacific salmon. Industrial pollution, erosion from logging roads, silt deposits due to clear-cutting, organic wastes, dams, changes in water temperature, and amplified changes in water flows owing to real estate development all threaten the reproductive success of salmon in their natal streams. Federal and provincial governments have patchwork authority to address these degradations, but they apparently lack the incentives to act in the absence of a public outcry. Politicians and regulators must balance the interests of land-based industrial interests, boat owners, canneries, environmentalists, specialized boat builders and gear suppliers, the increasingly activist aboriginal fishery, and various foreign interests in coming up with workable regulations. Given that any major regulatory shift is sure to redistribute wealth, the understandable result has been political and regulatory gridlock (Brubaker 1997, p. 154).

The recent worldwide trend in fisheries regulation is the creation of individual transferable quotas (ITQs) from a regulator-determined total allowable catch (TAC). ITQs allocate the right to either an absolute quantity of fish or a share of the allowable catch to quota owners. Because the quotas are transferable and, ideally, perpetual, they encourage holders to internalize the effects of their harvesting decisions and to consider the opportunity cost of retaining their quota rights in the face of attractive offers from interested buyers. Though falling short of full private property rights, ITQs avoid the rule of capture and eliminate the race to intercept salmon. Systems of ITQs have been successfully implemented for salmon and herring in Iceland, halibut in Alaska and British Columbia, scallops in eastern Canada, and orange roughy and other species in New Zealand. Interestingly, the move to ITQs in New Zealand is said to have been critical in allowing the government to compensate Maori tribes for their lingering claims to a share of the fishery (McClung 1997). At this time, however, ITQ allocation of the British Columbia salmon fishery is a mere hope and the ongoing crisis remains unresolved.

HISTORICAL BACKGROUND
OF THE NORTHWEST COAST TRIBES

The northwest coast tribes inhabited the many islands and inland waterways of the rugged Pacific Coast of North America. The region hosts countless rivers, many of which descend abruptly from rugged coastal mountains into the sea, though several, such as the Fraser River and the Columbia River, work their way over 800 miles inland. All support one or more species of Pacific salmon. From northern California to the Alaska panhandle, the Chinook, Makah, Coast Salish, Nootka, Kwakiutl, Nuxalk, Haida, Tlingit, and Tsimsian tribes, though diverse in linguistic origins, all relied heavily on salmon as their primary source of food and wealth.

During the prehistoric and early contact period, the northwest coast tribes are said to have been very warlike and possessive of their territories. As contact increased, however, there was a general trend away from violence. The British Crown ultimately reinforced this trend as part of the *Pax Britannica*, resulting in a worldwide prohibition on all aboriginal warfare and violence with draconian penalties for transgressors. Throughout the early contact period, the tribes enjoyed high and continuously rising per capita wealth unusual among North American natives. This was due in large part to the advent of European trade, but also to severe population decline from various epidemics (Boyd 1999). There can be no doubt of the tribes' commercial ambitions, which led them to nearly deplete the region's sea otter population when a prolific fur trade developed along the coast during the early decades of the 1800s. Between tribes they traded actively and aggressively in the expanding market economy and often successfully asserted exclusive rights over important trade routes, even against fortified Europeans. Exchange within tribes was generally regulated through an ever-shifting balance of reciprocal relations supported by kinship ties rather than with prices.

The most important social institutions found among the northwest coast tribes were the ubiquitous ceremonial potlatch system of reciprocal exchange, well-functioning capital markets, recognized property rights to salmon streams with hereditary title vested in the local group leader, and a corporate form of group structure that gave the tribe an identity separate from its members. To all this can be added a remarkably unabashed reverence for the accumulation of wealth and a shared system of cultural norms that accorded social prestige to those who most actively redistributed it through ceremonial potlatching.

The importance of salmon to the native economy cannot be overstated. Most tribes' livelihood revolved around the yearly cycle of salmon runs that began in early summer and continued late into fall.[4] With the exception of larger rivers such as the Fraser, the broader tribe normally claimed a large territory oriented around one or more contiguous rivers small enough to be owned throughout their entire length, with the river drainage establishing the limit of the tribe's territory. The tribe consisted of several shifting subdivisions, sometimes described as clans, which were in turn divided into local group houses that were dispersed across various winter villages with houses from other clans. Coastal tribes took much of the salmon harvest in tidal or fresh water with elaborate fish weirs and traps, or with dip nets, harpoons, and spears, primarily at upstream summer villages controlled by local clanhouse leaders. Either for lack of technology or economic benefit, the tribes had no means to harvest salmon in the open sea on a scale large enough to endanger stocks.

In many cases, local group leaders appear to have operated along the lines of franchisees to their clan leader, who had a similar relationship with the broader tribal leader. As local resource manager, the leader directed the harvesting and preservation of salmon and allocated a customary share of the output to each member of the house in return for his family's labor services. The same pattern repeated itself up the tribal hierarchy. The general expectation was that tribal leaders would share any residual above the opportunity cost of factor inputs on a discretionary basis with members of the local house, the clan, the tribe, and even between tribes, as variations in productivity and other circumstances dictated.

Almost uniformly up and down the coast, wealthier titleholders were known by a name that translated roughly into "river owner" (Drucker and Heizer 1967, p. 7) and were said to possess secret knowledge of "good" behavior, while the lesser chiefs were "without advice" (Suttles 1960, pp. 301–03). In spite of this designation and the "title" that went with it, tribal leaders had no right to sell rivers and other resource sites outright, although they could have their title divested by potlatch rivals.

Every year throughout the region, ranking titleholders performed the "first salmon rite" at the beginning of the spawning runs. The tribes believed the spirit of the salmon was immortal and voluntarily sacrificed its body for the benefit of man. If the salmon spirit was offended, the salmon run might not return full force in the following years. "Throughout the rite there was constant reference to the run and its continuance, and the first fish caught was usually placed with its head pointing upstream so the rest of the salmon would continue and not turn back to the sea" (Drucker 1965, at p. 95). Following this ritual, the tribal members began fishing, but not without restrictions by their leader on the number of salmon they could take and their allocation.

Potlatching has been described as "the ostentatious and dramatic distribution of property by the holder of a fixed, ranked, and named social position to other position holders" (Codere 1950, p. 63). Although there are many variations on the underlying theme ranging from informal feasts to elaborate regional events, potlatching in fact redistributed wealth both within and between tribes. Several cultural anthropologists have disputed whether potlatch gifts created an obligation to reciprocate, but reciprocation was nevertheless the norm. Any failure by a ranking titleholder to reciprocate, or any shortfall in the amount of the return gift, raised the potlatch rank and social prestige of the more generous party and lowered that of his rivals. The level of formality and the extent to which different tribes kept track of the balance of potlatch gift distributions varied along the coast, but relative success in potlatching was the primary basis for social prestige. As European contact increased, it appears the tribes expanded the formal potlatch system up and down the coast.

THE CASE LAW ON ABORIGINAL RIGHTS

English colonists to British Columbia brought with them the English common law which, beginning with the signing of the Magna Carta in 1215, had recognized the public right to fish in tidal waters and beyond, absent legislation to the contrary (Harris 2001, pp. 29, 31). The British Crown entered into a number of treaties on Vancouver Island in the 1850s through which several tribes ceded lands but explicitly negotiated to retain the right to "carry on [their] fisheries as formerly," an understanding embedded in subsequent nontreaty Indian reserve agreements (Harris 2001, pp. 34–43). Following British Columbia's entry into the confederation in 1871, however, Canadian regulators increasingly curtailed the tribes' fishing practices under the mistaken view that the natives regarded the salmon fishery merely as a "subsistence" activity aimed at securing enough food for daily consumption (Harris 2001, p. 16).

By 1879, Crown regulators had established mandatory licensing on the Fraser River in the name of conservation, with an exemption for natives as long as they fished according to traditional methods and did not sell their catch. Rather than being considered a right, however, fisheries regulators soon began to treat the aboriginal food fishery as a privilege subject to further restrictions. Allied with sport fishermen, the canneries succeeded in having specific conservation regulations imposed on the native food fishery,[5] especially the native use of fish weirs, which opponents alleged prevented the salmon from reaching their spawning beds and depleted stocks (Harris 2001). The affected tribes bitterly opposed these and other restrictions and were surprisingly effective at using the implicit threat of force, public opinion, and their considerable legal acumen to temporarily resist the tide of settlers. In at least one instance they stated publicly that they and their ancestors had cared for and nurtured their friends the salmon since time out of mind and had always made provision for them to reach the spawning beds. It was only with the coming of the whites that salmon stocks began to decline.[6] In spite of their resistance, the inexorable force of English settlement eventually prevailed, with several legal cases in the late 1880s finding that "Crown title underlay Native title" and natives therefore had no rights except those the Crown, in its benevolence, might allow (Harris 2001, p. 73). Concurrent with their eroding fishing rights, Canadian law under the Indian Act gradually restricted and ultimately prohibited ceremonial potlatching, ostensibly because it led the natives to dissipate their wealth and retarded their assimilation into Canadian society (Cole and Chaikin 1990).

The Canadian Constitution Act, 1982, included multiple provisions regarding the rights of all citizens known as the Canadian Charter of Rights and Freedoms; it was conceived somewhat along the lines of the American Bill of Rights. Section 35(1) was simply one provision aimed specifically at recognizing and affirming "existing aboriginal and treaty rights." Early cases under s. 35(1) upheld prior case law finding that "aboriginal title as a legal right derived from the Indians' historic occupation and possession of their tribal lands . . . and [had] survived British claims of sovereignty" (*Roberts v. Canada* [1989] at p. 340).[7] As a matter of affirmative policy, however, the Canadian Crown never extinguished aboriginal rights according to established common law principles—cession, conquest, or legislation; these rights continued to exist at the time of the Act and thereby received constitutional protection.

This left unresolved any number of related legal issues and led to three watershed Canadian Supreme Court cases during the decade of the 1990s.[8] The first of these was *R. v. Sparrow* (1990 at p. 385), a unanimous decision of the court. Sparrow, a member of the Musqueam tribe, was charged with fishing for salmon with a drift net exceeding the maximum length allowed under the tribe's food fishing license issued pursuant to regulations predating the act. Sparrow admitted the charges, but defended his actions as the exercise of a constitutionally protected aboriginal right to fish the Fraser River delta that had existed since "time immemorial." Though conceding Sparrow's factual claim to have been fishing in ancient tribal territory, the trial judge denied his defense and convicted him, finding that "existing" aboriginal fishing rights could not arise merely by historic use. The British Columbia Court of Appeal reversed, ordering a new trial, and Sparrow appealed to the Supreme Court of Canada.

The court identified the following four issues courts must address when assessing claims of aboriginal right: 1) whether the defendant has an existing aboriginal right; 2) whether the right has been extinguished; 3) whether there has been a prima facie infringement of that right; and 4) whether the infringement is justified by substantial and compelling legislative objectives. Based on factual expert testimony from a noted cultural anthropologist, the court had no difficulty concluding that Sparrow was exercising an existing right to fish in ancient tribal territory. And according to established case law, the sovereign's intent to extinguish an aboriginal right must be "clear and plain." Nothing in or under the Fisheries Act "demonstrates a clear and plain intention to extinguish the . . . aboriginal right to fish" (pp. 400–01). The court flatly rejected as "arbitrary" and "unsuitable" the Crown's view that the fishing regulations in place immediately prior to the passage of the act should determine existing aboriginal fishing rights. This "frozen rights" view would read into the constitution a patchwork of regulations differing from place to place and tribe to tribe. Instead, the court sought to interpret "existing aboriginal rights" in an abstract and flexible way that would allow for historical evolution to meet changing circumstances.

Having found an existing and unextinguished aboriginal right to fish, the court addressed the nature and scope of the right. On appeal, Sparrow argued that the Musqueam actively bartered salmon prior to contact and cited recent case law recognizing that holders of aboriginal hunting rights may exercise those rights for any purpose and according to any nondangerous method. To leverage these decisions, he asserted that his existing aboriginal right included the right to fish for commercial purposes. The court was sympathetic but cautious. In light of the anthropological evidence indicating that the tribe's fishing practices had always been an "integral part of their distinctive culture," the court agreed with the lower court's finding that the nature and scope of the aboriginal right to fish for food went beyond providing for mere "subsistence" using traditional methods (p. 402). In addition, it surely included the right to fish in a contemporary manner to provide for social and ceremonial needs. But because government regulation in proper keeping with s. 35(1) no doubt could be used to regulate constitutionally protected aboriginal rights, this was as far as the court would go. Noting mounting tensions between natives and participants in the mobile ocean fishery, it confined its decision to the aboriginal right to fish for food as the parties had characterized it at the trial, leaving the question of commercial fishing for another case.

The court then turned its attention to whether the net length regulation imposed by Sparrow's food fishing license demonstrated a *prima facie* infringement and, if so, whether the regulation was justified based on substantial and compelling legislative interests. In light of Sparrow's plausible assertion of a virtually unlimited constitutional right to fish, the court deemed it necessary to first establish a framework for interpreting s. 35(1). It began by reviewing the history of unjust political and legal treatment of Canada's aboriginal peoples, culminating in a 1973 policy statement by the Crown evidencing its newfound willingness to recognize aboriginal land claims regardless of formal documentation and to provide compensation for lands that had been taken. In the court's view, s. 35(1) was the constitutional manifestation of this political sentiment. At the very least, s. 35(1) protects natives from the legislative power of the provinces and provides a "solid constitutional base on which subsequent negotiations can take place." Beyond that, it mandates a "just settlement for aboriginal peoples" and renounces the "old rules of the game" in which the Crown acknowledged existing aboriginal rights but denied courts of law the authority to review its adverse assertions of sovereignty (p. 406).

Given the gravity of a constitutional amendment, the court reasoned that s. 35(1) must be construed in the light of its underlying purpose. A *purposive* approach mandates a "generous, liberal interpretation," with any doubt to be resolved in favor of the natives. In carrying out this charge, the court emphasized the importance of fair treatment and due regard for native traditions. But although the "honour of the Crown" establishes a fiduciary duty to native people in resolving aboriginal rights, these rights are not absolute. The Crown must retain its power to legislate in general and specifically with respect to aboriginal people. This framework demands compromise in balancing the *sui generis* nature of aboriginal rights against other substantial and compelling governmental interests, with the Crown bearing the burden of justifying any infringement or denial of aboriginal rights on a case-by-case basis.

The court emphasized the importance of being sensitive to the aboriginal perspective on fishing rights, which "are not traditional property rights. They are rights held by a collective and are in keeping with the culture and existence of that group. Courts must be careful . . . to avoid the application of traditional common law concepts of property as they develop their understanding of . . . the *'sui generis'* nature of aboriginal rights" (p. 411). Under the facts of Sparrow's appeal, the court found that a *prima facie* presumption of infringement would arise if the facts indicated an "adverse restriction" on the Musqueam in their exercise of the right to fish for food (p. 411).

Because Sparrow successfully raised this presumption, the court considered whether a substantial and compelling legislative objective justified the net length restriction. The party defending the restriction has the burden of proving that the legislative objective behind the restriction, and the restriction as applied, are both valid and consistent with the fiduciary duty owed to the native people. The court specifically identified conservation of the resource as a valid objective, noting its consistency with "aboriginal beliefs and practices." But even in the area of fisheries conservation, there must be an appropriate link between justification and the allocation of priorities to the fishery. Established case law would place paramount priority on conservation measures, followed by the native food fishery, the nonnative commercial fishery, and finally the nonnative sport fishery.

R. v. Van der Peet (1996) arguably raised the very issue of aboriginal rights to fish commercially that the court declined to resolve in *Sparrow*.[9] Van der Peet, a member of the Sto:lo tribe, was charged with selling ten salmon her husband had caught in the lower Fraser River under the authority of an Indian food fishing license that prohibited the sale, barter, or offer of sale or barter of any fish. She admitted the charges but claimed her constitutional right to fish for salmon included the right to sell fish. Relying on anthropological expert testimony, the trial judge determined that Van der Peet's constitutionally protected right to catch salmon for food and ceremonial purposes did not include a right to sell fish for money. He therefore found her guilty, with no further need to address the constitutionality of the licensing restrictions.

Van der Peet's appeal eventually made it to the Supreme Court of Canada, where she claimed the court below had turned an aboriginal "right into a relic" in defining aboriginal rights as "practices integral to the distinctive cultures of aboriginal peoples" rather than more generalized "legal rights," in finding that the purpose of the act was merely to protect natives' "traditional way of life," in requiring that claimants "satisfy a long-time use test . . . and demonstrate an absence of European influence," and in failing to "adopt the perspective of aboriginal peoples." With two justices dissenting, the court rejected Van der Peet's arguments, pointing out that the purpose of the act was not to accord aboriginal rights the same "liberal enlightenment" status as general rights accorded to all citizens under the Charter. In the court's words, its task is "to define aboriginal rights in a manner which recognizes [they] are rights but which does so without losing sight of the fact that they are rights held by aboriginal people because they are aboriginal" (p. 535). Although courts must be sensitive to the aboriginal perspective, they must "do so in terms which are cognizable to the non aboriginal legal system" (p. 551).

The court rejected any characterization of Van der Peet's actions as the sale of fish "on a commercial basis." Given the wording of the regulations and the defendant's pleadings, it was necessary to determine only whether she has the right "to exchange fish for money (sale) or other goods (trade)" (p. 563). Further, the court found that the test for establishing constitutional protection under s. 35(1) is whether the activity being claimed as a right was "an element of a practice, custom or tradition integral to the distinctive culture of the aboriginal group claiming the right." In addition, this test requires a trial court to determine the time period relevant to that inquiry. To be integral, an activity must be "one of the things that truly made the society what it was." To be distinctive, the practice cannot be true of every human society, nor can it be only "incidental or occasional" to the society, as the very point of the constitutional analysis is to reconcile the distinctive features of the aboriginal society with Crown sovereignty (pp. 553–54).

The moment for determining whether a practice is integral and distinctive to the society claiming the right is the moment of European contact, rather than the moment of European sovereignty, because contact caused those practices to depart from their unadulterated form. This does not mean the aboriginal society claiming the right must meet the impossible evidentiary burden of proving the exact nature of the practices in which they engaged prior to contact. It need only prove the practice was integral to their distinctive culture in postcontact times and had "continuity" with the precontact period. The continuity requirement is the primary means by which *existing* aboriginal rights can be interpreted flexibly to evolve over time rather than becoming "frozen," as the *Sparrow* court had warned. What is more, trial courts must adapt the rules of evidence to the "difficulties in proving a right" claimed to have originated prior to the existence of "written records" and must avoid undervaluing "the evidence presented by aboriginal claimants simply because that evidence does not conform precisely" to modern evidentiary standards (pp. 558–59).

The court reviewed the trial record to determine whether the sale of fish for money or other goods was integral to the distinctive culture of the Sto:lo. Drawing on anthropological expert testimony from the trial record, it noted that "trade was incidental to fishing for food [, and that] no regularized trade in salmon existed in aboriginal times.... It was the establishment by the Hudson's Bay Company at the Fort at Langley that created the market and trade in fresh salmon" (pp. 567–68). What is more, "such limited exchanges of salmon as took place in Sto:lo society [prior to contact] were primarily linked to the kinship and family relationships on which Sto:lo society was based." In the court's view, these findings support the conclusion that the exchange of salmon for money or other goods was not a significant, integral, or defining feature of Sto:lo society. Finding no evidence of "clear and palpable error" by the trial judge, the court held that Van der Peet had failed to carry the burden of proving her sale of salmon qualified as an existing aboriginal right constitutionally recognized and affirmed under s. 35(1).

In dissent, Justice McLachlin (as she was then) looked to existing precedent to determine, empirically, how common law courts had identified the scope of aboriginal rights in the past. She noted that the common law routinely recognized all kinds of aboriginal interests, even those "unknown to English law." As a matter of affirmative treaty policy, moreover, settlers had accepted "the principle that the aboriginal peoples who occupied what is now Canada were regarded as possessing the aboriginal right to live off their lands and the resources found in their forests and streams to the extent they had traditionally done so." The fundamental understanding behind settlement in Canada had always been that "aboriginal people could only be deprived of the sustenance they traditionally drew from the land and adjacent waters by solemn treaty with the Crown, on terms that would ensure to them and to their successors a replacement for the livelihood that their lands, forests, and streams had since ancestral times provided them" (p. 646).

According to Justice McLachlin, the aboriginal right to use the land and adjacent waters for sustenance is "safely ... enshrined in s. 35(1) of the

Constitution Act, 1982." But in her view, it includes the right to trade to the extent "necessary to provide basic housing, transportation, clothing, and amenities—the modern equivalent of what the aboriginal people in question formerly took from the land or the fishery, over and above what was required for food and ceremonial purposes" (pp. 648–49). Because she inferred from the evidence that aboriginal societies did not generally value "excess or accumulated wealth," this measure of aboriginal rights will seldom "exceed the basics of food, clothing and housing, supplemented by a few amenities." As to the allocation of further priorities, she found that "commercial and sports fishermen may enjoy the resource as they always have, subject to conservation," which is a necessary precondition for the resource to exist in the first place (p. 665).

Justice McLachlin took care in pointing out that her empirical approach has two distinct advantages over the principled approach favored by the majority. Where the court finds, as in *Gladstone* (a companion case to *Van der Peet*) that commercial fishing *was* integral to the tribe's distinctive culture, the aboriginal right has no internal limit under the principled approach. This will invariably require the court to establish an expansive concept of justification to "cut back the right on the ground that this is required for reconciliation and social harmony" (p. 659). When aboriginal and nonaboriginal claims to the commercial fishery conflict, for example, the court will ultimately find itself in the tenuous position of having to reconcile the conflict politically. But political expedience falls short of being a "substantial and compelling" legislative objective necessary to justify infringement of an existing aboriginal right.

In her view, an empirical approach avoids this problem because it places its own internal limit on the aboriginal right to engage in commercial fishing based on "equivalence with what by ancestral law and custom the aboriginal people in question took from the resource" (p. 665). Aside from truly substantial and compelling legislative restrictions—such as conservation measures necessary to ensure the resource continues to exist—the right is then regarded as a legally fixed entitlement. This, Justice McLachlin explained, represents the *Sparrow*'s court's "solid constitutional base upon which subsequent negotiations can take place." Further reconciliation of aboriginal and nonaboriginal interests should be left to negotiated settlements, which will naturally accommodate the aboriginal perspective, with the courts playing a less important role.

Delgamuukw v. British Columbia (1997) involved claims by hereditary chiefs of the Gistskan and Wet'suet'en tribes to aboriginal title covering 58,000 square kilometers land in central British Columbia. The case raised any number of issues critical to the settlement of aboriginal rights and generated a staggering trial record consisting of some 85,000 pages of testimony, exhibits, and argument. Owing to what the trial judge perceived as bias in favor of the claimants, as well as a general lack of credibility, he excluded the testimony of two anthropological experts regarding the nature of the tribes' relationship with their claimed lands. He admitted into evidence the tribes' oral histories regarding their ongoing occupancy of the claimed lands on a hearsay exception, but he found these histories deserved zero evidentiary weight. As a result, he concluded, the plaintiffs failed to establish the exclusive use and occupancy of these lands at the time of sovereignty required under the common law to establish aboriginal title.

On appeal, the Supreme Court of Canada was unwilling to overturn the trial judge's findings of fact regarding the credibility of the anthropological experts, but it rejected, as a matter of law, his refusal to give weight to the tribes' oral histories. In the court's words: "[t]he implication of the trial judge's reasoning is that oral histories should never be given any independent weight" (p. 1074). Given that these histories are often the only available record of the tribes' past, this would effectively bar all claims to aboriginal title. Because the trial judge made his evidentiary rulings prior to the court's judgment in *Van der Peet,* liberalizing the evidentiary burden on aboriginal claimants, he was unable to follow this approach. Reluctantly, the court found, a new trial was in order.

The court took the opportunity to elaborate on the content of aboriginal title under s. 35(1). To establish title, claimants must indeed demonstrate exclusive use and occupation of the land by, for example, establishing the construction of dwellings, cultivation and enclosure, or regular use for hunting, fishing, etc. "In considering whether occupation sufficient to ground title is established, the group's size, manner of life, material resources, and technological abilities, and the character of the lands claimed must be taken into account" (p. 1018). Unlike the requirement for establishing aboriginal rights, generally, the claimant need not independently show that the land is integral to its distinctive aboriginal culture; occupation, by itself, establishes this requirement. And whereas the time for the identification of aboriginal rights is first contact, the time for the identification of aboriginal title is the moment the British Crown asserted sovereignty over the land in 1846. Among other reasons, this is because occupation alone is sufficient to establish aboriginal title, with no need to distinguish between unadulterated aboriginal practices and those influenced or introduced by European contact.

Because aboriginal rights are held communally, according to the court, they may not be alienated to third parties but may be surrendered to the Crown in exchange for valuable consideration. Although aboriginal title encompasses the exclusive right to use the land for a variety of purposes, the uses to which the claimant puts the land must not be inconsistent with the nature of its attachment to the land so as to constitute equitable waste. Otherwise, the aboriginal peoples must surrender the lands to the Crown. Notwithstanding the exclusive occupancy requirement, joint title can arise from shared exclusivity, and shared, nonexclusive rights permitting a number of uses can be established if exclusivity cannot be proved. In this connection, "[t]he common law should develop to recognize aboriginal rights as they were recognized by either de facto practice or by aboriginal systems of governance" (p. 1019). In ordering a new trial, the court emphasized that it was not suggesting the parties should resolve their dispute through further costly litigation. Instead, it reminded them that negotiated settlements, "reinforced by judgments of this Court," will ultimately achieve s. 35(1)'s basic purpose of reconciling aboriginal rights with Crown sovereignty (p. 1124).

THE ECONOMICS OF NORTHWEST COAST TRIBAL PROPERTY RIGHTS

The study of primitive man, including the northwest coast tribes, has traditionally been considered the exclusive work of cultural anthropologists, who have questioned the relevance of economic theory to primitive societies because they lack organized exchange markets or monetary systems for which its analytical tools are thought to be specifically suited.[10] Beginning with Nobel Laureate Ronald H. Coase's pioneering work, *The Nature of the Firm* (1937), economists have made tremendous progress understanding the forces affecting nonmarket exchange. As Nobel Laureate Douglass C. North and coauthor Robert Paul Thomas state in their classic 1977 economic history essay, *The First Economic Revolution*, man's transition from hunting and gathering to settled agriculture "has been almost entirely the province of archaeologists and anthropologists.... There simply was no applicable [economic] theory that could be used to explain the Neolithic revolution.

This situation has changed with the recent development of theory to deal with . . . the evolution of property rights" (pp. 229–30). This theory is now widely known as the property rights approach to economic theory, a broad and scientifically powerful field of inquiry focusing on the role of social institutions in reducing economic frictions known as transaction costs.

The property rights approach postulates that individuals make decisions as if they consciously maximize *wealth*, defined as the capitalized value of future expected income.[11] Contrary to popular misconceptions, wealth consists of more than material goods; it includes anything of subjective value to the decision maker, whether tangible or intangible, present or future (Johnsen 1986b). More to the point, wealth reflects the stock value of a capital asset, such as the cumulative flow of services from a durable good or the future generations of a given population of salmon. One of the primary implications of wealth maximization is that individuals will undertake all investments that increase their expected wealth net of the transaction costs of capturing the associated returns.

Property rights in the broad economic sense result from the constraints social institutions impose on members of the group to assure those in a position to invest to promote the common wealth that they will capture a sufficient share of the returns to make the investment worthwhile. Formal law is one example of such an institution, but others include purposeful private ordering and a group's distinctive web of spontaneous cultural norms. Property rights in the narrower legal sense are a subset of economic property rights, just as law is one among many institutions that help to assure the capturability of investment returns (Barzel 1997). Although the exact scope of economic property rights over an asset depends on the context at hand, it generally includes some measure of the right to exclude, the right to transfer (or alienate), and the right to use the asset to derive income (Cheung 1969). Because numerous events beyond the owner's control can cause productivity to vary, the right to derive income is risky and is often characterized as the right to derive residual income, or the residual claim (Jensen and Meckling 1976).

Potlatching, Property Rights, and Salmon Husbandry

The famous ethnographer, Franz Boas (1966), and the many students of cultural anthropology that followed him to the Northwest Coast, deserve much of the credit for recording northwest coast tribal culture. Rather than engaging in the ethnocentric exercise of trying to explain tribal culture through the lens of Western civilization, however, Boas sought to record the tribes' culture from "their own perspective."[12] Because he and his followers (ethnocentrically) assumed the tribes inhabited a region superabundant with salmon and other natural resources easily exploited to meet material subsistence needs, they also "generally assumed . . . potlatch exchanges had little or no relationship to problems of livelihood" (Suttles 1990, p. 85). In Boas' view, ceremonial potlatching was primarily a means of establishing social rank. Codere, an adherent of this view, later went a step further. Observing that the tribes were very warlike and possessive of their territories in prehistoric and early contact times, and that warfare declined with contact while ceremonial potlatching increased, she argued the two were substitutes in tribal leaders' "limitless pursuit of a kind of social prestige which required continual proving to be established or maintained against rivals" (1950, p. 118).

In contrast, Suttles (1960, 1968) and Piddocke (1968), whose interests included the emerging field of ecology, proposed that potlatching provided a form of social insurance against local hardship resulting from variations in resource productivity, including the occasional failure of salmon runs. Drucker and Heizer (1967), who viewed potlatching strictly as a basis for social stratification, rejected this proposition. Given the tribes' superabundant resource base, they disputed the factual claim that variations in resource productivity were severe enough to cause local hardship. Donald and Mitchell (1975) performed the first empirical analysis of tribal resource productivity, finding that variability could indeed have been substantial and not unlikely to cause local hardship in the absence of potlatch wealth transfers.

Ceremonial potlatching evolved to define and enforce exclusive tribal property rights to salmon streams and—given the tribes' limited ability to intercept salmon in the open sea—their native salmon stocks. The historical record clearly demonstrates that the coastal tribes were extremely protective of their streams, with trespassers often being summarily executed. In the face of unpredictable stream-specific variations in resource productivity, however, the tendency was for unfortunate tribes to encroach on their more fortunate neighbors.[13] One tribe would see or hear of another enjoying relative prosperity and send its warriors to capture a share of the bounty (Ferguson 1979).[14] The tribes' oral histories and the records of early Europeans indicate that violence was the default method of property rights enforcement. But because violence imposes transaction costs on both encroacher and incumbent, the inexorable tendency is to replace it with less costly, institutionalized forms of property rights enforcement.

Even if fully able to defend itself in an absolute conflict, the problem the incumbent faced was that its cost of violently defending its territory was relatively high compared to the encroacher precisely because its marginal product of labor from fishing was relatively high.[15] The economic theory of property rights predicts that the incumbents should be willing to make concessions to encourage encroachers to leave in peace, a prediction clearly confirmed by widespread accounts of war parties being met with gifts and invited to an elaborate feast by their intended targets. With the incumbent having a comparative advantage in fishing and the encroacher having a comparative advantage in warfare, there were clearly gains from peaceful, as opposed to violent, exchange.

As an institutionalized form of reciprocal exchange, potlatching dramatically lowered the transaction costs of enforcing exclusive tribal property rights. To mitigate the encroachment problem, participating tribes essentially entered into a multilateral commitment that those among them who experienced unexpectedly high productivity would make protection payments to those whose productivity was unexpectedly low. Given that all tribes faced the possibility of a poor salmon run at one time or another due to factors at least partially beyond their control, the encroachment problem was reciprocal. Unless those tribes whose productivity was relatively low expected to be paid off, the system of recognized tribal property rights would have broken down, with enforcement reverting to mutually destructive warfare.[16]

Absent something more, this solution fails to explain why the tribes bothered to enforce exclusive property rights at all. Imagine early man's perception of the salmon fishery once the glaciers receded from the coast around 10,000 years ago. Each of five species of Pacific salmon has one or more life histories, many rivers support multiple populations of multiple species bound for spawning beds in different tributaries, and all salmon populations are subject to innumerable unknown influences during their life cycle. There would have been too much noise in the system for early observers to recognize salmon return to their place of birth to spawn and that protecting their upstream migration was therefore crucial to the productivity of future runs. The entire coastal salmon fishery would have appeared to be an undivided common resource base naturally subject to open access. A nomadic hunter-gatherer lifestyle was the likely response to local productivity variations, with "rights" to salmon being determined by what the group could capture and consume as it wandered the coast.

Rather than open access, the archeological evidence indicates that for thousands of years prior to European contact, the tribes were sedentary and enjoyed some measure of exclusive territorial property rights. But exclusive property rights do not simply happen. Because they are costly to enforce and require the owner to suffer unpredictable local variations in resource productivity, they must have generated offsetting benefits. The benefits came from the incentive they gave the tribes to invest in husbanding their salmon stocks. At some point, tribal leaders clearly recognized the anadromous character of the Pacific salmon. The widespread first-salmon rite, in which the chief warned that improper treatment of the salmon might result in their failure to return, provides casual support for this conclusion. But any doubt is laid to rest by a mid-nineteenth-century report that "[i]t is common practice among the few tribes whose hunters go far inland, at certain seasons, to transport the ova of the salmon in boxes filled with damp mosses, from the rivers to the lakes, or to other streams" (Sproat 1868). Transplanting fertilized ova would be a complete waste of time unless salmon were known to return to their natal streams to spawn.

By reducing the transaction costs of enforcing exclusive tribal property rights, potlatching encouraged tribal leaders to make stream-specific investments in husbanding their salmon stocks. The evidence suggests that they engaged in at least rudimentary husbandry. They surely recognized, for example, that too much or too little fishing effort would reduce the size of returning salmon populations and that proper husbandry was, in part, a matter of optimizing fishing effort. The tribes went beyond rudimentary husbandry, however, and actively specialized in accumulating stream-specific knowledge of salmon husbandry. This kind of prospecting for knowledge is unlikely to occur in the absence of exclusive property rights. As economic historians North and Thomas put it, when open-access rights exist over resources "there is little incentive for the acquisition of superior technology and learning. In contrast, exclusive property rights ... provide a direct incentive to improve efficiency and productivity, or, in more fundamental terms, to acquire more knowledge and new techniques. It is this change in incentive that explains the rapid progress made by mankind in the last 10,000 years" (1977, p. 241).

As Codere argued, ceremonial potlatching was indeed a substitute for warfare. But she failed to explain why either one generated social prestige, or why tribal leaders valued social prestige more than the wealth they spent to get it. Tribes that accumulated superior knowledge of salmon husbandry undoubtedly generated greater increases in the productive capacity of their salmon stocks than their potlatch rivals. This allowed their chiefs to gain social prestige by distributing more wealth at potlatches *and* to retain more for tribal consumption. Abstracting from differences in tribal leaders' managerial talent, over time wealth transfers through the potlatch system would have roughly balanced, with all tribes experiencing an absolute increase in wealth. The threat of losing social prestige was a cultural constraint on those who would free ride by strategically underinvesting in knowledge accumulation and hosting few or meager potlatches. But the desire for social prestige was not "limitless" nor was social prestige an end in itself; it was merely instrumental to the social goal of promoting the commonwealth of tribes.

Potlatching obviously transferred wealth from tribes whose circumstances were relatively good to those whose circumstances were relatively poor, as both Suttles and Piddocke proposed and Donald and Mitchell confirmed. But this would be unnecessary under an open-access regime in which all tribes fished an undivided common resource base. By assigning residual claims to specific streams, exclusive tribal property rights *created* stream-specific risk for individual tribes at the same time it increased their expected returns from accumulating knowledge about the avoidable causes of low productivity. This is a straightforward reflection of the standard risk-return tradeoff from financial theory, which also predicts that individuals will diversify away asset-specific risk if possible. Rather than providing insurance against local hardship as such, the potlatch system allowed the tribes to diversify stream-specific risk by giving them access to the market portfolio.

Because they are extremely "heritable," it would be difficult to find a genus in the animal kingdom better suited to scientific knowledge accumulation than Pacific salmon. As George P. Marsh reported in 1874, "[f]ish are more affected than quadrupeds by slight and even imperceptible differences in their breeding places and feeding grounds. Every river, every brook, every lake stamps a special character upon its salmon, . . . which is at once recognized by those who deal in or consume them" (p. 108). For Pacific salmon, the time between generations is short enough, and the struggle to reproduce keen enough, that over the course of a man's lifetime the characteristics of a given stock can evolve dramatically in response to even minor changes in its environment, whether induced by nature or by human influences.

The tribes' fishing technology was ideally suited to the accumulation of stream-specific knowledge of salmon husbandry to harvest salmon. Many tribes along the coast relied on fish weirs, which involved a substantial capital investment and in many cases were built to span an entire stream. The only way for salmon to pass was to enter a holding trap, which gave the attendants complete selectivity over which salmon were allowed to continue on to the spawning beds. Given the heritability of salmon, the use of fish weirs in privately controlled streams with no effective means to intercept salmon in the open sea would have given tribal leaders a relatively noiseless information feedback mechanism, and allowed them to accumulate stream-specific knowledge of salmon husbandry relatively rapidly. It is entirely plausible that the tribes actually engaged in purposeful genetic selection of salmon stocks to develop populations with preferred biological characteristics.[17]

Tribal organization, which was essentially corporate, was also ideally suited to knowledge accumulation. Tribal chiefs held title to streams and other resources on behalf of their tribe and, as professional managers, had the exclusive right of control over resources and the labor services of resident members. They uniformly demanded that anyone who wanted to pass through upriver sites seek their permission to do so and that under no circumstances were the salmon to be disturbed in their upstream migration or in the spawning beds. As we would expect of any entrepreneur, the chief received the residual income (Alchian and Demsetz 1972), which he shared with members on a discretionary basis. A tribal leader's reputation—social prestige, if you like—was part of his residual payoff from superior salmon husbandry. By allowing him to borrow against future expected income, it capitalized his superior management skill and thereby allowed him to finance wealth-increasing investment projects. It was therefore unnecessary for tribal members to incur transaction costs to carefully monitor their leader's managerial inputs; outputs conveyed the important information.

Equally important, tribal chiefs were widely known to possess a *corpus* of "secret" knowledge about how best to use their resources to create wealth. Children were taught to respect the salmon and to take great care in observing their habits and characteristics and, although primogeniture was the norm, chiefs often bequeathed resources and the associated knowledge to the child identified as having the best mental capacity. It is exactly this knowledge that the tribes revered and their chiefs touted at potlatches as the basis for their manifest prosperity. By perpetuating this knowledge, the tribe, like the corporation, had the potential for unlimited life supported by a perpetual capital stock.

Economics, Anthropology, and Law

Rather than being an exogenous fluke of nature, the observed "superabundance" of salmon on the Northwest Coast at the time of contact was the endogenous outcome of evolved property rights institutions that encouraged the tribes to husband their salmon stocks. Theorists can argue endlessly from first principles, but the true test of any scientific hypothesis is testability, that is, its ability to predict "phenomena not yet observed" and capable of not occurring (Friedman 1953). The available evidence regarding tribal institutions is consistent with the predictions of the property rights approach but inconsistent with the predictions, if any, of the theories put forth by cultural anthropologists. My hypothesis that potlatching served as an alternative to violence in enforcing tribal property rights predicts, for example, that the frequency and intensity of potlatching should have risen with the English prohibition on native violence, just as the historical record shows (Johnsen 1986a). And my hypothesis that the tribes engaged in salmon husbandry predicts that tribal property rights along the trunk section of larger rivers such as the Fraser—which was subject to "shared exclusive ownership" by multiple tribes and the interception of salmon by downstream tribes—would have been much less aggressively enforced than along the coast, where smaller river systems were subject to ownership in their entirety by a single tribe. The historical record clearly confirms these predictions (Johnsen 1986a, 2001).

Two pieces of casual evidence support the endogeneity of salmon abundance. First, contrary to the popular image of native North Americans as wise and mystical conservators of natural resources, in many cases they failed miserably as environmental stewards. The key to success or failure was the extent to which they developed exclusive property rights over resource stocks (Anderson 1996). With regard to salmon, the northwest coast tribes performed admirably, while other North American natives systematically hunted once-abundant large mammals to extinction (Smith 1975). With European contact and the advent of the fur trade, however, the northwest coast tribes quickly depleted the region's sea otter population, no doubt because of the high transaction costs of enforcing property rights to stocks that migrated across tribal boundaries.[18]

Second, not only did northwest coast tribes behave "as if " they maximized wealth, but uniformly up and down the coast they shamelessly revered the accumulation of wealth, which ultimately derived from their salmon streams and other resources. They were not content merely to meet "material subsistence needs," as most cultural anthropologists have assumed.[19] Instead, they actively sought to prosper, and took great pride in doing so (Grumet 1979). They achieved one of the highest standards of living among all North American natives, developed highly refined tangible and performance art, traveled widely for social purposes, and actively shared their aesthetic achievements and secret knowledge within an established network of allied tribes.

In the introduction to his otherwise excellent book on northwest coast tribal slavery, cultural anthropologist Leland Donald puzzles over the tribes' prosperity. In his words, "Although [the northwest coast tribes] were hunter-gatherers, their modes of subsistence and environments supported one of the densest known nonagricultural populations," exhibiting social traits "more usually associated with agricultural peoples" (1997, pp. 2–3). This leads him to ask how "the Northwest Coast peoples achieve[d] such rich and complex cultures on a foraging subsistence base?" North and Thomas (1977, pp. 230, 241) had already solved the puzzle twenty years earlier. In their words:

> [T]he transition from hunting/gathering to settled agriculture [was not] the crucial development occurring during the first economic revolution.... [I]t was not the type of economic activity so much as the kind of property rights that were established that accounts for the significant increase in the rate of human progress [by creating] an incentive change for mankind of fundamental proportions.

Seen in this light, when Europeans first made contact, the tribes had long since put the Neolithic revolution behind them. Having established both the property rights institutions and the knowledge base to husband their salmon stocks, they were not "hunter-gatherers" but institutionally sophisticated salmon ranchers.[20]

Much of what cultural anthropologists have found worth understanding about the northwest coast tribes is either pure white noise—neutral mutations with no explanatory power—or a reflection of arbitrary coordinating devices. Whether the tribes strictly followed matrilineal rules of descent or considered themselves the children of Coyote or Raven are simply irrelevant to helping Canadian courts understand their distinctive rights. The following statement of Lord Sumner from *In Re Southern Rhodesia* (1919) makes a telling, and necessarily ethnocentric, point:

> Some tribes are so low in the scale of social organization that their usages and conceptions of rights and duties are not to be reconciled with the institutions or the legal ideas of civilized society.... On the other hand, there are indigenous peoples whose legal conceptions, though differently developed, are hardly less precise than our own. When once they have been studied and understood they are no less enforceable than rights arising under English law.

The truth is that until native claims began making their way into Canadian courts, few cultural anthropologists considered tribal "legal conceptions"— or their contribution to tribal prosperity—worthy of serious attention.[21] How else can one explain their view of the tribes after over a century of intensive study as mere hunter-gathers and potlatching as mere ceremony? The property rights approach to economic theory is far better suited than cultural anthropology to understanding tribal legal conceptions because it provides a general theory to explain social institutions in a wide variety of settings, with the cost of transacting being the key explanatory variable. It is of course important to consider the aboriginal perspective in seeking to understand the facts regarding northwest coast tribes' legal conceptions but, according to the property rights approach, once having done this there is nothing especially unique or difficult to understand. Like all Neolithic societies, they aspired to prosperity, they relied on property rights institutions to exclude others from their resource stocks, and they actively accumulated knowledge to enhance their prosperity through long-term capital investment; only the transaction costs differed.

One culturally distinctive characteristic of the northwest coast tribes was their reliance on highly institutionalized reciprocity to enforce exclusive tribal property rights in the absence of formal legal enforcement by a hierarchical nation state. But this is nothing new to property rights economists. As Nobel Laureate Vernon L. Smith and others have shown, reciprocity is an important method of property rights enforcement in a variety of settings in which legal enforcement is unavailable (Hoffman, McCabe, and Smith 1998).[22] The truly distinctive thing about the tribes is that they succeeded in enforcing exclusive tribal property rights to entire salmon stocks. In this regard, their legal conceptions were far *more* precise than our own, which have treated the Pacific salmon fishery as an undivided common subject to open access under the rule of capture and persistently dissipated it ever since the canneries began intercepting salmon in 1871.

The tribes' exclusive stream-based ownership of salmon stocks represents the core of their distinctive culture. What began as an expectation by the early arrivals to the coast of the open-access "right" to capture salmon indiscriminately, and to exclude others from consuming only *those* salmon, ultimately evolved into the expectation of an exclusive right to harvest a specific river's salmon stocks in perpetuity. But a salmon stock does not exist independent of man's perception of it. It is an abstraction that relies on institutional arrangements for its practical "existence." Social institutions—whether formal law or formalized reciprocity—parse value flows from an otherwise undivided commons and reify them as cognizable assets in the sense that it pays their owner to specialize in identifying the causes of high and low productivity and to adjust accordingly to enhance their capital value (Johnsen 1995).[23] The tribes recognized salmon stocks as exclusive "property" because doing so increased their common wealth net of the transaction costs of enforcing the associated rights.

PRIVATIZING THE FISHERY: A NEGOTIATED SETTLEMENT

Exclusive ownership of "assets in place" includes the real option to take advantage of growth opportunities resulting from knowledge specific to the asset (Myers 1977). Even if the tribes did not engage in active commercial trade of salmon prior to contact, by securing exclusive ownership over salmon stocks, their tribal institutions gave them that option when contact occurred and they routinely recognized and actively took advantage of such opportunities. Although exclusive ownership of salmon stocks, including the real option to manage them for commercial purposes, is easily cognizable to the Canadian legal system and well within the limits of *Van der Peet*'s principled approach to aboriginal fishing rights, the court will probably be reluctant to follow through and apply the letter of its own law by restoring stock ownership to the tribes. The social upheaval from such a judicially orchestrated transfer of wealth would be devastating, and avoiding it may for all practical purposes be a substantial and compelling objective. Despite the looming crisis, incumbent mobile ocean fishermen have legitimate investment-backed expectations in the British Columbia salmon fishery for which they have shown themselves willing to organize and fight, both politically and otherwise, when necessary.

In arguing for a self-limiting conception of the aboriginal right to fish, Justice McLachlin's dissent in *Van der Peet* provides the court with a plausible fallback position. Her approach would divest the tribes of their real option on postcontact growth opportunities in the Pacific salmon fishery by converting their residual claim to a fixed priority claim (similar to converting a corporate equity claim to a debt claim) to enough salmon to provide a moderate livelihood roughly equal to what they would have enjoyed *but for* the arrival of English settlers.[24] This fixed claim against the fishery, together with the many tribal claims to native lands following *Delgamuukw*, reflect both a shift in property rights and a clarification of those rights that reduces the transaction costs of reassigning them to their highest valuing users in a privatization auction.

Privatization rests on the assumption that if the tribes were asked to rank the values they attach to various aboriginal rights in keeping with their distinctive cultural perspective, the current assignment of rights includes too much land and too little in the way of fishing rights. As Sproat commented in 1876 regarding early land negotiations with British Columbia's tribes, "If the Crown had ever met the Indians of this provinces [sic] in council with a view to obtain the surrender of their lands for purposes of settlement, the Indians would, in the first place, have made stipulations about their right to get salmon. . . . [L]and and water for irrigating it would have been, in their mind, secondary considerations" (Harris 2001, p. 34). The tribes have no culturally based advantage in managing vast tracts of land whose highest valued use is for hunting, mining, logging, hydroelectric generation, gaming, traditional agriculture, or commercial development.[25] They do, however, have a culturally based advantage in managing selected salmon stocks, both because their traditional stream-based property rights are vastly more efficient than the current mixed stock institutional structure and because they may yet possess accumulated knowledge, or at least general know-how, regarding salmon husbandry practices capable of completely revitalizing the British Columbia fishery.

The converse of the relatively high value the tribes place on the right to manage salmon stocks is that nonnatives place a relatively low value on such management—as evidenced by the long history of stock depletion and the current deplorable state of the fishery[26]—and a relatively high value on the vast tracts of land subject to tribal claims. There are clearly potential gains to incumbent commercial fishermen, the tribes, and Canadian society as a whole from recontracting because the transaction costs of doing so are sufficiently low in relation to the gains to make doing so worthwhile. One reason for the low transaction costs is the availability of a culturally correct mechanism for valuing and transferring the associated rights known as the "rivalry potlatch." Although the tribes' rights to resources were held communally and are therefore said to have been inalienable, title disputes invariably threatened to divest a tribe of its rights.[27] On such occasions, according to Drucker (1955, p. 128), the rival claimants held a potlatch to resolve the dispute, which he describes in the following passage:

> When two chiefs claimed the same place, the first one would give a potlatch, stating his claim; then the second would try to outdo him. Finally, one or the other gave away or destroyed more property than his opponent could possibly equal. The one who had been surpassed had no recourse. He could no longer contest his claim, for, in the native mind, it came to be regarded as ridiculous that an individual of few resources (and of course this involved not only the man, but his entire local group) should attempt to make a claim against someone who had demonstrated power and wealth.

The modern analogue of the rivalry potlatch is a second-price sealed bid auction in which the winner pays the loser an amount equal to the loser's bid rather than paying the proceeds to a third party. In general, a second-price sealed bid auction has the advantages of being incentive-compatible—both parties will bid their reservation price—while allowing the winner to retain the rents from its superior ability to enhance the asset's capital value.[28] A second-price compensatory auction would require the Crown to recognize those with vested interests in the mobile ocean fishery as an "incumbent" class of claimants and British Columbia's tribes as a "rival" class. The details are best left to investment bankers experienced in privatizations, but an approximation would be for the Crown to require each tribe interested in making an exclusive claim to a river system in which salmon spawn to create a tribal corporation that would issue a majority of common shares, say sixty percent, to its members and forty percent to a central British Columbia First Nations-holding company organized as a publicly traded corporation.

In exchange, the First Nations Corporation would issue back a controlling interest, say sixty percent, of its own stock to the shareholding tribes in proportion to an independent valuation of the shares they contributed to the holding company. Collectively, the tribes would control the holding company, and each tribe would individually control its own tribal corporation. With the Crown's mandate, the incumbent class could also be organized as shareholders in a representative corporation. After arranging financing, these corporations would then submit sealed bids for the exclusive and perpetual right to control and collect the residual income (say, the excess above the tribes' total current fixed claims according to Justice McLachlin's approach) from the British Columbia salmon fishery, with the winner paying the loser the amount of its losing bid.

If the incumbents were to win the auction, as the current owners of the residual claim they would in essence pay themselves the amount of the tribes' losing bid and thereafter hold the exclusive right as a group to commercially harvest salmon under the watchful eye of Canadian fisheries regulators, possibly pursuant to a plan to create ITQs. The tribes' traditional cultural practice would require them to relinquish any residual claim to the fishery in excess of their total current fixed claims. They would then content themselves with their subsistence fishery and the management of their new lands in nontraditional activities compatible with continued use by future generations. If the tribes were to win the auction—which is the most likely outcome—they would pay the incumbents their losing bid. Consistent with traditional cultural practice, they could then abolish the mobile ocean fishery by assigning exclusive stream-based tribal rights to salmon stocks in accordance with each tribe's traditional lands and subsequent intertribal negotiations.

Under plausible transaction cost assumptions, this institutional structure is far more efficient than mobile ocean fishing under the rule of capture. A privatization auction could reestablish the distinctive core of aboriginal rights in a culturally correct way that enhances the Canadian Commonwealth. There is no guarantee the tribes would win the auction. But the capitalized returns from husbanding selected salmon stocks in a system of stream-based tribal rights would so dramatically exceed those under ocean-based common group rights to mixed stocks under the rule of capture (and even under ITQs) that the resulting increase in the tribes' expected wealth would easily allow them to prevail. The incumbents would be compensated according to their revealed valuation of their residual claim to the British Columbia salmon fishery under its current institutional structure.[29]

To finance its bid, the First Nations Corporation could issue its remaining forty percent of common shares to outside investors, including tribal corporations, who could pay for it out of retained or pending cash settlements and other sources. It could also borrow from the Crown by pledging the fishery in its entirely as collateral. Presumably, the Crown would be willing to lend an amount equal to the incumbents' losing bid, which would necessarily reflect the capitalized value of the fishery in its best alternative use, that is, under the current institutional structure.[30] Alternatively, both to help finance the First Nations Corporation's auction bid and to secure the additional financing necessary to begin operations, the tribal corporations could borrow from the Crown by pledging much of their newly acquired land as security or by reselling those lands (or pending land claims) back to the Crown. If the tribes take their distinctive culture seriously, they should be willing to relinquish much of this land to reestablish their exclusive stream-based ownership of salmon stocks.[31] Finally, both the First Nations Corporation and the separate tribal corporations could issue nonvoting or low-vote common stock to interested outside investors.[32]

The analysis thus far assumes that each tribe asserts ownership to an entire river system. For the many smaller river systems once owned by single tribes, such as the Cowichan River near Nanaimo, this presents little problem. At the other extreme, the Fraser River presents problems of ownership by multiple tribes. Although the *Van der Peet* court's notion of "shared exclusive ownership" has been legitimately criticized as an oxymoron,[33] it accurately reflects the patterns of actual precontact ownership on the Fraser, albeit with the institutional details left unstated. The problem with the Fraser was that, in many places, salmon destined for upstream spawning beds were subject to interception by downstream tribes. The resulting institutional equilibrium was a substantial improvement on a pure open-access commons subject to the rule of capture. Granted, in many cases this was because of upstream tribes' threats of encroachment and severe retribution on downstream tribes, as well as the promise of reciprocal sharing for cooperative "conservation."[34]

In such situations, privatization would require all tribes with valid claims within any river system to begin by forming a common trunk corporation. Initially, the trunk corporation would harvest salmon at or near the trunk stream's mouth using a fixed net technology, being careful to avoid systematically discriminating against salmon destined for the spawning beds in any particular tribe's claimed territory. Even though the optimal point for effective husbandry is closer to the spawning beds because this reduces noise in the information feedback mechanism, trunk stream harvesting would be necessary because salmon destined for upper tributaries tend to deteriorate in quality the longer they remain in fresh water. But the rate of physical deterioration is probably not an immutable constant. By selectively harvesting individual salmon that deteriorate rapidly and leaving the slow deterioraters to spawn, upstream tribes could, conceivably, genetically engineer subspecies less prone to deterioration.[35]

Within the constraint of transaction costs, it is important to devolve control of individual salmon stocks to the separate tribes in the river system's upper reaches. This would require the trunk corporation to "underharvest" to allow upstream tribes to engage in more selective harvesting of their individual stocks to meet local conditions, with the trunk corporation gradually relinquishing control to upstream tribes. No doubt some management decisions are best made by the trunk corporation, as where it is necessary to bring suit against polluters that impose spillovers on all tribes' stocks. Eventually, however, the trunk corporation should find it worthwhile to spin off various tribal subsidiaries, leading to a corporate structure similar to the First Nations holding company.[36] In this way, the undivided population of salmon entering a larger river system could eventually be reified into selectively managed individual stocks subject to exclusive, as opposed to shared, tribal ownership. The overall system would constitute a nested hierarchy of corporate holding companies, with local tribal corporations exercising entrepreneurial control over salmon husbandry decisions to their own stocks.

This organizational structure mirrors the potlatch system, whose benefits included diversification of stream-specific risk and a reduction in the transaction cost of enforcing exclusive stream-based tribal ownership of salmon stocks. To achieve these benefits, each trunk corporation and, in turn, the First Nations Corporation, would have to hold a value-weighted portfolio of the individual "upstream" tribal corporations' stock based on the public prices of nonvoting outside tribal corporation shares. This is because the value of each tribe's stock in the First Nations holding company would be determined in appropriate part by the value of the other tribes' stock in the holding company portfolio. Just as in the potlatch system, this would diversify each tribe's stream-specific risk. And any action a tribe might take to inefficiently impose spillovers—to encroach—on other tribes, as, for example, by intercepting others' salmon or breeding its own race of exceptionally predatory salmon (say, aggressive ocean feeders), would lower the value of its holding company stock (Hansen and Lott, 1996). No doubt individual tribes would find it appropriate to hold ceremonial potlatches at which their tribal leader hosted other tribes to publicly declare his success at managing tribal resources when handing a check to the "downstream" corporation's manager for its share of the dividend distribution.

Tribal corporations' majority voting stock (held by tribe members) could be freely alienable to other coastal tribes or tribal members, but sale to nonnatives could be restricted. This would ensure the viability of an ongoing market for corporate control in which inefficient tribal management could be displaced by rival claimants, similar to the rivalry potlatch (Manne 1965). Outside, nonvoting "minority" shares in the various tribal, trunk stream, and First Nations corporations should be freely transferable. No doubt an active market for such shares could be relied on to value the "productivity" of the associated enterprises and to provide valuable information from a forward-looking efficient market regarding proper resource allocation. As always, the default rules of provincial corporation law in a federal system, together with privately tailored bylaws and articles of incorporation, could be used to ensure competitive governance and prevent majority interests from acting opportunistically toward minority interests.

Privatization stands to create tremendous value compared to mobile ocean fishing for several reasons. First, even under ITQs, mobile ocean fishing is a mixed stock fishery, subject to noisy information feedback. With exclusive stream-based husbandry of individual salmon stocks, noise can be dramatically reduced, with a corresponding increase in dynamic efficiency. Second, the increased productivity of stream-based stock ownership can, to some extent, be used to compensate dispossessed incumbent fishermen for relinquishing their vested interests. The corporate form of organization would allow them to purchase contingent claims, such as financial options on corporate stock, for example, and, as with the second-price auction itself, could be used to induce them to self-select for such claims based on their true reservation valuations. Third, part of the current threat to salmon stocks comes from stream degradation as a result of siltation and other forms of pollution. By assigning residual claims to the productivity of each river system to a specific tribal corporation, responsibility for pressing claims against polluters would be much more focused than under the current system. Experience in Iceland, Scotland, and elsewhere shows that owners of salmon stocks are inclined to take aggressive action against polluters and other transgressors where ownership is clear (Brubaker 1997).[37]

Fourth, by placing management of salmon stocks in private tribal hands, the ongoing involvement of command-and-control regulators subject to political influences in managing the salmon fishery can be avoided along with the problem of political gridlock. Fifth, under the current system, sport fishermen have the lowest priority to the salmon catch, but, pound for pound, they place a dramatically higher value on catching the marginal salmon. Yet the transaction costs of negotiating a value-enhancing reallocation are extremely high, making political resolution more likely. With privatization, the First Nations Corporation would in all likelihood be willing to issue saltwater sport licenses for reasonable fees, no doubt relying on sport fishermen to generate information regarding the movement of various stocks in inland waters. Trunk-stream corporations would surely be willing to sell fresh water sport fishing licenses as well. Finally, harvesting of salmon bound for natal streams in Canada by US fishermen would gradually select in favor of salmon that remain in Canadian waters while at sea, thereby reducing reliance on political solutions with United States fisheries regulators.[38] What is more, with Canadian fishermen leaving all salmon stocks in Canadian waters largely unmolested, international disputes would be far easier to address, possibly leading to similar privatizations in Alaska, Oregon, and Washington.

CONCLUSION

In *Van der Peet* the trial court accepted expert testimony from cultural anthropologists to determine whether the practice in question was "integral to the distinctive culture" of the defendant's tribe at the time of European contact. It is of course natural that Canadian courts have relied on expert testimony from cultural anthropologists to understand the nature and scope of the tribes' fishing rights. But although the world owes Franz Boas and his followers a great debt for their factual ethnographic work on the tribes, the theoretical work in cultural anthropology that followed has proven less than helpful, either to Canadian courts or to the tribes. By ignoring the relationship between tribal institutions and tribal livelihood, and by uncritically accepting the tribes' status as hunter-gatherers content with a subsistence livelihood—in spite of overwhelming evidence to the contrary—cultural anthropology has proven itself largely irrelevant to the legal resolution of aboriginal rights.

Economists have access to the same factual record as cultural anthropologists. But facts do not speak for themselves, and the power of economic theory in drawing inferences from the recorded facts completely transcends anything cultural anthropologists have to offer.

It is truly ironic that in an effort to understand the tribes from their own perspective, Boas and his followers inadvertently cast them as ambitious status-seekers indifferent to generating more than a subsistence livelihood from their environment. Though cultural relativism may have gotten them in the courthouse door, it has painted them into an ethnocentric corner in regard to their fishing rights. The apparent purpose of s. 35(1) is not simply to hand aboriginal peoples an entitlement, but to bring them into the modern era with a reasonable prospect of achieving prosperity through diligent and determined reliance on their distinctive cultural rights. Because tribal ownership of salmon stocks represents the core of these rights, the Crown's fiduciary duty requires that they be given the opportunity to reclaim them. By compensating incumbent fishermen to voluntarily relinquish their claims, British Columbia's tribes can once again aspire to prosperity, while contributing proudly to the Commonwealth of Canada.

NOTES

1. The author thanks David Haddock, Jon Klick, Moin Yahya, and participants in the Robert A. Levy Fellows Workshop at George Mason University School of Law for helpful discussions. This paper has benefited from presentations at the University of Calgary School of Law and the University of Alberta School of Law. The Donner Canadian Foundation and the Earhart Foundation provided generous support for the production of this Chapter.

2. Walker observes: "[l]ast April, the Nisga Treaty gave the band of 5,000 about 770 square miles of land in northern British Columbia, plus cash and benefits worth C$250 million, and the right to self-government." According to the BC Treaty Commission, claims by 55 BC First Nations are currently being addressed in 45 separate treaty negotiations (see British Columbia Treaty Commission 2004). Critics believe these claims are being given exaggerated legitimacy and have resulted

in unjustifiably generous land and cash settlements to a virtual handful of natives (see Lippert 1998).

3. Throughout this essay, I borrow freely from my earlier work to keep citations to a minimum.

4. The tribes possessed the knowledge to preserve large quantities of salmon through the winter months.

5. A similar process was at work in Washington State (Higgs 1982).

6. In several cases, tribal leaders on the Nass and Skeena Rivers refused to buy licenses to fish in their own territories and insisted regulators had an obligation to remit all fees they collected from nonnatives for the right to do so (Harris 2001, pp. 61–65). Harris reports that the increasing treatment of native fishing rights as privileges may have been the residuum of a broader eighteenth century shift in the English legal conception of sovereignty to treat all customary rights as privileges (2001, p. 73, no. 244).

7. See also *Guerin v. The Queen* (1984).

8. The last of these, *Delgamuukw v. British Columbia* (1997), addressed aboriginal title to traditional lands, although others specifically addressed the aboriginal right to fish.

9. *R. v. NTC Smokehouse Ltd* (1996) and *R. v. Gladstone* (1996) were two companion cases to *Van der Peet.*

10. Unlike cultural anthropologists, I use the term *tribe* rather loosely. First, I use it contextually to refer to any layer in a nested hierarchy of kinship groups that variously functioned as the resource managing unit, whether the local-house, the clan, or the broader tribe. Second, I generalize across tribal groups throughout the northwest coast based on patterns common to all of them. Cultural anthropologists emphasize the many differences between the tribes. These differences are overwhelmed by the similarities, which in any event are sufficient to establish the distinctive cultural basis of northwest coast tribal property rights.

11. To be more complete, wealth is the present value of an expected flow of net returns discounted at the appropriate interest rate (Johnsen 1986b).

12. Boas is regarded by many authorities as the father of cultural anthropology. The question I have always had about Boas is how he decided which aspects of culture were worth recording absent an underlying theory or intellectual issue to guide his work. It is now widely recognized that his lifelong agenda was to validate cultural relativism, and this no doubt guided his focus in recording tribal culture.

13. Even two streams within very close proximity can be differentially affected by natural environmental shocks such as flooding, drought, and variations in salinity or temperature.

14. Professor Ferguson's work on tribal warfare eluded me until very recently, which is unfortunate because it uniformly supports my analysis.

15. Even in the absence of productivity variations, there would always have been an incentive for the members of one clan to encroach on another's private fishing

territory because the marginal product of labor to an encroacher equaled the average product of labor to the incumbent (Cheung 1970).

16. Potlatching provided the ancillary incentive for the tribes within the system to assist in defending the territories of allied tribes from external aggressors.

17. Salmon have any number of biological characteristics subject to purposeful genetic selection, including the average size of fish, the timing of their upstream run, the duration of the run, etc. To increase the average size of fish in a run, a chief would have had to impose a rule on his labor force to harvest the smaller fish in the run, thereby leaving the larger fish to spawn. Because larger parents give birth to larger offspring, over time the average size of fish would increase. Note that it would take substantial experimentation to discern this result, which is counterintuitive. Being more desirable, the natural tendency would have been to harvest the larger fish now. Following a small-fish harvesting rule therefore involves an upfront investment the return from which, if any, would not be fully realized for several generations.

18. It seems likely that prior to the earliest contact, the tribes had established a fairly stable and violence-free system of tribal property rights, but that the advent of the fur trade set off a wave of violence as they struggled to establish ownership to elusive sea otter stocks. This hypothesis awaits further investigation and testing.

19. I can only speculate that this mischaracterization is responsible for Justice McLachlin's mistaken conclusion that the northwest coast tribes "were not generally societies which valued excess or accumulated wealth."

20. Their situation was similar to western ranchers on the American plains who turned branded cattle out onto the open range free from systematic molestation. See Anderson and Hill (1975) and Morriss (1998).

21. Two notable exceptions are Garfield (1945) and Oberg (1934, 1973).

22. Barzel, Habib, and Johnsen (2006) argue that modern investment bankers rely on a system of reciprocity very similar to potlatching to make initial public offerings of corporate securities, a setting in which encroachment by rival banks is problematic but where the legal system is unable to prevent it.

23. To make it worthwhile to incur the transaction costs of reifying value flows into cognizable assets, the productivity of the assets must be imperfectly correlated with the productivity of the undivided commons, thus generating gains from specialized ownership. Merely dividing the commons into *pro rata* claims that are, by definition, perfectly correlated does not reify assets.

24. This approach is supported by substantial legal precedent in Delaware corporation law regarding majority shareholders' fiduciary duty to the minority in cashout mergers. Minority shareholders' appraisal rights in a cashout merger are limited to a fixed valuation of their share of the enterprise at the moment the majority seeks to take advantage of its call option on the growth opportunities motivating the merger. The problem with this analogy is that, at least in hindsight, it is the tribes whose legal conceptions would have produced the greatest capital value for the Pacific salmon fishery.

25. Except for hunting, the tribes' distinctive culture never had much if anything to do with these activities and, although they asserted exclusive claim to hunting lands, as with sea otters, the migratory nature of most large prey left them unable to assert effective dominion or to exercise effective husbandry over most of the associated stocks.

26. In an essay apparently ignored by both case law and the academic literature, Walter, M'Gonigle, and McKay (2000) argue that the tribes' historical fishing rights included both the right to harvest and the right to *manage* the salmon fishery, and that, based on constitutional legal principles, the Crown's regulation of the Pacific salmon fishery constitutes equitable waste that fundamentally conflicts with these rights. I reach the same conclusion based on an empirical economic analysis of tribal institutions. It is truly remarkable when scholars far apart on the ideological spectrum as Professor M'Gonigle and I agree on such an assessment. Although Walter, M'Gonigle, and Kay characterize their solution as "environmentally sustainable" "community-based management" relying on "clean production," it ultimately unravels to exclusive tribal property rights to salmon stocks. And whereas they would urge the court to effect a huge wealth transfer from incumbent commercial fishermen to the tribes, I propose to have the tribes compensate the incumbents to voluntarily relinquish their residual claim.

27. Because tribe members had the option of shifting their residence and labor resources to the prevailing tribal leader, the rivalry potlatch may have been a close analogue to the hostile corporate takeover in which the acquiring firm displaces inefficient incumbent managers (Manne 1965).

28. A second-price compensatory auction is probably not purely incentive-compatible because the putative loser might be tempted to strategically raise its bid to just shade the likely winner's bid to capture a share of the differential rents. This strategy is obviously risky if the parties face uncertainty over one another's reservation values, and the problem may therefore be one of second-order smallness. Interestingly, if the auction is multilateral this problem would seem to vanish as the number of bidders rises. My thanks to David Haddock for this point.

29. The creation of ITQs represents a plausible growth opportunity to which the current institutional structure may convey a real option.

30. The appeal of this form of financing is that it automatically makes continued ownership of the salmon fishery contingent on the tribes' ability to generate returns in excess of the debt service on the capitalized value of the current institutional structure (Johnsen 1995; Habib and Johnsen 1999; Habib and Johnsen 2000). Looking forward, the First Nations Corporation's willingness to borrow on such terms would serve as an implicit bond of its owners' expectations.

31. It is possible that some tribes would prefer to retain their land rights and forgo the opportunity to reestablish their exclusive stream-based ownership of salmon stocks. If so, dispossessed incumbent fishermen could be given financial options to purchase stream-based fishing rights with a strike price roughly equal to the those streams' proportionate value of the incumbent corporation's losing bid.

32. No doubt an army of "socially responsible" investors would emerge to provide ample equity financing. For a discussion of how cross-portfolio holdings can be used to ensure socially responsible actions by portfolio companies, see Johnsen (2003).

33. See Lippert (1998).

34. The resulting equilibrium probably contributed to the unique "subsistence" ethic reported of the Musqueam and Sto:lo in *Sparrow* and *Van der Peet*. Any downstream tribe on the lower Fraser that took more than it "needed" faced retribution by upstream tribes if too few salmon appeared in the spawning beds. Shared exclusive ownership under an uneasy truce of subsistence-only harvesting was somewhat unique and by no means representative of other coastal tribes. A testable implication is that downstream tribes on the Fraser River followed a different ethic when fishing their wholly owned tributaries along the Fraser.

35. What is more, the effect of deterioration on the value of migrating salmon is not immutable. Upstream tribes could gradually develop relatively attractive markets for the flesh of more highly deteriorated salmon, which are lower in oil content than during their time at sea.

36. This would surely be true for tribes claiming territory and streams with spawning grounds near the mouth of the river system.

37. To the extent tribes sell their claims to extensive tracts of lands along river banks to finance purchase of the river's salmon stocks, they can impose restrictive covenants on the Crown and subsequent purchasers that reduce the transaction costs of mitigating externalities.

38. Fraser River sockeye that return through Johnstone Strait or hug the southern tip of Vancouver Island would gain a reproductive advantage. If this were a heritable characteristic, over time it would dominate the gene pool.

FIVE

Customary Land Rights on Canadian Indian Reserves

THOMAS FLANAGAN AND
CHRISTOPHER ALCANTARA

Leonard and Mary Anne Johnstone are members of the Mistawasis First Nation in Saskatchewan. They have been farming on the reserve since about 1960. In that period of time, they acquired control of thirty-three quarter sections of land, more than one-sixth of the 192 quarter sections on the reserve. They held thirteen of these quarters under Certificates of Possession issued by the Minister of Indian Affairs, while the other twenty were "ad hoc" or "customary" holdings approved by band council resolution at various points in the past. For about ten years (1986–1996), they also had a "Certificate of Right of Use and Occupation" issued by the Department of Indian Affairs for seventeen out of twenty of these customary quarters so that the Johnstones could borrow money from the Farm Credit Corporation; but these certificates were temporary in nature, not permanent like Certificates of Possession.

In the words of Justice Barclay of the Saskatchewan Court of Queen's Bench, the Johnstones:

... improved, maintained, nurtured and sustained the lands in their occupation and possession. The applicants have given their whole lives to nurturing the land. They have picked roots, cleared stones, fenced, drained and nurtured piece by piece, quarter by quarter, bush by bush, pasture by pasture, slough by slough to create a farming environment which would be an all-encompassing economic, family, and community lifestyle. (*Johnstone v. Mistawasis (2003), para. 24*)

Despite this decades-long investment by the Johnstone family, the Mistawasis band council decided in 2002 to take back the twenty customary quarters. The Johnstones applied to the Saskatchewan Court of Queen's Bench for an interlocutory injunction to block the reversion, but lost in a decision handed down on May 23, 2003. Justice Barclay held that "it is clear that the proper approval of the Minister, or his lawful designate, was never acquired with respect to the 20 quarter sections of land in issue" (para. 45). The Johnstones might have a claim for financial damages, he allowed, but that could be litigated later, and meanwhile the reversion of the land could proceed.

Welcome to the little-known world of individual property rights on Canadian Indian reserves, where various forms of quasi ownership are conferred by political authorities, where owners are frequently confused about what rights they possess, and where rights can be withdrawn on short notice without compensation.

What follows is a conceptual survey of traditional allotments on Canadian Indian reserves. This chapter discusses the emergence of customary rights, the range of their formalization, their treatment by Canadian courts, and how they have figured in economic development on reserves. In addition, we identify some limitations on customary rights and provide some suggestions for improvement. We draw upon the scanty literature and case law on the topic, and rely heavily on fieldwork conducted by Christopher Alcantara at Cowichan Tribes (British Columbia); Siksika Nation, Piikani Nation, and Blood Tribe (Alberta); and Sandy Lake Nation (Ontario) in 2002.

In one sense, this is a highly focused and narrow study of one type of property rights found on some Canadian Indian reserves. As such, it will be of special interest to people who possess these rights as well as to those who record, administer, and sometimes litigate them. But we also believe our work is of broader interest to the extent that it describes the spontaneous emergence of individual property rights in an officially collectivist legal setting.

In *Property and Freedom,* Richard Pipes argued: "Acquisitiveness is universal among humans as well as animals, and . . . it involves a great deal more than the desire to control physical objects, being intimately connected with the human personality by promoting a sense of identity and competence" (Pipes 1999, p. 65). Because of this, human beings spontaneously tend to create institutions of private property even if the law is silent about or hostile to individual property rights. Hernando de Soto in *The Mystery of Capital* devoted an entire chapter to what he called "an early American tradition— squatting," showing in detail how pioneers appropriated land for themselves in spite of hostile government regulations until the American authorities, "not always eagerly or consciously, gradually legitimized extralegal property norms and arrangements created by the poorest Americans and integrated them into the law of the land" (de Soto 2000, pp. 113, 148). In that context, our chapter is a case study of how human beings can create property rights for themselves without state sanction, even in the communal situation of an Indian reserve where the federal government has already declared the land to be the property of the Crown to be administered for the collective benefit of the band (for other examples, see Anderson and Simmons 1993; Acheson 1988).

THE MYSTERY OF CAPITAL

Hernando de Soto (2000) argues that, contrary to popular belief, millions of squatters living in third world countries are not poor. Rather, they have a substantial amount of capital in the form of houses, shanties, and land collectively worth about US$9.3 trillion. These assets, however, are not very useful because their ownership has never been properly recorded, legally recognized, or protected by the state. Recognition by the state is especially important because while people can organize to provide self-protection against other people, it is much harder for citizens to protect their property against a state that does not recognize and respect their property rights. Under these conditions, squatters cannot use their property as collateral for a loan or mortgage because financial institutions have no reliable way of collecting on a defaulted loan. In short, capital in these countries is "dead" (de Soto 2000, pp. 5–6).

Indeed, the problem is much greater than the inability to borrow as described by de Soto. In the absence of recognized and secure control over property, individuals lack incentives to use it in the most productive way. Why go to all the trouble and risk of developing a farm on your land or building a grocery store if you cannot count on reaping the profits of your enterprise?

In contrast, countries such as Canada and the United States have more reliable systems of individual property rights. Property is legally recognized, documented, and usually protected by the state, thereby allowing individuals to create networks within which they can negotiate for mutually profitable transactions. People with legal property can sell it to create investment capital or use it as collateral to secure a loan or mortgage. Banks accept property as collateral because it can be easily and legally seized in the event of default. People without legal property do not have any of these options (de Soto 2000, pp. 47, 58–61). More broadly, people with secure individual property rights have incentives to develop their property for economic purposes, thus serving the needs of others as they seek advantage for themselves.

In Canada, status Indians living on reserves have their own unique system of property rights (Flanagan and Alcantara 2004). Although ultimate legal title to reserve land resides in the Crown, Indian bands have the authority to administer their reserves according to the rules set out in the Indian Act of Canada, a federal piece of legislation governing the relationship between the Crown and Indians living on reserves.[1] Under the act, reserve land is to be enjoyed by the whole membership according to the wishes of the band council. The band council is responsible for managing all reserve land use, including housing, renewable and nonrenewable resource extraction, and leases.

Ownership and control of reserve land is vested in collectivities (the Crown and the band), but the legislation also provides for forms of limited individual ownership. Although not well understood by the general public or even by students of aboriginal affairs, these individual allotments are quite common and play an important role in the life of residents on many reserves. There are two main forms of individual allotment: Certificates of Possession authorized in ss. 20–29 of the Indian Act (Alcantara 2005), and customary or traditional allotments.

By means of a CP, a band member can gain lawful possession to an individual parcel of reserve land for the duration of his life and membership in the band (Alcantara 2003). To do so, the member must obtain the consent of both the band council and the Minister of Indian Affairs. Once that is achieved, a CP, which is the evidence that the member has lawful possession to a tract of reserve land, is issued to the member. A CP gives the member ownership rights somewhat akin to fee simple in that he can do what he wishes with it within the confines of Canadian law and band bylaws. In addition, CPs are legally recognized and protected by the courts. However, it is not quite fee-simple ownership since the holder is restricted in his ability to sell and lease his property, or devise it in a will (Alcantara 2005, pp. 186–87; Flanagan and Alcantara 2004). The main restriction—and it is a substantial one—is that a CP can be sold or devised only to other members of the band. Since 1955, over 140,000 CPs have been issued to band members living on reserves. CPs are in use on 301 of the more than 2300 Canadian Indian reserves, but the degree of usage is highly variable. Some reserves have only one or two CPs, whereas others have been divided up almost entirely (Payne 2002; Alcantara 2005).

Although many First Nations use CPs to some degree, traditional or customary rights are the most common system of property rights on Canadian Indian reserves. This system of allotment has no direct statutory basis; its justification in Canadian law comes from the authority of the band under the Indian Act to make use of reserve land for the benefit of its membership (Notzke 1985, pp. 48–49). In essence, band council resolutions create individual interests in parcels of reserve land. A member with such an interest can build on it, improve it, farm it, sell it to another member, and in some cases, devise it in a will. But, as shown in the Mistawasis case, the chief and council can evict a member from a customary holding at any time or for any reason because they have legal authority over all reserve land not held under CPs.

EMERGENCE AND FORMALIZATION OF CUSTOMARY RIGHTS

Customary rights emerged in more or less the same manner on many different reserves. Historically, band memberships were small enough and land was plentiful. The abundance of land meant that members, usually families, could claim parcels of land for themselves with little, if any, risk of conflict with others. Some of these claims even go back to the period before reserves were assigned and surveyed (Nemoto 2002, p. 214). On these lands, families built homes, grazed animals, and farmed. Land was also freely exchanged between members. In the event of death, land usually passed on to other members of the family.

Because land was abundant, conflicts were few, resulting in very little government involvement in customary claims. When governments did intervene, they did so in a minimal way. At Piikani Nation and Blood Tribe, for example, the tribal government's only involvement was to require members to erect fences around their properties within two years. Failure to do so meant that others could lay claim to the property. However, this two-year requirement was rarely, if ever, enforced. Prior to more recent government involvement in the allotment process, none of the customary allotments were surveyed or recorded in any type of registry. At all five First Nations in this study, familial customary claims to property were recognized by the community and recorded in their oral traditions (Ray 2002; Lands Committee 2002; Fox 2002; Owlchild 2002; Sullivan 2002).

As time progressed, almost all Indians in the ten provinces eventually moved onto reserves. On these new reserves, families once again claimed parcels of land for their own individual use. In cases where the government created reserves on lands where Indians already resided, members continued to occupy the parcels of land that they had historically lived on. Reserve status, however, created new stresses for community life. The fixed borders of reserves and the rising band populations increased the number of conflicts over land. As the number of conflicts grew, members turned to the band council to help resolve disputes. To minimize disputes and facilitate resolution, many bands established Lands Departments that had the task of administering all community and individual uses of land. Individual land-use policies and departments varied from band to band, depending on each reserve's population, culture, history, and territorial makeup. The result was wide variation in the formalization of customary rights, ranging from very little (Sandy Lake and Cowichan Tribes) to much greater (Piikani Nation, Blood Tribe, and Siksika Nation).

The level of formalization involves several factors: whether customary rights are recognized by the community, whether they are allotted to members by band council resolution (BCR), whether they have been surveyed

Table 5.1. Range of Formalization of Customary Rights at Five First Nations in Canada

First Nation	Recognized by the community?	Allotted by BCR?	Formally recorded in a land registry?	Surveyed?	Dispute resolution mechanism?
Sandy Lake, ON	Yes	No	No	No	No
Cowichan Tribes, BC	Yes	No	No	No	Yes
Piikani, AB	Yes	Yes	Yes	Yes	Yes
Blood Tribe, AB	Yes	Yes	Yes	Yes	Yes
Siksika, AB	Yes	Yes	Yes	Yes	Yes

and formally recorded in a land registry, and whether a dispute-resolution mechanism other than chief and council is in place to deal with conflicts. The range of formalization for the five First Nations examined in this study is summarized in Table 5.1.

The following section examines in more detail the emergence and extent of formalization for each of the five First Nations in this study.

Community Recognition

At all five First Nations, customary rights are recognized and respected by the community. Originally, families obtained usage rights to individual properties on these reserves by fencing or clearing the land (see also Nemoto 2002, p. 216). As time progressed, the community membership acknowledged that certain properties were owned by certain families or individuals. Community recognition was recorded in oral tradition and elders were unofficially given responsibility for verifying ownership of property. Today, community members continue to acknowledge that certain families and individuals have ownership or usage rights to certain parcels of land regardless of band council approval. Members respect these parcels, and will usually not trespass on them even though they could do so legally if they wished. Although there are many disputes over customary rights, most disputes are over boundaries rather than ownership as such. When disputes do occur over actual ownership, it is usually because there is a conflict between community and band council recognition of ownership (Owlchild 2002; Fox 2002: Lands Committee 2002; Sullivan 2002).

In contrast to the other four First Nations in this study, community respect for customary rights at Cowichan Tribes is waning. In 1876, Cowichan customary land tenure was changed when all of the land outside the seven villages in the reserve was allotted to members through Location Tickets, the predecessor of Certificates of Possession (CPs). Since then, almost all of the reserve has been allotted under CPs. At present, the band and the membership continue to respect the remaining customary properties in the villages. However, the band's long exposure to CPs and the large number of disputes over customary land has convinced the membership and leadership to begin the process of allotting all the village land through CPs (Sullivan 2002; George 2002).

Band Council Resolutions, Land Registries, and Surveys

At Cowichan Tribes and Sandy Lake, customary allotments were never formally recognized by the chief and council. Therefore, neither Sandy Lake nor the seven villages in Cowichan Tribes have ever been surveyed or recorded in any land registry (Sullivan 2002; Ray 2002).

In contrast, Piikani Nation, Blood Tribe, and Siksika Nation took over the customary allotment process in response to a growing membership and shrinking land base. At these three First Nations, existing allotments are respected. For new allotments, however, members must submit a land usage plan for consideration by the Lands Department and chief and council. If the plan is agreeable and if the member is in good standing with the band, the Lands Department forwards the application to the council. The chief and council then pass a BCR allotting the member the tract of land for individual use. At Piikani, a member receives "Occupation Rights and Utilization Privileges"; at Blood, a member receives a "Land Use Area"; and at Siksika, a member receives a "Land Use Agreement" (Lands Committee 2002; Fox 2002; Owlchild 2002).

Rather than requiring surveys, both Piikani Nation and Blood Tribe used to demand that their members fence off their land within two years. Failure to do so meant that other individuals could claim the property. Now, however, both reserves have been completely surveyed; a new survey for an allotment is only required when a lot is being subdivided. Siksika Nation, on the other hand, used surveys from the beginning when it first took over the customary allotment process and continues to use surveys whenever land is allotted to a member. For all three bands, once an allotment is made and surveyed, it is recorded in the band's Land Registry (Lands Committee 2002; Fox 2002; Owlchild 2002).

Dispute-Resolution Mechanisms

Dispute-resolution mechanisms at the five First Nations that we studied vary from no mechanism (Sandy Lake), through structured and somewhat effective (Piikani, Blood, Cowichan Tribes), to very highly structured and effective (Siksika). At Sandy Lake, there is no dispute-resolution mechanism other than the chief and council. Members plead their case to individual councilors or to the entire council at a formal hearing. The council either makes a ruling in the form of a BCR or declines to do so. Frequently, the chief and council prefer to allow members to work out their own disputes, leaving them to negotiate, exchange goods, or intimidate each other to come to an agreement (Ray 2002).

Piikani Nation, Blood Tribe, and Cowichan Tribes all have mechanisms that are effective to varying degrees. At Piikani, it is the Lands Committee, made up of the department head, three administrators, and a secretary, which has the task of resolving disputes. The committee allows disputants to present their case to it before sending its recommendation to the council, which then either accepts or rejects the recommendation. It is reported that, more often than not, the council rejects the committee's recommendation and uses its own criteria to make determinations (Lands Committee 2002).

In the past, Blood Tribe also used a committee made up of land department administrators to resolve disputes. However, because of the ineffectiveness of the committee, the chief and council and the Lands department are in the process of revising the dispute-resolution mechanism. In the interim, disputants are left with the option of resolving disputes themselves or obtaining a ruling from the chief and council (Fox 2002). At Cowichan Tribes, the Lands Investigation Committee, which is made up of eight elders, three councilors, and several Lands Department staff, holds hearings to resolve disputes. The committee acts as a court or mediator between the disputants, requiring them to make separate presentations to the committee, which the opposing party can observe but not interrupt. After the presentations by the disputants, the committee examines written records, oral tradition, and the recollections of elders. The committee then makes a decision and seeks the approval of the disputants. In the event that the parties do not support the decision, the committee sends its recommendations to the chief and council (Joe and Angus 2002). Recently, however, the council has refused to make decisions on customary rights disputes because many of the elders who have relevant memories have died. At present, Blood Tribe is seeking to allot all of its customarily held land through CPs (Sullivan 2002).

Siksika's mechanism seems to be the most effective. The band employs a committee made up of several Lands department officials to resolve disputes between members. The committee's mandate is to resolve disputes through consultation, mediation, and compromise. In cases where the committee cannot achieve agreement between the disputants, it makes a decision based on the evidence and sends a recommendation to the chief and council. The chief and council almost always affirm the recommendation because the Lands department has the most expertise in land management. However, most of the time, the committee is able to come up with a resolution that is agreeable to all of the disputants. The key to the committee's success is that disputants know that the chief and council will usually support the committee's decision, thereby motivating the parties to find some sort of compromise that is acceptable to both sides (Owlchild 2002).

Customary Rights in Canadian Courts

Although customary rights have existed on reserves for over a century and a half, the body of Canadian case law is quite small (Flanagan and Alcantara 2005). Courts have usually refused to hear cases involving customary rights because such rights have neither statutory nor common-law basis. They have made exceptions, however, when a customary right met the requirements needed for a CP, namely, band council consent and the approval of the Minister of Indian Affairs.

In *Leonard v. Gottfriedson* (1982), a member of the Kamloops Indian Band, Gottfriedson, occupied a parcel of land allotted to him through a BCR. Several years later, the band disputed the allotment. The court ruled that Gottfriedson was illegally occupying the land and ordered him off it, citing the fact that the original BCR allotting the land was invalid. The court found a clear conflict of interest because Gottfriedson and his father, both councilors, had signed the band council resolution. The court further ruled that he had no legal right to the land because a member can get enforceable occupation rights to reserve land only by fulfilling the requirements of s. 20(1) of the Indian Act. All in all, Gottfriedson had failed to acquire band council consent and the approval of the Minister of Indian Affairs (1 C.N.L.R, 73–74).

These rulings were confirmed in *Joe v. Findlay* (1987) and *Nicola Band et al. v. Trans-Can Displays et al.* (2000). In the first case, the Squamish band council had passed a BCR allotting the Findlay family a parcel of land for ten years. After the ten years passed, the band council ordered them to vacate, which they refused to do. The court ruled in the band's favor, stating that the band council has "the right to recover possession when the term granted has expired" (2 C.N.L.R. 75, 81). At issue in the second case was David Shuter's customary claim over land he had received from George Spahan. The Nicola band council challenged this transfer on the basis that the band did not recognize the legal enforceability of "traditional or customary entitlement to reserve lands outside of the provisions of the Indian Act" (para. 7). The court agreed that customary rights "cannot create a legal interest in the land that would defeat or conflict with the provisions of the [Indian] Act" (para. 151). Although customary rights have been historically used and recognized by the band in certain instances, "recognition of an individual's traditional occupation of reserve lands does not create a legal interest or entitlement to those lands unless and until the requirements of the Act [s. 20(1)] are met" (para. 162).

In *George v. George* (1996, p. 53), the court enforced a customary allotment approved by both the band council and Minister of Indian Affairs. An Indian couple who had been living in a matrimonial home on a reserve had separated. During the divorce proceedings, the wife sought compensation in the form of a portion or possession of the matrimonial home, among other things. The court found that, although no CP had been issued, the husband had lawful possession of the matrimonial property. The evidence produced was that the husband had signed an undertaking that stated: "He was in lawful possession of the land and had transferred his interest in the land to the band in order to obtain a CMHC [Canadian Mortgage and Housing Corporation] mortgage" (referenced in *Nicola v. Trans-Canada Displays*, at para. 137). According to government policy, both band council consent and the approval of the Minister are required for an undertaking to become legal. Therefore, the husband's customary claim to the property was enforceable by the court because the requirements of s. 20(1) of the Indian Act were satisfied.

This ruling was upheld in *Cooper v. Tsartlip Indian Band* (1997). In this case, Cooper purchased land on a reserve from two members who were not registered as owners of the land but had customary claims to it. The transfer was not recorded in the Reserve Land Register nor was a CP ever issued. However, the band membership generally acknowledged Cooper's ownership of it. Several decades later, descendents of the two members who had originally sold the property to Cooper transferred the same parcel of land to the band. This transfer was recorded in the Land Register and approved by the Minister. Cooper challenged the validity of this second transfer in court. The Federal Court of Appeal ruled that the first transfer was invalid because "the legal status of Indian reserve lands is based on the provisions of the Indian Act" (1 C.N.L.R. 50). Therefore, the second transfer was stronger because it met the requirements outlined in the Indian Act (1 C.N.L.R. 51).

In *Williams et al. v. Briggs* (2001), the court ruled that a customary claim did not need to have both band council and Ministerial approval to be legally enforceable. In this case, Annie Findlay, a band member, expressed in writing her desire to give her property to her granddaughter Marilyn Briggs, also a band member, whom she had been living with for four years. After Findlay's death, Briggs continued to stay in the home. However, Cheryl Helms, band member and sister to Findlay, produced a document entitled "Transfer of a Customary Interest in Non-Designated Reserve Land," signed by Findlay, which transferred the property to her. Using this form, Helms transferred the property to the band in exchange for C$35,000. The band then gave Briggs notice to quit. Relying on *Joe v. Findlay* (1981), *Nicola Band v. Trans-Can Displays*, and *Cooper v. Tsartlip Indian Band*, the court ruled that a member could not claim a right to possession of reserve land without band council consent and the approval of the Minister (para. 10). Therefore, Helms' claim was more valid because it had at least one element of the requirement under s. 20(1): the approval of the band council (para. 12).

Although disputes over customary rights primarily affect band members, their lack of legal enforceability can spill over onto non-Indian corporations. In *Heron Seismic Services Ltd. et al. v. Muscowpetung Indian Band* (1991, p. 308), the Heron company sought permission from individual band members to drill wells on their properties. The members, all of whom had customary rights to individual parcels of land, agreed, believing government grants would cover the costs. The grants, however, proved to be insufficient and the company sought the balance outstanding from the band. The band refused to pay, arguing that it had never approved the drilling. The court ruled that the company's contracts were never authorized in accordance with the provisions in the Indian Act and therefore the company was liable for its own costs (74 D.L.R. (4th), p. 313). The individuals' customary rights did not give them the right to authorize the drilling.

Customary Rights and Economic Development

Although the Canadian government and courts do not legally recognize customary rights, individual band members have been able to use them for personal farming and housing developments, as collateral for small bank loans, and to generate revenue through unregistered leases. The most common use of customary property for economic development is farming. Many members with customarily held land frequently lease it to non-Indian farmers through s. 28(2) permits. Section 28(2) of the Indian Act states: "The Minister may by permit in writing authorize any person for a period not exceeding one year, or with the consent of the council of the band for any longer period, to occupy or use a reserve or to reside or otherwise exercise rights on a reserve."

Such leases may be organized as a cartel. At Piikani, eighty percent of the band's five-year renewable agricultural and grazing s. 28(2) permits have been issued to off-reserve farmers on behalf of members who have customary rights to parcels of reserve land. To acquire a permit, a member with customary rights approaches the band council. The Piikani Lands Committee interviews potential farmers, conducts a credit check, verifies that the farmer has financial support from a bank, reviews the proposed crops to be grown and the soil quality of the land, and assesses how much the farmer plans to spend per acre. Once a farmer is chosen, the committee forwards its decision to the chief and council, which then passes a BCR approving the permit. The application and BCR are sent to Ottawa where the permit is registered in the Indian Lands Registry. Piikani permits run for a maximum of five years, at which time they can be renewed with any necessary adjustments. Farmers are charged land rent, ranging from $18.50 to $43.00 an acre. All of the land rent goes to the individual member, with the exception of a $1.00 per acre fee, which the band charges for administering the permits on behalf of the member (Lands Committee 2002).

Blood Tribe also allows members with customary rights to recruit off-reserve farmers to farm their land using s. 28(2) permits. The acquisition of a permit at Blood Tribe is identical to the process at Piikani except for the fees charged. Most of the farming permits are based on cash rent paid to individual members with occupancy rights. Very few of the permits are based on crop share. Land rent at Blood ranges from $20.00 to $42.50 an acre, with the band taking a five percent administrative fee. Recently, the chief and council determined that all new and renewing permits would have a set rate of $40.00 an acre and a renewable term of three years (Fox 2002; Cross Child 2002).

At both Blood and Piikani, members have been able to use their permits as collateral, called "grain assignments," for small bank loans up to $10,000. For example, an occupant has 100 acres of land rented to an off-reserve farmer for $40.00 an acre. The off-reserve farmer pays the occupant $4,000, less $200 (five percent), which goes to the band as an administrative fee. Payments are made to the member in three installments of $1,266.66 on the first of April, October, and December. A bank will lend the member an amount equal to up to a year and a half of a permit ($3,800 + $1,900), so in this case the member is eligible for a loan of $5,700. Once the first payment of $1,266.66 is issued to the member, he can pay off a portion of the $5,700 loan and borrow that same amount ($1,266.66) again, resulting in an endless cycle of borrowing and repayment until the permit expires permanently (Fox 2002). At Blood Tribe, the band does not play a role in these small bank loans. At Piikani, however, banks require members to have a BCR stating that all future rent monies coming from the permitted land are to go directly to the bank to pay off the loan (Crow Shoe 2002).

The second major use of customary rights is for securing financing for individual members to construct their own housing. Siksika has an On-Reserve Housing Program where eligible members can apply for a $35,000 grant from the Housing Department to subsidize the construction of their own house or to purchase a new mobile home. This $35,000 comes from a federal fund administered by the band. Eligible members must be registered band members or eligible members under Bill C-31, have the ability and credit rating to pay off a bank loan, and be able to contribute at least twenty-five percent of the total cost. The member is also given $28,200 to service his site. In addition, the band will guarantee an individually obtained mortgage from a bank for up to $75,000 over a twenty-five-year amortization period. In exchange, the member signs an agreement stating that in the event of a default or an action to foreclose, he will relinquish to the band his claim to property and house. A member who wishes to access this program but does not yet have a customary right to land must submit three sites where he would be willing to build his house. The Lands Department chooses an unencumbered site and grants the member customary rights to the land and the house. All applications under this program must be approved by the chief and council (Royal 2002; Siksika Chief and Council 2002; Owlchild 2002).

Members at Cowichan Tribes have also been able to use customary rights to build a small number of houses through personal mortgages from the Canadian Mortgage and Housing Corporation (CMHC). To acquire a ministerial guarantee for a mortgage, the member must demonstrate to the Lands Investigation Committee that he has a legitimate claim to the land. Once this has been established, the holder must transfer his right to the land to the band in return for guaranteeing the mortgage. Possession of the land is returned to the member when he pays off the mortgage and meets any other conditions set by the band. This use of customary rights to acquire personal mortgages is quite rare, however, so the band is moving toward subdividing all of the reserve under CPs (George 2002; Sullivan 2002).

At Piikani, customary rights played a somewhat smaller but still important role for the housing needs of two members. In 1995, the houses of two members were destroyed by flooding. Using the insurance money paid to them and their customary rights to their property, the members were able to acquire a ministerial guarantee to secure mortgages from a bank to rebuild their homes. The key to these arrangements was the presence of the down payment and the traditional land holdings (Crow Shoe 2002).

The Lac La Ronge Indian Band (Saskatchewan) recently introduced an innovative housing program based on the experience of two Ontario bands. Building on the record of the Bay of Quinte Indian Band and Six Nations (Alcantara 2005), the Lac La Ronge Indian Band applied for and received a $1.7 million grant from DIAND (the federal Department of Indian Affairs and Northern Development) to start a revolving loan fund. The purpose of the fund is to loan monies to individual members so that they can renovate or build their own homes on the reserve. The fund is meant to be self-sustaining. As members repay their loans, other members can make use of the returned monies to build their own houses.

A member seeking to build a house on the Lac La Ronge reserve must apply to the band for a customary allotment. The band issues a letter to the individual, stating that the land is available to the member for six weeks pending financing. The member then must apply to the Bank of Montreal for a mortgage. If approved, the member can access up to twenty percent of the down payment from the revolving loan fund. As an incentive for repayment, the band adds 0.5 percent to each monthly payment the member makes. The member must also sign a lease with the band stating the details of the mortgage and the repayment schedule for the funds borrowed from the revolving loan fund. During and after the life of the mortgage, the member owns the house and any improvements he makes to the land (shed, fence, etc). The member can sell the home, but only to fellow band members. Non-band members, including spouses and children, cannot own the house.[2] Title to the land remains with the band, which will intervene only if the terms of the lease, such as failing to make regular repayment, are violated (MacLeod 2005).

Beyond such uses, Indians on reserves have also used customary rights to engage in informal and unregistered contracts called "buckshee leases." These agreements, signed by band members with nonmembers, nonIndian businesses, or corporations, are used for a variety of purposes including farming, timber extraction, and erecting advertising billboards. The danger with these leases is that they are not registered with Indian Affairs and therefore do not receive any of the legal protection afforded to registered leases. Some band councils, such as at Siksika, and to a lesser extent Cowichan Tribes, actively oppose buckshee leases because they go against the cultural identity of the band. They see such leases as benefiting the individual at the expense of the entire community (Owlchild 2002; Wilgress 2002) because no revenue flows from such leases to the band administration. Nonetheless, many members prefer to use buckshee leases rather than registered leases to avoid the transaction costs of dealing with the band and the Department of Indian Affairs and Northern Development.

Advantages and Limitations of Customary Rights

Many native people defend customary rights as being consistent with their perception of their culture. With the exception of Cowichan Tribes, all of the bands we studied have resisted adopting Location Tickets or CPs, citing fears that CPs are destructive to the reserve's land base and antithetical to the Nation's culture (Owlchild 2002; Fox 2002; Lands Committee 2002; Ray 2002). These fears seem to be less prevalent in those parts of eastern Canada where the indigenous culture included agriculture and family ownership of land (the Six Nations reserve, for example, is almost entirely subdivided into CPs); but they are particularly acute on the western prairies, where cultural traditions originally based on buffalo hunting included individual ownership of chattels but not of land.

At Piikani, Blood, and Siksika, band members reportedly feel that the community rather than the individual should benefit from the land. Customary rights give the band some tools to accomplish this because the band has legal control over all land not held under a CP. At Piikani, for example, the band council wanted to build a school on land to which a member had occupation rights and utilization privileges. The property was perfect for the school because it was on a major road and was in a central location near most of the homes on the reserve. The member agreed to give up his occupation rights and utilization privileges, provided that the band compensated him with $20,000. The band refused to negotiate and evicted the member. The member responded by obtaining legal advice. He was told, however, that he had no basis for a legal suit because the courts have refused to recognize customary rights unless they meet the requirements of a CP (*Nicola Band et al. v. Trans-Can Displays et al.* [2000]). The member therefore had no legal recourse and no means of preventing eviction or extracting compensation. Nonetheless, the band did provide him with some compensation (Lands Committee 2002). Customary rights, in short, are easily subordinated to collective purposes. This may be an advantage in the sense of being congruent with the prevailing cultural beliefs and political system on many reserves.

Customary rights fit into the communal control prevalent on reserves such as Blood Tribe and Siksika Nation. At these two First Nations, all members share in the revenue generated from oil, gas, and farming activities. If oil or gas is found on an individual's property, the band takes control of it and extracts the resource. For farming permits, the band takes a portion of rent paid to individuals. Members access these funds through various band services such as free housing, housing repairs, and band council jobs (Fox 2002; Owlchild 2002).

Individual band members also value customary rights because these rights give them a direct connection to their precontact cultural heritage. Indians employed customary property rights based on usage and traditional occupation long before the arrival of Europeans (Benson 1992; Hickerson 1967; Trigger 1990; Donald 1997; Miller 2001; Harris 2002; Alcantara 2003). On all the reserves examined in this study, most of the individual properties were obtained prior to the band council regulating the allotment practice, resulting in many members having rights to land based on their traditional occupation or fencing of it. In almost all cases, the band council has respected these traditional holdings because they are seen as being an integral part of the band's cultural and social makeup. In contrast, band officials see CPs as a foreign instrument based on western European notions of land tenure and ownership and designed to achieve cultural assimilation and the destruction of Indian life. Officials at Piikani, Siksika, Blood, and Sandy Lake mentioned how CPs are a foreign institution that could destroy their reserve's land base. They were emphatic about their intentions to keep their customary land tenure systems as these systems supported their cultural beliefs and practices (Lands Committee 2002; Owlchild 2002; Fox 2002; Ray 2002).

Customary rights have another very practical advantage over CPs or leases. Since customary rights are completely administered by the band, DIAND is rarely, if ever, involved in land transactions. Therefore, in contrast to First Nations which extensively use CPs and leases, bands with customary rights do not experience the additional time delays involved in waiting for Ministerial approval. Compared to CPs (see Alcantara 2005), customary land tenure is more time-efficient—an advantage of what in the United States would be called tribal sovereignty.

Customary rights have several limitations. Firstly, they are not enforceable in Canadian courts unless they amount to an incomplete CP. Courts will sometimes enforce customary rights if such rights have been approved by the band council through a BCR recorded in the band's land registry and/or have been approved by the Minister, but otherwise there is a legal vacuum. Of the five First Nations examined in this study, only Siksika has a customary allotment system that mimics the requirements of a CP. In principle, this limitation might be overcome by a system of American-style tribal courts that could enforce customary rights, but such courts do not exist in Canada at the present time.

The fact that the chief and council are the source of authority for customary rights is another problem, especially in light of Canadian courts' unwillingness to recognize customary rights. The relative smallness of most of these communities means politicians are usually well connected to many of the members in the band. Thus, politics can and does intrude in the allotment of customary holdings, and more importantly, in dispute resolution. For instance, common to all five First Nations examined in this study is the problem of boundaries. None of the allotments at Cowichan Tribes and Sandy Lake were ever surveyed, registered, or recorded. For places such as Blood and Piikani, where DIAND unilaterally imposed a square survey onto the reserves, disputes occur over the validity of the DIAND survey as compared to the original allotments based on physical features, fencing, and oral tradition. In the end, members are forced to turn to the chief and council for resolution. Frequently, however, the council chooses not to make a decision, passing the buck to the band's Lands department because it does not wish to antagonize the disputants at election time. When the chief and council make a ruling, decisions are sometimes based on nepotism (Lands Committee 2002; Fox 2002; Ray 2002). Even then, losing disputants may wait for a more friendly council to get elected in two or four years before appealing a ruling because BCRs can be overturned by the council at any time (Fox 2002). Band constitutions establishing stable decision-making processes might alleviate some of these difficulties, as they do in larger democratic systems.

Another limitation of customary rights is that the lack of security of tenure discourages individual band members from pursuing on-reserve development. This insecurity of tenure comes in three forms. First, although a member can transfer customarily held land to another member through a quit claim, band council must approve it. Second, a member's ability to devise his property is limited, because wills devising customarily held land are not legally recognized or enforceable. Some Nations have developed more secure ways to get around this problem. Piikani, for example, uses conditional quit claims in which a member states he will sell his property to another member upon his death for a fee. However, these documents are restricted and must be approved by the chief and council, thus limiting their usefulness. Nonetheless, the council at Piikani more often than not respects these conditional quit claims. In contrast, Siksika's chief and council are vehemently opposed to any type of document that devises customarily held land in the event of a member's death (Lands Committee 2002; Owlchild

2002). Also, as mentioned previously, the individual is constantly threatened by the council's ability to seize land at any time and for any reason, leaving the member with no legal recourse, beyond the band council, to seek justice. Councilors can be easily swayed into action or inaction due to the smallness of Indian communities.

The insecurity of tenure and the lack of legal protection afforded by the courts are the key weaknesses of customary rights. Without security of tenure, the individual has little incentive to engage in innovative projects to raise his standard of living. The threat of the band stepping in and taking over an economic development project or house saps the entrepreneurial spirit of the individual. The danger of politics intruding in the cancellation of an allotment, quit claim, or will is a constant fear, especially in a small community where politicians are well connected to many members of the community. This, in turn, affects the entire community, as members may move away or invest off-reserve, taking away potential sources of employment for other members.

Finally, customary rights in practice tend to produce band-owned rather than individually owned and financed housing. As noted previously, there are some exceptions. At Cowichan Tribes, one member was able to use his customarily held land as collateral for a band-guaranteed mortgage from the CMHC to build his own house (Sullivan 2002). At Piikani, two members used a cash down payment and a transfer of their customary interest in land to the band to acquire band guarantees for bank mortgages to rebuild their flooded houses (Crow Shoe 2002). However, the bulk of housing on reserve is band-owned rental housing. Rather than building their own homes, members prefer to receive rental housing with rates of $307 a month at Siksika, $487.50 at Blood Tribe, and $600 at Cowichan Tribes. Because members can stop paying with little fear of retribution, nonpayment rates for band-owned housing range from medium to very high. At Cowichan Tribes, fifty of 400 members living in rental homes are not paying (George 2002); at Siksika, the rate is sixty percent (Day Chief, Jr. 2002); and at Blood, the rate is approximately seventy-five to eighty percent (Little Chief 2002). At Piikani, ninety-seven percent of members living in rental housing are not paying (Crow Shoe 2003). Members do not fear that the band council will evict them for nonpayment because the evicted members can punish councilors by voting against them in the next election. In addition, in all of the reserves studied, the community is said to frown upon the use of evictions, thereby further weakening the council's will to act. In some cases, Indian bands have had to turn to external institutions to recoup unpaid rent. For instance, the Champagne and Aishihik First Nation filed a $100,000 lawsuit against their own citizens "after all other efforts to recover unpaid rents failed." The lawsuit targeted five Champagne and Aishihik citizens who each owed between $10,000 and $30,000 in unpaid rent. Chief James Allen blames DIAND for developing a dependency through "handouts to our First Nations people." The result is "an odd situation where some First Nation citizens seem to be making distinctions based on who's collecting the rent. Down the street, you may have a First Nations person with a white landlord and they're willing to pay that white landlord every month. But when it comes to paying your own First Nation, it's a different story" (Canadian Broadcasting Corporation 2005).

Nonpayment of rent reduces the amount of capital available to First Nations to build more housing and engage in repairs. According to one estimate, Cowichan Tribes is losing approximately $600,000 a year from nonpayment. For those First Nations that have few economic development resources available, this problem is even more acute. At Piikani, which is poor compared to the other Treaty 7 First Nations, the high nonpayment rate has crippled the housing department, leading to deteriorating housing conditions and very few new housing constructions per year (Crow Shoe 2003). For Blood Tribe, which does have some agricultural and oil and gas developments, nonpayment resulted in the closing of the housing department for one full year (Fox 2002; Cross Child 2002; Day Chief, Jr. 2002). Siksika, on the other hand, has managed to keep its housing stock in good condition and has done a relatively good job in meeting the demands of its membership for new construction and repair. However, they have accomplished this because they have extensive oil and gas reserves that help make up for the lost revenue in uncollected rents (Owlchild 2002; Ayoungman 2002; Smith 2002).

SUGGESTIONS FOR IMPROVEMENT

Customary property rights on Indian reserves are probably less economically efficient than the fee-simple system that prevails generally in Canada, or even than the Certificates of Possession that are a legal option under the Indian

Act. However, we do not believe it is fruitful to try to impose institutions upon people from the outside. James C. Scott, in *Seeing Like a State,* has given an imposing catalog of "how certain schemes to improve the human condition have failed" (Scott 1998; see also Anderson and Parker (this volume) on the Dawes Act). We do not want to repeat what Scott calls the "high modernist" error of ignoring the local knowledge incarnated in rural people's customs, practices, and folklore. Rather, we offer a few suggestions for how customary rights could be made to work better for those First Nations that find them to be a good fit with their culture but who also wish to participate successfully in the modern economy.

The main problem limiting the usefulness of customary rights is the lack of security of tenure. Customary rights result in a large number of disputes and are subject to the authority of the band council, itself frequently and inordinately influenced by band politics because of the small size of reserves and the political costs involved with making decisions on individual land use. This insecurity of tenure and lack of legal protection afforded by the courts has created economic disincentives for individuals.

The first and most important counter to this pervasive insecurity would be for bands to document customary rights more fully. The band council could create a process to allot all customarily held land to members. This process could be overseen by a Lands Department or committee, made up of nonelected officials with the authority to act independently according to guidelines set out by the band council and approved by the membership. Using oral tradition, written documents, and any other relevant materials, the department or committee would hold hearings to determine exact ownership and boundaries of new and existing allotments. Once a determination is made, the allotment application would be sent to the band council, which should approve it through a BCR. The land should then be properly surveyed and registered in a band land registry.

The next step would be for band councils to adopt a policy of treating these allotments as legally binding written contracts, which the chief and the head of the Lands department sign with the allottee. The allotment contract should include the survey, an exact description of the land, the name and band membership number of the individual, the land usage options that the member is allowed to pursue, and a clause stating the exact circumstances under which the band council can retake the land. At Siksika, the chief and council treat their allotments as agreements legally binding on both the band and the individual. The band will only retake land in certain instances. In every Land Use Agreement allotment, there is a clause stating that the band "reserves the right to access and use land for purposes that represent the best interest of the tribe as a whole. Purposes could include public buildings, economic development projects, and the harvesting of natural resources." In the event that this clause is invoked, the council uses a consultation process designed to acquire agreement from all parties regarding compensation (Owlchild 2002). In this way, the individual has some measure of security. He has clear expectations of what he can do with the land and under what circumstances the band can retake the land. In addition, through the formalization of his customary right and an exact contract recognized by the band council, the member might have the legal means to pursue an action in court if he feels that his property rights have been unjustifiably breached. The prospect of legal enforcement of customary rights should, in turn, confer greater security of expectations, which gives members the incentive to pursue on-reserve business and housing development projects for their own betterment and for the benefit of the entire reserve.

Although these two improvements may give the member access to legal protection from Canadian courts, this should only be used as a last resort. Rather, the disputants should be steered to a band-created arbitration system before pursuing justice from the courts. Arbitrators might be nonelected officials from the reserve or, even better, neutral adjudicators from other native communities (Benson 2000). A land-use and dispute-resolution policy should be established by the Lands department and chief and council, and approved by the membership. Subject to judicial appeal, the decision of the arbitrator should be final in practice, with council merely giving formal approval. This lends decisions legitimacy because Lands department officials or external adjudicators are at least somewhat insulated from the political pressures that face band councilors. If their jobs are not dependent on winning the political approval of the membership, they can focus on deciding whose claim is more valid.

Arbitration, of course, is but one type of judicial process. It would also be possible to set up First Nations courts in Canada, like the Indian tribal courts that exist on some reservations in the United States. There are no full-fledged native courts in Canada today, but there is a wide variety of justice initiatives in many First Nations, including local policing, sentencing circles, healing lodges, family conferencing, and mediation (Dickson-Gilmore 2005;

Cummins 2003). Adjudication of conflicts arising out of customary land rights would be an appealing responsibility for First Nations courts if they were created eventually.

For many First Nations, however, full-fledged courts, or even formalized registration and arbitration systems, might be too expensive. As Demsetz (1967) pointed out, property rights, like other institutions, are subject to considerations of cost and benefit. When land is abundant relative to population, it may make more sense to treat it as a common pool resource rather than to go to the expense of assigning and enforcing individual property rights. That was undoubtedly the original situation on most Canadian Indian reserves, which were large in comparison to their founding populations. It is still the case on many remote northern reserves. However, it is not the case on many southern reserves, where population growth has rendered land scarce and valuable.

But even where formalization would be desirable, it may be difficult to attain due to the very small size of most reserves. The average First Nation in Canada has a population of little more than a thousand (Flanagan 2000, p. 78). In spite of the ambitious term "Nation" now used to describe them, most are really tiny rural municipalities without the resources or expertise necessary to create and enforce formal systems of property rights. First Nations should be able find their way out of this impasse by pooling their resources to create property rights systems covering many reserves, but progress may be slow because the transaction costs of such cooperation are high for communities separated from each other by barriers of language, culture, and administrative inertia.

These real-world problems of small size and lack of resources are also impediments to participating in another approach to improving customary rights, namely formalizing them under the First Nations Land Management Act of 1999 (FNLMA). Fourteen First Nations have drafted and ratified their own land codes and, after having had them accepted by DIAND, are now operating outside the Indian Act.[3] Dozens more have made inquiries and some of these may eventually take complete control of their land under the FNLMA. The process, however, is neither simple nor straightforward. In order to receive approval for their land codes, bands have to demonstrate a high level of legal and administrative capacity, which many smaller bands find hard to afford. First Nations administrators also worry that, if they enter the FNLMA, they assume complete legal responsibility for their actions and lose the protection of the Crown's fiduciary responsibility. Poor administration of even a well-drafted code might open the band to crushing liability in litigation (Flanagan and Alcantara 2004, pp. 512–17). It seems likely that the FNLMA will provide a way for some larger and better-off First Nations to formalize their customary land rights but will not become a practical option for the majority of bands.

Another major problem that needs to be addressed in relation to customary rights in many aboriginal jurisdictions is the nonpayment of housing rent. As mentioned, customary rights tend to produce mainly band-owned rental housing rather than individually owned housing. At all of the communities examined in this study, nonpayment was a major problem, ranging as high as ninety-seven percent of members not paying. The solution is to evict members who have the ability to pay but are not doing so. Evictions have been shown to reduce the nonpayment rate on reserves (Alcantara 2005; Flanagan and Alcantara 2004). Reducing the nonpayment rate would give bands the necessary capital to fund new construction as well as repairs on existing units.

Improvements along these lines would make customary land rights more useful for those First Nations that wish to retain them. Such incremental improvements are likely to be more effective in practice than the imposition of unfamiliar and undesired institutions of individual property. Although individual property rights are essential to successful market economies, they can vary greatly in detail while still serving to promote individual freedom and economic initiative.

NOTES

1. Section 2 of the Indian Act states that a reserve is a "tract of land, the legal title to which is vested in Her Majesty for the use and benefit of a band."

2. In a related issue, several band councils and Canadian courts have denied Indian women an interest in matrimonial property in the event of a relationship or marriage breakdown. See Alcantara (2006); *Sandy v. Sandy* (1978, p. 363); *Darbyshire-Joseph v. Darbyshire-Joseph* (1998); *Derrickson v. Derrickson* (1986); *Paul v. Paul* (1986).

3. Those fourteen First Nations are: Nipissing; Opaskwayak; Lheidli T'enneh; Westbank; Scugog Island; Muskoday; Georgina Island; Beecher Bay; Tsekani (Mcleod Lake); Ts'kw'aylaxw (Pavilion); Sliammon; Tsawwasscn; Kinistin; and Whitecap Dakota Sioux.

SIX

The Wealth of Indian Nations: Economic Performance and Institutions on Reservations

TERRY L. ANDERSON AND DOMINIC P. PARKER[1]

From first contact, Europeans struggled with how to interact with the indigenous population. When the Pilgrims landed, there was little choice. Out of supplies and outnumbered, they had to act peacefully to survive and indeed were able to gain substantially from trading with the Indians. Eventually, formal government caught up with the early settlers in the New World and tried to organize relations with the Indians. In particular, the British Crown attempted to keep local colonies from negotiating with Indians, tried to avoid conflict by recognizing Indian land claims, and formed alliances with tribes against other colonizing nations.

After the Revolutionary War, the new national government developed its own policy with respect to Indians. Chief Justice John Marshall set the stage for the present Indian policy by asserting that tribes were sovereign nations. In 1831, he wrote in his famous *Cherokee Nation v. Georgia* opinion that Indian tribes were "nations within a nation," but he went on to call them "domestic dependent nations," implying that they had alienated their power to negotiate with foreign nations by virtue of treaties with the federal government. Although implying that the tribes had retained their internal powers to govern themselves, Marshall described the relationship between tribes and the United States as "that of a ward to his guardian." Under this interpretation, the federal government attempted to monopolize treaty negotiations with tribes in order to reduce conflicts over land and forced the tribes into a subservient position by declaring them "wards."

Tribal sovereignty might have allowed Indians to devise their own property rights and governance structures had the federal government not established the trust relationship with Indians, and had it been willing to grant full autonomy to Indians to control their property. Indeed, many tribes were establishing institutions compatible with agricultural production after they were placed on reservations and before they were subjected to bureaucratic controls under the Dawes Act of 1887 (see Anderson 1995, pp. 113–16). Under this Act, reservation lands were allotted to individual Indians, but were held in trust until the allottees were deemed "competent" by federal agents to become private property owners. Perhaps fee-simple ownership could have eventually substituted for institutions evolving under tribal systems, but the possibility of fee-simple ownership ended in 1934 with the passage of the Indian Reorganization Act. Land that was allotted but not released from trusteeship was frozen in trust status, thereby retaining the federal government's stronghold on reservation assets and establishing bureaucratic layers of red tape that impede productive land use to this day.

Since 1934, the Department of Interior has struggled to find ways to fulfill its trust responsibility and to eliminate corruption, but no one would argue that there has been much success. Not only does the trust authority raise the cost of managing Indian lands, timber, minerals, and wildlife, but it also provides opportunities for corruption in the use of those resources and the funds generated therefrom. As a result, the Department of Interior and its Bureau of Indian Affairs (BIA) have been embroiled for years in a lawsuit charging mismanagement of Indian trust funds. With so many assets controlled by bureaucrats and politicians in Washington, it is not surprising that little wealth is generated from these assets for reservation Indians.

Despite the fact that many reservations are resource-rich and receive transfer payments from federal assistance programs, nearly all reservations remain among the lowest of income strata in the United States. For example, Stephen Cornell and Joseph Kalt (2000, p. 444) estimate that the Crow tribe in the early 1990s had $27 billion in coal assets or over $3 million per tribal member, but that these assets earned a paltry 0.01 percent annual return. Despite being resource rich, fifty-five percent of Crow tribal members receive public assistance.

A full explanation of why reservation Indians have remained the poorest of America's minorities has remained elusive. As with many explanations of economic development, early focus on reservation economies was on physical and human capital. The argument was that Indians were left with poor land, little capital, and inadequate education to take advantage of the assets they did have. A growing body of data suggests that this explanation is inadequate for developing economies or reservation economies because it ignores the institutional environment in which resource allocation decisions are made.

This chapter focuses on the institutional environment and how it influences economic performance on reservations. It follows the lead of an extensive and robust literature focusing on institutions, formal and informal, as a primary reason why economies prosper or stagnate. After providing a brief review of Indian institutional history, we survey the literature on economic performance and property rights in developing countries. Within this context, we consider the ways in which property rights and the rule of law influence tribal economies. This institutional theory of economic development guides our empirical analysis of Indian income as it relates to institutional and other control variables. Though our empirical findings support the theory that institutions and economic performance are inextricably related, getting from here to there, especially in the context of American Indian politics, is very difficult.

THE EVOLUTION OF RESERVATION
LAND TENURE

Hollywood depictions of pre-Columbian Indians living in communal organizations where individuals contributed to the best of their abilities and shared equally in the fruits of communal endeavors offer a mystical, if not a mythical, view of how tribes were organized.[2] Although it is difficult to fit pre-Columbian Indian institutions into the modern context of law, government, and property rights, anthropological evidence suggests that they understood the importance of institutions for getting the incentives right. Frank Speck

(1939, p. 259) referred to Indian property rights as a "naked possession" and concluded that this possession led to "the maintenance of a supply of animal and vegetable life, methods of insuring its propagation to provide sources of life for posterity, the permanent family residence within well-known and oftentimes blazed property boundaries, and resentment against trespass by the family groups surrounding them who possessed districts of their own." Whatever term is used to describe pre-Columbian Indian institutions, it is clear that they understood the importance of incentive-compatible rules that limited access to the commons and encouraged productivity.

Even after contact with Europeans and confinement to reservations, but before the national government dictated what property rights they would have, American Indians developed institutions that enabled them to produce, using the resources they had. For example, the Blackfeet began accumulating individually owned but communally herded cattle. When the federal bureaucracy took control of how property rights were held, "the tradition of individual ownership was so well established that Indians resisted government efforts to establish common property from 1910 to 1920" (Carlson 1992, p. 74). The more sedentary tribes, such as the Cherokee, "showed much aptitude and success in farming" (Hurt 1987, p. 230). Among tribes with an agricultural tradition, "the Indian concept of land tenure enabled various villages to make the best possible use of the land in order to meet their own specific needs" (Hurt 1987, p. 75).

Trusteeship of Indian Lands

Institutional autonomy for reservation Indians in the nineteenth century was short-lived as Congress and federal agencies began molding property rights from Washington. With the Allotment Act of 1887, the government made its first major attempt at bureaucratic control over how reservation land would be allocated. Under this Act, reservation land was allotted to individual Indians, but held in trust until the secretary of interior deemed the individual Indian "competent" to hold the land in fee simple. Surplus land, which is reservation land in excess of what was necessary to give individuals the minimum parcel (usually 160 acres), was opened to homesteading by non-Indians. When allotted land was freed from trust, it could be alienated in any way the Indian owner saw fit, including sale to non-Indians. Comments from Senator Dawes himself sum up the reason why many non-Indians supported the Act: "Till this people will consent to give up their lands, and divide them among their citizens so that each can own the land he cultivates, they will not make much progress" (quoted in Otis 1973, pp. 10–11).

Because so much Indian land was released to non-Indians through sale and homesteading, Congress passed the Indian Reorganization Act in 1934 (IRA). Between 1887 and 1933, Indian land holdings declined from 136,394,895 acres to 69,588,421 acres. Under the IRA, those lands that had not been released from trusteeship were to remain under the trust authority of the BIA.

The IRA left reservations with a mosaic of land tenure including fee-simple land that was released from trusteeship prior to 1934, individual trust land that was allotted to individual Indians but not released from trusteeship, and tribal trust land that was owned by the tribe but held in trust. As we shall see, trusteeship by the BIA is a mixed blessing. On the one hand, it stopped Indian lands from being transferred to non-Indians; on the other hand, it continues to subject decisions regarding Indian use of Indian resources to a federal bureaucracy that may not always have the best interest of Indians at heart.

Owners of fee-simple lands have complete autonomy over their land use decisions within the limits of the law. Production decisions regarding these lands are controlled by the owner, and the land can be sold or encumbered as collateral in the capital market.

In contrast to fee-simple land tenure, trust lands are subject to regulation by the BIA. It grants or denies permission to change land use, approves lease arrangements, and agrees to capital improvements. When held in trust, land cannot be sold and generally cannot be encumbered as collateral for loans. Making matters worse, individual trust lands have often been inherited many times over, leaving multiple owners, all of whom must agree on land management decisions. This "fractionation" or "heirship" problem increases the costs of establishing a clear owner and manager who can control land use decisions and reap the benefits of good management.

In the case of tribal trust land, management decisions are made by tribal governance institutions, which further reduce any individual decision maker's incentive to maximize the net value of production. From a case study of the Navajo reservation, Gary Libecap and Ronald Johnson (1980, p. 83) conclude that the politics of the Navajo Tribal Council and its grazing committees have essentially legislated "a common property condition for the range," wherein access is open to all tribal members and overuse occurs. Given these constraints, we would expect the higher transaction costs associated with management decisions to thwart optimal land use decisions.

This three-part tenure system—fee simple, individual trust, and tribal trust—yields very different productivity for several reasons. First, because the costs of organizing production under fee-simple tenure are lower than under individual or tribal trust tenure, the fee-simple owner's choice of a mix of land, labor, and capital should be approximately optimal. Second, because trust constraints raise the cost of capital by restricting the ability of owners to transfer land title, productivity should be lower on trust lands. Third, because the returns from individual and tribal trust lands are distributed among many owners, each has less incentive to monitor land management, thus making output lower. Finally, because trust land cannot be freely alienated, the size of farms and ranches will remain too small to be optimally productive (see Trosper 1978). For all of these reasons, we would expect the legacy of the allotment process and trusteeship to play an important role in reservation productivity.

The IRA, Termination, and Public Law 280

In addition to halting the transfer of Indian land to fee-simple ownership, the IRA permitted tribes to enact their own tribal codes and constitutions (although most tribal constitutions were drafted by BIA officials who used a template constitution). The resurgence in self-governance put pressure on tribal governments to manage resources responsibly and to create an environment that encouraged investment.

Before it could be put to the test, however, tribal sovereignty on some reservations was stripped away by Congress during the termination period, which extended from about 1945 to 1961. During this period, Congress passed numerous resolutions seeking to make Indians subject to the same "privileges and responsibilities" as ordinary US citizens (Getches, Wilkinson, and Williams 1998, p. 205).

Public Law 280 legislation, enacted in 1953, epitomized the prevailing Indian policy of the termination period by transferring jurisdiction from some tribal courts to state courts.[3] It extended state jurisdiction over civil disputes and criminal offenses arising on reservations in Alaska, California, Minnesota, Nebraska, Oregon, and Wisconsin. Tribes in these "mandatory"

Public Law 280 states did not have the opportunity to formally consent to the transfer (see Goldberg-Ambrose 1997).[4] Reservations in the mandatory states were targeted first either because they were perceived to lack adequate tribal forums and to have rampant lawlessness (see Goldberg-Ambrose 1997), or simply because the transfer of jurisdiction to these states could take place without legal impediments.[5]

Public Law 280 legislation gave other states the option to assume jurisdiction, but the procedure for doing so was more complicated than in mandatory states (see Strickland and Wilkinson 1982). Some optional states had disclaimed jurisdiction over Indian country in their constitutions as a prerequisite to acquiring statehood. Would these states need to amend their constitutions to adopt Public Law 280? Other states wished to assume jurisdiction over some of the affairs named in the legislation. Was the assumption of partial jurisdiction allowed under the legislation? Furthermore, some states conditioned their assumption of jurisdiction on tribal consent. How was tribal consent to be obtained and how long would it be valid?

The Supreme Court decisions validated the assumption of partial jurisdiction under Public Law 280, deemed constitutional disclaimers unnecessary as a matter of federal law, and clarified other legal uncertainties.[6] Taking into account these Supreme Court decisions and considering state legislative actions, Florida, Iowa, and Washington appear to have most credibly assumed jurisdiction over most contractual disputes and tort claims arising between Indians and non-Indians on the reservation (Strickland and Wilkinson 1982). Tribal authority to adjudicate such cases remains intact in many states including Arizona, New Mexico, North Dakota, and South Dakota.

To most scholars of American Indian law, Public Law 280 is a profound and deleterious example of Congress stripping tribal sovereignty without tribal consent (see Goldberg-Ambrose 1997; Jiménez and Song 1998). Carole Goldberg-Ambrose (1997) argues that the law has diminished BIA funding for law enforcement, stunted the development of tribal courts, and created a burden some states have been reluctant to accept. For these reasons, she contends that Public Law 280 has caused higher crime rates on some reservations. More generally, she concludes: "Tribes in Public Law 280 states are at a disadvantage compared with tribes elsewhere in the United States" (Goldberg-Ambrose 1997, p. 37).

Alternatively, Public Law 280 may have advantaged the economies of tribes for which jurisdiction was assumed by the states if state jurisdiction meant a more stable rule of law. As Haddock (1994) and Haddock and Miller (this volume) argue, sovereignty is paradoxical in that, on the one hand, it is necessary to give government the power it needs to enforce property rights and the rule of law but, on the other hand, it gives government the power to take property rights and arbitrarily enforce the law. Not only is sovereignty paradoxical, but it also creates a dilemma for governmental officials; the dilemma is whether to use governmental sovereignty to enforce property rights and the rule of law, thereby increasing the size of the economic pie, or to use it to redistribute the pie, thereby discouraging productivity. The temptation to take property is even greater in cases where investments are immobile, as with oil and gas development.[7] Because Public Law 280 authorizes nontribal adjudication of contractual disputes, it conveys a credible commitment to non-Indians that Indians will not opportunistically change the terms of contract after investments are made.[8]

To the extent that investors, mainly non-Indians, perceive state courts to be more stable and impartial or perhaps even biased in their favor, state jurisdiction under Public Law 280 can improve the investment climate on Public Law 280 reservations, thus bringing outside wealth and economic growth to Indian Country.[9]

The Era of Self-Determination

Public Law 280 and other policies of the termination era alarmed many Indians and their supporters and led them to rally for yet another Indian policy change—self-determination. President Nixon officially announced a new era of self-determination, asking Congress in 1970 to "strengthen the Indian's sense of autonomy without threatening his sense of community. We must assure the Indian that he can assume control of his life without being separated involuntarily from the tribal group" (quoted in Getches, Wilkinson, and Williams 1998, p. 227).

Self-determination goals were manifested in congressional legislation and a series of Supreme Court decisions during the 1970s and 80s. Congress passed legislation allowing tribes greater control over forest, mineral, and other natural resources. Tribes were allowed to enter into development agreements without as much reliance on Department of Interior authorization. Congress also enacted several bills intended to assist Indian education by funding tribally controlled schools, and to give tribal courts and councils more exclusive control over child custody cases, environmental standards, and substance abuse and health care programs (see Getches, Wilkinson, and Williams 1998; Strickland and Wilkinson 1982).

Policies regarding gambling, however, have probably had the greatest effect on reservation commerce in recent years. Casino and bingo gaming were initiated by the Indian Self-Determination and Education Act of 1975 and a series of court decisions recognizing tribal authority to run gaming facilities in the 1980s. By 1987, over a hundred tribes had opened high-stakes bingo facilities, and a few allowed poker and other card games. The Indian Gaming Regulatory Act of 1988 (IGRA), however, may have been the strongest impetus to tribally operated gaming on a large scale. The IGRA acknowledges the right of tribes to run gaming operations on federal trust land under certain conditions (see Johnson, this volume) and distinguishes among three classes of gaming. Class I and II include bingo and relatively low-stake gaming. Class III allows for "Vegas style" gaming including slot machines and craps (see Johnson, this volume; Evans and Topoleski 2002). At the end of 2003, about 201 tribes were engaged in Class II or Class III gaming.[10]

Many recent Supreme Court decisions have also reaffirmed the federal policy of self-determination. In a handful of cases involving the contractual or tort claims of non-Indians engaged in business in Indian Country, the Supreme Court insisted that tribal remedies be fully exhausted before state or federal courts could be invoked.[11] The court, however, has recognized state court adjudication over such matters arising on reservations in Public Law 280 states.[12] Nevertheless, the Supreme Court has struck down attempts by Public Law 280 states to regulate economic activities or to tax reservation businesses (including casinos).[13] In contrast and consistent with self-determination policy, the court affirmed the right of tribes to levy taxes on non-Indian individuals and businesses in key decisions in the 1980s.[14] Finally, the court has often ruled to affirm the sovereign immunity status of tribes, sometimes in cases where the tribe has signed sue-or-be-sued clauses and ostensibly waived immunity (see McLish 1988; Haddock and Miller, this volume).

Through these congressional actions and Supreme Court decisions, the era of self-determination has empowered tribal governments and courts. Hence, we expect institutions governing reservation economies to affect reservation prosperity more so than ever before.

INSTITUTIONS AND ECONOMIC GROWTH

Though any reader of Adam Smith should recognize the importance of institutions to the "wealth of nations," it has only been recently that economists have refocused attention on institutions as a driving force in the economic growth process. Douglass North's work in general and his book *Institutions, Institutional Change, and Economic Performance* (1990) in particular, have helped refocus attention on institutions.

With increasing attention paid to the effect of markets, property rights, law, and politics on economic growth, some political economists have begun trying to quantify the extent to which these institutions influence economic performance across countries. They have employed measures of institutional quality such as the risk from governmental expropriation of assets (see Coplin, O'Leary and Sealy, 1996), the degree of separation of powers within governmental branches (see Keefer and Knack, 1997), and the degree of economic freedom (Gwartney, Lawson and Emerick, 2003). The common thread weaving these studies together is the focus on property rights, the rule of law, and constraints on government that limit its ability to redistribute wealth.

Whichever measure, the general conclusion is that economic performance is positively correlated with a government's inability to redistribute property rights and the gains from contracting.[15] Acemoglu, Johnson, and Robinson (2001, p. 1369) summarize this conclusion: "countries with better '*institutions*,' more secure property rights, and less distortionary policies will invest more in physical and human capital, and will use these factors more efficiently to achieve a greater level of income."

Though statistical measures of the correlation between institutions and economic performance on Indian reservation are less well developed, institutions are equally important to reservation economies. Like so much of the literature on economic development, explanations of stagnation on Indian reservations have focused on the lack of physical capital, human capital, or natural resources. Such explanations, however, are at best insufficient and, at worst, inconsistent with the data. As pointed out above, Indian reservations often have abundant natural resources including fertile land, energy, scenery, and wildlife habitat, but these resources may contribute little to economic growth.

Some scholars recognized the importance of institutions to growth on reservations and have tried to empirically estimate their importance. Ronald

Trosper (1978) was one of the first economists to mention the potential role of institutions in his study of Indian cattle ranching efficiency. Dismissing a lack of human capital as the reason for Indian cattle ranching inefficiencies, Trosper (1978, p. 239) concludes that "land tenure or other institutional problems" should be examined as a possible explanation.

Anderson and Lueck (1992) focused specifically on the impact of trusteeship on agricultural productivity. They estimated the impact of tenure on a cross-section of reservations using the total value of reservation output per acre. Controlling for a number of other variables that might affect productivity, they found that the per-acre value of agricultural output was from eighty-five to ninety percent lower on tribal trust land than on fee-simple land, and from thirty to forty percent lower on individual trust land than on fee-simple land. The magnitude of these numbers supports the contention that bureaucratic constraints on trust land reduce agricultural productivity. The inability to transfer title of trust lands, the difficulty in using trust land as collateral, and the transaction costs resulting from multiple ownership of small parcels all make it difficult to maximize productivity. The results are especially significant on tribal trust land and suggest that tribal governance institutions have not significantly offset the difficulties of making collective decisions that promote productivity.

Cornell and Kalt (2000) searched for the "glue" that promotes economic growth by considering a broader range of institutions. They analyzed a cross-section of sixty-seven reservations with populations of 1000 or more, explaining variations in 1989 unemployment levels and income growth from 1977 to 1989. They measured variation in governance using qualitative variables deciphered from their analysis of tribal constitutions. In addition, Cornell and Kalt employed a qualitative variable indicating whether the tribe's judiciary was created as a separate and independent branch of tribal government.

Cornell and Kalt's conclusion was generally consistent with the international studies discussed, namely, institutions matter. They found that natural, human, and financial capital does matter in the growth process, but that "resources and knowledge tautologically set the upper bound on society's potential for growth at any point in time. As is increasingly reflected in the economic development literature, however, how far away a society's performance is from this upper bound depends centrally on the legal, social, and political institutions that are imposed on it or selected by it" (2002, pp. 416–47). After trying to measure the impact of formal and informal institutions on economic development, Cornell and Kalt concluded that "generous resource endowments, human capital, and access to financial capital will be virtually useless if tribes are incapable of making collective decisions and sustaining collective action, and if they lack the institutional structures necessary to maintain a hospitable environment for human and financial investment" (2000, p. 267). In other words, economic development for Indian nations, as for other nations, depends on institutions that create a stable legal environment in which productive behavior is rewarded.

Following the lead of these institutional studies, we examine the effects of different political, legal, and landownership regimes on American Indian incomes. We analyze a cross-section of reservations with populations of 1000 or more, explaining variations in the level of income in 1999 and variations in income growth from 1989 to 1999. Census Bureau surveys conducted in 1990 and 2000 provide estimates of Indian income and population for 327 reservations.[16] BIA surveys provide estimates of reservation acreage held in tribal trust, individual trust, and in fee simple. Data on tribal government employment were generously provided by Stephen Cornell and Joseph Kalt from their Harvard Project on American Indian Economic Development. To this we add data from our analysis of Public Law 280 and related legislation and from a gamblers' directory of American Indian casinos.[17]

Dependent Variables

Each reservation serves as a single observation in our cross-sectional analysis. As Table 6.1 shows, we limit the analysis to reservations with populations of 1000 or more. Doing so eliminates 246 (seventy-five percent) reservations listed in the Census Bureau data and approximately ten percent of the 512,431 individuals identified as American Indians living on reservations.[18]

We use two measures of economic performance. Our first measure of prosperity on reservations is per-capita income of American Indians in 1999 (1999 AI PER-CAPITA INCOME).[19] To measure economic growth, the percentage growth in American Indian per-capita income from 1989 to 1999 is used. Table 6.2 shows summary statistics for these dependent variables and Table 6.3 lists the data for each reservation. Note that the Crow Creek Reservation in South Dakota had the lowest 1999 per-capita income at an impoverished $4,043. The lowest real income growth rates occurred on the Crow Creek

Table 6.1. American Indian Populations on Census Reservations, 1999.

State	All Census Reservations		Reservations with population > 1000	
	Number of Reservations	Number of Population	Reservations	Population
Alabama	2	198	0	0
Alaska	1	1,204	1	1,204
Arizona	20	244,253	12	240,318
California	98	14,219	1	2,180
Colorado	2	3,073	2	3,073
Connecticut	3	217	0	0
Florida	11	1,170	0	0
Georgia	1	55	0	0
Hawaii	5	25	0	0
Idaho	4	6,964	3	6,910
Iowa	1	619	0	0
Kansas	3	1,209	0	0
Louisiana	3	344	0	0
Maine	5	1,615	0	0
Massachusetts	2	62	0	0
Michigan	10	4,853	2	2,378
Minnesota	14	17,064	4	13,765
Mississippi	1	4,108	1	4,108
Montana	8	43,373	8	43,373
Nebraska	5	4,305	2	3,640
Nevada	25	7,297	1	1,198
New Jersey	1	0	0	0
New Mexico	22	30,044	11	25,813
New York	9	7,375	3	5,720
North Carolina	1	5,832	1	5,832
North Dakota	2	7,127	2	7,127
Oklahoma	1	6,338	1	6,338
Oregon	10	4,844	2	4,380
Rhode Island	1	7	0	0
South Carolina	1	358	0	0
South Dakota	9	44,264	8	43,947
Texas	3	1,107	0	0

(Continued)

Table 6.1. (*Continued*)

State	All Census Reservations		Reservations with population > 1000	
	Number of Reservations	Number of Population	Reservations	Population
Utah	4	3,087	1	2,824
Virginia	1	33	0	0
Washington	26	25,949	9	21,390
Wisconsin	11	13,446	5	10,377
Wyoming	1	6,394	1	6,394
TOTAL	325	512,431	81	462,289

SOURCE: US Census Bureau (2000).

NOTE: 1) The Census does not report any American Indian reservations in the following states: Delaware, Illinois, Indiana, Kentucky, Maryland, Missouri, New Hampshire, Ohio, Pennsylvania, Tennessee, Vermont, and West Virginia. 2) In cases where reservations straddle multiple states, the reservation is considered part of the state in which the majority of reservation residents live.

and the Santa Domingo Pueblo reservation in New Mexico, both at about negative nineteen percent. In contrast, the Isabella Reservation in Michigan's Upper Peninsula had the highest 1999 per-capita income at $17,436 and the highest real income growth rate from 1989 to 1999 at 138 percent.

Independent Variables

The independent variables of primary interest measure differences in landowner incentives and constraints, the rule of law, and the government's role in transferring reservation wealth. The following sections describe the variables in more detail. Table 6.8 gives definitions and indicates sources, and Table 6.2 shows summary statistics.

Landowner incentives and constraints

As discussed above, much of the land on reservations is owned by individual Indians or by the tribe, but is held in trust by the federal government. Reservation land not held in trust is owned in fee simple by Indians and non-Indians. Although we expect the fee-simple lands to be more productive than trust lands (see Anderson and Lueck, 1992),[20] we cannot precisely

Table 6.2. Summary Statistics for American Indian Reservations.

Variable	Number of Reservations	Reservations with American Indian populations > 1,000				
		Min	Max	Median	Mean	St. Dev
Dependent Variables						
1999 AI PER-CAPITA INCOME ($s)	81	4,043	17,436	8,383	8,814	2,484
89–99 AI PCI GROWTH RATE	80	−19.8%	137.9%	6,390	31.7%	24.6%
Landowner Incentives & Constraints						
PERCENT FEE SIMPLE	81	0%	98.5%	13.1%	29.3%	33.4%
PERCENT FEE SIMPLE × % EMPLOYED IN RESOURCE INDUSTRIES 99	81	0%	533.45%	23.4%	68.9%	100.5%
% EMPLOYED IN RESOURCE INDUSTRIES 99	81	0.11%	15.1%	2.3%	2.9%	2.7%
External Adjudication & Rule of Law						
STATE JURISDICTION	81	0	1	0	0.31	0.46
Transfer Payments & Rent Seeking						
PER-CAPITA BIA PAYMENTS (1999 $s)	80	0	2,646	524	616	461
% EMPLOYED BY TRIBAL GOV. 89	71	0.17%	25.5%	7.8%	9.3%	6.4%
Control Variables						
1989 AI PER-CAPITA INCOME (1999 $s)	80	3,674	14,648	6,390	6,817	1,926
ADJACENT COUNTY PCI 1999	80	14,251	26,847	18,678	18,764	2,422
ADJ. COUNTY PCI GROWTH 1989–99	80	−1.7%	47.2%	16.3%	18.4%	8.5%
MILES TO METRO AREA	80	3.2	341.0	96.2	116.6	82.9
RESERVATION ACRES	81	832	15.6 M	276,928	851,047	1.86 M
SLOTS PER AI RESIDENT	81	0	3.43	0.05	0.23	0.53
PERCENT HS GRADS	79	28.6%	86.7%	66.7%	65.8%	10.0%

SOURCE: US Census Bureau (1990, 2000).

Table 6.3. American Indian Income and Income Growth by Reservation.

Reservation	State	Am. Indian Pop. (1999)	Per-Capita Inc. (1999 $s)	Percent of Adj. County PCI	Real PCI Gr. Rate (1989– 1999 [%])
Acoma Pueblo	NM	2740	8680	48.3	59.6
Allegany	NY	1203	12298	63.5	19.3
Annette Island	AK	1204	14940	NA	2.0
Bad River	WI	1069	10584	60.8	53.8
Blackfeet	MT	8259	8383	48.7	32.3
Cattaraugus	NY	1936	12318	63.8	33.2
Cheyenne River	SD	6095	6609	40.9	20.7
Coeur d'Alene	ID	1214	10023	53.7	29.4
Colorado River	AZ-CA	2304	9459	44.8	18.2
Colville	WA	4479	10120	54.4	−0.4
Crow Creek	SD	1856	4043	22.3	−19.0
Crow	MT	5193	7942	42.3	39.3
Eastern Cherokee	NC	5832	12008	68.7	40.0
Flathead	MT	6701	9811	55.2	13.6
Fond du Lac	MN-WI	1262	12649	67.9	72.5
Fort Apache	AZ	11597	5724	27.9	12.0
Fort Belknap	MT	2792	7848	51.2	28.8
Fort Berthold	ND	3849	7915	44.8	21.5
Fort Hall	ID	3609	8978	44.9	45.0
Fort Peck	MT	6271	6970	42.3	8.6
Fort Yuma	CA-AZ	1304	8858	41.6	48.9
Gila River	AZ	10317	5746	27.0	34.7
Hoopa Valley	CA	2180	9757	55.1	22.3
Hopi	AZ	6470	7803	47.9	27.2
Hualapai	AZ	1241	7793	38.5	59.8
Isabella	MI	1371	17436	97.4	138.0
Isleta Pueblo	NM	2633	11947	80.9	25.1
Jemez Pueblo	NM	1924	7938	41.1	23.7
Jicarilla Apache	NM	2431	8791	43.4	14.4
Lac Courte Oreilles	WI	1959	9119	52.6	59.7
Lac du Flambeau	WI	1559	10741	59.6	92.6
Laguna Pueblo	NM	3668	8615	57.7	5.4
Lake Traverse	SD-ND	3429	7786	41.3	42.8
Leech Lake	MN	4456	8180	43.2	29.4
Lower Brule	SD	1197	6129	39.2	−5.9
Lummi	WA	2028	10145	49.9	38.7

(Continued)

Table 6.3. (*Continued*)

Reservation	State	Am. Indian Pop. (1999)	Per-Capita Inc. (1999 $s)	Percent of Adj. County PCI	Real PCI Gr. Rate (1989– 1999 [%])
Makah	WA	1076	9835	45.4	12.7
Menominee	WI	2813	8096	39.7	27.2
Mescalero	MI	2848	7541	39.1	28.8
Mississippi Choctaw	MS	4108	6864	39.5	15.1
Muckleshoot	WA	1029	9194	36.5	84.4
Navajo Nation	AZ-NM-UT	174847	6807	41.2	35.7
Nez Perce	ID	2087	10369	54.8	26.5
Northern Cheyenne	MT-SD	3948	6730	36.2	11.8
Omaha	NE-IA	2220	6328	38.7	37.9
Oneida	WI	2977	14771	69.7	54.7
Osage	OK	6638	12203	64.1	25.5
Pascua Yaqui	AZ	2928	5627	26.8	33.6
Pine Ridge	SD-NE	14255	5619	32.6	34.3
Payallup	WA	1386	12439	49.5	1.8
Pyramid Lake	NV	1198	10878	44.8	50.9
Quinault	WA	1023	9117	44.0	−4.6
Red Lake	MN	4903	7876	40.6	36.7
Rocky Boys	MT	2534	6951	42.1	20.9
Rosebud	SD	8687	5613	35.5	11.7
Salt River	AZ	3381	7680	36.4	35.6
San Carlos	AZ	8769	4970	24.4	16.6
San Felipe Pueblo	NM	2482	7615	39.9	44.4
San Juan Pueblo	NM	1326	11275	55.7	49.5
Santa Clara Pueblo	NM	1313	9544	49.9	7.4
Santo Domingo Pueblo	NM	3106	5620	29.1−	19.8
Sault Ste. Marie	MI	1007	7229	43.7	31.1
Southern Ute	CO	1405	13043	80.6	58.5
Spirit Lake	ND	3278	6259	36.1	NA
Spokane	WA	1535	9724	51.7	21.1
St. Regis Mohawk	NY	2581	12016	56.2	30.0
Standing Rock	SD-ND	5753	6322	39.3	37.6
Taos Pueblo	NM	1342	9512	47.8	50.7
Tohono O'odham	AZ	9783	6520	31.1	77.4

(*Continued*)

Table 6.3. (*Continued*)

Reservation	State	Am. Indian Pop. (1999)	Per-Capita Inc. (1999 $s)	Percent of Adj. County PCI	Real PCI Gr. Rate (1989– 1999 [%])
Tulalip	WA	1875	10623	39.6	15.0
Turtle Mountain	MT-ND-SD	7675	8330	54.5	32.5
Uintah and Ouray	UT	2824	6934	37.0	14.2
Umatilla	OR	1373	12032	64.2	70.1
Ute Mountain	CO-NM-UT	1668	8159	55.5	25.5
Warm Springs	OR	3007	8535	38.9	16.7
White Earth	MN	3144	9127	53.8	38.2
Wind River	WY	6394	7304	36.1	25.3
Winnebago	NE-IA	1420	7662	43.6	16.2
Yakima	WA	6959	8730	46.4	31.9
Yankton	SD	2675	6170	43.3	62.0
Zuni	NM-AZ	7377	6029	35.8	14.9

SOURCE: US Census Bureau (1990, 2000).

NOTE: 1) This table shows data for only those reservations with American Indian populations exceeding 1,000. 2) Adj. County PCI is the per-capita income of nonreservation residents living in the same county and any county adjacent to the county or counties containing the reservation. 3) The NAs signify that data are unavailable to make the necessary calculations.

infer the effect of land tenure on American Indian incomes because we do not know which or how many fee-simple acres are owned by Indians. In lieu of an ideal measure of land owned by Indians in fee simple, we construct a variable that denotes the percentage of reservation land that is not held in trust (PERCENT FEE SIMPLE). We construct this variable by subtracting trust and government-owned acres (reported by the regional BIA offices) from the total acres of the reservation (reported by the Census Bureau) and dividing the difference by the total acres.[21] This variable provides a relative measure of land that is free from bureaucratic constraints across reservations.

We also interact PERCENT FEE SIMPLE with a variable that indicates the proportion of the adult population of American Indians employed in agricultural, forestry, mining, and hunting and fishing industries (% EMPLOYED IN RESOURCE INDUSTRIES). The interaction term helps us infer whether fee-simple ownership is especially important on reservations whose economies depend on land-based production.

External adjudication and the rule of law

As with cross-country institutional studies, we would expect a positive relationship between indexes of an impartial and consistent rule of law and economic growth on reservations. Although tribal courts vary considerably in terms of appointment procedure, training, and length of office (see Skari 1992), it is difficult to quantify a meaningful stability index from these differences. Even if we had such a measure, the actual stability of a tribal court may do little to encourage investments from non-Indians contemplating business with reservation Indians because non-Indians may perceive all tribal courts to be biased or unpredictable regardless of the actual track record of an individual court (Haddock and Miller, this volume). This perception is a major obstacle to economic development because much more wealth lies outside rather than inside Indian Country.

The effect of an unstable rule of law may have been reduced for some tribes by Public Law 280. We test for this effect with the variable STATE JURISDICTION. The variable denotes reservations in the mandatory Public Law 280 states, reservations in optional states that have most credibly asserted jurisdiction over contractual and tort claims in Indian Country, and reservations in New York, where the state has had jurisdiction over civil disputes since at least 1950 (see Strickland and Wilkinson 1982, p. 372).[22]

Government transfer payments and political rent seeking

To evaluate the extent to which governmental activity on reservations reduces productive activity, we use PER CAPITA BIA PAYMENTS, which indicates the number of dollars per-capita the BIA allocated to tribes.[23] This measure would be biased if BIA payments were determined by reservation incomes, but they are not. To be sure, a preferred measure would be all federal dollars allocated to tribes including those from other agencies such as Health and Human Services, Housing and Urban Development, and Department of Justice, but such aggregate data are not readily available.

To the extent that BIA payments go to infrastructure, education, and so on, they could contribute to economic growth, but more payments also discourage productive activity and encourage rent seeking (see Tullock 1993). That is, the greater the federal payments to the tribes, the more resources will spend to garner political clout on the reservations. Our empirical estimates suggest that these negative rent-seeking effects offset the positive benefit from payments as discussed below.

Another proxy of the tribal government's ability to transfer wealth is the percent of tribal members over twenty-five years of age employed by tribal government in 1989, % EMPLOYED BY TRIBAL GOV. 89. Like PER CAPITA BIA PAYMENTS, we expect this variable to negatively affect per-capita income growth if the employment is related to rent-seeking rather than productivity.

Control variables

To control the effect of gaming on Indian income,[24] we estimate the number of slot machines at reservation casinos per American Indian resident (SLOTS PER AI RESIDENT).[25] This variable does not precisely measure variation in the economic benefits accrued from gaming because it does not measure tribal revenues or profits from gaming. Nonetheless, it does proxy expected net revenues from gaming on each reservation to the extent that tribes are unlikely to invest in more slot machines without expecting that they will make a profit. For example, it is unlikely that Class III casinos will be built on rural reservations, and it is more likely that tribes will invest in Class III casinos if they have a credible commitment from the state or other tribes to limit competition.

Cornell and Kalt (2000) note that resource endowments determine the "upper bound on society's potential for growth." The size of the reservation, RESERVATION ACREAGE, is used to control for this resource endowment effect. Of course, because land quality is heterogeneous across reservations, this is not a perfect proxy. Moreover, small reservations could have significant amounts of oil or minerals or be located near metropolitan areas, thus making our measure less than perfect.

Differences in human capital and exogenous demand for inputs (e.g., labor or natural resources) and outputs across reservations are also likely to affect Indian income. The variable, PERCENT HS GRADS 89, controls for human capital by measuring the number of American Indians who graduated from high school as a percentage of the 1989 reservation population over twenty-five years of age. Exogenous demand is measured by per-capita income earned by nonreservation residents in counties in or adjacent to the reservation, ADJACENT COUNTY PCI. Similarly, the distance from a reservation to a city with a population of 100,000 or more, MILES TO METRO AREA, provides a measure of the exogenous demand for reservation inputs and outputs.

Empirical Specifications and Regression Results

The impact of these independent variables on Indian incomes is estimated using an Ordinary Least Squares (OLS) procedure. The regression analysis relies on several different specifications to estimate the following generic model:

$$\text{American Indian Income} = \beta_0 + \beta_1(\text{landowner incentives \& constraints})$$
$$+\beta_2(\text{external adjudication \& rule of law})$$
$$+\beta_3(\text{government transfers \& rent-seeking})$$
$$+\beta_4(\text{controls}) + e$$

Table 6.4 shows our OLS estimates of 1999 per-capita income. Column 1 employs the variable, PER-CAPITA BIA PAYMENTS, while the other specifications omit this variable. Column 3 employs the interaction term, which measures the marginal effect of an increase in the percentage of fee-simple land when coupled with an increase in the number of American Indians employed in resource industries.

The coefficients shown in Table 6.4 have simple interpretations because the dependent variable is specified in dollars. For example, the Column 1 coefficient on STATE JURISDICTION means that reservations with state jurisdiction over contract disputes and tort claims are estimated to have per-capita income levels $2,242 greater than those that do not.

Table 6.5 shows our OLS estimates of real per-capita income growth on reservations from 1989 to 1999. Column 1 uses PER-CAPITA BIA PAYMENTS, Column 2 uses % EMPLOYED BY TRIBAL GOV. 89, and Column 3 uses PERCENT HS GRADS 89. These variables are used separately because of the relatively high pair-wise correlations between them and because analyzing them in separate regressions allows us to utilize more observations per-specification. Column 4 differs slightly from Column 2 because it employs the variable interacting fee-simple ownership with employment in resource industries. All of the Table 6.5 coefficients can be interpreted in terms of their impact on income growth. For example, the Column 1 coefficient on STATE JURISDICTION means that per-capita incomes on reservations with state court jurisdiction grew at rates about fifteen percentage points faster than those lacking state jurisdiction.

Table 6.4. OLS Estimates for American Indian Per-Capita Income, 1999

	Dependent variable = 1999 AI PCI		
	(1)	(2)	(3)
Independent Variables			
CONSTANT	9,699	9,263	10,215
	(4.59)**	(4.40)**	(4.82)**
Controls			
ADJACENT COUNTY PCI 1999	−0.426	−0.036	−0.090
	(0.41)	(0.35)	(0.84)
MILES TO METRO AREA	−6.00	−6.94	−7.66
	(2.00)*	(2.35)**	(2.50)**
SLOTS PER AI RESIDENT	1,400	1,378	1,636
	(3.08)**	(3.04)**	(3.56)**
RESERVATION ACRES	−0.0009	−0.0001	−0.0001
	(0.81)	(0.68)	(0.91)
Landowner Incentives & Constraints			
PERCENT FEE SIMPLE	4.12	2.89	−9.33
	(0.55)	(0.40)	(0.92)
PERCENT FEE SIMPLE × % EMPLOYED IN RESOURCE INDUSTRIES 99	—	—	5.87
			(1.90)*
External Adjudication & Rule of Law			
STATE JURISDICTION	2,242	2,178	2,149
	(4.27)**	(4.16)**	(4.14)**
Transfer Payments & Rent Seeking			
PER-CAPITA BIA PAYMENTS	−0.75		
	(1.54)	—	—
Observations	79	80	80
Adjusted R^2	0.38	0.37	0.40
F-Statistic	7.85	8.83	7.49

NOTE: 1) Absolute value of *t*-statistics in parentheses. ** Indicates statistically significant coefficients at 5% level for a one-tailed *t*-test. * Indicates statistically significant coefficients at 10% level for a one-tailed *t*-test. 2) Although not shown, specification 3 also includes the variable % EMPLOYED IN RESOURCE INDUSTRIES 99 as an independent regressor. The estimated coefficient on the variable is 23.4 with a *t*-statistic of 0.24.

Table 6.5. OLS Estimates for American Indian Per-Capita Income Growth, 1989–1999.

Dependent variable = 89–99 AI PCI GROWTH			
(1)	(2)	(3)	(4)

Independent Variables

	(1)	(2)	(3)	(4)
CONSTANT	73.19	87.66	25.60	73.62
	(6.30)**	(6.70)**	(1.48)	(6.07)**

Controls

	(1)	(2)	(3)	(4)
1989 AI PCI	−0.006	−0.008	−0.008	−0.006
	(3.86)**	(5.22)**	(4.89)**	(3.55)**
ADJ. COUNTY PCI GROWTH 89–99	−0.079	0.197	0.041	−0.09
	(0.31)	(0.72)	(0.16)	(0.34)
MILES TO METRO AREA	−0.031	−0.015	−0.062	−0.029
	(1.08)	(0.57)	(2.18)**	(0.95)
SLOTS PER AI RESIDENT	21.36	31.45	22.01	21.49
	(4.63)**	(6.31)**	(4.87)**	(4.37)**
RESERVATION ACRES	−4.47e-08	−5.67e-07	−9.55e-07	−1.74e-08
	(0.04)	(0.51)	(0.78)	(0.01)
PERCENT HS GRADS 99	—	—	0.97	—
		(3.07)**		

Landowner Incentives & Constraints

	(1)	(2)	(3)	(4)
PERCENT FEE SIMPLE	0.042	−0.125	−0.089	0.021
	(0.55)	(1.51)	(1.02)	(0.18)
PERCENT FEE SIMPLE × % EMPLOYED IN RESOURCE INDUSTRIES 99	—	—	0.008	(0.22)

External Adjudication & Rule of Law

	(1)	(2)	(3)	(4)
STATE JURISDICTION	15.35	15.78	13.79	15.66
	(2.84)**	(3.02)**	(2.62)**	(2.82)**

Transfer Payments & Rent Seeking

	(1)	(2)	(3)	(4)
PER-CAPITA BIA PAYMENTS	−0.013			−0.013
	(2.77)**	—	—	(2.51)*
(%) EMPLOYED BY TRIBAL GOV. 89	—	−1.29	—	—
		(3.32)**		
Observations	79	71	78	79
Adjusted R^2	0.40	0.54	0.40	0.40
F-Statistic	7.37	11.37	7.58	7.37

NOTE: 1) Absolute value of *t*-statistics in parentheses. ** Indicates statistically significant coefficients at 5% level for a one-tailed *t*-test. * Indicates statistically significant coefficients at 10% level for a one-tailed *t*-test. 2) Although not shown, specification 4 also includes the variable % EMPLOYED IN RESOURCE INDUSTRIES 99 as an independent regressor. The estimated coefficient on the variable is -0.36 with a *t*-statistic of 0.34.

In Table 6.4, the coefficient estimates on PERCENT FEE SIMPLE are not statistically significant by conventional standards. However, the coefficient on the interaction term, PERCENT FEE SIMPLE × % EMPLOYED IN RESOURCE INDUSTRIES, is statistically significant and positive.[26] The Table 6.4 result suggests that BIA trust constraints on reservation land have stunted economic development on reservations where land-based production is relatively more important, but neither PERCENT FEE SIMPLE nor the interaction term is a significant determinant of per-capita income growth from 1989 to 1999. If ways can be found to relax BIA trust constraints to make it easier for Indian owners to lease land and use it as collateral in credit markets, the negative effects of trust status could be reduced.

The coefficient estimates on STATE JURISDICTION suggest a large and statistically significant effect on economic growth. Table 6.5 coefficients, for example, show that per-capita incomes on reservations with state court adjudication grew at rates from 14 to 16 percentage points higher than reservations with only tribal court adjudication.[27]

The coefficients on government transfers payments and tribal employment are negatively correlated with our dependent variables. The coefficient of −0.013 on PER-CAPITA BIA PAYMENTS in Table 6.5 implies that a one-hundred dollar increase in payments from the BIA to tribal leaders caused a 1.3 percent decline in per-capita growth rates. The negative coefficient on % EMPLOYED BY TRIBAL GOV. 89 implies that a one percentage point increase in the size of tribal government as measured by employment caused a decrease of 1.29 in per-capita income growth rates. To understand the magnitude of this relationship, consider that an increase of one standard deviation in % EMPLOYED BY TRIBAL GOV. 89 (6.4) is associated with an 8.3 percentage point decline in 89–99 AI PCI GROWTH.

The control variables generally perform as expected. MILES TO METRO AREA is negatively correlated with our dependent variables, implying that tribes in isolated locations have fewer economic opportunities. The coefficients on the gaming activity variable are statistically significant in all regressions. This finding, although less sophisticated, is consistent with Evans and Topoleski (2002), who show that reservation Indians benefit economically from having gambling facilities. PERCENT HS GRADS 89 is positively correlated with per-capita income growth, suggesting that investments in human capital can help reservation economies. The negative coefficients on 1989 AI PCI in Table 6.5 imply convergence, meaning that low-income tribes adopt the economic development strategies of higher-income tribes or that the lower income tribes earn a higher return per-unit of physical and human capital employed (see Barro 1997).

Robustness checks help us infer the extent to which the hypothesis tests are affected by the omission of certain observations, particularly those most likely to wield a large degree of influence on the results shown in Tables 6.4 and 6.5 (e.g., the Navajo reservation because it is so large). The independent variables with the highest variability across the sample help identify outliers. These variables include SLOTS PER AI RESIDENT, RESERVATION ACRES, % EMPLOYED IN RESOURCE INDUSTRIES (and the interaction term), and PER-CAPITA BIA PAYMENTS. Two-dimensional graphs (not shown) of the regression residuals with respect to these variables show that each may be a source of heteroskedasticity and therefore bias our results.

Tables 6.6 and 6.7 show the results of simple robustness checks. The regressions employ the same independent variables as Tables 6.4 and 6.5, but omit certain outliers. Outliers are defined as observations for which the value of any of the four independent variables listed above is greater than one standard deviation from the mean. For example, any reservation not receiving PER-CAPITA BIA PAYMENTS between $155 and $1,077 is excluded from the first column of Tables 6.6 and 6.7 because the mean of PER-CAPITA BIA PAYMENTS is $616 and the standard deviation is $461 (see Table 6.2). Perhaps most striking, the negative (but insignificant) Table 6.6 coefficients on SLOTS PER AI RESIDENT reveal that the estimated effect of gaming activity on levels of per-capita income is quite sensitive to the omission of outliers.[28] The Table 6.7 coefficients, however, show that the effect of SLOTS PER AI RESIDENT on 1989 to 1999 income growth are less sensitive to outliers. As shown in Tables 6.6 and 6.7, STATE JURISDICTION and % EMPLOYED BY TRIBAL GOV. 89 are insensitive to the outliers as is the variable PERCENT FEE SIMPLE × % EMPLOYED IN RESOURCE INDUSTRIES in Table 6.6. The variable PER-CAPITA BIA PAYMENTS, however, is less robust to omission of the outliers.

SUMMARY AND CONCLUSION

Our empirical findings show a significant relationship between institutional variables and 1999 American Indian per-capita income and income growth from 1989 to 1999. The relationship holds even when we control for income in

Table 6.6. OLS Estimates of American Indian Per-Capita Income with Outliers Omitted, 1999.

	Dependent variable = 1999 AI PCI		
	(1)	(2)	(3)
Independent Variables			
CONSTANT	7,033	9,213	9,418
	(3.09)**	(4.40)**	(4.31)
Controls			
ADJACENT COUNTY PCI 1999	0.101	−0.017	−0.028
	(1.90)	(0.16)	(0.25)
MILES TO METRO AREA	−4.39	−5.36	−5.18
	(1.33)	(1.73)*	(1.58)
SLOTS PER AI RESIDENT	−2,190	−1,102	−598.26
	(1.25)	(0.76)	(0.40)
RESERVATION ACRES	−0.0004	−0.0004	−0.0006
	(0.99)	(1.34)	(1.88)*
Landowner Incentives & Constraints			
PERCENT FEE SIMPLE	4.69	4.82	−11.80
	(0.58)	(0.65)	(1.20)
PERCENT FEE SIMPLE × % EMPLOYED IN RESOURCE INDUSTRIES 99	—	—	10.76
			(1.96)*
External Adjudication & Rule of Law			
STATE JURISDICTION	2,075	2,157	2,074
	(3.10)**	(4.00)**	(3.70)**
Transfer Payments & Rent Seeking			
PER-CAPITA BIA PAYMENTS	−0.23		
	(0.24)	—	—
Observations	55	71	66
Adjusted R^2	0.26	0.29	0.35
F-Statistic	3.78	5.80	5.29

NOTE: 1) Absolute value of t-statistics in parentheses. ** Indicates statistically significant coefficients at 5% level for a one-tailed t-test. * Indicates statistically significant coefficients at 10% level for a one-tailed t-test. 2) The regression shown in specification 1 excludes observations outside of one standard deviation from the mean for the following variables: SLOTS PER AI RESIDENT, RESERVATION ACRES, and PER-CAPITA BIA PAYMENTS. 3) The regression shown in specification 2 excludes observations outside of one standard deviation from the mean for SLOTS PER AI RESIDENT and RESERVATION ACRES. 4) The regression shown in specification 3 excludes observations outside of one standard deviation from the mean for SLOTS PER AI RESIDENT, RESERVATION ACRES, % EMPLOYED IN RESOURCE INDUSTRIES 99, and the fee-interaction term. 5) Although not shown, specification 3 also includes the variable % EMPLOYED IN RESOURCE INDUSTRIES 99 as an independent aggressor. The estimated coefficient on the variable is −35.8 with a t-statistic of 0.39.

adjacent counties, distance to metropolitan areas, education levels, gambling, and other factors. Although we emphasize a different set of institutions, our findings are generally consistent with Cornell and Kalt (2000), who also shift the focus of economic performance from physical and human capital to institutions.

Table 6.7. OLS Estimates of American Indian Per-Capita Income Growth with Outliers Omitted, 1989–1999.

	Dependent variable = 89–99 AI PCI GROWTH			
	(1)	(2)	(3)	(4)
Independent Variables				
CONSTANT	72.37	90.81	35.31	76.50
	(4.87)**	(6.15)**	(1.96)*	(4.53)
Controls				
1989 AI PCI	−0.006	−0.008	−0.008	0.006
	(3.25)**	(4.73)**	(4.42)**	(3.09)**
ADJ. COUNTY PCI GROWTH 89-99	−0.005	0.171	0.171	0.025
	(0.02)	(0.57)	(0.57)	(0.09)
MILES TO METRO AREA	−0.035	−0.021	−0.050	−0.037
	(1.00)	(0.67)	(1.56)	(1.04)
SLOTS PER AI RESIDENT	9.01	22.22	18.19	9.62
	(0.45)	(1.36)	(1.14)	(0.47)
RESERVATION ACRES	−2.00e-08	−1.65e-06	−6.68e-07	−8.61e-07
	(0.00)	(0.39)	(0.16)	(0.18)
PERCENT HS GRADS 99			0.75	
	—	—	(2.28)**	—
Landowner Incentives & Constraints				
PERCENT FEE SIMPLE	−0.013	−0.085	−0.034	−0.021
	(0.16)	(0.93)	(0.38)	(0.18)
PERCENT FEE SIMPLE × % EMPLOYED IN RESOURCE INDUSTRIES 99	—	—	0.02	(0.50)
External Adjudication & Rule of Law				
STATE JURISDICTION	18.18	15.26	12.18	18.13
	(2.47)**	(2.46)**	(2.13)**	(2.37)**
Transfer Payments & Rent Seeking				
PER-CAPITA BIA PAYMENTS	−0.011			−0.013
	(1.08)	—	—	(1.10)

(*Continued*)

Table 6.7. (Continued)

	Dependent variable = 89–99 AI PCI GROWTH			
	(1)	(2)	(3)	(4)
(%) EMPLOYED BY TRIBAL GOV. 89		−1.29		
	−	$(3.17)^{**}$	−	−
Observations	55	63	69	55
Adjusted R^2	0.18	0.29	0.20	0.15
F-Statistic	2.51	4.17	3.15	1.97

NOTE: 1) Absolute value of t-statistics in parentheses. ** Indicates statistically significant coefficients at 5% level for a one-tailed t-test. * Indicates statistically significant coefficients at 10% level for a one-tailed t-test. 2) The regression shown in specification 1 excludes observations outside of one standard deviation from the mean for the following variables: SLOTS PER AI RESIDENT, RESERVATION ACRES, and PER-CAPITA BIA PAYMENTS. 3) The regressions shown in specifications 2 and 3 exclude observations outside of one standard deviation from the mean for SLOTS PER AI RESIDENT and RESERVATION ACRES. 4) The regression shown in specification 4 excludes observations outside of one standard deviation from the mean for SLOTS PER AI RESIDENT, RESERVATION ACRES, % EMPLOYED IN RESOURCE INDUSTRIES 99, and the fee-simple interaction term. 5) Although not shown, specification 3 also includes the variable % EMPLOYED IN RESOURCE INDUSTRIES 99 as an independent aggressor. The estimated coefficient on the variable is 0.14 with a t-statistic of 0.10.

One of our strongest findings suggests that allowing non-Indian litigants access to state courts in contract and tort cases stimulates economic growth. This finding is consistent with cross-country empirical studies showing the positive effect of a stable rule of law on economic growth (see Acemoglu, Johnson, and Robinson 2001; Keefer and Knack 1997) and with the thesis of Haddock and Miller (this volume). Though this does not necessarily mean that tribes should submit to state courts or certainly that Congress should force them to do so, it does quantify a cost of judicial sovereignty.

There is also a robust negative relationship between the size and scope of tribal government and income growth. This finding is consistent with Tullock's (1993) discussion of the deleterious effects of rent-seeking on economic productivity and with the Gwartney, Lawson, and Holcombe's (1999) finding of a negative relationship between governmental power and economic growth across a sample of sovereign nations.

Finally, our empirical analysis suggests that BIA trust constraints on land have stunted the long-run economic development of reservations whose economies depend on natural resource use (including farming and ranching).

Table 6.8. Variable Definitions and Sources.

Variable	Definition	Source
Dependent Variables		
1999 AI PER-CAPITA INCOME	1999 per-capita income of American Indians and Alaskan Natives living on the reservation	US Census Bureau
1989 AI PCI	Same as above for 1989. CPI adjusted and specified in 1999 dollars	US Census Bureau. CPI data come from the Bureau of Labor Statistics
89–99 AI PCI GROWTH	The percentage growth in CPI adjusted American Indian and Alaskan Native PCI from 1989 to 1999	Calculated from the two sources listed above
Landowner Incentives & Constraints		
PERCENT FEE SIMPLE	The difference between total acreage and the sum of trust, tribal, and federal land in 1999 divided by the acreage of the reservation in 1999	Land tenure data came from individual reports sent to US by the real estate divisions of each regional BIA office
External Adjudication & Rule of Law		
STATE JURISDICTION	= 1 if state courts have jurisdiction over contract cases and tort claims arising on reservations	This variable denotes reservations in mandatory states of Alaska, California, Minnesota (excluding Red Lake Res.), Nebraska, Oregon (excluding Warm Springs Res.), and Wisconsin (excluding Menonimee Res.), reservations in optional states that have assumed relevant jurisdiction (Florida, Idaho, Iowa, and Washington), with reservations in New York Sources are Public Law 83-280 (18 U.S.C. s. 1162, 28 U.S.C. s. 1360) Strickland and Wilkinson (1982, pp. 362–63), and 25 U.S.C. s. 233

(Continued)

Table 6.8. Variable Definitions and Sources. (*Continued*)

Variable	Definition	Source
Transfer Payments & Rent-Seeking		
PER-CAPITA BIA PAYMENTS	The sum of inflation-adjusted dollars allocated to a tribe on an individual reservation in 1995 and 2000 divided by the 1999 American Indian population on the reservation	Bureau of Indian Affairs of the US Department of Interior: Budget Justifications and Annual Performance Plans for Fiscal Years 2000 and 1995. We aggregate the payments to tribal leaders earmarked for tribal government, human services, education, public safety and justice, community development, resources management, and trust services
% EMPLOYED BY TRIBAL GOV. 89	1989 tribal government employees divided by 1989 American Indian population over the age of 25	The tribal government employment data were compiled by Steve Cornell and Joseph Kalt of the Harvard Project on American Indian Economic Development. The 1989 American Indian population data came from the US Census Bureau
Control Variables		
SLOTS PER AI RESIDENT	Number of slot machines on reservation for casinos that opened prior to 2000 divided by the 1999 American Indian population	The primary source is a gamblers' web site: http://www.gambl inganswers.com/casinos/country/US/ (visited on November 10, 2003). We gathered data on the opening dates of casinos with LexisNexis searches of newspaper articles in relevant locales. We also cross-referenced the gambling web site data by calling casino managers, gleaning information from casino web sites, and investigating the web sites of gaming regulatory agencies in the different states

1999 PCI IN REGION	The 1999 per-capita income of non-Indians living in reservation counties or counties directly adjacent to the reservation	US Census Bureau
89–99 PCI GROWTH IN REGION	The percentage growth, from 1989–1999, in real per-capita income as described above	US Census Bureau. CPI data came from the Bureau of Labor Statistics
MILES TO METRO AREA	The minimum number of miles, by road, from the geographic center of a reservation to the nearest city with a 1999 population of at least 100,000	
RESERVATION ACREAGE	The total acreage of the reservation	US Census Bureau
PERCENT HS GRADS	The number of American Indians with high school degrees (or higher) divided by the Indian population that is over 25-years old	US Census Bureau

These results are consistent with empirical findings of Anderson and Lueck (1992) regarding reservation agricultural productivity. We find little evidence, however, to suggest that BIA-trust constraints have impeded economic growth on resource-based reservations in the last decade. More research is needed to determine why, but we can speculate that the BIA has relaxed some of these constraints in recent years, creating more opportunities for Indians to use land as collateral in credit markets.

The wealth and income of Indian nations will remain low as long as economic development policies remain focused on cultural differences, resource endowments, and welfare payments, and continue to give short shrift to institutions. A growing body of literature documents that property rights and the rule of law, albeit informal, were at work both before and following European contact. Federal trust authority, however, undermined property rights on reservations, and tribal political institutions have sometimes failed to create a stable rule of law.

The data presented here suggest that the same variables important to economic prosperity in developing countries are important on Indian reservations. Fee-simple landownership, an impartial and stable legal environment, and a government that can resist the temptation to engage in transfer activity, improve income levels, and economic growth rates. These results are consistent with other studies of American Indian institutions and are likely to find more support, as better data for measuring the impact of institutions on economic performance are forthcoming. This is not to say that culture is unimportant; indeed as Cornell and Kalt (2000) note, culture may be an important part of the catalyst for economic development. Without formal and informal institutions that lower transaction costs and reward productivity, however, Indian economies are likely to remain enclaves of poverty in a sea of prosperity.

NOTES

1. The authors are grateful to Tony Cookson for excellent research assistance.

2. For a more complete discussion see Wilson (1992) and Anderson (1995).

3. See US Senate Report No. 699, July 29, 1953. The Report accompanies H.R. 1063, which was enacted as Public Law 280. Also see the records of the US Senate floor debate on H.R. 1063, especially the dialogue on August 1, 1953.

4. The Public Law 280 scholar Goldberg-Ambrose (1997, p. 1) argues: "Tribes neither requested nor approved states' Public Law 280 jurisdiction." At the time the legislation was passed, however, Department of Interior officials claimed that "The Indian groups in those [mandatory Public Law 280] states were, for the most part, agreeable to the transfer of jurisdiction..." (Senate Report No. 699, July 29, 1953). The report also names tribes that objected and were afforded exemptions. The reservations that were ultimately exempted include the Red Lake Reservation in Minnesota, Warm Springs Reservation in Oregon, and Menominee Reservation in Wisconsin (18 U.S.C. s. 1162[a]).

5. See the record of Senate floor debate on H.R. 1063 from August 1, 1953. The records show that senators from several nonmandatory states, including South Dakota and Wyoming, believed that their states could not assume jurisdiction without amending their state constitutions.

6. See *Washington v. Confederated Bands of Yakima Indian Nation* (1979) and *Kennerly v. Montana District Court* (1971).

7. See Haddock (1994) for further discussion of this point.

8. See Klein, Crawford, and Alchian (1978) for a discussion of post-contractual opportunism.

9. To be sure, Public Law 280 may make Indians uneasier about doing business with non-Indians. However, American Indians on reservations have fewer alternative business partners than non Indians living outside reservations. If they refuse to contract with non-Indians for fear of impartial court judgments, American Indians will forgo a greater number of potentially beneficial transactions (see Haddock and Miller, this volume).

10. This information comes from the web site of the National Indian Gaming Association. It is available at: http://www.indiangaming.org/library/indian-gaming-facts/index.shtml.

11. See especially *Iowa Mutual Insurance Co. v. LaPlante* (1987) and *National Farmers Union Ins. Companies v. Crow Tribe of Indians* (1985).

12. See especially *Williams v. Lee* (1959) and *Kennerly v. District Court of Montana* (1971).

13. See especially *Santa Rosa Band of Indians v. Kings County* (1975), *Bryan v. Itasca County* (1976), and *California v. Cabazon Band of Mission Indians* (1987).

14. See especially *Washington v. Confederated Tribes of the Colville Indian Reservation* (1980) and *Merrion v. Jicarilla Apache Tribe* (1982). Note, however, that a more recent Supreme Court decision rescinds some tribal taxing authority over non-Indians in Indian Country (see *Atkinson Trading Company, Inc. v. Shirley* (2001)).

15. See, for example, Acemoglu, Johnson, and Robinson (2001); Hall and Jones (1999); Gwartney, Lawson, and Holcombe (1999); Keefer and Knack (1997).

16. According to the Census, a reservation is land that has been set aside for the use of the tribe, either by tribal treaties, agreements, executive orders, federal statutes, secretarial orders, or judicial determinations. Although Alaska and Oklahoma have

large indigenous populations, most American Indians and Natives in these states do not live on federally recognized reservations and are therefore omitted from our sample.

17. The directory is available online at: http://www.gamblinganswers.com/casinos/country/US/.

18. Eliminating sparsely populated reservations from our analysis decreases the likelihood that the results will be heavily influenced by per-capita income observations that may be biased by a small denominator.

19. Census income data include "Social Security or Railroad Retirement income; Supplemental Security Income (SSI); any public assistance or welfare payments from the state or local welfare office; retirement, survivor, or disability pensions; and any other sources of income received regularly such as Veterans' (VA) payments, unemployment compensation, child support, or alimony."

20. An obvious potential bias in this measure is that fee-simple lands might be the better quality lands on the reservation. Anderson and Lueck specifically address this point and find no systematic bias. Indeed, when the raw agricultural potential of reservation lands is compared with surrounding counties, they find Indian lands are not of lower quality.

21. For a few reservations, the acres of trust land reported by BIA regional offices exceeded the Census account of total reservation acres for reasons we could not explain. In these instances, we assumed the reservation to have zero fee-simple acres.

22. In a few cases, it is not entirely clear whether the state has jurisdiction over civil disputes involving non-Indians and Indians arising on reservations. Thus, our categorization of reservations requires some judgment. Our statistical results, however, are not very sensitive to different interpretations of Public Law 280 status (see Anderson and Parker, 2005).

23. To account for annual fluctuations in BIA allocations, the variable reports the average allocation over 1995 and 1999.

24. Precisely measuring the effect of gambling on income is a difficult task outside the scope of our study. Factors such as when the casino was opened, how close the reservation is to urban centers, whether tribal members directly share in the profits, and whether the tribal-state gaming compacts restrict competition are likely to be important (Johnson, this volume). Those interested in a systematic study of the effects of casino gambling on American Indian employment and non-income measures of economic well being should consult Evans and Topoleski (2002).

25. The directory is available online at: http://www.gambl inganswers.com/casinos/country/US/. We used various methods to verify whether the listing of casinos is complete and to add data on casinos that were missing. In addition, because this source does not indicate when gaming activity was initiated, we used various methods to find out when casinos were opened. Our methods included conversations with casino management, gleaning information from casino web sites and the web sites of regulatory agencies overseeing gambling, and searching LexisNexis for

newspapers accounts of casino openings. To verify accuracy, we cross-checked all sources of information.

26. The magnitude of this coefficient is not easy to interpret. Additional regression (not presented here) suggest that a one percent increase in PERCENT FEE SIMPLE is correlated with a $27 increase in Indian per-capita incomes on the twenty-five percent of reservations for which % EMPLOYED IN RESOURCE INDUSTRIES is greatest (e.g., on the twenty reservations whose employment base is most dependent on natural resources). The regression results are available upon request.

27. In other research, we find that reservations with state court adjudication outperformed other reservations even before the casino boom. We also find that reservation economies in states that have assumed jurisdiction through both mandatory and optional Public Law 280 legislation have outperformed other reservations, and the results are robust to different interpretations of optional Public Law 280 status. See Anderson and Parker (2005).

28. Reservations with large casinos in Michigan, Minnesota, Wisconsin, Idaho, and Washington are omitted by the criteria.

SEVEN

Sovereignty Can be a Liability: How Tribes Can Mitigate the Sovereign's Paradox

DAVID D. HADDOCK AND ROBERT J. MILLER[1]

Political rhetoric often treats strengthened tribal sovereignty as an unambiguous advantage to tribal members and governments. This chapter offers a cautionary note—the sovereignty that US law recognizes in tribes comes in varieties, some that threaten those who might most aid impoverished Indians, namely, potential investors. An offer to limit one's own discretion—in other words, an offer to weaken one's own powers—may be necessary and desirable in order to achieve consensual, mutually beneficial undertakings. Limitations on sovereign power will prove more credible if a judiciary focuses on the future opportunities that might be gained rather than the possibility of extracting recompense from present investors for historical inequities not of their doing.

In contrast to private relationships, however, to rely on a court to discipline its sovereign is tantamount to relying on the sovereign to discipline the sovereign. That is the sovereign's paradox—all else equal, the greater a sovereign's power to insist on an outcome that is favorable to itself during potential future disputes, the less its present power to conclude agreements that require time to reach fruition (Barzel 1992, 1997; Haddock 1994). Some sovereigns do manage to firmly discipline themselves through their court system, but across history and geography most do not. Correctly or incorrectly, many investors are skeptical that either tribal or federal courts fully perceive the value to Indian sovereigns of such discipline. Here we suggest a self-help initiative that willing tribes could adopt both to ameliorate doubts about their own courts and to make the involvement of a potentially unreliable national court system unnecessary.

A tribal government's power can be enhanced via distinct routes that are different in important ways—at the expense of the national government, at the expense of the government of the state or states that overlap the tribe geographically, or at the expense of private parties, whether Indian or non-Indian, who have or might form interests on the reservation. A power is an option, not an obligation; a sovereign may or may not elect to utilize one of its powers, as it prefers. Increasing any sovereign power may well afford benefits, but will surely impose costs, and thus may either appreciate or depreciate the prospects that face citizens (Barzel 1992; Haddock and Hall 1983; Haddock 1998). When permitted by courts, a wise and benevolent government would seek to exploit its sovereign power if and when the benefits to its citizens exceed the costs. At the same time, that government would attempt to control the costs of the subset of sovereign powers that it elects to exploit.

The several facets of sovereignty remain blurred unless one distinguishes nonconsensual constraints that were imposed by more powerful sovereigns from constraints that are assumed willingly in order to draw corresponding commitments, in other words, constraints imposed on the sovereign by the sovereign. Every tribe could point to the past to rationalize policies that disappoint individuals who may have played no role in earlier inequities. That is a hazardous practice with consensual interactions, where cooperation will be rare if unprincipled tribal sovereignty is feared. An investor who simply foregoes on-reservation opportunities avoids tribal policy easily and at low cost, but tribal residents holding site-specific complementary resources are then exposed to substantial opportunity costs.

Emerging tribes endeavoring to form good reputations can more easily calm investor fear if courts, both tribal and federal, will help insure the *ex post* veracity of *ex ante* tribal proclamations, as courts do for other citizens.

Profligate use of a first mover's power more easily injures other tribes than investors. If courts neglect that danger, they could trap some tribes in a prisoner's dilemma where the best choice becomes prompt overexploitation of tribal power (Haddock 1994). Just a few bad examples might easily convince many potential investors that all tribes are untrustworthy.

Yielding sovereignty implies increasing constraints in one of several distinct ways:

1. For instance, when William the Conqueror seized power from King Harold, dominion was gained by the one and *ipso facto* lost by the other. Harold would have been displeased by the expectation and (had he survived) by its realization, wishing that someone could halt William's incursion at Hastings.

2. William, hoping to retain the loyalty of his Norman lieutenants, granted them limited sovereignty over parts of his new realm by disenfranchising Saxon lords. The new-minted Norman lords were sovereign over their serfs and the lesser nobles below them in the feudal estate, but at the same time subjects of William. William expected both he and his lieutenants would be advantaged, but the displaced Saxons must surely have rued the day both *ex ante* and *ex post*, wishing that some still higher authority had forbidden William's expropriations.

3. Saxon peasants limited their future options in exchange for Norman or Saxon merchants limiting their present options, as by an exchange of food during famine for an offer to repay with interest once yields recovered. Survivors would be advantaged *ex post* by avoiding repayment but, in sharp distinction to the two earlier examples, disadvantaged *ex ante* were that anticipated, for then merchants would predictably provision only those who could pay spot prices. Merchant injury would be reduced to the extent that their provisions could instead be sold where no similar threat existed. Thus, every famished peasant would ardently vow to repay, but after the famine had passed, an unscrupulous peasant's incentive would be to disavow the promise. The peasants' loss of sovereignty would be beneficial *ex ante*—their problem would be making their promises credible so as to avoid starvation.

With respect to tribal governments, analogues are: 1) unilateral extension of authority over Indians by the United States government; 2) delegation of a part of that authority to state governments; and 3) tribal member or government dealings with investors, whether Indian or not. There is plenty of reason to think that tribes were disadvantaged by involuntarily yielding sovereignty to the United States and might benefit by recapturing it. State governments typically exchange little if anything, at least directly, for the limited sovereignty over the tribes that is granted them by the national government. Tribes might benefit by recapturing that.

However, nonfraudulent voluntary agreements between a tribe and either a private party or a state are mutually beneficial *ex ante*. If the long run injury could be confined to untrustworthy tribes and those foolish enough to contract with them, opportunism would be of minor importance. But federal Indian law is a unified whole and investors have difficulty distinguishing among tribes, so untextured deference to Indian tribal sovereignty diminishes credible tribes' reputations as well.

SOVEREIGNTY RECAPTURED FROM THE UNITED STATES

If sovereignty is taken to mean independent of and unlimited by any other, no Indians inside the United States borders have been completely sovereign since Geronimo's dwindling band surrendered in 1886. Like William's lieutenants, the sovereignty of tribes has been conditional since they were subjugated by the United States government—whatever the United States is prepared to recognize, which can change in a moment. In 1831, the Supreme Court characterized tribes not as sovereign nations but as "domestic dependent nations" (*Cherokee Nation v. Georgia*). Recognized as governments, they were and are able to deal directly with the national government, but certainly not as equals. And they can deal directly and bindingly with any other individual or government—state or foreign—only if and when authorized to do so by the national government.

Since *Cherokee Nation v. Georgia*, the tribes' plight has actually increased:

The contention [that Congress could not divest tribal lands in violation of treaty terms] in effect ignores the status of the contracting Indians and the relation of dependency that they bore and continue to bear towards the government of the United States. To uphold the claim would be to adjudge that the indirect operation of the treaty was to materially limit and qualify the controlling authority of Congress ... and to deprive Congress ... of all power to act, if the assent of the Indians could not be obtained. (*Lone Wolf v. Hitchcock* [*1903*])

Popular perception is that treaties do indeed "materially limit and qualify the controlling authority of" the signatories. Intersovereign dealings often lack an impartial third-party enforcer and as a result ultimately rely on credible threats (Umbeck 1981a, 1981b; Haddock 2003, p. 180), but such bald-faced acknowledgment never facilitates treaty negotiations.

A transfer of sovereignty from the United States might well benefit tribes. But to the extent it may seem from time to time to occur, it is a mere delegation of authority and readily withdrawn. Sometimes the United States government chooses not to intervene in tribal affairs, but it always can. In that sense, the tribes are older, but nonetheless treated by the government as lesser sovereigns than states. Though the Constitution's Supremacy Clause permits the national government to set aside a great deal of state law, there remain reserved rights that protect state action in the absence of a constitutional amendment. *Lone Wolf*, in contrast, grants the national government extraordinary discretion unilaterally to frustrate tribal decisions.

SOVEREIGNTY RECAPTURED FROM STATES

State sovereignty over tribes would seem a more promising target for the tribes, given the United States government's availability as third-party enforcer. A few reservations are more easily measured in acres than square miles, and it seems unlikely that their sovereignty could be completely disentangled from that of the surrounding state. But at the opposite extreme, sixteen reservations are geographically larger than Rhode Island; ten of them larger than the Canadian province of Prince Edward Island; and eight larger than Delaware. The largest reservation, Navajo, is similar in size to New Brunswick, Nova Scotia, or West Virginia, and well over twice the size of any New England state other than Maine. Just as it has long been possible for all those states and provinces to govern themselves rather than lean on geographically larger neighbors, it seems at least plausible that the largest reservations could similarly stand completely apart from states if US trust authority over Indians were terminated.

In fact, most reservations predate the states that were layered atop them. States attain sovereignty over tribes only to the extent the Congress transfers it to them and retain it only so long as it is not rescinded—the legal default remains that tribes are senior to states. When Congress or courts override the default, empowering both tribe and state independently to regulate or tax a reservation activity, a successive monopoly problem becomes a threat. Removing authority of either the state or the tribe should lower burdens on individuals but actually increase aggregate regulatory benefit or tax revenue (Machlup and Taber 1960).

An alternative would be for the United States to require those two lesser sovereigns to negotiate with each other but, as tribal gaming illustrates, that can lead to substantial dissipation through rent seeking (Johnson, this volume). With a casino in San Diego County where state law prohibits most gambling, the Barona Reservation's median annual household income now exceeds $100,000, two and one-third times the national average.[2] Just off the Boston-New York City interstate in eastern Connecticut, receipts from Foxwoods, the world's largest casino, enable the Mashantucket Pequot to send all tribal children to a private school, a school whose insolvency was avoided as a result. But most reservations, frequently the most impoverished, are remote with few passers-by. Consequently, less than one-third of the tribes participate in gambling.

> For the majority of tribal governments that do run gambling facilities, the revenues have been modest.... The 20 largest Indian gambling facilities account for 50.5 percent of total revenues with the next 85 accounting for [only] 41.2 percent. Additionally, not all gambling facilities are successful. Some tribes operate their casinos at a loss and a few have even been forced to close money-losing facilities. (*National Gambling Impact Commission Report 1999, pp. 2–10*)

Moreover, states increasingly are threatening to license competing operations in order to extract side payments from tribes (Johnson, this volume). A once thriving tribal enterprise may find survival increasingly difficult as a result. Beyond question, gaming has proven lucrative for a few tribes, but the bounty is quixotic. Tribes that by pure luck are well situated enjoy very attractive returns, while their unlucky brethren languish in poverty. Though ameliorating reservation poverty in individual locales, tribal gambling establishments are far from a panacea.

Much of the rest of the tribe-state record is similarly discouraging. A Supreme Court that typically loves competition among private enterprises is skeptical of competition among political enterprises. Thus *Washington v. Confederated Tribes of Colville Indian Reservations* (1980) held that activities on a reservation would be subject to state taxation if a substantial part of the business was motivated by nonmember customers' intention to evade the state levy. Though a state cannot tax a transaction if the reservation-based enterprise can reliably document that the customer is a member of the tribe, doing so is a costly undertaking and thus uneconomic for low-value items, such as tobacco. That cost must be borne by the tribal enterprise rather than the state.

Thus the court has outlined an Orwellian form of sovereignty—all sovereigns are equal, but some are more equal than others. There is no question that Indiana can tax liquor brought into that state for local consumption, but Indiana must bear the cost of policing the policy. But imagine the court informing Illinois that Indiana could tax the entire Illinois retail liquor sector except for those parts that, at substantial cost, Illinois enterprises documented were not sold to Hoosiers. Imagine the court informing North Carolina that New York could tax all North Carolina tobacco sales in an analogous way. The court's reasoning in *Washington v. Confederated Tribes* was distinct only in viewing reservations as a part of states that were layered atop them, though in most other cases the court treats a reservation as a hole in the state's sovereignty.

The import of *Washington v. Confederated Tribes* is that both a reservation and a state can tax a lot of on-reservation sales, while only the state can tax off-reservation sales, even those made to tribal citizens living on the reservation. State-taxed liquor stores and bars thrive along one side of many reservation borders, while double-taxed smoke shops along the opposite side fail.[3]

Vacillating policy means that even tribal sovereignty retrieved from the states, as in *Montana v. Blackfeet Tribe of Indians* (1985), may quickly be lost, as through *Cotton Petroleum Corp. v. New Mexico* (1989). Those cases were similar in that each plaintiff challenged a state's ability to tax mineral production on tribal reservations. In 1924, Congress reversed the legal default that tribes are senior sovereigns to states and permitted nondiscriminatory state taxes on royalties from minerals withdrawn from reservations. Did that power to tax survive subsequent legislation that streamlined leasing of tribal minerals but was completely silent regarding state taxes? The Supreme Court's Canons of Construction of Indian Law require that "ambiguous expressions must be resolved in favor of the Indian . . . and Indian treaties must be liberally construed in [their] favor" (Wilkinson and Volkman 1975, p. 617). In *Montana v. Blackfeet Tribe*, the court decided the state taxing power could not survive the Canons and thus a state could not tax tribal royalties unless and until Congress reinvigorated the authorization. Sovereignty regained from states.

Could states tax mineral extraction companies making those severances? In *Cotton Petroleum*, the court held that the reservation hole in state sovereignty was too shallow to shield the companies, who were thus simultaneously subject to both sovereigns.

Assuming that states, tribes, companies, and consumers—everyone, that is, except courts and lawyers—are interested in average revenue paid and received and the level of output rather than in filamentary legal distinctions, then rudimentary economic theory implies that *Cotton Petroleum* simply unraveled *Blackfeet Tribe*. Each case dealt with the distribution between state and tribe of returns from leasing Indian mineral rights, but the cases reached diametrically opposing outcomes. *Blackfeet Tribe* implied that states were entitled to no share of economic rents from tribal minerals; *Cotton Petroleum* implied that by taxing an intermediary firm, the states could tax at whatever rate they decide would maximize state revenue. Sovereignty lost to states once more.

That model may be unduly optimistic. Throughout the United States, specialized companies undertake nearly all mineral extraction, hinting that other forms of organization are more costly. Drilling on government land utilizes specialized private companies. Ranchers do not drill their own water wells, much less oil wells; specialized companies do. A tribe-owned company, however, is exempt from state taxes. The incoherence of the cases could result in small-scale and inefficient tribe-owned extractors (Haddock 2005). Every cent of tax a tribe saved would be a cent that a state would never receive, hence a mere transfer rather than an economic gain, while mineral withdrawals would become more costly than withdrawals beyond reservation borders, an unadulterated waste.

SOVEREIGNTY OVER VOLUNTARY RELATIONSHIPS

> "Truth is stranger than fiction ... Fiction is obliged to stick to possibilities."
>
> —MARK TWAIN (1897, CH. 15)

A derisively dismissed fictional account would be greeted with gape-mouthed wonder if gleaned instead from the media or a court record. Events transpiring more or less as usual are not news. To appear in a news report an event must be extraordinary, something that a statistician would characterize as drawn from the distribution's tails. That is to say, editors are constrained in the amount of information that they can report to the public, and consequently consider only the most remarkable aspects of the most remarkably bad or good events to be worth including. The sorts of normal events that must comprise the bulk of a credible work of fiction are by their nature unremarkable, and thus unremarked by the media in the nonfictional world. The legal record censors data even more severely—arrangements that work remarkably well are rarely litigated but occasionally may be newsworthy. Thus things seem bizarrely risky on reservations because those living elsewhere hear only of aberrational features of aberrational events, not the many humdrum events of daily reservation life.

But if perceptions are unfairly biased against reservations, those perceptions form the environment within which a tribe must seek capital. Indisputably, given enough time a tribe can invest in its reputational capital. However, in the meantime, many potential investors can afford little research to distinguish among tribes. To them, a tribe is a tribe is a tribe. Thus one tribe's investment in reputation benefits hundreds of other tribes, while the cost of another's opportunism spreads across hundreds.

Hence the prisoner's dilemma—if all others invest in reputation, a given tribe's most lucrative decision may be to behave opportunistically due to the diluted impact on its own reputation; if no other tribes invest in reputation, the demanded risk premium will be daunting in any case. So a tribe must pay for a poor reputation whether or not it has earned one. In such an environment, it makes sense to take what must be paid for in any event, defiling all other tribes' reputations before they have an opportunity to execute the reverse tactic. The judiciary could help defeat that dilemma.

The diversity that might permit a litigant to remove a case to federal court for trial is often useless in cases contesting Indian rights, where remedies at tribal law commonly must be exhausted before a federal appeal can be lodged. An appellate court readily reverses errors of law but is far more deferential toward trial court findings of fact. In common parlance, that means the trial court's findings do not have to be air tight, merely supported by substantial evidence though there may also be a good deal of evidence pointing in the opposite direction. In the presence of substantial evidence supporting the decision, litigants will be assumed to have behaved as the trial court perceived. The appellate court will then overrule only errors of law, in other words where the trial court has been in error in its holding that a losing party lacked a right to behave as the court believed it had, or alternatively where the trial court has been in error in its holding that a winning party possessed a right to behave as it had. If crucial facts have not been found at all, the appellate court typically will not find them, but will remand the case to the trial court for further findings of fact. Thus the motivating behavior is rarely an issue on appeal, only its damnability.

That leaves tribes on the horns of a dilemma:

1.   Given the issue and tribe, some tribal courts apply law based on tribal customs that are often unpredictable to non-Indian investors.[4] Admittedly, after exhausting tribal remedies a litigant may sometimes successfully challenge that court's jurisdiction. Then, depending on subject-matter jurisdiction, the case essentially begins anew in a federal district or state court. Courts may treat litigation—in this instance duplicative litigation—and lost time as costless, but investors do not.

2.   Due both to animus and statistical discrimination, there is a long history of jury, even judicial, bias against Indians in state courts, especially pronounced in states with large Indian populations.[5] Fearing bias, individual Indians and tribes hesitate to form agreements that potentially will require them to litigate before state courts, while non-Indian investors resist agreements that may require them to litigate a case under an unfamiliar tribal law.

A widened range of disputes that require exhaustion of tribal remedies mitigates Indians' fear of state courts but exacerbates non-Indians' fear of tribal courts. When disputes concern strictly off-reservation matters, tribal members must litigate against nonmembers in state or federal courts. Perhaps it is only fair that disputes concerning matters on a reservation require nonmembers to litigate against members in tribal courts. But a tribe cannot deposit "fair" in the bank. Non-Indians will barely notice if the tribal members refuse to come off their reservation, but the tribe cannot help but recognize that many non-Indian investors refuse to come onto the reservation.

In recognition, many tribes endeavor to meet high ethical standards.[6] Making that known to investors, however, is a long, tedious and expensive process, and even those laudable efforts by individual tribes are thwarted if an opportunistic renegade tribe chooses to make a quick strike, enriching itself while sullying the reputations of Indians as a group.

As with states or the nation itself, tribal governments can only be sued after clearly and expressly waiving sovereign immunity (unless Congress has waived it for them). Why then are private parties not hesitant to deal with state and national governments? In part, it is because investors find a larger legal record in those venues and thus find it easier to evaluate the sovereign's reputation (Haddock 1994); and in part, it is because states are much larger economic entities. States sacrifice substantial future prospects if they behave opportunistically at the moment. Being smaller and more impoverished, however, many reservations have few attractive prospects. If an individual reservation behaves opportunistically against present investors, in other words, it sacrifices few future opportunities. If that is foreseen, however, no present investors will be available to treat opportunistically. Stated in more technical terms, states have substantially more hostages to bond their behavior, and as a result the likelihood that a state will renege on its promise is less threatening to investors.[7]

Of course, states do occasionally renege on their commitments. Though every state can borrow from private lenders, even on occasions when it refuses to waive its immunity, states that have reneged on commitments are regarded as more risky than others, and in consequence pay higher risk premiums due to their poor record. The matter thus is not only whether a tribe can attract investors, but also the terms under which it can obtain their capital.

Exacerbating their problem, tribal governments face strenuous constraints as a result of their trust relationship with the United States, often leaving them powerless to endow reservation assets to individual members. So, regardless of the preferences of its members or the tribal government, a tribe typically owns or controls most reservation land, natural resources, and business (Miller 2001). Most reservation enterprise is in consequence unavoidably controlled by an entity with sovereign immunity, and that naturally invites heightened investor scrutiny.

Unlike states or the United States, which can adopt general class-wide waivers to attract investors who may be unknown to them in advance, an individualized process is required for waivers that affect trust property. With tribal trust property, the United States is the legal owner, and the tribe or individual merely the beneficial owner. Thus Bureau of Indian Affairs' (BIA) approval must be sought (and potentially refused) after an investor has incurred the cost of negotiating a contract with a tribe. Investors will assume the risk that the BIA may frustrate their costly negotiations with the tribe only when the expected payout is appropriately enhanced.

Though it may place them under the oversight of a potentially hostile state court, most tribes will waive their immunity if a proposal promises sufficient return, though projects that offer marginal positive benefits are more likely to go forward off the reservation than on it.[8] For instance, to reassure a public at risk of injury in their casinos, resorts, and such, many tribes have adopted Tort Claims Acts mandating procedural limitations similar to those of states and the US government. Some tribal governments have contracted to provide members with services formerly coming from the US government. Congress has provided that the employees of those undertakings are to be treated as though they were US employees, with injured persons having a remedy against the US government in the federal courts. Many tribes carry liability insurance and expressly waive immunity with respect to their carriers.

Carefully drawn arbitration clauses in contracts have successfully waived tribal sovereign immunity, as in *C & L Enterprises, Inc. v. Citizen Band Potawatomi Indian Tribe* (2001). The Potawatomi and C & L contracted for construction of a tribal commercial building to be located out of Indian country. The contractual language did not mention sovereign immunity at all, but the court held unanimously that a waiver was clear due to two provisions. First, "[a]ll ... disputes ... shall be decided by arbitration in accordance with the Construction Industry Arbitration Rules of the American Arbitration Association.... The award rendered by the arbitrator ... shall be final, and judgment may be entered upon it in accordance with applicable law in any court having jurisdiction thereof." Second, a choice-of-law clause read: "The contract shall be governed by the law of the place where the Project is located."

On the other side of the ledger, however, one finds immunity nightmares. Pursuant to a management agreement, Tamiami Partners, Ltd. (TPL) invested $6.5 million dollars in 1990 to buy land for the Miccosukee Tribe and to construct a bingo hall. Disputes arose, and the Miccosukee soon filed a suit in a tribal court. TPL immediately filed a federal lawsuit to enforce the agreement's arbitration clause and to enjoin the Miccosukee from taking control of the operation. The federal court ruled that the Miccosukee had waived sovereign immunity by agreeing to arbitration, but stayed its proceedings until TPL exhausted its tribal court remedies. The Miccosukee appealed to the Eleventh Circuit, which ruled there was no federal subject matter jurisdiction (*Tamiami Partners, Limited v. Miccosukee Tribe of Indians of Florida* [11th Cir. 1993]).

TPL then filed a new complaint. The federal trial court concluded that it had subject matter jurisdiction, but sovereign immunity barred TPL's suit against the Miccosukee, the tribal business council, and the tribal gaming agency, but not against individual defendants. All parties appealed (*Tamiami Partners, Limited v. Miccosukee Tribe of Indians of Florida* [11th Cir. 1995]). The appellate court agreed that the trial court had subject matter jurisdiction over three of TPL's new claims but the management agreement that waived immunity applied only to suits regarding arbitration, defeating TPL's breach of contract claim. TPL's claim against individual tribal officers was permitted to proceed—prospective injunctive relief can be had against a government official to prevent violations of law (*Ex Parte Young* [1908]).

But after four years of further litigation, the Eleventh Circuit found the second amended complaint to be "a thinly-disguised attempt . . . to obtain specific performance of the Tribe's obligations" by suing individual defendants. Because the suit was thus construed to actually be against the Miccosukee, sovereign immunity protected the individuals (*Tamiami Partners, Ltd. v. Miccosukee Tribe of Indians of Fla; Dexter Lehtinen et al.* [11th Cir. 1999] at pp. 1225–26). The court remanded the case again for trial on the arbitration issues. The reach of tribal immunity rather than fact is still being litigated.

Whichever party ultimately wins, TPL undoubtedly regrets having become involved with the Miccosukee; whichever party should win, widely available reports of the litigation in newspapers nationwide must have troubled anyone contemplating new investments on any reservation, not just that of the Miccosukee.

Few people have direct knowledge of the merits of the *Tamiami Partners v. Miccosukee Tribe* dispute, nor could they until the case proper can surmount seemingly endless procedural hurdles. What investors do understand only too well is that issues that led TPL to apparently interminable litigation with an Indian tribe would have been irrelevant had they contracted instead with a private party at any off-reservation location.

Political upheaval can also upset investor projections. The Rosebud Sioux and Sun Prairie negotiated a lease to place pork production facilities on tribal lands in order to employ members (*Rosebud Sioux Tribe v. McDivitt* [8th Cir. 2002]).[9] Construction commenced within five days of a BIA lease approval after its determination that the operation would have no significant environmental impact. Environmental groups promptly brought suit. The Assistant Secretary of Interior for the BIA voided the lease, claiming that the BIA—not Sun Prairie—had failed to comply with the National Environmental Policy Act.

Acting in unison, the Sioux and Sun Prairie sued, winning a permanent injunction restraining the BIA from interfering with construction or operation of the project. As the BIA appealed, a tribal referendum was narrowly decided against the project and a newly elected tribal council voted to support the BIA. Though no issues of fact had been decided, the court then held that Sun Prairie acting alone could not contest the BIA's lease invalidation, dismissed its complaint, and lifted the injunction. Thus, a tribal election occurring after the contract was signed doomed Sun Prairie's chances even to litigate the case. The tribal council then asked the BIA to close completed facilities that had cost roughly $20 million dollars to construct. Sun Prairie continues to litigate.

Politically motivated diminution of property rights deleteriously affects the investment climate on reservations. Perhaps investment could be had more easily if tribes adopted a constitutional provision such as that of the US Constitution (Art. I, s. 10) that bars government alteration of vested contractual rights. What other ways to mitigate the problem are available to ambitious tribes?

SELF-HELP

A far-sighted sovereign has an incentive to form a reputation that shows that investors within its realm will not find the returns from their investments confiscated or destroyed as a result of the sovereign's opportunism or capriciousness. Such a reputation arises most directly from a history of observed court successes by aggrieved coinvestors when their suits against the sovereign are meritorious; but being small and poor, with relatively few investment opportunities, many tribal reservations possess thin legal histories on point. Tribal sovereigns could instead rely on a stronger sovereign to bond their good behavior. But as the plight of Tamiami Partners and Sun Prairie illustrated above, investors might well doubt that federal courts dependably provide that bond. How then might a tribe avoid paying investors high-risk premiums, resorting to costly tribal ownership, or foregoing an opportunity altogether? Perhaps the answer is to make the federal and state court systems largely extraneous.

Tribes would seem to have it within their power to reverse the default regarding waivers of tribal immunity, and in that way encourage the US courts to honor tribal commitments. At present, the default is that waivers of sovereign immunity must be clearly specified in tribal undertakings with private parties and, as detailed above, the tribes' problem is that courts too often seem determined *ex post* to read waivers much more narrowly than the parties had intended *ex ante*. When courts implicitly encourage tribal opportunism in that way, investors become apprehensive, and then refuse to deal with tribes at all or charge risk premiums that have been correspondingly enhanced.

Tribes, however, are empowered to adopt tribal constitutions, which could include a stipulation that, as to commercial agreements, the tribe may be sued in US courts as though it were a private party, unless and to the extent the agreement delineated those immunities that the tribe was reserving. Such a provision would leave waivers of immunity completely at the tribe's discretion, but would serve to make unambiguous which (if any) facets of immunity had been retained. If a reservation of immunity had not been explicitly stipulated in the agreement, then it had not been retained. The tribe would not be compelled to waive any immunity, but it could dependably do so whenever waivers were to its advantage.

Those who are approached about investing on reservations that have included such clauses in the tribal constitution would be much less concerned about instances, such as those discussed above, in which the US courts have "found" implicit retentions of immunity that arguably neither party had intended *ex ante*. The investor would not need to infer the individual tribe's reputation from a scanty body of decided and recorded cases in tribal and federal courts, but could infer it directly from the tribal constitution and the clauses in the agreement being proposed to the investor by the tribe.

Alternatively, an association of like-minded tribes determined to assure investors that they were reliable sovereigns could, in effect, magnify their reputation by forming themselves into a group. The group members would commit to bring disputes before a predesignated arbitrator under a limited number of well-specified options regarding sovereign waivers of immunity.[10] A member tribe that selected an option that waived more immunity for a particular undertaking could expect to pay investors lower risk premiums; a tribe opting to waive less would of course pay more.

Stated differently, investors would willingly undertake more projects in the realms of tribes willing to waive more of their sovereign immunity in arbitration, and would charge less interest for a project of given promise. Ideally, the options would be formulated with explicit textual discussion that made the intent quite transparent to the investors and the arbitrator. The group of tribes collectively could bond commitments by individual member tribes by agreeing to hold a portion of each tribe's assets within the jurisdictions of other members.

Suppose that a member tribe refused to abide by an arbitrator's decision, forcing the matter into court. As discussed, *C & L Enterprises, Inc. v. Citizen Band Potawatomi Indian Tribe* demonstrated that at least some arbitration commitments are secure in federal court, but even then enforcement is delayed by the litigation, and both delay and the litigation itself are costly. To discourage such suits the group's charter would stipulate that bringing a previously arbitrated dispute to court would serve immediately to evict the suing tribe from group membership, forcing it henceforth to rely entirely on its own besmirched reputation.

The other members would then permit the aggrieved investor to bring suit in their own tribal courts, where assets of the offending tribe that were being held within those jurisdictions could be used to pay a judgment. An action in federal court seeking to overturn those tribal awards would force one sovereign to sue other sovereigns who, as a condition of their group membership, would categorically have refused to waive any immunity against that suit. There would of course be no charter stipulation barring a tribe from initiating a suit to enforce an arbitrator's award that was favorable to the tribe.

[T]rusted private arbitrators provide an alternative to a court system, not by directly enforcing contracts but by generating the public information necessary to allow reputational mechanisms to enforce them. Third parties [need not] investigate a dispute in detail in order to learn who was at fault.

They [need only] find out which party the [arbitrator has] ruled against. . . . If private enforcement of contracts via reputation and social pressure is less expensive and more reliable than enforcement via the court system, people whose social institutions make such private enforcement practical have a competitive advantage over those who must rely on the courts. (*Friedman 2000, p. 146*)

Even if the group were of modest size to begin with, early improvements in the members' ability to attract investors would induce additional tribes to apply for membership. As new tribes joined, investors' awareness of the group would gradually increase and the value of membership would grow. With scrupulous *ex post* enforcement of their clear *ex ante* intentions, the tribal group might soon find that investors considered its members more desirable investment sites than some less dependable states. Because state and national courts would rarely be required to adjudicate member-investor disputes, the tribal group would unilaterally have retrieved an important measure of the sovereignty that had once been taken from them without consent.

CONCLUSION

Indian tribes are sovereign, subordinate to the national government, in many ways parallel to states. Over the past several decades, tribal sovereignty has gradually been enhanced as tribes have recaptured limited sovereignty from states and exerted more extensive tribal power over consensual arrangements.

Enhanced tribal sovereignty, however, is a two-edged sword because it gives tribes more power to act opportunistically. Because tribes compete against states for investment, investors can easily vote with their feet by moving if states comprise a more secure jurisdiction. An expectation that tribes act opportunistically imposes a price in the form of less investment on reservations and a higher risk premium demanded by those investors who remain.

States, of course, can also act opportunistically, but they are far less likely to do that for three reasons, two that concern investors' information cost, and one that concerns the magnitude of the consequence of acting opportunistically. First, states have a great deal of ongoing enterprise that has tested state inclinations over the years, and that provides a mature body of precedent for their courts to employ. That precedent would signal investors to avoid a state that had pursued an opportunistic path. Because vastly fewer cases have been litigated under tribal law, investors have less tribal precedent upon which to rely, leaving them uncertain of the tribe's dependability. Second, tribal precedents often have been poorly recorded, making the relatively sparse body of tribal precedent difficult for investors to discover. Third, having much larger economies, each state risks substantially more than any tribe in the way of future investments that will be lost as a result of opportunistic behavior.

It would seem that a tribe could overcome much of that legal weakness by waiving sovereign immunity and specifying that state law governs its contracts, thus enabling the tribe to rely on the reputation of a state. That path, however, presents two problems of its own. First, though a state may deal fairly with investors, some states have a poor reputation for dealing fairly with tribes. As a result, tribes are fearful of enhancing state power over tribal affairs. Second, given the infinity of possible future states of the world, contracts are inevitably incomplete, and courts are often asked to select the default for a missing clause. Courts characteristically find against a waiver of sovereign immunity only when the sovereign's commitment is precisely on point. That is to say, the sovereign wins if there is no clear reason for it to lose, though there may be no clear reason for it to win either. Sovereigns that are states can rely on their reputations for dealing fairly with investors to smooth that difficulty, but investors are uncertain of the credibility of tribal waivers of sovereign immunity.

Unless tribes can find ways to bind themselves against opportunistic behavior, reservation economies will continue to languish. A tribe acting individually has too little incentive to enhance its reputation for fair dealing, because doing so generates mainly external benefits for other tribes, while opportunistic behavior by other tribes continues to tarnish the fair-dealing tribe's reputation.

We suggest two ways for tribes to enhance their reputations, both approaches aimed at assuring investors before on-reservation investments are sunk that tribal commitments would prove reliable if unforeseen issues arise thereafter. First, a tribe could insert a clause into its constitution that reverses the default employed for waivers of tribal sovereign immunity. When a tribal court decision is appealed, the federal courts would be instructed by the clause to abandon the default that sovereign immunity is retained in every state of the world except where a waiver was clearly detailed in the contract with an investor. Instead, sovereign immunity would be understood to have been waived except where a contract makes clear that it has been retained by the tribe—the tribe would lose a claim of sovereign immunity unless there was a clear reason for it to win. Second, if tribes prefer to dispense with courts altogether, they can band together and commit to bring disputes before a predesignated arbitrator.

Such approaches are consistent with the goal of tribal self-determination, and they are consistent with the rule of law necessary for sustained financial investment and growth of reservation economies.

NOTES

1. The authors have benefited from the contributions of Bruce Benson, Ronald Johnson, Miriam Jorgensen, Lewis & Clark Law School's 2003 Conference on Community Development, the Northwestern University Economic History Workshop, and attendees at the Southern Economic Association and the ISNIE (International Society for New Institutional Economics) conventions.

2. *Seminole Tribe v. Butterworth* (1981) and *California v. Cabazon Band of Mission Indians* (1987) are important early cases concerning tribal ability to operate a reservation gaming establishment with less stringent operating limits than are exercised by the surrounding state. Congress quickly acted to affirm those court initiatives, with substantial modification, through the Indian Gaming Regulatory Act of 1988 (18 U.S.C. ss. 1166 et seq.; 25 U.S.C ss. 2107 et seq.).

3. Belluck (2003) reports on one of a number of recent tribe-state encounters regarding a state's ability to tax sales made on reservations.

4. In some cases the Constitution's Supremacy Clause supplants tribal with federal or even state law, and when there is no tribal law on point some tribes permit their courts to adopt federal law, the law of other tribes, or occasionally state law. Nonetheless, the "Supreme Court's mandate to lower federal courts to defer to tribal courts for initial resolution of most reservation disputes has placed increased responsibility on tribal courts . . . [that] must compete for limited resources with other vitally necessary tribal programs. . . . There is a widespread feeling held by many non-Indians that tribal judges are biased against them. There are also complaints of incompetence, and even corruption in some tribal courts. Tribal traditions of deference to the consensus-building process within the tribe may constrain the process of judicial review of executive and legislative branch actions" (Getches, Wilkinson, and Williams 1993, p. 522).

5. "Because of the local ill feeling, the people of the states where they are found are often their deadliest enemies" (*United States v. Kagama* [1886] at p. 384).

6. See the discussion in Haddock and Miller (2004) regarding the Mississippi band of Choctaw Indians.

7. The use of hostage assets to bond agreements was discussed in Williamson (1983, 1984).

8. Though studying United States rail history rather than the history of Indian reservations, an exhaustive empirical study by Fogel (1964) led to the conclusion that dependable economic progress more likely arises from a multitude of relatively unimpressive projects than from a few individually impressive ones.

9. A number of similar examples are discussed in Haddock and Miller (2004).

10. Though their legal systems left domestic investment highly insecure, present and former communist countries greatly improved their ability to enter capital markets by inserting contractual clauses that compelled arbitration, a Swiss arbitrator often being designated, with extraterritorial assets at risk (Böckstiegal 1984; Benson 1999).

EIGHT

Indian Casinos: Another Tragedy of the Commons

RONALD N. JOHNSON

> "I think it is fair to say, that 15 years ago nobody could have seen that by 2002 Indian gaming revenues would grow to be $14.5 billion."

—SENATOR BEN NIGHTHORSE CAMPBELL[1]

American Indian reservations often conjure up an image of extreme poverty, with economies based largely on transfer payments and governmental services. Casino gaming, however, has brought a new source of wealth to a number of formerly impoverished Indian tribes. A key factor contributing to the success of Indian gaming is the sovereign status enjoyed by Indian tribes.

Although Indian tribes do not have the sovereign status of a foreign nation, they have retained vestiges of aboriginal sovereignty. The sovereign status of Indian tribes and the special nature of their relationship to both federal and state governments were recognized in the well-known cases of *Cherokee Nation v. Georgia* (1831) and *Worcester v. Georgia* (1832). In the *Cherokee* case, the US Supreme Court recognized the sovereign status of Indians, albeit as domestic nations dependent on the federal government. The *Worcester* case established that, within the boundary of an Indian reservation, Congress was recognized to have plenary authority and state law did not apply. The history of Indian tribal relations with the federal government, however, hardly resembles that of two sovereigns on equal footing.[2] United States Indian policy since the 1830s has shifted from removal and subjugation, to allotments and assimilation, to reorganization, and to tribal termination in the 1950s. In the early 1970s, Indian policy shifted again when the federal government began to support tribal self-determination and self-governance.

The shift in federal Indian policy has been concomitant with the growth of legalized gambling in the United States. Backed initially by a series of court decisions, Indian tribes have leveraged their sovereign status to participate in this growth industry. But many states opposed Indian gaming and the battle shifted to Congress. The result was passage of the Indian Gaming Regulatory Act of 1988 (IGRA).[3] Although the Act allows tribes to engage in certain gaming operations, such as bingo halls, independent of state oversight or regulation, a tribe wanting to engage in the potentially more lucrative operation of Las Vegas-style casinos, with slots and house-banked table games, must negotiate a compact agreement with the state where the casino is to be located. In essence, jurisdiction over Indian-operated, Las Vegas-style casinos would involve three sovereigns: the federal government, the state in which a tribe has land, and the tribe itself.

From a property rights perspective, the Act allows for too many claimants, as in a commons, a situation that encourages the socially costly pursuit of gaming profits—a type of activity often referred to as "rent seeking" (Tullock 1967; Tollison 1997).[4] At the heart of the problem of the commons is the absence of clearly defined property rights. Reducing the number of sovereigns to one would reduce the potential for conflict over resource development and rent seeking. The theory of property rights addresses both individual behavior and the organizational forms individuals use to capture and exploit assets.[5] Because property rights are always in danger of appropriation, collective action may be necessary for their protection. Indeed, the origin of the state and the evolution of property rights can be attributed to the need to protect property against outside threats and enhance the prospect for wealth accumulation. A sovereign with the ability to protect the property of its citizens from outside forces, while itself refraining from excessive confiscation, would encourage the expansion of aggregate wealth. But modern governments, especially democratic ones, do not have clearly defined residual claimants, a situation that can lead to excessive demands by the competing parties. Despite the potential for conflict inherent in the IGRA, however, Indian gaming has been a growth industry.

The focus of this chapter is on whether Indian tribes are likely to sustain and continue to develop profitable gaming operations. That is, can gaming tribes withstand the onslaught from both external and internal forces that are likely to challenge their success? The recent and largely unanticipated success of Indian gaming has prompted state politicians to seek revenue sharing and other concessions from gaming tribes. In response, gaming tribes have become major contributors to political campaigns. However, there are also internal governance problems that challenge the success of Indian gaming. Rather than a strong sovereign state that protects individual property rights, Indian tribes are more like a commons, subject to internal forces that can lead to dissension and challenge the accumulation and productive use of wealth.

THE RISE OF INDIAN GAMING

In the mid-1970s, casinos and off-track betting were illegal in all US states except Nevada (Eadington 1999). Although bingo was typically permitted by churches or fraternal organizations, only New Hampshire had a state lottery. The legal climate for gambling, however, was about to change. In 1976, New Jersey voters authorized casino gaming in Atlantic City and, by 2004, non-Indian, Las Vegas-style casino gaming was permitted in eleven states, and seven states allowed racetrack casinos (American Gaming Association 2004a).[6]

Although some may be tempted to associate the dramatic increase in legalized gaming with a decline in social mores, Raymond Sauer (2001) points out that gambling regulation over the past 400 years has been episodic in character. The original colonies, and later many states, used lotteries to raise revenues, but were subsequently challenged by antilottery groups. Gambling establishments thrived on the frontier, but were later subject to substantial restrictions. Even Nevada banned gambling in 1909, repealing the ban in 1931. Between 1890 and 1910, horse racing was challenged in most major racing states. According to Sauer, this episodic nature of gaming regulation reflects a change in the willingness of voters to accept gaming as a source of government revenues.[7] Since the 1970s, there has been a steady progression of states instituting lotteries, and by 2001, forty states had legal lotteries. Importantly, the states' growing interest in using legalized gambling to raise revenues set the stage for the rise of Indian gaming.

Starting in the 1970s, Indians assumed a greater role in managing their own affairs. The Indian Self-Determination and Education Act of 1975 (88 Stat. 2203) codified procedures allowing tribes to engage in contracting for various services free of local Bureau of Indian Affairs (BIA) control, and provided greater tribal control over educational programs. During the 1980s, both the Reagan and Bush administrations reaffirmed the policy of self-determination, even if it included gaming operations (Mason 2000, p. 58). The idea was to encourage tribes to develop their own enterprises, while also lowering federal expenditures on Indian programs. Gaming, if properly regulated, offered an opportunity to accomplish both those objectives.

In 1979, the Seminole Indians of Florida opened a relatively high stakes bingo operation that became an instant success (Cordeiro 1989). But the stakes offered exceeded state limits on bingo and, shortly after the tribe opened its bingo operation, the Broward County sheriff threatened arrests on the Seminole reservation. The Seminole tribe sued the county, seeking a declaratory judgment and injunctive relief (*Seminole Tribe v. Butterworth* [1981]). Although the Seminoles claimed tribal sovereignty, the state of Florida and Broward County argued that Congress had granted the state jurisdiction in this matter. During the tribal termination era of the 1950s, Congress enacted Public Law 280 (67 Stat. 588–90) that granted certain states, including Florida, criminal jurisdiction over a limited category of activities occurring on reservations. Although Florida had a statute regulating bingo, the state needed to show that bingo was prohibited through criminal sanctions. Because the Florida statute allowed regulated bingo games, the federal circuit court concluded that Florida's approach to bingo was civil-regulatory in nature, rather than criminal-prohibitory. The state could not therefore assert its jurisdiction over the Seminoles' bingo operations. In essence, the court reinforced a "regulatory" versus a "prohibitory" distinction that became critical in a series of later cases.

After *Seminole*, tribes across the United States seized the opportunity to get into high-stakes bingo gaming in states where bingo was not expressly prohibited by law. By 1987, over 100 tribal bingo facilities, grossing close to $200 million, were in operation (Cordeiro 1989, p. 1). Moreover, by the mid-1980s, tribes were seeking to expand their gaming activities to include card games. This expansion produced yet another state challenge to tribal gaming.

The Cabazon Band of Mission Indians was operating a bingo and draw-poker parlor on its reservation when the state of California and the county of Riverside attempted to apply state and local statutes governing bingo, poker, and other card games. The Cabazon tribe sought declaratory relief, and the federal district court granted summary judgment against the state (see *California v. Cabazon Band of Mission Indians* [1987]). The case was appealed to the US Supreme Court. Using the civil-regulatory, criminal-prohibitory test relied on in *Seminole*, the court affirmed the district court's decision. Because California operated or allowed a state lottery, parimutuel horserace betting, and bingo, and did not expressly prohibit poker-type card games, the court reasoned that such games were presumably not contrary to the state's public policy. The *Cabazon* case came to represent the idea that, if a state allowed some types of gaming activities, a state's policy on gaming in general would be interpreted as civil-regulatory with tribal gaming, therefore, beyond state enforcement.

Federal court rulings, starting with the *Seminole* case, were generally favorable to Indian gaming. But states had an alternate venue to proclaim their concerns about the harmful effects of Indian gaming: the United States Congress.[8] In November 1983, Rep. Morris Udall of Arizona proposed a bill (H.R. 4566) to regulate Indian gaming. The bill expressed concern that Indian gaming would attract organized crime and other undesirable elements. Although it did not make it to the floor, the efforts on behalf of this bill and the efforts that followed revealed mounting opposition from the states, many of which regarded Indian gaming as a threat to their own tax revenues from commercial gaming operations and state-run lotteries. This was clearly a justifiable concern as a state may not impose a tax on tribal property or on activities on Indian lands, nor are most tribal enterprises subject to federal taxes (GAO 1997). Naturally, the states were joined in their opposition to Indian gaming by casino operators in Las Vegas and New Jersey. With the ongoing *Cabazon* case as a backdrop, Congress debated the merits of regulating Indian gaming. Shortly after the decision in the *Cabazon* case was handed down, Congress enacted the IGRA. It was clearly a compromise, but one that gave the states more influence over Indian gaming than the courts had given them.

The IGRA divided gaming into three classes, each class subject to differing degrees of tribal, state, and federal jurisdiction and regulation. Class I gaming is defined to include social and traditional Indian games played for minimal prizes by individuals at tribal ceremonies and gatherings. Class I games are under the exclusive jurisdiction of the tribes. Class II gaming includes bingo (whether or not electronic, computer, or other technological aids are used) and if played in the same location as bingo, pull tabs, punch board, tip jars, instant bingo, and other games similar to bingo. Class II gaming also includes nonbanked card games, that is, games that are played exclusively against other players rather than against the house or a player acting as a bank. The Act specifically excludes slot machines or electronic facsimiles from the definition of Class II games. Tribes have the authority to conduct, license, and regulate Class II gaming so long as the state in which the tribe is located permits such gaming for any purpose, and the tribal government adopts a gaming ordinance subject to oversight by the National Indian Gaming Commission (NIGC), a federal agency created by the IGRA.

The definition of Class III gaming is broad. It includes all forms of gaming that are neither Class I nor II. Games commonly played at Las Vegas-style casinos, such as slot machines, black jack, craps, and roulette, would clearly fall in the Class III category. Before a tribe may lawfully conduct Class III gaming, the following conditions must be met: 1) the particular form of Class III gaming that the tribe wants to conduct must be permitted in the state in which the tribe is located; and 2) the tribe and the state must have negotiated a compact that has been approved by the Secretary of the Interior. The state, upon receiving such a request, is required under the IGRA to negotiate in "good faith." The terms of the compacts may specify, among other things, the types of gaming devices allowed, hours of operation, and local impact mitigation.

In the event that the state fails to negotiate a compact in good faith, the IGRA originally allowed tribes to sue the state in federal court. However, in *Seminole Tribe of Florida v. Florida* (1996), the Supreme Court ruled that the IGRA's judicially forced negotiation scheme violated the Eleventh Amendment's guarantee of state sovereign immunity. This decision, which covers a plethora of legal issues, has been widely interpreted. It did not, however, declare invalid nor set aside any part of the Act, nor did it set aside any Class III gaming pacts already negotiated.[9] States and tribes may continue to enter voluntarily into new compacts. In some states such as California, tribes opened Class III casinos without a compact. State governments are not empowered to act against Indian tribes if the tribes are operating Class III gaming establishments without a compact as enforcement is a federal responsibility, and states have complained that the federal government refuses to act aggressively in these matters. It is not surprising that the IGRA's requirement that the two parties negotiate compacts for Class III gaming has been a source of continuing controversy. On the one hand, federal courts have ruled that Indian tribes have a right to establish gaming facilities on their reservations; on the other hand, IGRA requires that compacts be negotiated between the tribes and the states, obviously requiring the state's consent for Class III gaming. Accordingly, the IGRA created a situation wherein property rights are ill defined.

THE REVENUES AT STAKE

Data on Indian gaming net revenues, sometimes referred to as net win (dollars wagered minus payouts), as shown in Table 8.1, indicate a very rapid rise in revenues, especially in the years immediately following the passage of the IGRA. The data are from the NIGC and are for both Class II and Class III operations.[10] Although bingo operations remain a significant contributor to Indian gaming revenues, Class II operations account for only about twelve percent of total Indian gaming revenues (GAO 1997, p. 9). The distinction between Class II and Class III operations, however, can be murky. Tribes operating without a Class III compact have attempted to use gaming devices that function like video slot machines.[11] The tribes involved argue that these machines are a facsimile of pull-tabs or instant bingo that are permissible under Class II. In most cases, the rulings have gone against the tribes.[12] Nevertheless, some tribes continue to use gaming devices that violate classification opinions and others are constantly in search of new gaming devices that would fall within the permissible Class II category. Thus, the distinction between Class II and III operations is murky and constitutes another venue where both tribes and states expend resources defending their positions.

The rapid but diminishing annual rate of growth in Indian gaming revenues shown in Table 8.1 reflects, in part, the fact that Indian gaming has been capturing an ever-larger share of total gaming industry revenues. The growth of Indian gaming has been so expansive that their revenues are now

Table 8.1. Indian Gaming Revenues, FYs 1988–2003.

Fiscal year	Revenues in constant 2003 dollars (dollars in millions)	Annual percent change (%)
1988	$188	–
1989	445	135
1990	688	55
1991	973	41
1992	1,966	102
1993	3,431	75
1994	4,242	24
1995	6,586	55
1996	7,387	12
1997	8,542	16
1998	9,589	12
1999	10,820	13
2000	11,689	8
2001	13,226	13
2002	15,055	14
2003	16,826	12

NOTE: The Consumer Price Index was used to convert to constant 2003 dollars.
SOURCE: For the years 1988 to 1995, GAO (1997); for 1996 to 2002, NIGC (2004c); for 2003, NIGC (2004b).

approximately equal to the gross gaming revenues from slot machines and table games in Nevada and New Jersey casinos combined. The $16.8 billion garnered by gaming tribes in 2003 accounts for about twenty-three percent of total legal gaming revenues in the United States (NIGC 2004b).[13] Between 1982 and 1997, revenues from all forms of legalized gaming grew at an average annual rate of 7.45 percent (Eadington 1999, p. 174). However, the rate of growth has diminished in recent years. As a consequence, the future rate of growth of Indian gaming will be more constrained by the overall rate of growth in the demand for gaming than it has been in the past.

Although Indian gaming revenues are impressive, amounting to about $8,500 per enrolled tribal member in 2002, revenues are concentrated.[14] Of the 562 federally recognized Indian tribes in 2002, only 224 were engaged in gaming.[15] However, 226 tribes are located in Alaska, where only two tribes are engaged in gaming and, according to the NIGC, sixty-four percent of gaming revenues were earned by thirteen percent of the 330 Indian gaming establishments in 2003. Indeed, slot revenues from Foxwoods Casino together with its Connecticut neighbor, Mohegan Sun Casino, account for about $1.6 billion or over nine percent of total Indian gaming revenues (State of Connecticut, Division of Special Revenue 2004).

Nevertheless, despite the fact that some large tribes, like the Navajo, do not yet participate in gaming, the tribes in the lower forty-eight states that are engaged in gaming represent approximately seventy percent of enrolled tribal members.[16] Today, Indian gaming can be found in twenty-eight states, and twenty-five states have signed compact agreements. Only Hawaii and Utah appear to prohibit gambling to the extent that even Class II operations would likely be in violation of the IGRA. Many of the tribes that have chosen not to participate are located in remote sections of the country, distant from major population centers. Of course, Las Vegas was not considered to be in close proximity to anything when it first opened casinos. Today, it is considered a destination resort. That concept, although on a smaller scale, is increasingly utilized in Indian country. Thus, the potential to get into gaming is present for most tribes in the lower forty-eight states.

Besides the obvious distributional issues, the $16.8 billion shown in Table 8.1 for 2003 is a gross measure from which ordinary operating expenses should be deducted. Estimates of tribal gaming costs and expenses were made by the GAO (1997) based on financial statements submitted by the tribes to the NIGC for 1995. According to the GAO, net income was approximately thirty-eight percent of gaming revenues. This figure compared very favorably with their analysis of non-Indian casinos in Atlantic City and Nevada, but the GAO noted that the tribal advantage appeared to be largely due to state gaming taxes as well as property taxes and other fees paid by non-Indian casinos. Thus, net returns to Indian casinos appear to be large and growing.

CARVING UP THE PIE: THE EXTERNAL THREATS

The traditional concept of rent seeking (Tollison 1997) stresses the costs, such as lobbying and litigation expenditures, associated with the use of the political arena by firms and individuals to obtain monopolies or favorable regulations that can generate monopoly type rents. Firms would be willing to expend up to their expected gain in profits derivable from the monopoly in order to secure such an advantage. Conceivably, lobbying and litigation expenditures could equal potential profits, resulting in the complete dissipation of rents. In contrast, a powerful sovereign could auction off the rights to the monopoly. If competition for the monopoly is sufficiently intense, the sovereign could capture the potential rents, avoiding their dissipation. Likewise, it is possible that a sovereign could tax away the potential profits. Because tax revenues are conventionally treated as a transfer, to the sovereign in this case, dissipation would again be avoided.

The conditions, however, under which complete dissipation or the complete capture of rents can occur are very demanding. For example, competition for the monopoly position is essential for both full capture or complete dissipation. But more to the point, full capture of the rents implies the existence of a well-defined transferable right to the monopoly. As the discussion in the preceding sections indicates, there are three sovereigns with potential claims to Indian gaming revenues. Consequently, the sovereignty Indian tribes possess is dependent on political ambitions and court decisions. Although complete dissipation is unlikely, the various claimants can be expected to expend costly resources on either protecting or attempting to confiscate gaming rents.

The margins for dissipation are many, but in addition to the traditional forms of rent seeking, politicians can also induce exchanges by threatening to write laws or undertake actions that could disadvantage certain individuals or firms (McChesney 1987). Whether the initial sponsors of the IGRA were so motivated is beyond the scope of this chapter. But, as the examples offered in this section indicate, state politicians have used a variety of threats, including the threat of expanding gaming to non-Indians, in order to obtain concessions from gaming tribes.

By granting the states a degree of veto power over Class III operations, the IGRA essentially gave the states, and therefore their politicians, the right to claim part of the residual. However, the states do not have absolute veto power. For one thing, compacts must be approved by the Secretary of the Interior, and the department has made clear that attempts to extract excessive amounts from the tribes would be met with a denial of the compact. The IGRA allows states to assess tribes for the cost of regulating and monitoring Class III operations, but the Act (25 U.S.C 2710 [d][4]) is explicit in denying a state or any of its political subdivisions authority to impose any tax, fee, charge, or other assessment on an Indian tribe's gaming operations. Without obtaining a share of gaming revenues, however, a number of states balked at signing compacts, a stance that was later reinforced by the 1996 *Seminole* decision. Moreover, in 1988 most states prohibited casino-style gaming. If such gaming were to be allowed, these laws would have to be modified or repealed and, if repealed, it could open the door to non-Indian gaming operations and the proliferation of casinos would offend voters who were opposed to gambling.

Accordingly, politicians will seldom act as a perfect broker for any single interest group (Peltzman 1976, p. 211). Moreover, as Bruce Yandle (1983) has pointed out, regulation often involves a coalition of strange bedfellows such as bootleggers and Baptists. Hence, a political tradeoff, one that allowed a limited amount of gaming carried on by Indians who were often viewed as having been victimized by federal and state policy, was the more palatable outcome for politicians in a number of key states. Importantly, restricting the number of gaming establishments and devices was also essential if tribes were to become major contributors to political candidates and campaigns. Too much competition would drive net returns to zero and reduce the willingness of gaming tribes to contribute. Although they are unlikely to agree on the same number of devices, both politicians and gaming tribes have an incentive to restrict entry.

The key to achieving a compact agreement in a number of important cases has been a tribe's willingness to share gaming revenues with the state. In exchange and to obtain the blessings of the Department of the Interior, gaming tribes have been granted "substantial exclusivity" for Class III type gaming in the state or localities within the state (Martin 2003). To date, the Secretary of the Interior has approved compacts with revenue-sharing provisions in six states. In approximate chronological order of their approval, the states are Connecticut, Wisconsin, New Mexico, California, New York, and Arizona (see Table 8.2). All compacts with revenue-sharing components involve the granting of exclusivity by the state. Importantly, should the state renege on the exclusivity agreement, revenue-sharing payments from tribes cease. Indeed, Michigan tribes were at one time making revenue-sharing payments to the state under a court-approved consent decree, but these tribes stopped making payments when the voters in Michigan authorized three non-Indian casinos in Detroit. The experiences of the six revenue-sharing states illustrate the tradeoffs imposed by the IGRA on gaming tribes and state politicians.

Table 8.2. States with Approved Revenue Sharing Compacts.

State	Net revenue sharing rates	Approximate state revenues/remarks
Arizona[a]	From 1 to 8% percent. The 8% rate applies to a tribe's net revenues in excess of $100 million	Compacts approved January 24, 2003. Estimated state revenues, $102 million per year
California[b]	Based on the number of devices operated by the tribe on September 1, 1999. From 1 to 200 gaming devices, 0%. From 201 to 500 devices, 7% on the excess over 200 devices. The top bracket is 13 percent on the excess over a 1000 devices	First payments were due September 30, 2002. Revenues are expected to exceed $100 million annually
Connecticut[c]	25% of net revenues	$403 million in FY 2004
New Mexico[d]	3 to 8 %. The 8% rate applies to revenues in excess of $4 million	$35 million in 2003
New York[e] (Seneca Nation Compact)	18% in the first 4 years of operation; years 5–7, 22%; and years 8–14, 25%	Compact approved October 25, 2002. Estimated state revenues of $50 million per year per new casino
Wisconsin[f]	Varies across tribes. In general, graduated rates rising to 5%. The top rate is 8 % in later years	Newly negotiated compacts are expected to generate $118 million in the fiscal year 2003–2004[g]

NOTE:

[a]Arizona Tribal-State Gaming Compacts (http://www.gm.state.az.us/compact.final.pdf).

[b]California Gambling Control Commission, *Model Tribal-State Compact* (http://www.cgcc.ca.gov).

[c]State of Connecticut, Division of Special Revenue (http://www.dosr.state.ct.us).

[d]New Mexico Gaming Control Board (http://www.nmgcb.org).

[e]Nation-State Gaming Compact between the Seneca Nation of Indians and the State of New York, approved by the Secretary of the Interior on October 25, 2002.

[f]State of Wisconsin Gaming Compacts, 2003 Amendments (http://www.doa.state.wi.us).

[g]Estimated revenues are currently in question because the Wisconsin Supreme Court struck down key portions of the compacts in 2004.

The precedent for states to obtain a share of Indian gaming revenues was established early on by the Mashantucket Pequot tribe of Connecticut.[17] Shortly after obtaining tribal recognition, the Pequots opened a bingo hall in 1986 with seating for 5,000 near the town of Ledyard, about 120 miles from New York City. The bingo hall was an immediate success and, following passage of the IGRA, the tribe sought to expand beyond bingo. At the time, the state of Connecticut allowed charity gaming under the rubric of "Las Vegas Nights." The games allowed included blackjack and roulette, but not slots. The Pequots argued that, because the state allowed Class III gaming, it was compelled to negotiate a compact agreement. The state of Connecticut resisted but a series of court decisions and support from the Department of the Interior and a court-appointed mediator eventually led to a compact agreement and the opening of a casino that offered a variety of games, including poker and parimutuel horserace wagering, which was banned in Atlantic City, but not slots.

Foxwoods Casino opened in February 1992. Its success and the fact that no taxes were paid to the state stimulated efforts to capture some of the newfound wealth. Shortly after Foxwoods opened, a Las Vegas casino operator initiated a campaign to open a non-Indian casino in Bridgeport, Connecticut, a severely depressed community at the time. The area was promised jobs and the state substantial tax revenues. The Pequots recognized the threat and the opportunity to expand into slots. They commenced their own lobbying effort, outspending their competition. In the process, they revealed the extent to which gaming tribes were capable of becoming major sources of campaign funding. The Las Vegas interests spent $357,000 in 1992. The Pequots' lobbying expenses were $363,000 (Eisler 2001, p. 178). The Pequots' campaign paid off. Although the Governor of Connecticut, Lowell Weicker, had declared he was adamantly against allowing slots, the campaign revealed public support for Indian gaming. Importantly, the Pequots offered the state $100 million a year or twenty-five percent of the winnings, whichever was greater, if the tribe were granted the exclusive rights to operate slot machines in the state. It was an offer that was difficult to refuse, especially because the state was running a large deficit at the time and there was public support for Indian gaming. Following the introduction of slots in January 1993, revenues poured into Foxwoods and state coffers. However, arguments were continually raised that a non-Indian casino in Bridgeport, located closer to New York City, could yield even more revenues for the state even though the Pequots would no longer have to contribute twenty-five percent of their revenues. Again, the Pequots commenced a lobbying campaign, one that cost the tribe over $2 million (Eisler 2001, p. 225). Their objective was to open a casino in Bridgeport, but that effort failed. Moreover, the only other federally recognized tribe in Connecticut, the Mohegans, were also attempting to open their own casino. Although the Pequots did not welcome the competition from the Mohegans, the threat of a non-Indian casino in Bridgeport was real and the Pequots agreed to maintain the compact if the Mohegans were also required to pay twenty-five percent of their net revenues to the state. The efforts by state politicians to establish a non-Indian casino in Bridgeport subsided with the opening of the Mohegan Sun Casino in 1996. Today, the Pequots operate one of the world's largest casinos, and Foxwoods' revenue-sharing contribution to the state of Connecticut in fiscal 2004 was $197 million. The Mohegan Tribe, which operates the Mohegan Sun Casino, paid $206 million to the state over the same period (State of Connecticut, Division of Special Revenue 2004). The total of $403 million far exceeds Indian revenue sharing in any of the other states.

In 1991, the Governor of Wisconsin signed the first compact agreements allowing Class III gaming in the state. The compacts called for revenue sharing and were to be renegotiated every five years. Until recently, however, the tribes paid very little to the state. The eleven tribes, operating twenty-four casinos, paid about $24 million to the state in FY 2001–2002, an amount that represents only 2.2 percent of net revenues (Thompson and Schmidt, 2002). Recent shortfalls in the state's budget spurred Governor Doyle to go after additional revenues from the gaming tribes. Of the eleven tribes, eight have so far agreed to new compacts. During the negotiations, there were threats to amend or repeal state law that prohibits casino gaming other than by compacted tribes. Although the tribes agreed to increases in revenue sharing (see Table 8.2), the newly negotiated compacts also give the tribes expanded hours and games and have no expiration date.

There were protracted and bitter conflicts over Indian gaming in New Mexico. The state repeatedly refused to negotiate a compact. As had occurred in Connecticut, the tribes took their case to the public, whose response to polls showed they strongly favored legislation allowing Indian gaming (Mason 2000, p. 161). In 1997, the state finally agreed to a compact that would grant a degree of exclusivity to the tribes in exchange for the state receiving a sixteen percent share of net revenues. In commenting on

New Mexico's 1997 gaming compacts, Secretary of the Interior Bruce Babbitt stated, "My most serious concern is the state's insistence that the tribes make large payments to the state" (US Department of the Interior 1997). Although Babbitt allowed the forty-five-day statutory deadline for disapproval of the compact to expire, essentially allowing it to go into effect, he made his disapproval clear. A number of the tribes also felt that the revenue-sharing agreement was excessive in light of the presence of other gaming establishments in the state and refused to make timely payments. The issue again returned to the courts and the state legislature. The terms of the compact were renegotiated and, in 2001, ten New Mexico tribes agreed to new terms offering the state up to eight percent of net gaming revenues (see Table 8.2). However, these compacts are constantly under threat of pending legislation that would expand slot numbers and hours at non-Indian casinos located at New Mexico racetracks. Once again the state and tribes are faced with the tradeoffs that exclusivity and revenue sharing impose.

Similar confrontations occurred in California. When the IGRA passed in 1988, California had a state lottery and allowed wagering on horse races, bingo for charitable purposes, and nonbanked card games. However, California's state constitution essentially prohibited slot machines and house-banked card games. Accordingly, tribes were essentially free to establish Class II gaming operations but would have to induce the state to sign compact agreements and, eventually, amend the state constitution before they could legally engage in Las Vegas-style gaming operations. A stalemate ensued for almost ten years. Finally, in March 1998, Governor Wilson signed a compact agreement with the Pala Band of Mission Indians, and later with a few other tribes. However, these compacts did not allow slots and greatly restricted the number of video lottery devices that were considered legal by the state. Most of the larger and established gaming tribes objected to the Pala Band compacts. Their recourse was to take the issue to the voting public via a pro-gaming ballot initiative.

If passed, Proposition 5 would permit tribes to offer certain electronic gambling devices (California Secretary of State 1998). Importantly, this type of gaming could only occur on Indian lands, essentially granting gaming tribes exclusive rights to slot machines in California. Proposition 5 was opposed by a variety of interest groups, including church groups and Nevada gaming interests. The major coalition organized against Proposition 5 managed to raise over $26 million for its defeat (Mason 2000, p. 252). The tribes were even more resourceful; their coalition raised over $59 million. Moreover, the voters had a clear sense that reparation was in order, and that this was a way to accomplish it. In November 1998, voters overwhelmingly approved Proposition 5 with 62.4 percent of the vote. In August 1999, however, the Act was ruled unconstitutional by the California Supreme Court.[18]

The California Supreme Court ruling did not come as a surprise and efforts were immediately undertaken to place another initiative before the voters to amend the state constitution. In the meantime, Governor Gray Davis quickly signed compact agreements with fifty-seven tribes. On March 7, 2000, the voters of California approved proposition 1A by a margin of sixty-four percent. The state constitution was amended to allow slot machines on federally recognized tribal lands (Art. IV, Sec. 19(f)). The amendment essentially granted tribes exclusive rights to operate slot machines in the state. The compact agreements state: "In consideration for the exclusive rights enjoyed by the tribes, and in further consideration for the State's willingness to enter into this Compact, the tribes have agreed to provide the state, on a sovereign-to-sovereign basis, a portion of its revenue from Gaming Devices" (California Gambling Control Commission 1999, Preamble E).

California's compact agreements call for gaming tribes to contribute a percentage of their net win depending on the number of gaming devices the tribe operated on September 1, 1999. There were a total of 19,005 gaming devices statewide at that time (California Gambling Control Commission 2003). Each tribe's contribution was based on a scale that was highly progressive (see Table 8.2). First payments into the fund were due September 30, 2002. Revenues to the fund were initially expected to exceed $100 million annually and were to be used mainly for programs to address problem gambling, regulatory costs, and to help local governments deal with impacts of casinos such as roads.

Indian gaming revenues in California were approximately $4.7 billion in FY 2003 and are growing rapidly.[19] This newfound wealth, coupled with a large state budget deficit, prompted newly elected Governor Arnold Schwarzenegger to seek additional revenues from the tribes. In July 2004, the state of California ratified new compact agreements with five tribes. If approved by the Department of the Interior, the new compacts would provide an additional $100 million annually to finance a $1 billion bond for the state and could generate up to $200 million a year in recurring revenue from additional slots permitted under the new compacts. Governor Schwarzenegger's ability to extort additional funds was aided by the presence of two gaming initiatives on the November 2004 ballot that would have expanded casino gaming to non-Indians. After signing the new compacts, the Governor expressed his opposition to those initiatives. The expansion of Indian gaming in California, however, is a concern for the tribes currently engaged in gaming, and some are opposed to the new compacts (Barfield 2004). Indeed, attempts to control the expansion of Indian casinos in California and preserve potential rents has been an underlying force in the development of the current rules.

As of July 2003, sixty-one of the 107 federally recognized tribes in California had entered into compacts with the state, and fifty-three tribes had gaming operations in place. Although some tribes are located in very rural locations and are unlikely to engage in gaming, there is considerable room for expansion by tribes not currently in the game. This potential competition was clearly seen by the major gaming tribes, and the compact agreements establish a benefit scheme for noncompacted tribes. The Revenue Sharing Trust Fund provides up to $1.1 million annually to tribes that operate less than 350 gaming devices. Payments into the fund are in addition to the revenue-sharing contributions to the state, and tribes are required to contribute based on the number of gaming devices operated. Although the fund is proclaimed as evidence of California's gaming tribes' willingness to share their wealth with other Indians, equal payment is provided to each of the nongaming tribes, independent of tribal population. Moreover, the established gaming tribes have challenged the efforts of other tribes to open casinos in their vicinity. The gaming tribes have complained about the negative environmental and local impacts of new casinos, the very same complaints issued against the established casinos (Barfield 2003c). But some of their most adamant opposition is left for tribes attempting to establish casinos off their existing reservations, particularly in urban downtown areas or on major interstate highways where they could compete with other gaming tribes (Barfield 2003b).

There is, of course, a clear incentive for each individual gaming tribe to want a casino closer to their patrons. Tribes may purchase land and add it to their reservation base. However, if left unchecked, this could create a rush by tribes to expand into urban areas, resulting in a chase for the same patrons and the dissipation of rents. Section 20 of the IGRA, however, prohibits tribes from conducting Class II or Class III gaming activities on lands acquired in trust after October 17, 1988, unless one of several exceptions applies.

Importantly, the governor of the state in which the gaming activities are to take place has veto power. Between 1988 and July 2003, only three applications have been approved (Martin 2003). There are, however, a number of applications pending, and newly recognized tribes and those who claim their ancestral homes were illegally confiscated may eventually succeed in locating a casino in a major urban area.[20] But they will likely have to overcome the veto power of state governors and that could be very expensive.

In New York, only one tribe, the Seneca, currently has a revenue-sharing compact. In exchange for sharing up to twenty-five percent of the revenue with the state, the compact grants the tribe exclusive rights to open three casinos in western New York (see Table 8.2). The tribe has one off-reservation casino in Niagara Falls and plans another off-reservation casino in suburban Buffalo. The off-reservation site in Niagara Falls was provided by the state of New York to the Seneca tribe. Apparently, both the tribe and the State recognize the potential for substantial revenues from a downtown location. Two other major gaming tribes in New York, the Oneida Nation and the St. Regis Mohawks who have gaming compacts since 1993, are not required to make revenue-sharing payments to the state. Any new ventures, however, such as those planned for the Catskill region of southern New York, would be subject to revenue sharing.

Gaming compacts were negotiated with Arizona tribes in 1992. Under these compacts, limited gaming was permitted, but there was no revenue-sharing component. As elsewhere, the issue was placed before the voters of Arizona, who expressed their willingness to grant gaming tribes exclusivity in exchange for a share of the revenue. The new compacts (see Table 8.2), approved by the Department of Interior in July of 2003, are exemplary. They provide exclusivity and limit the number of gaming devices tribes may operate, but make those rights transferable. Should Arizona state law be modified to allow non-Indian casinos, tribal contributions to the State would immediately be reduced to 0.75 percent of gaming revenues.

Elsewhere, the recent boom in Indian gaming revenues has caused states to renegotiate their compacts when they expire or reopen negotiations by threatening tribes with competition from non-Indian casinos and racinos (race tracks that offer video lottery terminals or actual slot machines). In the state of Minnesota, all casinos are operated by Indian tribes but there is no explicit revenue-sharing agreement. It is likely that this is a temporary situation as efforts are underway to capture part of the rents by allowing non-Indian casinos whose revenues can be more readily taxed, or entering into a revenue-sharing agreement with the tribes.

The tribes are not defenseless, but competing head to head with non-Indian gaming establishments in some states, for example, Nevada and Montana, does not appear to have been a particularly fruitful endeavor.[21] On the other hand, gaming tribes have more than held their own in states like Michigan and Mississippi that allow Las Vegas-style non-Indian casinos, but restrict their locations. A key factor contributing to the survival of gaming tribes in states where they compete with non-Indian casinos is that the tribes do not pay taxes on gaming revenues, nor do they pay corporate or property taxes. This group, which represents about forty percent of Indian gaming revenues, pays regulatory fees that are relatively small and may also pay local impact charges.[22] Thus, tribes negotiating the amount of revenue sharing and the degree of exclusivity have a fallback position that limits the amount states can extract. Accordingly, the percent of revenues tribes share with the states should be relatively small compared to the revenues extracted from non-Indian casinos.

Table 8.3 reveals considerable variation in gaming revenue tax rates imposed on non-Indian land and riverboat casinos in the eleven states that allow Las Vegas-style casinos. Tax rates for the casino industry in 2003, applied as a percent of gaming revenues, ranged from 6.75 percent in Nevada to a high of 70 percent in Illinois.[23] The average tax rate across the eleven states with major casino operations is 16 percent, a figure that is high compared to most of the rates shown in Table 8.2. The evidence suggests that even though gaming tribes with revenue-sharing compacts have been targeted by states as a revenue source, most have managed to avoid the higher rates paid by many non-Indian casino operators. Moreover, those tribes have obtained a degree of exclusivity in exchange for their payments to the states.

Although the initial prices in terms of revenue sharing appears to be relatively low, there are other costs to dealing in the political marketplace. Obtaining a share of Indian gaming revenues can enhance a politician's reelection chances among voters who oppose gambling, or those who think it a preferable source of state revenue. But making demands of gaming tribes can also generate campaign contributions, which aid reelection efforts. The casino industry has long been a major contributor to political campaigns. During the 2002 election cycle, the casino industry, including gaming tribes, contributed $14.9 million to federal office seekers, ranking twenty-seventh

Table 8.3. Non-Indian Casino Tax Revenues, 2003.

State	Gaming tax rates on net revenues	Casino net revenues (millions)	Gaming tax revenue (millions)
Colorado	Graduated tax rate. Maximum of 20%	$698	$95.6
Illinois	Graduate tax rate from 15% to a maximum of 70%, plus $3–5 patron fee.	1710	719.9
Indiana	Graduated tax rate. Maximum of 35%, plus $3 per patron admission tax.	2230	702.7
Iowa	River boats, maximum of 20%.	1020	209.7
Louisiana	Maximum of 21.5%	2020	448.9
Michigan	Effective tax rate 22%	1130	250.2
Mississippi	Maximum state tax of 8%. Local governments can impose additional 4%	2700	325.0
Missouri	20% tax rate, plus $2 per patron charge	1300	369.0
Nevada	Tax rate of 6.75%, plus annual fees on gaming devices	9600	776.5
New Jersey	8% plus investment contribution of 1.25%	4500	414.5
South Dakota	8% plus $2,000 per gaming device tax	70	5.4
Total		$27000	$4320

SOURCE: American Gaming Association (2004b). Tax revenue data are from state gaming regulatory agencies, as are some of the casino revenue figures. For those states that do not report industry gaming revenues, the revenue figures were estimated by the American Gaming Association.

among all industry groups, up from seventy-fifth in the 1990 election cycle (Center for Responsive Politics 2002). As the Pequot tribe demonstrated early on, gaming tribes have access to sufficient funds to make them a potent interest group. During the 1990 election cycle, gaming tribes contributed only $1,750; in the 2002 election cycle, they contributed $6.8 million, or forty-five percent of the industry total.

The terms of the IGRA, however, make clear that most of the obstacles to Indian gaming are at the state level. Hence, one should expect campaign contributions at the state level to be even higher than they are at the federal level. Indeed, since 1998, tribes in California alone have contributed well over $100 million to candidates and initiative campaigns, making them one of the largest contributors in the state.[24] Total contributions, however, pale in comparison to the net returns to tribal governments. As mentioned previously, the GAO (1997) estimated that net returns, or gaming revenues minus operating expenses, were around thirty-eight percent of gaming revenues. Testimony by the Chairman of the National Indian Gaming Association in 2003 suggests net returns in the range of twenty-five to thirty-five percent (Stevens 2003). Applying the twenty-five percent figure to the $14.7 billion in Indian gaming revenues earned in FY 2002 yields a net return of $3.7 billion. According to the Institute on Money in State Politics, total tribal government contributions to candidates and state ballot initiatives in the 2002 election cycle was $41.5 million.[25] Although individual tribes in some states may rank in the top twenty of all campaign contributors, total rents are clearly not being completely dissipated via campaign contributions.

In general, gaming tribes have been successful in warding off efforts by the states to extract sufficiently high payments, either in the form of revenue sharing or campaign contributions, that net returns to the tribes would be reduced to zero. Moreover, economic impact studies indicate that Indian gaming has reduced unemployment in counties where an Indian casino opens and has increased per capita incomes on reservations with gaming.[26] Both the high returns from gaming and the related employment opportunities continue to stimulate tribes to get into gaming, a market signal that the residual rents are positive. This success raises another question: What is this money used for?

INDIAN TRIBES AS A COMMONS: THE INTERNAL OBSTACLES

There has been confusion over the usage of the term "commons." It has, at times, been used to denote a condition whereby no one has the ability or right (which amounts to the same thing) to exclude anyone from use of a resource (Hardin 1968). Today the convention is to denote the latter condition as an open-access regime (Ostrom 2000; Eggertsson 2003). In contrast, a common property regime is a societal arrangement whereby members of a clearly demarked group have the ability to exclude nonmembers from using a particular asset. The commons can have legal standing or recognition by a higher authority that facilitates the exclusion of nonmembers. Members of a common property regime typically manage the asset in a collective manner and individual rights are usually stinted. Common property regimes seldom give members full rights of alienation or transferable titles to shares of the assets, making them a very different organizational form than that of a corporation. Because individual property rights within the organization are not well specified, these regimes often confront high internal governance costs.

Indian tribes operate much like a common property regime. In particular, the tribe, and only the tribe, may determine who is a member, and who may directly benefit from gaming revenues. The ability to exclude has taken on new importance as gaming profits have soared, and there are numerous accounts of individuals seeking tribal recognition only to be rejected (Barlett and Steele, 2002). The most frequently used system for determining membership requires applicants to prove blood ties but the standards vary across tribes. There is also variation in how tribes are governed (Cornell and Kalt, 2000). Although all tribes elect their leaders, some tribal leaders operate with few checks or balances. Although tribes have the right to control their own membership numbers, how gains are distributed remains a vexing problem.

The IGRA (25 U.S.C. 2710 [b][2][B]) constrains the use of net revenues to funding of tribal government operations and programs that provide for the general welfare of the tribe and its members. Gaming tribes have used their funds to build schools, provide housing for their members, and pay for a variety of other programs. Although some of these programs have been tainted by allegations of extravagant spending, if not outright corruption (Testerman 2004; Barlett and Steele 2002), much of the media attention has focused on the enormity of some tribes' per capita payments. Net gaming revenues may be distributed in the form of per capita payments to members of an Indian tribe provided the Indian tribe has prepared a Tribal Revenue Allocation Plan that has been approved by the Secretary (25 U.S.C. 2710 [b][3]).

Although these payments are considered confidential, a number of tribes and individuals have released information on payments and they reveal a general pattern. At the top of the list are the Shakopee Mdewakanton Sioux in Minnesota, who operate the very successful Mystic Lake Casino. In 2002, each of the 170 adult tribal members received over $1 million (WCCO-TV

2003). More moderate are the per capita payments distributed by the Viejas tribe, who operate a very successful casino and adjacent shopping mall about a half-hour east of San Diego. The tribe, with about 280 members, makes per capita payments of around $10,000 per month, while most members also work for the casino (Barfield 2003a). Other tribes have distributed much smaller payments. Indeed, as of December 2001, only about one-third of gaming tribes were making per capita payments.[27] There are a number of factors that likely contribute to that outcome. Unlike tribal revenues, per capita payments are subject to federal individual income tax. Thus, if the tribal government is capable of providing the services enrolled tribal members want, even if they valued them at somewhat less than their cost, there would be little pressure to provide per capita payments. But, for the highly successful gaming tribes, there are limits to what tribal governments can provide in the way of worthwhile services, and relinquishing direct control may be the politically prudent action for tribal leaders to take. Although data are limited, it appears that it is the relatively smaller tribes with highly successful casinos that tend to distribute per capita payments.

The fact that few tribes are making per capita payments suggests, as many tribes have claimed, that the real tax rate on Indian gaming revenues is 100 percent, with the taxing authority being the tribal governments. For those who believe that individual sovereignty, in contrast to tribal sovereignty, is the route to real prosperity, the success of Indian gaming is unlikely to contribute to the former status, at least not directly. Indirectly, gaming has provided jobs and work experience, and the more successful tribes have typically set up educational funds for their members. Both employment and education contribute to human capital, which belongs to the individual and increases mobility. Gaming has also allowed tribes and their members to gain business experience. This learning experience has led some tribes to moderate their claims of tribal sovereignty. Although at first tribes objected to gaming regulation by states or outside entities and many still consider it an affront to their sovereignty (Soto 2003), a number of tribes have come to recognize that regulation is an integral part of the gaming business. The gaming public wants to know that the game is legitimate and what the chances of winning are. For example, casino patrons will often research guides to learn the average payback percentage of slot machines at various casinos (Bourie 2003). However, providing reliable information on slot machines generally requires audits by a state gaming agency or some reputable independent auditor. The top Indian casinos like Foxwoods and Mohegan Sun have followed the lead of Las Vegas and make public their average payback percentages on slots that are based on data audited by the state. Compared to Las Vegas strip casinos, the average payback percentages at these two Connecticut casinos tend to be somewhat lower, approximately 91.8 percent compared to 93.8 percent, but that is substantially better than the payback percentage of eighty percent or less rumored to hold at smaller Indian casinos.

Relinquishing a degree of sovereignty has also been essential to financing the construction of casinos. As David Haddock (1994, p. 140) explains: "... economically small and immature sovereignties comprise unpromising environments for long-term, immobile private investment." Sovereign political entities may renege on agreements with private parties, leaving them very limited abilities to appeal. The US Supreme Court has repeatedly held that Indian tribes are immune from suit in state or federal court on contracts performed on or off the reservation.[28] When attempting to construct the Foxwoods Casino, the Pequots were confronted with the reluctance of US banks and financial houses to make loans to Indian tribes (Eisler 2001, pp. 149–56; Benedict 2000, pp. 216–17). The Pequots turned to a Malaysian group experienced in the operation of casinos. The terms gave the Malaysian group the ability to construct a hotel on private land adjacent to the proposed casino, and the right to take over and manage the casino should the Pequots default on the loan. The latter required the approval of the BIA, but the agency ultimately agreed. The key to overcoming the potential for confiscation by the sovereign was the willingness of the Pequots to explicitly grant an exemption to its claims of sovereignty. Following that lead, US banks and financial institutions are today actively engaged in making loans for Indian casinos provided they include exemption clauses in the contract.

Common property regimes can certainly present problems in allocating wealth and are another venue for rent seeking, but they are not inherently inefficient (Eggertsson 2003). Any conclusion as to the efficiency or inefficiency of these entities depends on the real-world alternatives. Although it will take time to see how well tribal members take advantage of these new opportunities, the success of gaming enterprises holds out the promise that tribes may eventually break decades of institutional dependence upon federal programs and bureaucracies. Since the passage of the IGRA in 1988, federal spending on major Indian programs and services, adjusted for inflation, has actually increased, suggesting that one of the goals of the IGRA, self-sufficiency, has yet to be achieved.[29]

CONCLUSION

The rise of legalized gambling over the past thirty years in the United States reflects, in large part, the willingness of the voters to accept limited gaming in exchange for state revenues. Indian gaming was initially viewed much like charitable gambling, but the success of Indian gaming operations appears to have gone well beyond what most state and federal politicians anticipated. Now that it has been demonstrated how successful Indian gaming operations can be, there is no reason to suspect that gaming tribes will be spared the political pressures that beset the commercial gaming industry or any other successful industry dependent on governmental support or acquiescence. Under the IGRA, gaming tribes are not the only residual claimants of Class III gaming revenues. The Act paved the way for rent seeking by both state and federal politicians as the states seek additional gaming revenues. Indian tribes, however, have sovereign status and are largely tax-exempt. In contrast, non-Indian gaming operations are heavily taxed. Although that provides an umbrella for Indian casinos, sovereignty does not provide exclusivity or preferred locations. To gain these advantages, tribes have signed compact agreements with revenue-sharing components that have generally paid off for the tribes.

The tribes appear to understand well the rules of the game. While they proclaim their sovereign status, tribes have shown a willingness to pay for exclusivity and other activities that benefit their gaming operations. Given the voting public's conditional acceptance of gaming, however, the tribes will likely have to contribute more in terms of revenue sharing with the states and payments for local impacts. But there is no reason to believe that the states or the federal government will be able to capture the entire residual, or that competition for it would result in its full dissipation. The IGRA granted tribes attenuated rights to gaming and the tribes have used those rights to develop highly profitable operations. Unlike so many other attempts at Indian enterprise development, gaming is likely to remain profitable. How well gaming tribes utilize these proceeds to advance the welfare of their individual members and Americans Indians in general is ultimately a more important question, but that question may take the passing of a generation to answer.

NOTES

1. United States Senator from the State of Colorado, Chairman, Senate Committee on Indian Affairs, Oversight Hearings on the Indian Gaming Regulatory Act of 1988. Washington, DC, July 9, 2003.

2. See Anderson (1995, pp. 166–76) on the ambiguity inherent in the notion of tribal sovereignty and the tensions that policy has created.

3. P.L. 100–497, codified at 18 U.S.C. 1166 et seq. and 25 U.S.C. 2701 et seq.

4. With excessive rent seeking, development of a potentially valuable resource can be severely retarded. In contrast to the more traditional case where there is over usage of a common or open-access resource, the absence of the right to exclude can also result in under usage. Buchanan and Yoon (2000) have referred to this problem as the tragedy of the anticommons. Given the growth of Indian gaming, the tragedy of the anticommons appears to have been avoided.

5. In its most complete form, a property right implies the ability of the owner to derive value from the asset, exclude others from using it, and transfer ownership. See Barzel (1997) for the distinction between economic and legal rights. North (1990) discusses the importance of institutions (property rights) for promoting the accumulation of aggregate wealth.

6. Parimutuel wagering is also allowed in forty-three states.

7. Direct revenues to states from gambling, including lotteries, was around $27 billion in 2001. Recent state budget deficits have caused states to seek even more funding from gaming operations, both Indian and non-Indian (Binkley, Hilsenrath, and Forelle, 2003).

8. See Mason (2000, pp. 53–69) for a more detailed description of the events leading up to passage of the IGRA.

9. Following the 1996 *Seminole* decision, the Department of the Interior published a rule on April 12, 1999, at CFR Part 291, authorizing the Secretary to intervene in situations where a tribe and a state cannot reach agreement. This rule has been used only sparingly and is the subject of current litigation (see Blackwell 2001).

10. Although the NIGC collects data on the various tribes' gaming operations, these detailed reports are protected from release under the Freedom of Information Act. However, the GAO (1997 and 2001) was allowed access to the tribes' financial reports. In addition, industry-reporting groups such as Christian Capital

Advisors LLC (http://www.cca-i.com) keep track of the gaming industry, and there are numerous newspaper accounts of tribes' gaming successes and failures. Together, these sources allow for the construction of an overview of the industry.

11. For example, the Seminole Tribe of Florida has two hotel and casino facilities, operated in conjunction with Hard Rock Cafes, which have the appearance of Las Vegas-style casinos. Most, but not all, of the gaming devices they have utilized are considered to be Class II devices (Testerman 2004).

12. See National Indian Gaming Commission, *Classification Opinions* at http://www.nigc.gov/nigc/nigcControl?option=OPINIONS.

13. Gross industry revenues were $72.9 billion in 2003. The figure includes parimutuel wagering (on horses, greyhounds, and *jai alai*), lotteries, casinos, legal bookmaking, charitable games, and Internet gambling (Christian Capital Advisors LLC 2004).

14. Enrolled tribal members is a better measure of the affected group than US Census counts. Among American Indians, enrolled members are the group most likely to benefit directly from gaming revenues. The figure in the text was computed using enrollment data from US Department of Interior (1999).

15. See National Indian Gaming Association, *Indian Gaming Facts*, at http://www.indiangaming.org/library/indian-gaming-facts/index.shtml.

16. The figure in the text was computed using enrollment data from US Department of Interior (1999) and the NIGC's (http://www.nigc.gov) list of gaming tribes.

17. The Pequot's rise to prominence is described in Benedict (2000) and Eisler (2001).

18. *Hotel Employees & Restaurant Employees Internat. Union v. Davis* (August 1999).

19. The NIGC does not provide revenue data on a state-by-state basis. However, they do report gaming revenues for six regions. Region II is composed of California and Northern Nevada. Because the Indian gaming establishments in Nevada numbered only two in 2003 and are relatively small, the regional gaming revenues of $4.7 billion can be attributed largely to California (NIGC 2004a).

20. Not unexpectedly, following passage of the IGRA, there was an increase in the number of applications for federal tribal recognition (GAO 2001).

21. See Zoellner (2003). Of the thirteen tribes in Nevada, only two tribes are currently engaged in casino gaming and they have relatively small operations.

22. The forty percent figure was derived by using regional data from the NIGC, state revenue data (see sources in Table 8.2) and various reports. In 2001, tribal governments claimed they spent over $163 million enforcing regulations. Tribes also reimbursed states $40 million for regulatory costs and contributed $8 million via fee assessments to fund the NIGC (NIGC 2002).

23. Illinois raised their maximum tax rate to seventy percent in July 2003. There are, of course, limits as to how high a rate a state can set before actually losing revenues, and Illinois may have reached that limit. Revenues were reported down

in late 2003, and patrons are reportedly heading out of state to gamble (Gruszecki 2003).

24. California Common Cause (2003). The actual contributions may be understated. For example, the Agua Caliente tribe has challenged a California Fair Political Practices Commission ruling that the tribe had failed to report millions of dollars in contributions, arguing that its sovereign status exempts it from FPPC rules (see *FPPC v. Agua Caliente Band of Cahuilla Indians* at http://www.fppc.ca .gov/index.html?id=385). This case is on appeal, but it is noteworthy that foreign nations are generally prohibited from making campaign contributions.

25. This figure is calculated using the institute's power search. Online web site: http://www.followthemoney.org/database/power_search.phtml?sl=10&f= 12#sector. Cited: 15 November 2004.

26. See, for example, Evans and Topoleski (2002) and the studies referenced therein.

27. See National Indian Gaming Commission, *Frequently Asked Questions* at: http://www.nigc.gov/nigc/nigcControl?option=ABOUT_FAQ.

28. Most recently in *Kiowa Tribe v. Manufacturing Technologies, Inc.* (1998).

29. Walke (2000, Graph 22, p. 235) presents time-series data on federal budget allocations for major Indian-related programs, including the BIA. Although the overall budget declined in the 1980s, allocations rebounded during the 1990s.

NINE

"Doing Business with the Devil": Land, Sovereignty, and Corporate Partnerships in Membertou, Inc.[1,2]

JACQUELYN THAYER SCOTT

Cape Breton Island, northeast of Nova Scotia's mainland, is internationally known as a place of great beauty, but the same cannot be said for its largest city, Sydney (regional population about 125,000), on its eastern shore. This city's industrial glory days of coal and steel are gone, and out-migration of people and capital has left a legacy of rundown buildings, empty storefronts, and a ragged infrastructure of pot-holed roads, boarded-up schools, and weed-choked parks.

A small southeast-Sydney community, however, stands in sharp contrast. The potholes are filled, new curbing and buildings abound, and construction work includes a new trade center adjoining a new market, a food-retailing center, and a gas bar. New buildings also house an economic development corporation, local government chambers, and a gaming commission. The lobby walls of the community's main administrative office building are covered with architectural sketches and posters advertising consultation sessions about a new community plan, as well as Career Days at the local school where students can talk with representatives of community partners like

SNC-Lavalin and Lockheed Martin. There are plans for a community arena and multipurpose center, including a new health clinic and seniors' activity area, and a new housing subdivision. Welcome to Membertou, Inc.[3]—a 1,000-member Mi'kmaq Reserve.[4]

During the past decade, Membertou has gone from massive operating debt and welfare to labor shortages, budget surpluses, capital reserves, and annual dividend payments to band members (with those of minor children banked in a healthy trust fund for future education and other expenditures). One factor in this remarkable turnaround is gaming. Band revenues in 2003–2004 are expected to approximate Canadian $41 million, and gaming will produce an estimated $15 to $19 million of this total. However, it would be a mistake to conclude that Membertou's turnaround is simply due to gambling.

Dramatic changes in the institutions and processes of governance have occurred on the reserve, and they are paying off through a number of new business enterprises and partnerships. In many ways, Membertou's new organizational structure is more like a corporation than a government. Even though it provides many local goods and services to band members, Membertou is managed through corporate divisions similar to the way a "company town" is managed by a large mining or manufacturing firm. Indeed, it is the first aboriginal government in Canada, and possibly the world, to achieve and maintain ISO 9000 certification.[5] And while its headquarters are thoroughly grounded on the reserve, national and international business is more familiar with Membertou's Corporate Division offices, where the band's CEO is based: the glass-walled 17th floor of Purdy's Wharf Tower on the Halifax waterfront, hundreds of kilometers away.

Membertou also has been gaining new respect from its Sydney neighbors. Sydney merchants see band members spending their wage and dividend checks instead of welfare checks in local stores. Recently, the band contributed $25,000 to the regional hospital's campaign for a new MRI and bone densitometer equipment, a move warmly received by the local community, as was a $15,000 contribution to a sports fund for young people. Local radio talkback shows hear Sydney residents suggest that Membertou CEO, Bernd Christmas, or Chief Terry Paul would make a great mayor for the regional municipality. Most band-owned market and gas bar customers are from Sydney, and they are not in Membertou to avoid paying sales taxes. Membertou collects and remits the same sales taxes for nonresidents as do other Sydney businesses. "We're competing on concept, service, and quality,"

Christmas says, "not on any price advantages that may be considered unfair by other local businesses" (Christmas 2003). The message: We are a part of the larger community, even though we are apart from it.

That sentiment—"a part, but apart"—was not always so. Until recently, poverty was the norm in Membertou, and band members faced the choice of leaving home for work or going on welfare. There were no jobs for Mi'kmaq in the steel mill, the mines, or other local stores and businesses, and few young people completed high school. Furthermore, Mi'kmaq who settled in the Sydney area were forced to engage in a long-running struggle over reserve lands. Throughout the late nineteenth century and the early part of the twentieth century, the reserve's neighbors and Sydney municipal officials tried to force the Department of Indian Affairs (DIA) to remove the Mi'kmaq from one of the urban parcels that they occupied (Indian Reserve No. 28 on King's Road), which had become commercially valuable, to somewhere else, preferably outside the town limits. In 1916, the Exchequer Court of Canada ordered the relocation of 125 band members and, in 1926, the community was moved to its present site. The struggle over Reserve No. 28 continued, however. In the 1930s, the city requested a lease of the land for the Community Club to plant a garden, which the DIA granted for $1 per year. Dr. F.J. Kelley, a local physician, offered to purchase the property for $6,500 in 1963 to build a clinic and, after a series of negotiations, meetings, and encouragement by the city, the band apparently approved the sale in 1964 for the purpose of building a medical clinic. "Apparently" is the key word here, as voting and documentation irregularities are alleged, and an ongoing land claim dispute by the band further alleges that Indian Affairs:

> . . . alternately colluded in the removal of the Mi'kmaq by invoking s. 49A, and ignored its duty to ensure the highest and best use of the property for the Mi'kmaq by leasing the land at a nominal rent. Finally, it ignored the clearly expressed desires of the band that if the reserve was to be surrendered, it be surrendered only on condition that a medical clinic be constructed on the land. By negotiating to include the conditions in the acceptance of the surrender by the Governor in Council, the terms of the surrender were invalidated.[6]

Membertou residents also contended that they had been denied access to treaty-established rights regarding hunting, fishing, trapping, and other traditional uses of surrounding lands, an issue settled in 1999 in the Donald

Marshall decision by the Supreme Court of Canada, upholding these claims.[7] The idea of running the band as a corporation, partnering with major multi-national corporations on economic development projects, and developing cordial and cooperative relations with their neighbors may seem particularly surprising, given the history of local discrimination against the band and the perceived betrayal of trust.

TURNING POINTS

Perhaps the first key step toward Membertou's socioeconomic growth and self-confidence came in 1970, when the chief and council of the day began to take direct control of delivery of federal programs and services. This assertion of sovereignty did not have immediate consequences, but it set the stage for what would occur in the mid- and late-1990s. Economic progress at Membertou required more than band control of its resources (collective property rights) and decision making. Significant changes in the way it managed those resources and made decisions were needed, changes that required a strong leadership and a pool of managerial and technical skills. This does not imply that new leadership was needed. In fact, the chief and council have been mostly the same individuals for the past twenty years or more. The current Chief took office in 1984, for instance. Over time, however, significant institutional changes were made to alter the structure and processes of band governance so that band leadership could make and implement economically sound decisions. Formerly, the band was organized much like many other reserve governments, with divisions replicating the departmental divisions at Indian and Northern Affairs Canada (INAC). After all, almost all of the band's revenues came from INAC and, until the mid-1990s, there was no cadre of well-educated Membertou managerial talent ready to undertake thoughtful, long-term, institutional and governance change.

The band's budget of $4 million in 1993–1994 included an operating deficit of $1 million. Indeed, deficits had been accumulating since at least 1984–1985 despite band and INAC efforts in the 1980s to attract companies and jobs to Membertou. These efforts were typical of programs that have been failures in other aboriginal or rural communities. For instance, a fast-talking consultant with no fisheries experience sold the band on getting into a short-lived silver hake fishery experiment, assets of which were eventually sold for five cents on the dollar. Later, an irrigation pipe company attempted to establish a manufacturing plant on the reserve, but the location displaced a traditional gathering space, and the firm required a 24 × 7 workforce for which band members were not prepared. When it collapsed, the band was unable to meet its payroll.

After a seven-year hiatus on major development projects and accumulation of substantial debt (see Figure 9.1) and with the specter of third-party management of the band looming, the time was right for change. Band leadership recognized that they had to take responsibility for at least some of the failures of the past and do something to avoid similar failures in the future, so in 1994–1995 Bernd Christmas was recruited to serve as the band's CEO and General Counsel. Christmas, a Membertou native, had earned his law degree at York University's Osgoode Hall Law School. He was practicing law with Lang Michener, a large and influential Toronto law firm, where he implemented the firm's aboriginal law practice group and specialized in corporate/commercial and aboriginal law. Christmas proposed organizing the band like a large business and treating its members as shareholders, with

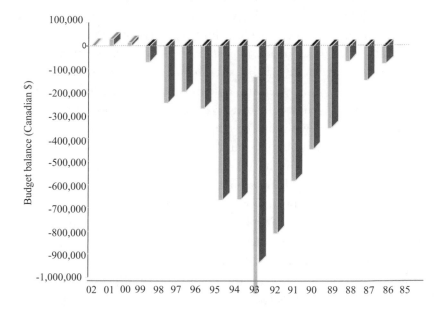

Figure 9.1. Deficit Reduction, Membertou First Nation, 1985–2002.
SOURCE: Membertou First Nation, Auditor-General presentation. March 31, 2003.

INAC as an investor and not a funder. The new organization was consciously modeled as a corporate structure, with accountability for decisions as a primary objective. Qualified people, most of them educated younger band members, were sought to fill roles and the chief and council became the board of directors. These changes in governance are discussed in more detail below, but first consider the changes in economic activity and performance that followed.

Bandleaders recognized that erasing deficits was a necessary step toward the band's self-determination, in part because the Canadian federal government continued to control virtually all decision making due to the debt the band had built up. Figure 9.1 indicates the deficit accumulation and retirement progress from 1985–2002.

One potential means of resolving the band's budget problems arose in 1994 when the province first offered the opportunity for gaming operations to reserves. A referendum was held to decide whether the band should be involved. It failed, as band members apparently feared that the benefits would be highly concentrated among a few. Such fears were motivated by experiences on other reserves where licensing of individuals to place gaming machines in commercial and community locations was practiced, with bands receiving set fees, while those individuals with licenses retained the profits. Membertou's initial proposal was reworked so that the band would develop gaming within its new corporate structure, by owning the Gaming Commission and operating all premises, with all profits going back to the band. The second referendum passed with eighty-seven percent support.

By 1999–2000, band revenues had grown to $9.08 million, by 2000–2001 to $11.8 million, by 2001–2002 to $12.86 million, and by the end of fiscal year 2003, to $21 million. Gaming revenues provide a major part of this growth, as approximately one-third of band revenues come from the Membertou Gaming Commission and Membertou Bingo and Tobacco. Another third still comes from INAC, mostly statutory program payments. This percentage dropped from close to 100 percent in less than ten years. The balance of band revenues is generated through its other business operations, as well as smaller grants from the Department of Fisheries and Oceans (DFO) and Health Canada for program or project purposes. Revenues in 2003–2004 are expected to approximate $41 million, with gaming accounting for an estimated $15 to $19 million. By June 2004, the band's 88 VLT machines were bringing in $400,000 per week.

In FY 2002–2003, slightly over one-third of expenditures went to programs and services and about forty-five percent to corporate and commercial operations, with the biggest expenditures being $6.2 million for the Gaming Commission and $2 million for the Membertou Commercial Fishery. About $1 million was paid in dividends to band members shortly before the Christmas holidays in 2002, another million dollars was set aside for the planned MultiPurpose Community Centre, and $800,000 was invested in road improvements.

During the past decade, the band has used its growing revenues to diversify its investments, and several nongaming initiatives have also been successful. Some of these now showing profits or promise thereof include:

1.   Membertou Fisheries, which employs from fifteen to twenty people on a seasonal basis. It brought in $2.8 million in sales and another $1.2 million in contract income from the federal DFO in 2002–2003, as well as supplying substantial amounts of food for community members. For instance, salmon and moose are harvested, with those who participate in the harvesting getting first choice of personally distributed goods, then elders, then the community's needy. A portion is set aside and stored for special community occasions and feasts. The fish food harvest includes shellfish, lobster, trout, and groundfish, as well as salmon. Commercially, the band has four lobster, three snowcrab, one shrimp, and one bluefin tuna license, and they also are fishing swordfish. Captains are nonaboriginal but the plan is to train aboriginal successors. Recently, Membertou Fisheries launched two new 58-foot band-fishing boats, built under close quality supervision in Newfoundland. Both are Class B ice-breakers and, at $900,000 each, represent a significant investment, although the price appears to be a bargain compared to monies paid for lesser quality boats by many other bands. The band is currently doing a review of commercial fishing, and is building a strategy for its negotiations with DFO when most of its "post-Marshall decision" licenses expire in FY 2003–2004. They also hope to expand their unique partnership with Clearwater Fine Foods, which includes contract harvesting (50–50 profit split) and potential branding of Membertou-fished products, while employing from twenty to sixty people seasonally.

2.   Mi'kmaq Gas Bar & Convenience, a food retailing and gas bar concept, which is unique in its merchandising format in the Sydney

area. It employs from fifteen to twenty people, and for the financial year ended March 31, 2004, was expected to bring in $300,000–400,000 in revenues, with profits of about 16.5 percent.[8]

3. Membertou Trade and Commerce Centre (MTCC) and Business Park. This is a $6.23 million complex that will anchor many of the band's joint-company partnerships and provide land and facilities for long-term lease to other companies. The Gaming Commission also will lease space in the facility to host their bingo games and additional VLT operations. Its design includes convention space intended to serve some of the midrange meeting requirements (up to 900 delegates) for the regional municipality, a Fisheries Science Centre that will contain a GIS Mapping Centre of Excellence (training partnership for technicians with Eastcan Geomatics), marine lab and classroom facilities, an aboriginal tourism office, and a 140-seat restaurant.

4. An Economic Development Fund. This fund is managed by the Corporate Division to assist band members interested in establishing or expanding a business enterprise, and several small businesses have received support, including CJIJ-FM radio station (an aboriginal broadcasting company on the reserve), Marshall's Paintball, Eugene Simon Auto Body, Safety Associates, Junior & Bucks Convenience Store (owned by Donald Marshall, Jr.), and George Christmas' recording project (George Christmas is a musician).

5. The Aboriginal Employment Agency. It will be owned and operated by Membertou and run out of the corporate office in Halifax.

6. Natural resource development. The band is negotiating forestry agreements with the Crown and with Stora-Enso, the pulp and paper company with major facilities in Port Hawkesbury, and is investigating the possibilities for mining opportunities on Crown land.

7. Corporate partnerships offering training and profit participation to the band and its members. Examples include:

· An SNC-Lavalin/Membertou partnership to develop environmental technologies, including some of the large-scale monitoring and cleanup operations associated with the Sydney Tar Ponds Project and remediation of the Cape Breton Development Corporation lands. (In addition to pursuing more environmental work, Membertou is attempting to develop its own expertise through this partnership in construction and design engineering services generally.)

- A partnership with Lockheed Martin (LM), to bid for the $3.1 billion Maritime Helicopter Project, and to provide additional IT skills at Membertou.

- Membertou Technologies, Inc. (MTI), a joint venture, fifty-one percent owned by the Membertou Development Corporation and forty-nine percent owned by Fujitsu Consulting. It is being used by LM as an integral part of its business with Canada's Department of National Defence (DND), with a first project, worth approximately $500,000, to consolidate and secure health records for Canada's military personnel, starting in 2004.

- Membertou and Sodexho-Marriott, one of the world's largest catering firms, joined together to pursue catering contracts for the offshore oilrigs, with plans to train several community members in the hospitality program of the Nova Scotia Community College and in Sodexho client kitchens. To date, this partnership has not experienced real commercial success, but it is now reorienting to add marketing of its hospitality services (e.g., catering, housekeeping, janitorial, laundry, etc.) onshore in the Maritimes, to universities, secondary schools, and health care facilities.

- A Grant Thornton LLP/Membertou business alliance is designed to offer workable solutions to other First Nations for financial management problems, with a focus on building internal financial capacity (accumulated deficits among First Nations in Atlantic Canada alone reached a combined $59 million in 2002, and across Canada some 138 native communities were experiencing some form of comanagement or third-party intervention).

- Techlink Entertainment, a Sydney-based gaming technology company, agreed to showcase their new generation PERFORMER I VLT machine exclusively in Membertou as part of a government-sanctioned ninety-day pilot project, which will include a number of support activities that Membertou has been involved with designing.

- The Laurentian Group, a local consortium that owns Sydport, a major ports facility for the Sydney Harbour, and the band have linked on a number of potential future projects.

In all, Membertou and its band-owned enterprises now employ more than 362 individuals on reserve, of whom from fifty-five to sixty are nonaboriginal. Major employers include the Band Council with about 100 full-time and twenty part-time or seasonal employees, the Membertou Gaming Commission with sixteen full-time and nineteen part-time/on-call workers, and other organizations and the new market/gas bar employing about fifty people.

COMMUNITY GOVERNANCE: MERGING BAY STREET AND UNAMA'KI[9]

Band business success has been demonstrated in less than ten years since the development of its new corporate governance structure in 1994–1995, even though the changes were not implemented without some difficulty. The new ideas offered by the band CEO were foreign to band members and many on the Council. However, over time, nine departments were created: Finance and Administration, Education Services, Social Services, Corporate Division (Halifax), Public Works & Housing Services, Health Services, Natural Resources, Employment & Training Services, and the Gaming Commission.

A key watershed decision for changes in operational management practices was to seek ISO 9000 certification, which was achieved in early 2001. This was done, at least in part, to serve as a signal of band credibility, thus enhancing the opportunity to work with multinational partners and in global markets. But it also had significant impacts on band governance and performance. For managers, the exhaustive certification process forced cultural change. That process includes an external audit of management processes, including links between policy decision making and implementation, human resource and communications practices, evaluation activities, and so on. Although at one level the organization is measured against its own statement of mission and objectives, the audit attests to use of appropriate management processes and standards in achieving those outcomes.

The ISO 9000 process requires that customers and stockholders (band members, in this case) be treated with respect. It demands that management focus on a vision or plan, and that the interconnecting roles be understood within the organization in order to enhance the chances of achieving objectives. The vision must be known to all and progress must be measured regularly so that mitigating action can be taken. Prior to Membertou's attempt to achieve ISO 9000 certification, departments just carried out their separate functions. Now, managers meet weekly, set objectives, document progress, and evaluate performance. Governance has become more results-oriented and less process-oriented. Long-time band management personnel receive training and are taught to fully utilize the planning cycle. For instance, the band now has a five-year rotating plan for preventative maintenance for housing and other band buildings, resulting in better service and fewer complaints. Another telling example: Cape Breton's harsh winters, with multiple freeze-thaw cycles, result in more potholes and road cave-ins than in many other parts of Canada. Nova Scotia's roads are notorious for their history of poor maintenance and Sydney's streets resemble slalom courses without flags, especially at night. Often, there is a six-week "break-up" period during which the most egregious potholes cannot be repaired, and car owners often suffer broken axle boots, flat tires, and other structural damage to vehicles. In spring 2003, at Membertou, "customer orientation" meant workers were sent out with spray cans of orange phosphorescent paint to spray around potholes and crumbling shoulder-beds so drivers could spot-and-avoid. A Nova Scotia first!

MEMBERTOU AS A TEST CASE

Although critical studies of aboriginal economic success are still quite limited in Canada, for more than fifteen years the Harvard Project on American Indian Economic Development[10] has been studying the conditions under which sustained self-determined social and economic development is achieved among First Nations. Over the years, its work has tracked the performance of Indian nations that use one of two models of reservation economic development.

The first, which it calls the "Standard Model," has predominated since the 1920s. In this model, the focus is short-term and nonstrategic. It looks for income and jobs, but lets others set the development agenda. Development is viewed primarily as an economic problem and indigenous culture is considered an obstacle to development. Starting businesses is more important than sustaining them, and there is a "flavor-of-the-month" approach to sectoral investment. Stephen Cornell (1999) describes the development planning and process in this model as:[11]

1.   Ask the tribal planner to identify business ideas and funding sources.
2.   Apply for outside grants, and respond to outside initiatives.
3.   Start whatever can be funded.
4.   Appoint your supporters to run projects.
5.   Micromanage.
6.   Pray.

Membertou may have fit this model quite well before 1994.

In contrast, the second approach, labeled the "the Nation-Building Model,"[12] utilizes *de facto* sovereignty and self-governance to gain control

of and direct tribal resources; to form effective governing institutions in order to establish objectives and allocate resources effectively in the pursuit
of those objectives in the context of a long-term strategic orientation; and
to perform a matching of contemporary indigenous culture with strategy
in order to pursue the kinds of goals that will maintain support of tribal
members. Cornell and Kalt (1998) maintain that economic development is,
first and foremost, a political problem the solution to which requires: 1) asserting sovereignty, by assuming control of the agenda and property rights
in resources and then coupling decisions and consequences with concrete,
bottom-line payoffs; 2) building institutions that are characterized by stability, separation of politics from business management, employment of a
competent bureaucracy, and effective nonpoliticized dispute resolution; 3)
cultural match of institutions and strategies with indigenous ideas about
how legitimate authority should be organized and exercised; and 4) strategic
action by shifting from reactive to proactive, from short-term to long-term,
and from opportunistic to systemic thinking and operating with a broad
societal focus.

The Harvard Project's tracking of performance concludes that the Standard Model typically results in failed enterprises, a politics of spoils, outside perceptions of incompetence and chaos, and continuing poverty. The
Nation-Building Model offers more effective access to and use of resources,
increases chances of sustained and self-determined economic development,
provides a more effective defense of sovereignty, and results in societies that
work.

Jorgensen and Taylor (2000) studied some seventy Indian enterprises
in the United States, including those studied by the Harvard Project,
and concluded that three independent variables are strong predictors of
performance:[13] 1) enterprises with unmet technical assistance needs usually
perform more poorly; 2) nonpoliticized boards of directors tend to perform
better; and 3) tribal-owned entities tend to perform more poorly.

Some examples of successful Indian nations using the Nation-Building
Model described by Cornell and Kalt (1998, p. 2) include both large and small
nations, as well as those well-endowed with natural resources and those not so:

- The Choctaws, with large gaming revenues that are being invested in a
  diversified portfolio of other enterprises, both on and off the reservation,
  are one of the largest employers in the state of Mississippi. They also
  employ several thousand non-Indians in their enterprises.

- The White Mountain Apaches of central Arizona and the Mescalero Apache of New Mexico employ most working-age tribal members in multiple-use forestry-based enterprises with integrated timber, wildlife (fee hunting and fishing), cattle ranching, and tourism (skiing, boating, golf, gaming, etc.) activities. These enterprises outperform private competitors as well as state and federal resource management bureaucracies (forest service, fish and game departments).

- The Flathead Reservation in rural Montana has many of the same enterprises as the White Mountain and Mescalero Apache, as well as an outstanding tribal college.

- The Cochiti Pueblo in New Mexico employs most of its members in tribal-owned enterprises.

One senior INAC official who has carefully studied the Harvard Project and other US literature on aboriginal enterprises believes some of the earlier conclusions have been altered with additional enterprise experience. Ten years after his first tour of successful US enterprises, Gordon Shanks recently revisited some of the same reservations. "The Harvard studies have clearly demonstrated that natural resource wealth is not required for a reserve to be successful in socioeconomic terms," he said. "But the single real predictor of success appears to be leadership" (Shanks 2003). That is, where leadership has been strong and consistent, socioeconomic success continues. In cases where political change has occurred and, with it, a decline in the quality of leadership vision and strength, success also has declined. And firewalls are more apparent than real in the long-term Harvard cases, he concludes.[14]

Development is arguably a multivariate process, and various disciplinary perspectives also abound. Although management and sociological theorists often cite the role of leadership and human capital development, institutional economists have long debated whether democracy and other checks on government must precede, or follow on, human and physical capital accumulation to initiate evolutionary growth. Proponents of both perspectives agree that, whatever the process, it is ultimately necessary to secure property rights to support investment. Those who advocate for the procedural preeminence of democracy and good institutions point to the comparative growth of European nations and to other examples of political institutions of limited government causing economic growth.[15] Those who argue that growth in income and human capital causes institutional development cite numerous evidential examples that human capital is a more basic source of growth than are the institutions, and that poor jurisdictions escape poverty through good policies "often pursued by dictators" and subsequently improve their political institutions (Glaeser et al. 2004, p. 1).[16]

The Membertou case provides evidence for the view that human capital development (and leadership) is an *a priori* condition that has led to institutional development for economic growth. As noted later in this chapter, Chief Paul had an early and sustained commitment to postsecondary education for younger band members, several of whom now have returned and carry the technical managerial vision for improved institutions, though some elements of institutional development, including a regime that encourages inward capital investment, remain farther out on the evolutionary curve.

Applying the Harvard Project's Nation-Building Model to Membertou demonstrates similarities to relatively successful US corporate tribes. These similarities are:

- Asserting sovereignty over land and resource claims, effectively managing financial assets, and focusing on goal-setting and evaluation processes.
- Building institutions in the context of a corporate "holding company" approach to enterprises, a program of educational and cultural authorities and programs, use of legal contracts, and development of a long-term community plan, combined with stability and an able bureaucracy.
- Matching culture to enterprises as with the collective structure of its gaming enterprises, the band-as-capitalist-corporation approach to enterprise development, and the band's use of Mi'kmaq language in official activities and naming, to the extent practically possible.
- Acting strategically as in the band's contracting practices with partners, its attention to community and nonaboriginal relationships, its targeted media attention, and its infrastructure and human capital planning.

The Membertou Model

Membertou's approach to socioeconomic development emphasizes a strong ideological foundation. Bernd Christmas calls it a "First Nations Progression Model" that is based on a business approach to government, management, and economic development in order to achieve community objectives (see Figure 9.2).

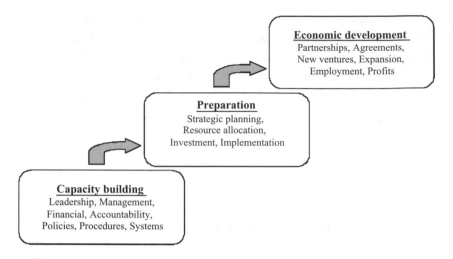

Figure 9.2. First Nations Progression Model.
SOURCE: Membertou First Nation, Auditor-General presentation. March 31, 2003.

According to Christmas, the model rests on four value pillars: conservation, sustainability, innovation, and success. Although the last two would be commonly recognized at any corporate AGM, the first two are intended to embed cultural values. Nonetheless, the band's leadership recognizes that success requires integration into the mainstream economy. The intention is to measure success through profit and return on investment, but to do so within their customary system of values.

Management also recognizes three other operating values that they believe are key to the model: transparency, accountability, and legitimacy. They feel that integration of mainstream and aboriginal concepts in a socioeconomic model requires enormous amounts of explanation, education, and consensus building. Band members, especially the Elders, must be able to voice their opinions and know that the leadership are not hiding anything. Decision makers must be trusted.

Historically, in most advanced western societies, economic development and political change occurred in an evolutionary environment where each affected the other. As merchants gained wealth, kings granted them special privileges (economic and political rights) to encourage them to invest that wealth within their jurisdictions. Wealth spread to other groups (capitalists, labor, etc.) and these groups subsequently were able to gain access to the political process too. Thus, political institutions evolved away from feudalism and toward democracy as more groups gained wealth and then political franchise.

For Canadian aboriginal communities, however, this simultaneous evolution of economic and political institutions has been stifled by creation of reserves and the Indian Act, which allows political evolution, but not an evolution in economic rights. The Indian Act instead establishes a particularized form of feudalism, which disallows sovereignty and provides no incentives for innovation and change. Add to that, some would suggest, the dispossession of culture through the continuing legacy of the residential schools, band relocations and historical seizures of resources, and we might begin to understand why aboriginal communities appear to seek extraordinary means to protect what they perceive to be important cultural values, and why they so often continue to occupy the lowest quartiles of all national socioeconomic indicators.

Membertou has attempted to break from the constraints imposed on economic development by the Indian Act, while maintaining its cultural ideologies. But how does this integration of modern economic values and traditional values work in practice, beyond issues of management style? Some specifics are contained in the statement of the objectives of the band's Corporate Division, shown in Table 9.1. Many of these elements are recognizably part of any corporate private-sector regime.[17] Similarly, although a

Table 9.1. Objectives of Membertou's Corporate Division.

- To create wealth and development for the Membertou First Nation community.
- To disseminate Membertou's corporate vision and strategy to its community and to the corporate world.
- To define and develop relationships with potential partners in the corporate sector.
- To promote efficiency and profitability within Membertou's current businesses.
- To establish investment protocols for all profits created by the corporate strategy to the maximum benefit of the Membertou Band and its community.
- To create partnerships with other Mi'kmaq First Nations to ensure that those communities share in Membertou's intellectual properties and corporate success.
- To develop a strategy that ensures that all of Membertou's corporate entities are operated in a fashion that conveys our commitment to excellence.

SOURCE: Membertou First Nation web site:
http://www.membertou.ca/corporate/index.html/. Cited: July 7, 2003.

corporation presumably attempts to generate benefits for its "community" of stockholders, the Membertou focus is clearly on community benefit. The most important benefits for corporate stockholders take the form of increased material wealth: dividends and capital gains. Band members cannot capture capital gains because, unlike stocks, membership is nontransferable, but "dividends" can be and are paid. Increased wealth for the Membertou community includes support of nonmaterial cultural values, too, such as its outreach with respect to sharing intellectual property and economic benefits with other Mi'kmaq First Nations.

A closer look at some of the band policy or practices not already examined may illustrate the Membertou approach more clearly in terms of its consistency with the Nation-Building Model.

Pursuit of Sovereignty: Membertou's Ongoing Aboriginal Rights Agenda

The name of one of Membertou's leading citizens, Donald Marshall, Jr., is synonymous with aboriginal rights in Canada, and the band's focus on governance and socioeconomic development has not deflected its attention from the rights agenda. Membertou has pursued this agenda in three ways. First, it has pursued its own specific land claim with regard to the sale of the King's Road property, as well as providing key leadership in overall Mi'kmaq treaty claims. Second, it has pursued opportunities opened up through court judgments in fishing, hunting, forestry, and mineral resources. Most recently, Membertou has entered the long-standing interjurisdictional morass over the Sydney Tar Ponds cleanup. Citing archaeological evidence of Mi'kmaq hunting and fishing in the Muggah Creek watershed and Sydney Harbour, Membertou intends to press senior levels of government for remediation action under its own treaty rights.[18]

Sovereignty and Long-Term Objectives Through Partnerships

Band officials closely observed early partnership agreements between many aboriginal governments and corporations. They concluded that such arrangements often failed because all that was created was a shell company. No long-term human resource benefits to the band in the form of transfers of business skills or capacity occurred. Any benefits tended to be short term—the band might get a bonus check or finder's fee. Furthermore, aboriginal skills and perspectives were not transferred back to the corporate partner in order to create the potential for greater understanding and stronger long-term relations. In this light, Membertou has attempted to establish symbiotic relationships with their corporate partners, and bandleaders feel they have accomplished this, having gained confidence with experience. Key features are training and internship experiences for front-line and managerial staff, joint-venture structures, profit sharing, branding, and the opportunity for global reach. Working capital investments by Membertou in these (and other business) ventures from consolidated band revenues are seen by the band management as "shareholder loans."

Bandleaders feel that they have many of the basic partnerships needed in key areas for employment and growth. They will continue to consider new arrangements that fill additional needs, but they are only interested in major new partnerships if they provide diversification and new opportunities by being very different from existing relationships. After all, sophisticated and integrated partnerships are costly to establish and time-consuming to maintain, so Membertou is trying to be careful not to commit ahead of its growing management capacity levels.

Institution-Building and Community Governance

Only Education Services and the Gaming Commission have any distance from direct governance by the chief and council. In the case of Education Services, there is a strong relationship to Mi'kmaw Kina'matnewey, the tribal educational authority that covers ten of the Nova Scotia bands. The Gaming Commission, while it is wholly owned by the band and its manager reports directly to the CEO and Council, holds its own assets. For tax purposes, other band enterprises are either wholly owned or joint-ventured through its holding company, Membertou Development Corporation (MDC). At the end of the fiscal year, all operations are consolidated on the balance sheet and audited financial statements are published on the band's public web site (a move that has earned them criticism from some other chiefs, as published audited financial statements are not a hallmark of many Canadian aboriginal community governments).

Chief and council's management practices borrow from Bay Street, standard Canadian governance practice, and aboriginal values. Sometimes, the mix may appear to external observers to have internal contradictions. For example:

- Regular Council meetings are always held in camera rather than publicly, though band members and others may petition to appear before the Council.

- Band meetings are held only at the call of chief and council–approximately annually, but Chief Paul is thinking about more frequent public meetings.

- Major issues involve lengthy (in terms of lapsed time) consultation with smaller groups of band members, iteratively: first, with the Elders, then with other groups, including youth.

- The band publishes a weekly online newsletter with notices and messages from all administrative divisions, from the latest corporate division activities and encouragement to parents to attend parent-teacher meetings with tips on helping children with homework, to job postings and reports on hiring for seasonal jobs. Sections of the newsletter can be inputted directly by band members, for example, letters of concern about speeders or mild vandalism, cards of thanks, and birthday and get-well wishes.

- On most reserves, members with a problem line up directly outside the chief's office door (or home), but over time, Membertou's divisional managers have taken on more troubleshooting and problem-solving roles. Band members have been gently encouraged to go through channels first, and the chief and council have become "court of last appeal."

- Although the MDC was created for tax purposes, real governance of the band's enterprises is exercised by the chief and council, who also act as the board of directors for any economic activity. Firewalls between economic and political activity are practically nonexistent. This has also meant a learning curve for corporate partners, who often are unaware of how band governance works in Canada. Staff are encouraged by chief and council to provide information and explanations to band members.

Cultural Match and Skill-Building Through Leadership, Education, and Recruitment

Chief Paul has held his office for twenty years. He is widely respected both on and off the reserve, with a reputation as a trustworthy "man of the people." Unusual for his generation, he has always been a fluent Mi'kmaq speaker and grew up living, in turn, on all five Cape Breton reserves. Then, like other young Mi'kmaqs, he left the island to find work, spending five years in Boston where his views about the necessary integration of cultural tradition with hard work, education, and self-sufficiency were solidified. When chief Paul returned to Membertou after the idea-rich environment of Boston, he was shocked at how little had changed. His early years as chief were spent laying the groundwork for the more recent changes. In particular, among the Mi'kmaq chiefs, he has been a leader in promoting postsecondary education. When access and outreach programs were developed with the nearby University College of Cape Breton (UCCB),[19] tiny Membertou had five times the number of participating students as larger reserves such as the Eskasoni, the biggest aboriginal community east of Québec. Those early graduates, too, had to go away for work and experience. As the band has been able to recruit some of those educated young people, their "going away" experience has been an important factor. Those who did so gained skills and perspective on the emerging knowledge-based economy, and experienced a different culture of work and achievement than existed in mainstream industrial Cape Breton society.

Although the management team developed under Bernd Christmas' leadership is tight-knit, there is an inner circle of bright and energetic people whose skills are complementary. The remaining members of the management group (as distinguished from members of Band Council) are competent managers with a team ethic, differing from private-sector corporate counterparts by their zeal and passion for the ideological model. Personal integrity and credibility are expressed as high personal values, and this is regularly reinforced in the team-building process. One might think of this as a "Principled Technocrat" model of basic institutional capacity building.

Long-Term Strategic Action for Human Capital Development

The early commitment to advanced education (both university and skilled trades) allowed the band to reap measurable benefits in implementing current socioeconomic development success. That commitment continues. The stated goal of Education Services is to have twenty percent of band members complete post-secondary education. While the current total is four percent, students now in-course are more diversified in their program choices. In 2000–2001, eighty-three percent of Membertou postsecondary students were enrolled in arts programs but, by the following year, it had dropped to fifty-three percent. By 2002–2003, it was only thirty-eight percent. Importantly, nearly one-third of current students are enrolled in science-based programs, nearly all at UCCB, which pioneered an integrative science program in cooperation with Mi'kmaq educational leaders and Elders. Membertou's total represents a significant proportion of all aboriginal science students in Canada.[20]

To highlight the band's focus on continued human resource development, the division holds an annual community forum on education that includes youth and focuses on "what can we do better?" Past suggestions have resulted in increased focus on meaningful summer employment for young people, which develops long-term thinking skills, more scholarships, and an annual Career Day that involves Membertou's corporate partners. In addition, training programs associated with corporate partners require participants to work outside the community and off-island, as outside work and cultural experience are still seen as a critical part of the attitudinal change process. Focus is also placed on family intervention to promote homework skills and on better communication between parents and teachers.

A Lack of "Firewalls" Between Business and Band Governance

Separation of politics from business management is a key element of the Nation-Building Model; but, according to senior INAC officials, few true "firewalls" between business operations and political governance exist in Canadian First Nations. For purposes of this discussion, a "firewall" involves creation of a truly arm's-length institutional mechanism, governance of which is not directly impacted by a political authority (in this case, the Band Council). That is, the institution is separately incorporated, governed by its own board of directors (with most or all appointed for multiyear terms or elected by institutional membership), and has the capacity to raise funds independently and to manage the organization's affairs in a sound and accountable manner. At least two Membertou managers cited the location of their Corporate Division in Halifax as a "virtual firewall" created by geographical distance, and an important perceptual one for potential corporate partners. Potential partners look for a demonstrated record of transparency, accountability, and legitimacy as protection against arbitrary political actions by sovereign First Nations.

The issue has not presented huge problems for the Membertou to date (except, perhaps, for those families impacted by band competition with their individual businesses) because of Membertou's political stability (long-serving chief and council, little turnover), quality professional management, and the value-based symmetry between the two. However, the institutional vulnerability exists for the future. There may have been little interest by other band members in political life when their government had only debt and problems to share, but now that the band reasonably anticipates significant annual profits, other noses may sniff the political opportunities—not all of whom may be committed to the personal integrity and accountability that has characterized the present government and administration. Without firewalls between the band Council's legitimate political activities and its economic enterprises, there is always the real and perceived risk of political interference in business operations. This risk to investors and business partners normally is ameliorated through federal government financial assistance, often in the form of loan guarantees or other sureties. This practice, however, leads to cynicism among nonaboriginal businesses and taxpayers, and leaves the federal government in a powerful position regarding business and economic development choices by the band.

Another risk exists. The "financial firewall" issue has been raised recently in many First Nation communities where business failures have impacted a band's ability to maintain delivery of essential services funded by other levels of government. Although Membertou has some protection through incorporation of its holding company, if push comes to shove in legal terms (given that business and band decision makers are the same), they might have some difficulty shielding the band's main government operations from the consequences—either a recovery of funds by other levels of government (who would presume that program funds were diverted to either support or maintain business operations), or an inability to provide essential public services to band members.

More critically in the Membertou example, there is no immediate or near-term anticipation that the "no firewall" situation will or should be changed. In part, some managers say, this is because the community is so small and tightly knit: it is hard to have effective firewalls when everyone knows the chief and where he lives. More fundamentally, the dominant value between both chief and managers is that business and economic activities must be closely attuned to community values and readiness to proceed. In their view, this requires the political-development symmetry that now exists. In other words, the leadership sees a tradeoff between internal support and cultural match on the one hand, and external credibility through separation of political and economic activities on the other.

The band's dispute resolution processes with partners also has yet to be tested, although these are contractually embedded. The outcome of any future contractual challenges will be an important signal to potential business partners, as the predictable rule of law (or judicial review) in enforcement of contracts is a critical feature in a stable economy, putting limits on political and administrative discretion, and increasing the accountable autonomy of individuals and organizations. Contractual business partnerships are still a relatively new phenomenon for Membertou, but the reserve is on a track for "global reach" in their economic activities. When business activity is small and local, the number of relationships is also limited and governed, in part, by local convention and mores. When that economic activity grows in size and beyond local borders, Membertou is likely to find that it is judged by investors as to the predictability of contractual enforcement through law, much as is the case for international states whose economic fortunes are affected by the integrity with which laws are passed and enforced in their jurisdictions.

In addition, few partnership joint ventures are, as yet, located on reserve. With the construction of the Membertou Trade and Commerce Centre, this will change and may present new issues for band management. It remains to be seen whether long-term leases in a firewall-free environment will be sufficient to overcome a desire for embedded individual and corporate rights to property. History elsewhere would encourage skepticism. At least one scholar has argued that bands should be willing to temporarily forgo their sovereign immunity that protects tribal assets from litigation in order to convince investors and partners they are playing on a level field (Bernardi-Boyle 2002).[21]

Reserve Land and Band Rather than Individualized Property Rights

Band leadership is quite clear in its decision that property ownership on the reserve is not available to either outside companies or band members for commercial purposes. For instance, they say they are unlikely to issue any more Certificates of Possession.[22] Although specifics were hard to come by, best estimates suggested that almost all long-time business land properties and over ninety-five percent of housing land is band-owned, with no individual rights beyond those in lease arrangements. The band is willing to provide long-term commercial leases either to outside companies or band-member entrepreneurs. The community newsletter, for example, has several times encouraged would-be entrepreneurs to identify themselves to chief and council and work with advisers for assistance through the Community Economic Development Fund, with the proviso that the band collectively also benefits from their future success, usually through payment of leasing fees.

The argument for continued communal land ownership policies at Membertou has two extralegal roots. One is that the band has already lost too much land, so they are now trying to buy land and they refuse to sell or give it away. Others cite a cultural value of "sharing" as a fundamental principle that governs food, shelter, and possessions. Others must not be deprived because of the perceived personal greed of some individuals.

Commercially, three examples illustrate the band's allegiance to this point. Referenced earlier, the decision to become involved in gaming only proceeded after a second band referendum, the first having been defeated because members felt individuals would benefit from gaming franchises. The subsequent successful proposal assured all gaming would be owned and controlled by the band. The second example is the Membertou Market (gas bar/convenience/food retailing). This was the first and most visible economic development project once the band gained control of its deficit. However, this small reserve already had an extremely successful privately owned (by a band member) gas bar and convenience store that had, at times, employed thirty-five or more band members. When asked why Membertou Market was the band's first commercial foray in an already-occupied niche, the answer from managers was that people in the community felt one family was benefiting too much from the use of reserve land. The third example is the band's decision to pursue commercial fisheries activities collectively, even though a private fishery company, WABN Fishery, owned by a band member exists on the reserve.

The status of private land control by band members for housing seems less clear to managers. Practice varies across the country, but some reserves (e.g., Six Nations, Fort Alexander, Westbank, Kamloops, Whitecap)[23] have developed either an internal real estate market within the band, or provided conditional surrender and long-term leases, up to 100 years. Membertou began arranging twenty-five-year mortgages for members allocated housing on reserve in 1988 because housing program monies from INAC fell far short of demand for housing. When asked what happened to an individual's status with respect to their house once the mortgage was paid, replies were definitive but varied. Most believed that the mortgage payment was a form of rent—the individual family would simply cease paying this rent after the twenty-five years but no CP would be given. Some individual band members consulted during this study who were paying such mortgages felt "the house would be mine" at the end of the period.

The actual mortgage document signed by the occupants of a home confirms the view that "ownership" *of the house* lies at the end of the lease period, when the premises may be purchased for one dollar by exercising a written option within 365 days of making the last rent payment. The band then undertakes to issue to the tenant a CP. Whether this will eventually result in the development of an internal housing market at Membertou remains to be seen, but it at least presents that possibility and pragmatically, it recognizes that younger band members are likely to be influenced in the matter of potential home ownership on reserve by mainstream Canadian culture, which places a high value on home ownership.

As will be noted below, the limited recognition and acknowledgement of land and property rights is a central concern, along with development of arm's-length institutional mechanisms, if Membertou is to sustain its stability and growth either through next stages of development or future political leadership changes, however unlikely these may seem to be at the present time. Economists such as the Peruvian Hernando de Soto (2000) would probably argue that individuals, as well as corporations, will ultimately require the ability to leverage their own capital independently through transferable property rights—perhaps more so when a marginal jurisdiction lives within the framework of a culturally distinct (and property-based) mainstream regime. Certainly, the lack of ability to leverage personal and business capital assets will constrain individual and band experiments with entrepreneurialism and change. Individuals may improve their homes or business premises, establish their reputation and expertise, and improve property that others recognize as having a historical relationship with them or their families. However, without formal title to the land and, therefore, without the capacity to leverage their own assets, individual reserve citizens will be greatly dependent upon the largesse of Band Council in approving loans, grants, or guarantees for investment and working capital. If an individual falls out of favor politically with key powerful individuals in the band government, it will limit or preclude their ability to obtain leaseholds, capital, and business licenses. As in earlier times, if for different reasons, reserve citizens will then be forced to leave Membertou in order to pursue economic freedom, regardless of their cultural, linguistic, and blood ties to the community and its land.

Additionally, whatever value and goodwill may be built up in an on-reserve environment, without formal title, the individual or family has no way of establishing the value of what they have through transactions at a distance from the community. This inhibits, potentially, building relationships with suppliers, partners, and future buyers. It restricts all value created by the individual to an internal on-reserve market only, or to a larger market that is still "internal" to aboriginal communities only (within which some surrogate instruments may be developed for barter or exchange without transfer of formal title).[24]

A corporation can hold private property rights, of course, and historically, many have actually developed entire communities, owning the land and the houses. Some of these company towns have been quite successful as the corporate management has an incentive to maximize the value of the community's amenities in order to attract and hold a stable workforce (Benson 1986). But the corporation can alienate its property (indeed, many company towns have been sold to residents) and therefore use it as collateral in loans. The ability to transfer property rights is an important determinant of access to capital, and Native American communities asserting sovereignty generally cannot or will not consider transferability. As development evolves in such communities, they are likely to need mainstream financial markets to be willing to deal with them, and the restricted potential for using reserve and reservation lands as collateral may limit access to these markets.

THE CHALLENGES AHEAD

Membertou is undeniably a great success story today, and one that resulted from good long-term planning and skill, in addition to any timely luck. Strong and patient leadership, human capital development, and governance changes have all played a part in this story. Looking ahead, their story does point to some future challenges for this successful band. One looming challenge is attitude change and continued human capital development. Things are going well at the moment, but nearly all Membertou-related interviewees agreed that old community attitudes lurk just below the surface. There is still deep suspicion about the "corporate model" and a lingering notion among older band members that business development is a bad thing. Some Elders, although trusting the current leadership, feel change is coming too fast and may erode culture and loosen the traditional bearings that have sustained the community through hard times. Other band members still retain vestiges of "the government victimized us and, under the treaties, they owe us a living," or still harbor the belief that governments should provide jobs through grants and subsidies to enterprise. In this latter sentiment, there is reinforcement from persistent (if fading) similar views among many in Sydney and other industrial-area Cape Breton communities.

A corollary of this kind of short-term thinking shows up in a new human capital development issue. In the old days, people in Membertou did not get educated because they did not feel it would make a difference to their future. Then, with encouragement, band members found they could get good jobs "away" if they were well educated and highly qualified. Now the band has lots of jobs. At present, many are still comparatively low-paying in retail and service operations, but a family with several lower-income earners living in subsidized housing at the periphery of an urban area can live well. Educators and councilors are having a tougher time convincing young people that they should complete postsecondary training, when the lure of an immediate paycheck is stronger.

A final attitudinal problem could adversely affect the band as it seeks to extend its influence and success in the future. Membertou's chief and managers are committed to sharing their success with other Mi'kmaq bands. Reactions from other Mi'kmaq to that success are, however, mixed. Those cultural attitudes that value collective success over individual achievement mean that members (and governments) of other bands may applaud Membertou's skills and accomplishments, but bitterly resent their prosperity and the media attention it brings. Cape Breton's nonaboriginal communities are notorious for their intraregional jealousies, backbiting, and sabotage, which adversely affects the entire subregion. This pattern, exacerbated by Membertou's continuing success, could result in the same fate for Cape Breton

Mi'kmaq bands in their relationships to senior governments and corporations. Managing resentment could be a major forward challenge.

Finally, the issue of firewalls and the evolutionary strengthening of property rights (with their implication for capital leverage) will not go away. At the moment, human vice is addressing Membertou's immediate cash needs through gaming revenues. This may sustain growth for a long period as vice seems unlikely to become unfashionable. But the Membertou vision seeks diversification of enterprises, occupational opportunities, and cultural interaction through global economic participation. As long as its gaming operations are confined to their immediate geographic area, those revenues are likely to peak and level off within a few years. Will there be enough capital to continue their great leap forward? Perhaps, as the band is small, but prospects for more global dreams may be dimmed by these fiscal realities. A longer period of high growth is likely to require more capital, and that may require innovation and compromise on the property rights issue, as well as separation of political and business decision-making authorities.

Chief Paul is not overly worried. "Change takes a long time, and we're adaptable because we know who we are. If we need to organize ourselves differently in the future for better advantage, we can do that."

NOTES

1. The author wishes to thank the Mi'kmaq Research Ethics Commission for its approval of this research application, and Chief Terry Paul and CEO Bernd Christmas of the Membertou First Nation, who supported and encouraged this study's preparation, and provided access to documentation, without in any way interfering with the research process or conclusions. Thanks are also extended to many individuals in the federal government and the Cape Breton community who made themselves available for interviews and questions, not all of whom are directly quoted or acknowledged in the text of this chapter. The encouragement, support, guidance, and editorial wisdom of Dr. Brian Lee Crowley, President of the Atlantic Institute for Market Studies, made this study possible, and contributed greatly to any merit it may bring to the dialogue on these issues. Any errors and omissions are, of course, the sole responsibility of the author. An earlier version of this chapter was published in July 2004 by the Atlantic Institute for Market Studies at http://www.aims.ca.

2. This article represents a "snapshot" in time: interviewing, other research and substantive writing were completed during the period from April to October 2003, and some initiatives and partnerships have evolved or changed since then.

3. The community is named commemoratively for Grand Chief Membertou (1510–1611). It was legally created in 1959 as the Sydney Band. The name was later changed and three existing Indian Reserve lands were allocated to the band.

4. The Mi'kmaq are a First Nations people indigenous to northeastern New England, Canada's Maritimes, and the Gaspé Peninsula of Quebec. Membertou's on-reserve population grew 137 percent between 1980 and 2002, and continues to expand. In the same period, housing units have expanded from fifty-six to 218 on reserve (source: Membertou Band documents).

5. ISO 9000 certification is granted by accredited auditors of the International Organization for Standardization, whose secretariat is located in Geneva, Switzerland. The certification primarily is concerned with "quality management," meaning what the organization does to fulfill the customer's quality requirements and applicable regulatory requirements, while aiming to enhance customer satisfaction and achieve continual improvement of its performance in pursuit of these objectives. Established in 1987, the ISO 9000 certification process focuses on generic management system standards. Achieving ISO 9000 certification requires an organization to undergo an exhaustive internal process, under the guidance of an independent, external ISO auditor (e.g., a qualified major accounting or consulting firm), which then certifies (or not) that the organization's management system has been audited and conforms to the requirements specified in the standard.

6. Quoted from page 68 of *Indian Reserve No. 28, King's Road, Statement of Fact and List of Sources Consulted*, prepared by legal counsel for the Membertou First Nation as part of its current land claim lawsuit against the government of Canada.

7. Judgments were rendered on September 17 and November 17, 1999, in 26014 *Donald John Marshall, Jr. v. Her Majesty The Queen—and—The Attorney General for New Brunswick, the West Nova Fishermen's Coalition, the Native Council of Nova Scotia and the Union of New Brunswick Indians (N.S.)*. The case overturned, by a 5–2 decision, Marshall's 1996 conviction for catching and selling eels off-season. Marshall, Jr., is a resident of Membertou.

8. The name of the enterprise was changed during 2004 to The Membertou Market. Instead of the profits projected, the Market ran a deficit of $153,262 in FY2004. The formats of the band's financial statements have also changed so that only net revenues or expenditures are reported for some enterprises, including this one. Thus it is not known if the operating deficit occurred because revenues were less, or expenditure more, than expected. Net gaming revenues for FY2004, however, significantly exceeded budgetary targets by $2.5 million, totaling $5.58 million.

9. Unama'ki is the Mi'kmaq name for the Cape Breton division of the Mi'kmaq Nation.

10. See http://www.ksg.harvard.edu/hpaied/.

11. Cornell is Professor of Sociology and of Public Administration and Policy, and Director of the Udall Center for Studies in Public Policy at the University of Arizona. His list is drawn from a set of slides he prepared for distribution in

1999 by the Economic Development Administration, United States Department of Commerce.

12. Developed and discussed by Stephen Cornell and coauthor Joseph P. Kalt, Henry Ford Foundation Professor of International Political Economy at the John F. Kennedy School at Harvard University.

13. Jorgensen and Taylor's study employs a statistical analysis of enterprise survey data, utilizing multiple regression of dependent success variables, environmental, and policy variables.

14. Long-term research findings from the Harvard Project support the notion that leadership plays a role in successful development. See especially Cornell and Kalt (2000), Jorgensen (2000), and Jorgensen and Taylor (2000a).

15. For example, see DeLong, Bradford, and Shleifer (1993). More recently, Knack and Keefer (1995) and others have argued that the political institutions of limited government cause economic growth.

16. See also Lipset (1960), Djankov et al. (2003), and Alvarez, Cheibub, and Limongi (2000).

17. Other bands would have been encouraged to adopt many of the administrative and development practices of Membertou through elements of Bill C19, *The First Nations Governance Act*, tabled by the INAC Minister in June 2002, and Bill C-61, *The First Nations Fiscal and Statistical Management Act*, tabled by the Minister in August 2002. At the time of writing, however, these bills had been effectively killed as a result of protests by the principal Chiefs' organization, the Assembly of First Nations, and other groups who disagreed with provisions pertaining to elections, accounting and governance practices, and to policies of transparency, disclosure, and redress with more access to information by individual band members. Bands also would have had additional financial instruments to raise long-term private capital for infrastructure, and a First Nations Tax Commission would have been available to resolve problems arising from band taxation of nonmembers. A fuller discussion of the broader issues of governance taxation and these bills is contained in Richards (2003).

18. The *Cape Breton Post* reported on June 17, 2003 that Chief Paul had sent a letter to Ottawa on May 28 requesting monetary reimbursement for the community for loss of fishing due to contamination of the site. Chief Paul was quoted as saying: "All we're saying is that there is a legal obligation for the federal government to consult with us (about remediation) and to mitigate issues satisfactorily . . . the government has no choice because it has a legal obligation to deal with us" (Macdonald 2003).

19. Subsequent to the preparation of this chapter, UCCB's name has been officially changed to Cape Breton University.

20. This emphasis on education and its direct connection to economic growth is supported by a recent study of this same relationship in sixteen emerging economies by the United Nations Educational, Scientific and Cultural Organization (UNESCO) and the Organization for Economic Cooperation and Development (OECD). It concludes that, overall, investments in education during the

past two decades may have accounted for about half a percentage point in the annual growth rates in those countries studied. Its results also indicate: "high levels of upper-secondary and tertiary attainment are important for human capital to translate into steady growth." See UNESCO (2003) that looks at Argentina, Brazil, Chile, China, Egypt, India, Indonesia, Jamaica, Malaysia, Paraguay, Peru, the Philippines, Thailand, Tunisia, Uruguay, and Zimbabwe.

21. See also Haddock and Miller (this volume); Johnson (this volume); and Huffman and Miller (this volume).

22. Certificates of Possession (CPs) are one instrument available under the current Indian Act for distribution of a form of individual property rights within a communal environment. A CP provides the individual with undisturbed use of the land for personal or commercial purposes, as indicated in the documentation. The federal government's interpretation of the Indian Act on this speaks exclusively to "land," not to the asset that may be placed on the land such as a house. This is a contentious issue and has raised many complexities for matrimonial property rights on reserves. For example, an individual band member may have a house fully paid for from personal resources (through a bank mortgage or other means) on a plot of reserve land for which there is a CP, but the underlying title to the land is held in common for all band members.

23. Interviews with various present and former INAC officials, including Steven Joudrey, Regional Director-General for Nova Scotia; Dennis Wallace, former Assistant Deputy Minister (ADM) of INAC and, at time of interview, President of the Atlantic Canada Opportunities Agency); Gordon Shanks, INAC ADM of Economic Development and Special Initiatives at the time of the interview and now Senior ADM Regional Operations Support and Services; and Robert Frelich, Executive Assistant to the INAC Minister for Atlantic Canada.

24. For more discussion of de Soto's theories and their impact on other Atlantic Canadian communities, especially coastal communities, see Crowley (1995).

TEN

Indian Property Rights and American Federalism

JAMES L. HUFFMAN AND ROBERT J. MILLER

Two recent developments affecting economic prosperity in Indian country warrant thoughtful examination of the place of Indians in the American federal system. One is the rapid economic development that some tribes have experienced while others have remained little more than wards of the federal government. The other is the evolving and still uncertain sovereign status of the tribes and, in particular, the nature of their control over their land and other natural resources. Most tribes that have experienced rapid economic growth have relied primarily on gaming. In some cases, gaming profits have allowed tribes to diversify their economic base, but most tribes without gaming have been left to struggle with the economic realities of limited resources, isolation from markets and, perhaps most importantly, uncertainty about property rights and the reach of their sovereignty.

From a theoretical perspective, property rights are a form of sovereignty. As Morris R. Cohen observed in his 1927 article "Property and Sovereignty," "the essence of private property is always the right to exclude others" (p. 10). One need not embrace Cohen's conclusion that "dominion over things is also *imperium* over our fellow human beings," to acknowledge that private property recognizes in property owners the power to make resource allocation decisions. Depending on the scope and content of government regulation, these private decisions are the heart and soul of a free market. As we have witnessed over the course of the last century, the restriction or elimination of private property, which is to say the restriction or elimination of free markets, has devastating effects on economic prosperity and human welfare.

Putting aside the peculiar history of property rights and sovereignty in Indian country, there are all manner of good reasons thought to warrant restrictions on private property. Accepting that some of these reasons do justify restrictions on private property, it should nonetheless go without argument that a system of private property is essential to economic development and prosperity. Even without the widespread assaults on liberty and human dignity committed by eastern European and other dictatorships, the most well intentioned of centrally planned economies have proven disastrous in terms of economic prosperity and human welfare. To the extent that some socialist regimes of western Europe have provided well for their citizens, it is testimony to the persistence of the private economies of those states, not to the wisdom of the central planners. Without property rights, we can have no markets and, without markets, we are doomed to having too much of this and too little of that and finally a dispirited, unproductive, and impoverished population.

Although believers in natural rights will contend that property rights exist independently of, or at least prior to, the state, the reality is that the state has a huge impact on the assignment and enforcement of property rights. And in a federal state, the matter can be more complex than it is in a state with a single centralized level of government. In the American federal system, the common law of property passed to the state governments, and those governments have retained primary authority over private property. But the federal government has played a significant role, particularly in the West, where virtually all lands were once owned, and roughly half are still owned, by the federal government. As will be explained at some length below, the matter is further complicated in the case of Indian lands because of the trustee status of the federal government and the federal role in privatizing some of those lands in the past. Both the federal and state governments have imposed various regulations, which effectively restrict private property, as have innumerable local governments.

Most discussions of American federalism are rooted in the constitutional structure of vertical separation between the state and federal governments.

From a constitutional perspective, local governments are creatures of the states without independent constitutional significance. But from a practical perspective, it is useful to think of federalism (or at least of vertically divided government) as the complex of local, state, regional, and national governments. All of these governments can and do have impacts on private property rights, and most are themselves owners of property. Adding to the complexity, of course, are Indian governments that own property and regulate private property. The nature of Indian sovereignty—its scope and clarity—is part and parcel of the institutional structure within which Indian economic development occurs. For the purposes of this chapter, we adopt this broad conception of American federalism.

Although the states are the primary source of property law, property rights are defined and enforced by a combination of laws emanating from all levels of the federal system. This makes it challenging to have the clearly defined and freely transferable property rights necessary to the achievement of economic prosperity through a free market. Notwithstanding their status as sovereign entities, Indian tribes do not have full control of their economic destiny. They must work with every level of government in the federal system to create the legal infrastructure they require for economic success. Indeed, it is useful to think of tribes as an integral part of our federalist system. Like the states, the tribes are not fully sovereign, but like the states they have limited sovereignty, which impacts on many aspects of governance including definition and enforcement of property rights.

The building of sustainable and healthy Indian communities depends in significant part on the building of productive and sustainable economies, which in turn depends on having a legal infrastructure necessary to economic development and participation in the larger economies of the state, nation, and globe. Clearly defined and enforced private property, combined with a well conceived allocation of sovereign powers in the federal system, are the key ingredients of this legal infrastructure.

REGULATORY SYSTEMS IMPACTING INDIAN COUNTRY PROPERTY RIGHTS

Tribal, individual Indian, and non-Indian property rights holders encounter myriad layers of governmental regulatory authority in Indian country.[1]

Clearly, such property rights holders, including tribes themselves, experience the effects of this complicated and pervasive regulatory scheme. It is beyond question that the multiple levels of regulation from federal, tribal, and state and local entities complicates and burdens the exercise of property rights.

The primary property right that most people would identify with—landownership or real property—exists amid a complicated patchwork of regulatory schemes in Indian country. Most tribal governments, for example, own the majority of the land on their reservations. Tribes in the lower forty-eight states own about forty-five million acres of land. However, they own most of this land in the context of a trust relationship in which the United States exercises influence and control over many tribal and individual Indian assets. In this situation, the United States is the trustee for the tribe and owns the legal estate in the land. The tribe, as the beneficiary of this trust, owns the beneficial estate. Some tribes have purchased other lands on and off reservations and hold the fee-simple estate. Fee simple is the usual form of landownership and means the owners have complete control and ostensibly can do whatever they wish with their property as long as what they do does not interfere with the recognized rights that others possess. Owners in fee simple can sell to whomever they wish for whatever price they wish, can exclude others from their property, and have the right to the quiet and undisturbed enjoyment of their land.

Individual ownership of land in Indian country is also complicated. A member of Tribe A, for example, can own land on the reservation of Tribe A in fee simple. Indians who are members of other tribes might also own land on reservation A in fee simple. In addition, both types of Indians, called member and nonmember Indians, can own land on reservation A in trust status. Hence, they individually own the beneficial estate of the property, and the United States is their trustee and owns the legal estate. About eleven million acres of land in Indian country are owned by individual member and nonmember Indians in trust with the United States. Moreover, due to federal policies from 1887–1934, large numbers of non-Indians own land in fee simple on many reservations. On some reservations, in fact, the majority of the land is owned in fee simple by non-Indians. Obviously, these various types of landownership complicate real estate transactions and provide ample opportunities for mischief from governmental regulation of real property rights in Indian country.

In the following sections, we examine the interface between property right in Indian country and various levels of government, namely federal, tribal, state, and local.

Federal Government

The federal government has wide-ranging powers and responsibilities over Indian tribes, Indian citizens, and lands and assets within Indian country. Thus, federal laws and policies have an enormous impact on real and personal property rights in Indian country. Many commentators think this has negatively affected reservation property rights.

The United States has officially pursued many different economic policies toward tribes and Indians over the past 225 years. These policies have directly and often purposely interfered with the private property rights of tribes and individual Indians. At the very formation of the United States, the Constitution provided that "Congress shall have Power . . . To regulate Commerce . . . with the Indian Tribes." The first Congress quickly exercised this power and enacted the Trade & Intercourse Act, which is still in effect today, to prevent tribal and Indian lands from being sold without federal approval (25 U.S.C. s. 177). In addition, in many of the more than 390 treaties that the United States signed with tribes, the federal government included language giving the United States control of all commerce with the tribe. The federal government implemented this regulatory authority over trade with tribes, particularly in the years 1795–1822, by operating twenty-eight official trading posts across the Indian frontier. These trading posts not only gave the United States a direct means of trade with tribes, but also limited private access to tribal trade by requiring governmental licenses and bonds for private traders.

For almost one hundred years, from 1790 to 1887, the United States intentionally removed Indian country from the American economic marketplace (Miller 2001, pp. 808–10). Noted Indian law expert Vine Deloria, Jr. (1985, pp. 243–44) has stated that Congress became "a surrogate for Indian decision making in . . . economic relations with the settlers."[2] This occurred because almost all Indian treaties made the regulation of tribal trade "the sole and exclusive right" of the United States.[3] This did not necessarily benefit Indian people and their tribes economically. For example, reservation timber and minerals could not be harvested and tribal lands could not be leased during this time period. Furthermore, many treaties with tribes required that the tribe limit or curtail their previous trading relationships, or trade only with the United States government. For example, the Makah Tribe of northwestern Washington was required to give up trading with Canadian tribes and citizens and to give up its practice of holding slaves.[4] Many other tribes agreed in treaties to trade only with federally licensed American citizens.[5] Several tribes later realized that they were suffering from an absence of trade and successfully negotiated new treaties to address this problem.[6]

By 1887, the United States realized that it needed to open Indian lands and resources to the American market. Thus, Congress enacted the allotment policy in which reservations were taken from tribal and communal ownership and partitioned into small "allotments" deeded to individual Indians. These deeds contained twenty-five-year restrictions on alienation and state taxation. Most reservations were large enough that allotting the land to small tribal populations still left large amounts of "surplus lands" which the United States then sold to non-Indians, thus inviting these people to come live in Indian country. Congress further opened Indian country to the American marketplace by enacting laws from 1890 onward that allowed leasing of tribal lands to non-Indians, allowed timber and mineral harvesting, and granted easements for railroads, utilities, and state highways. These federal actions often severely limited tribal and individual Indian property rights.

Today, many reservations are a "checkerboard" pattern of tribally and US-owned trust lands, intermingled with a small amount of tribally owned fee lands, individually owned trust and fee lands held by member and non-member Indians, a fairly large amount of non-Indian-owned fee lands, and a small percentage of state and federally owned lands all mixed together. This mixture of landownership including multiple governmental owners invites conflicting and counterproductive land use planning and regulation, causes battles over jurisdiction, and makes it difficult and costly for property owners trying to comply with all the various regulatory regimes.

When discussing problems that arise from Indian and tribal trust lands, such as federal bureaucratic delays and possible obstacles to economic development, one must remember the 200-year history of federal/tribal interaction. It is entirely possible that without the federal trust responsibility and the federal trust ownership of tribal and Indian lands that much of the remaining tribal land base today would have been lost in the past. Hence, while many people criticize trust ownership, it has most likely been a valuable tool for maintaining the lands that tribes and Indians own today. Still, it is appropriate to discuss how to minimize the negative impacts that arise from federal trust ownership on the maximization of modern-day economic development and private property rights on reservations.

One of the problems arising from the trust status of tribal and Indian lands is that this fact gives the federal government a central role in the regulation of real property rights in Indian country. As a matter of federal law, the United States Department of the Interior must approve any sales, leases, and most developments of trust lands owned by a tribe, a tribal member, or a nonmember Indian (25 U.S.C. ss. 81, 177, 415). This gives the Interior Department and its Bureau of Indian Affairs (BIA) near veto power over land and other property rights and over a wide array of issues of tribal and Indian economic development. In the current era of federal Indian policy, generally referred to as self-determination, tribes can usually convince the BIA to approve tribal development plans. Until recently, however, the BIA was a very paternalistic agency with immense power over tribes, and the BIA often told tribal councils what they could and could not do with their lands. Also part of this not so distant past was the federal government's willingness to grant easements across reservations and to allow tribal and Indian property rights to be used for highways, utilities, and dam reservoirs that primarily benefited non-Indians off reservations.

The federal government is also required to comply with the National Environmental Policy Act and other federal environmental laws in approving almost all actions on trust lands. This added regulatory procedure for most types of development on trust land adds time, expense, and uncertainty to these transactions. For example, building individual housing on trust land with Department of Housing and Urban Development funds requires environmental reviews, and Secretarial approval for leases of restricted tribally or individually Indian-owned lands is conditioned on environmental considerations.[7] This burden is not placed on similar activities conducted by tribes, Indian people, or non-Indians for land not held in trust status.

A few tribal governments have taken advantage of federal delegations of authority in the environmental arena and have secured federal enforcement of tribal environmental standards that have impacted Indian and non-Indian property rights on and off reservations. The Northern Cheyenne Tribe of Montana, for example, received the approval of the Environmental

Protection Agency (EPA) under the Clean Air Act for a class one "pristine" standard for its reservation air shed in 1977. The US Ninth Circuit Court of Appeals upheld the EPA's action of approving the heightened standard even over arguments that it negatively impacted persons, mining companies, and a neighboring tribe located outside the Northern Cheyenne reservation. In addition, the Isleta Pueblo in New Mexico secured EPA approval for its heightened environmental standard under the Clean Water Act for the Rio Grande River and the EPA then required upriver activities off the reservation to comply with the tribe's heightened water quality standards. The Tenth Circuit Court of Appeals upheld the Isleta Pueblo/EPA standard even though it allegedly could cost the city of Albuquerque $250 million to comply. Finally, the Salish and Kootenai Tribes in Montana secured EPA approval of heightened water quality standards for their reservation, including the beautiful Flathead Lake, and the standards are being enforced by the EPA on-reservation against all Indian and non-Indian property rights holders.

Landowners in Indian country can also be subject to other federal laws that do not apply off reservation. Two such examples are the Archaeological Resources Protection Act (ARPA) (16 U.S.C. ss. 470aa–470mm), and the Native American Graves Protection and Repatriation Act (NAGPRA) (25 U.S.C. ss. 3001–13). ARPA applies only to federal and Indian trust lands and it protects archaeological resources and sites by requiring a federal permit before anyone disturbs or excavates such sites. NAGPRA protects human remains and cultural items that are embedded in federal and reservation lands, including land privately owned by Indians and non-Indians. These laws can significantly impact private property rights on reservations.

Like all property rights, tribal, Indian, and non-Indian real property rights in Indian country are subject to regulatory limitations under various federal laws that apply nationwide. But as the foregoing discussion indicates, tribal, Indian and non-Indian property rights in Indian country are also subject to federal regulations applicable only in Indian country.

In addition to having approval power over many economic activities on trust lands, the United States also approves and controls to greater and lesser extent other types of contracts and property rights by controlling interactions between tribes, Indians, and non-Indian entities. Again, this can lead to inefficiencies, delays, and lost business opportunities because the federal bureaucracy is large, cumbersome, and not business-oriented. In addition, although federal employees do not necessarily have business expertise or experience, they often find themselves passing judgment on tribal and Indian business decisions.

The Indian Gaming Regulatory Act, for example, requires federal approval by the chair of the National Indian Gaming Commission of management contracts with tribes and, surprisingly, even requires federal approval of tribal ordinances and regulations regarding gaming. Moreover, many tribes still have to have their contracts and fee arrangements with their outside attorneys approved by the United States. And, to this day, the federal government still possesses approval and licensing power over any person who wants to trade in Indian country. The federal government also has authority over tribal and individual Indian property rights in native arts and crafts and thus controls the ability of non-Indians to engage in commerce relating to these often-valuable properties.

Timber, mineral, and grazing land resources on trust lands are also heavily regulated under federal law. The federal government has extensive oversight of tribal and individual Indian trust properties regarding these assets and has the responsibility to ensure that contracts and activities concerning timber management are conducted on a sustained yield basis and that mineral resource decisions are in the best interests of tribes and individual Indians, and that grazing resource decisions preserve and improve the range while also returning the highest yield. Pursuant to these duties, the federal government must review and approve many tribal and individual Indian contracts regarding trust land development of mineral, timber, and grazing resources.

Treaty tribes and their members possess specifically defined property rights to various natural resources according to terms in their particular treaties. The Supreme Court has implicitly recognized in *Menominee v. United States* (1968) that treaty rights are property rights for which a tribe can maintain a suit for money damages against the United States under the Fifth Amendment if the rights are taken by the federal government.

An example of the federal government arguably taking tribal treaty rights exists in the Columbia River system. The United States may be liable for taking Indian treaty fishing rights through the construction of dams and the operation of the Columbia River system that allegedly has decimated salmon runs and led to a precipitous decline in the exercise of Indian treaty fishing rights. Northwest tribes have threatened a takings lawsuit to recover damages for the loss of this commercial property right. Although ostensibly well justified, the United States has also limited tribal treaty property rights by enacting several animal protection statutes such as the Endangered Species Act, the Bald & Golden Eagle Protection Act, and the Marine Mammal Protection Act.

Many treaties also promise tribes health care, education, and agricultural assistance. Yet a 2003 study by the United States Commission on Civil Rights demonstrates that federal spending on Indian and tribal health care, education, and other such programs has not even kept up with inflation over the past decades and seriously lags, in per-capita spending, behind the amount the United States spends on all American citizens in these categories (United States Commission on Civil Rights 2003). This has occurred even though the United States has specific treaty and fiduciary trust responsibilities toward tribes. It appears evident that the United States has not met its duties toward tribes in some of these areas and has caused an ongoing negative impact on tribal treaty property rights.

In 1908, the US Supreme Court determined that American treaties with Indian tribes impliedly reserved enough water for tribes to maintain a permanent existence on their reservations (see *Winters v. United States* [1908]). Thus, tribes, and the federal government as their trustee, own very valuable water rights in the arid west of the United States. In the modern day, the United States often helps tribes enforce and protect their water rights. However, from 1908, when the right was first recognized, until the early 1960s, the federal government did almost nothing to protect tribal treaty property rights in water (US National Water Commission 1973, pp. 474–75). In fact, the United States did just the opposite under the 1902 Reclamation Act because it worked diligently to create irrigation projects in the arid sixteen western states and actively promoted the policy of settling the west by building dams and water projects that favored non-Indians and encouraged migration that came at the expense of tribal water rights.[8] For example, dams were built without concern for tribal treaty rights in lucrative and traditional fisheries, and Indian issues were almost totally ignored when siting dam reservoirs because, although they benefited off-reservation farmers almost exclusively, they were often placed on reservations and seriously disrupted reservation life and displaced tribal populations.[9] Since the 1960s, however, the federal government has pursued water projects, negotiated settlement agreements that were enacted into federal law, and litigated court cases to try to salvage tribal water rights.

Tribal Governments

Today, over 565 American Indian governments are in operation and carry out sovereign functions. This might be surprising because historically the United States, and most certainly the non-Indians it invited to permanently settle on Indian reservations, never expected tribal governments to survive to the present day. In contrast, tribes are a thriving and growing presence in modern-day American life.

Moreover, it is no surprise that tribal governments are and always have been treated as sovereign governments by the United States. The history of European and American colonial practice was to deal with tribes diplomatically by treaties and as governments that controlled their populations and territories. The United States continued this practice and ultimately entered into more than 390 treaties with tribes to buy land, to arrange for trade, and to secure peace. Moreover, the US Constitution's Interstate Commerce Clause defines tribal governments as being among the governments over which Congress has the power to regulate commerce. The Supreme Court has described tribes at various times since the 1830s as "political states," "domestic dependent nations," and "distinct political communities" that have territorial boundaries, and "inherent sovereigns" with the power of self-government and territorial management. The anomalous situation of the sovereignty of Indian tribes, which finds tribes physically located within states and within the United States, and oftentimes with many non-Indians living on reservations, leads to intriguing and complex issues of jurisdiction and governmental control in Indian country. Tribes have wide-ranging, but not absolute, jurisdiction, police power, and regulatory authority in Indian country. In fact, the US Supreme Court has decided several cases in the past few decades that have limited tribal sovereignty and jurisdiction as to nontribal members operating within Indian country to a level far less than what state government A can exercise against non-state citizens when they are within state A. For example, tribes do not have criminal jurisdiction over non-Indians and are thus not able to completely control law and order issues in Indian country (*Oliphant v. Suquamish Indian Tribe* [1978]). In certain circumstances, tribes also lack legislative, zoning, and judicial authority over all persons who live or conduct activities within Indian country.[10] This leads to confusion about property rights and conduct in Indian country and which government can impact and control them. Notwithstanding the Supreme

Court's recent decisions on this subject, there are numerous circumstances in which tribes have regulatory and jurisdictional control and an effect on private property rights.

Tribal governments possess the same rights to control and use the lands they own in fee simple as does any landowner. Even on trust lands owned in conjunction with the United States, tribes are given fairly wide latitude by the federal bureaucracy consistent with the official federal policy of Indian self-determination to pursue their own objectives. Hence, tribes control their own real property rights to a great degree.

Tribes also have the inherent sovereignty to regulate the real property rights of tribal citizens, and to some extent the rights of nonmember Indians and non-Indians, who are located on reservations. The Indian Civil Rights Act requires that, in doing so, tribal governments must not deny the equal protection of their laws to anyone within their jurisdiction nor deprive any person of liberty or property without due process of law (25 U.S.C. s. 1302[8]). Thus, tribal members, nonmember Indians, and non-Indians should have the protection of well-defined principles of American law when it comes to tribes regulating or taking property rights.

A tribe's power to regulate all the property rights located on a reservation, however, is less far reaching than that enjoyed by state and federal governments within their territorial limits. The US Supreme Court has decided several cases in the past two decades that have significantly limited the reach of tribal regulatory, legislative, and even judicial jurisdiction within reservations. The court set out a rule in *Montana v. United States* (1981) that tribes do not have civil regulatory jurisdiction over non-Indians and their conduct if it occurs on non-Indian-owned fee land within a reservation.[11] The court created two exceptions when a tribe can regulate a non-Indian's conduct on non-Indian-owned fee lands: first, if the non-Indian has entered a consensual, commercial relationship with the tribe or its members; or, second, if the conduct of the non-Indian threatens or directly affects the economic security, political integrity, or the health or welfare of the tribe. If the non-Indian falls within either of the *Montana* exceptions, a tribe can regulate, tax, and/or zone their activities even on non-Indian-owned fee lands within a reservation. Tribes also have the authority to regulate almost all activities of tribal members on reservations. Thus, tribes can regulate, legislate, adjudicate, and have a significant effect on many real property rights in Indian country.[12]

In exercising their regulatory authority, many tribes have created land, grazing, forestry, and water departments that issue use permits and settle reservation disputes. Decisions by these tribal agencies can impact private property rights. Certain federal laws have also given tribes even more authority over reservation real property rights. In addition to the environmental statutes mentioned above, which allow tribes through the EPA to enforce their environmental standards against persons on or near reservations, tribal governments can also take over the National Historic Preservation Act (NHPA) functions for their reservations, a job that would otherwise be performed by state historic preservation officers. This way, tribes can increase their authority and role in dealing with reservation historic properties. Tribes also have a statutory right to actively participate in the NHPA process regarding their historical and cultural sites even when they are located outside Indian reservations. Thus, tribes can take an active role under this law and impact property rights on and off reservations.

Tribes have the authority to tax, zone, and regulate persons and businesses and their conduct on reservations under the requirements of the *Montana* test described above. Consequently, many Indian and non-Indian businesses and property rights holders on reservations can be affected by tribal regulation of their commercial and noncommercial activities. Federal courts in the past have allowed tribes to regulate non-Indian reservation-based activities in several different instances. Furthermore, tribes generally have the normal "police power" inherent in sovereign authority to extensively regulate tribal members. In 2003, for example, the Mohawk Tribe in New York suspended for one year a permit issued to a tribal member to sell cigarettes in her reservation store and fined her $1.1 million for violating the terms of her tribal permit (Newsday.com 2003).

Tribes do not have any specific authority over most private contracts entered into with tribal members or other persons just because they are signed in or are to be performed in Indian country. Of course, tribes control the negotiation and approval of all contracts signed with the tribe or tribal agencies. Tribes can impact private contractual rights, however, as their courts develop the principles of contract law that apply to litigation in tribal courts. This might affect reservation contractual rights in a different manner than analogous litigation in a state or federal court. Tribes can also impact private reservation contractual rights based upon the degree of protection tribal courts and bureaucratic systems give to economic and contractual rights.

Obviously, water is one of the most significant property rights, particularly for tribes located in the arid west. Tribes and tribal members possess very valuable treaty-derived water rights and have become very active in the past few decades in protecting and exercising those rights. Much of this activity has arisen because of a Supreme Court decision in 1963, which adopted a method to quantify the amount of water a tribe owns. Since then, significant protracted litigation and disputes have accompanied tribal claims to water.

For many decades, however, most tribes have had only "paper" water rights in the sense that they have not been able to turn their legal right to a certain amount of water into real "wet water" on their reservations. This problem stems from several sources. First, most tribes have not yet had their legal right to a defined amount of water determined by a court. Litigation involving tribes, states, and private individuals is ongoing in many state court systems and has already consumed decades and millions of dollars with no end in sight. Second, many tribes do not yet have the physical capacity to draw out the water they might be entitled to because they lack delivery systems for making water useable on reservation and/or they lack capital to build the necessary infrastructure. Finally, many tribes lack sufficient on-reservation economic activity to put all the water they own to beneficial use even if they could withdraw it.[13] Thus, such tribes watch their "paper water" right flow down the river to be used for free by other users. Tribes have, with varying success, tried to sell or lease this "paper water" so as to benefit in at least some way from the water they own.

Many tribes have pushed for more federal involvement and federal funding for projects to deliver "wet" water to reservations. Water rights stream adjudications have forced the federal, tribal, and state governments into settlement negotiations in attempts to avoid decades of litigation and acrimony. Often, the parties have been able to settle these difficult issues and Congress has enacted the resulting agreement into federal law and provided for federal funding to build projects that deliver water to reservations.[14] As in any negotiation, however, some tribes have given up valid claims to undetermined water rights to secure the guaranteed delivery of lesser amounts of water and to secure other economic rights such as the right to lease or sell water that they cannot yet utilize on their reservation.

Other tribes have also used their treaty-reserved water rights to get a seat at the table to help settle water issues for whole regions. In Oregon, for example, the Warm Springs Tribe was extensively involved for fifteen years with the federal, state, and local governments in negotiating an innovative settlement regarding water use for the Deschutes River Basin. The federal government cooperated by providing funding for expert studies to help the Tribe establish its water claims and Oregon enacted legislation to help advance this ground-breaking effort.[15] The Tribe was able to quantify and protect its consumptive uses and, in what is probably a first, the Tribe also secured nonconsumptive instream flow rights to protect its traditional fishery. This process was a proactive example of tribes protecting and exercising their water rights and of the Tribe and Oregon working together "to develop creative solutions while maintaining differing positions . . . " (Driver 1998, p. 3).

In other instances, tribal water boards and agencies regulate water use on their reservations, and some non-Indians have felt that their property rights have been put at risk. In the mid-1990s, for example, water issues at the Lummi reservation in Washington led to the involvement of Washington Senator Slade Gorton and threats against tribal interests. In 2001, the Coeur d'Alene Tribe gained the assistance of the United States to sue Idaho and ultimately proved it owned the southern third of Lake Coeur d'Alene. Now the tribe controls all uses of that part of the lake, including permitting authority for boat docks, piers, pilings, and navigational aids. In another example, in late 2002, the Montana Supreme Court decided that the state could not issue water permits for non-Indians on the Flathead reservation until the Salish and Kootenai tribal water rights were quantified. These few instances amply demonstrate that tribal water rights and actions can affect private property rights on reservations.

Tribes, as governments, have inherent sovereignty to control hunting and fishing rights on tribally owned and tribal member owned lands within their reservations. States have sometimes unsuccessfully attempted to exercise this same power on reservations.[16] Tribes have even been allowed to enforce their regulations off-reservation against member Indians in unique situations. Courts have also held that tribes and Indians possess reserved treaty property rights in some off-reservation privately owned lands. Under treaties between the United States and tribes in Oregon, Washington, and the Great Lakes area, for example, treaty tribes possess easement rights to take fish, shellfish, and other resources on public and private lands off reservations. This property right impacts non-Indian private and public property rights because the Indians cannot be excluded from these lands when they are exercising their treaty rights. In addition, the federal courts have held, in the context of salmon fishing and shellfish gathering in the Pacific Northwest, that the tribal members of the treaty tribes have a property right to take fifty percent of the harvestable catch.

State and Local Governments

The Supreme Court stated in 1832 that state laws could "have no force" in Indian territory. Congress and the Supreme Court, however, have retreated from that clear rule of law. Today, in fact, state and local governments strive to tax, regulate, and exercise power over tribes, Indians, and non-Indians in Indian country. Thus, states and tribes are locked in the classic governmental competition over power and money. Our concern here is only the extent that states and their local governments extend their authority into Indian country and impact private property rights.

States have been somewhat successful, with the approval of Congress and the federal courts, at reaching into Indian country and gaining authority over some of the real property rights of tribes, Indians, and non-Indians. The exercise of state authority in Indian country is necessarily a limitation on tribal sovereignty.[17] This result not only limits specific property rights, it causes great confusion over which government and how many governments have a say in the exercise of rights in Indian country. This creates a serious stumbling block for the development of rational and coordinated plans for developing, controlling, and utilizing property rights on reservations.

Federal law has long allowed states to condemn individual Indian trust lands on reservations for state public works, and to enter reservations to enforce various state health, educational, and sanitation interests. Furthermore, if a tribe purchases land in fee simple, to avoid the restrictive trust ownership relationship with the United States as trustee, the Supreme Court has held that states can then impose their annual ad valorem property taxes on those lands.

In 1989, the Supreme Court unsettled the entire subject of zoning jurisdiction in Indian country. In *Brendale v. Confederated Tribes and Bands of the Yakima Indian Nation*, the Court rendered a fractured decision that has left the lower federal courts with very little guidance regarding future cases. In three vastly different opinions, the Court explicated two different conclusions and allowed a Washington county to reach inside a reservation to zone a private development project proposed by a non-Indian who lived on the Yakima Indian reservation. The Court then also allowed the tribe to zone a different private development proposed by a nonmember Indian for property he owned on the reservation. The different results were based on very specific factual situations that may never be seen again. But the decision left completely up in the air the question of the power of tribal governments to zone lands within their reservations and also left uncertain the power of state agencies to reach into Indian country to control zoning. Since *Brendale*, federal courts have struggled to determine how much authority states and tribes have to zone lands in Indian country. Such uncertainty is detrimental to the profitable and expeditious exercise of property rights.

Tribes, Indians, non-Indians, and states have often engaged in protracted disputes regarding water. Nearly all of the western states are currently or have been embroiled in water rights issues with tribes. Congress did not help tribes in this situation when, in 1953, it enacted the McCarran Amendment, which waived federal sovereign immunity to allow federal water rights issues to be litigated in state courts. In 1980, the Supreme Court decided that "federal water rights" included tribal treaty water rights. Needless to say, tribes are distrustful of having their water rights litigated in state courts. Many state stream adjudications have dragged on for more than twenty years, cost millions of dollars to litigate, and resulted in restrictions on the federal water rights tribes and Indians possess. In Oregon, for example, the state has taken the position that it will not take any steps to protect unadjudicated water rights, including Indian rights, until they are quantified and identified by a court decision, no matter how much time might elapse before any such decision. State control over tribal water rights is unsettling for tribal and Indian property rights holders and the future of many economic activities in Indian country.

One might think that states would have no voice in the exercise of federal tribal treaty rights and would have no authority over fishing and hunting on reservations. The Supreme Court, however, has allowed states to exercise a small amount of control over some aspects of treaty rights and to sometimes reach into Indian country to regulate hunting and fishing. In 1968, the Supreme Court held that state regulations that served conservation purposes and that applied to all fishers without discrimination could be applied to Indians exercising treaty fishing rights on and off reservations.

In the 1981 *Montana* case discussed above, the Court allowed the state to regulate all hunting and fishing on the Big Horn River, which runs through the Crow reservation, because the Court held that the state owned the riverbed. The Court also allowed the state to control non-Indian hunting on non-Indian-owned fee-simple lands within the Crow reservation. In 2002, the State of Montana Supreme Court demonstrated its understanding of this principle when it held that the state could regulate hunting by a non-Indian on non-Indian-owned fee-simple lands within the Flathead Indian reservation (*Montana v. Shook* [2003]). Consequently, states are able in certain circumstances to reach into Indian country and control some aspects of hunting and fishing activities.

States have sometimes interfered with tribal and individual Indian economic property rights in Indian country. States get involved in these economic activities because they want to tax and regulate such activities. The collection of state cigarette taxes for sales on reservations has led to a long-running and acrimonious battle between some tribes and some states. The United States Supreme Court addressed this issue three times over an eighteen-year span and ordered tribes to collect and pay the state cigarette taxes for sales to non-Indians and nonmember Indians.

States have also actively tried to tax other economic activities on reservations. The US Ninth Circuit Court of Appeals even allowed Arizona to tax the proceeds on sporting and social events held at a tribally owned arena on reservation. In *Cotton Petroleum Corp. v. New Mexico* (1989), the US Supreme Court allowed New Mexico to tax companies for using state highways even after the companies had already paid the tribe royalties and taxes on their oil and gas extraction activities on reservation. These kinds of state actions can have a dramatic impact on reservation economic activity, cause uncertainty, increase the risks of unprofitability for businesses operating on reservations, and injure tribal and private reservation economic development property rights. To date, the Supreme Court has not been swayed by arguments citing this negative impact and thus it has not stemmed the tide of efforts by states to reach into Indian country to tax tribes, Indians, and non-Indians and to impact private and tribal property rights.

CONCLUSION

It is clear that both tribal and individual Indian property rights are defined by the direct and indirect impacts of multiple laws and regulations with resulting high levels of uncertainty about the definition and certainty of property rights. This uncertainty has the inevitable consequence of stifling and discouraging the private enterprise that is so critical to economic prosperity and improved human welfare on reservations and among Indian tribes.

As a constitutional matter, there is no doubt that the federal government has the power to preempt state and local governments to create a more predictable and consistent system of property rights. But there is virtually no prospect of this happening as a political matter, and it is not clear that centralization of property rights definition and enforcement is a good idea. The existing system of state government dominance of property law has worked reasonably well as a general matter. Because existing markets have developed within the context of the property rights regime, it makes little sense to depart from that regime if the objective is to encourage and facilitate economic development in Indian country. But this does not necessarily lead to the conclusion that states should have the same dominant position with respect to Indian property rights. An alternative that warrants consideration is the recognition in tribes of a sovereignty over property somewhat like that presently exercised by the states.

Because of the long history of federal intervention with resulting social welfare support systems, this is not an idea without risks to the development of a strong system of property rights. The tendency for some tribes may be the replication of the federal social welfare model to which they have become accustomed. But several tribes have demonstrated the possibilities for economic development offered by free enterprise. The tribes have strong incentives to create and maintain well-defined and secure property rights, incentives not necessarily shared by the states where vested economic interests might not perceive the benefits of stronger tribal economies.

If we conceive of tribal governments as comparable to state governments, at least for property rights purposes, we may discover that tribes will embrace a commitment to private property in the interest of improving the welfare of those who live and work in Indian country. It is a version of what the Europeans call subsidiarity, pursuant to which political power in a federal system is lodged where it can be most effectively exercised. If our objective is to improve the lives of those living in Indian country, more power should be lodged with those who stand to be the beneficiaries. Building and maintaining a strong system of property rights is not a bad place to start.

The studies discussed in the other chapters of this book support the argument for creativity and flexibility in the allocation of sovereign power over property rights in Indian country. Jacquelyn Scott explains how the Membertou have been "a part, but apart" in adaptation of mainstream business practices and in their relationship with their urban region. Tom Flanagan and Christopher Alcantara discuss how customary rights arose spontaneously on Canadian Indian reserves. In both these cases, an important advantage of local sovereignty in the definition of property rights is the ability to have the rights system reflect important cultural differences.

Bruce Benson describes the impact on the American bison of poorly defined property rights in game and land due to a lack of clearly defined sovereignty among American Indian tribes. There were no institutions in place to define property rights, with warfare the resulting approach to dispute resolution. Ann Carlos and Frank Lewis tell a similar story about the lack of effective property rights in beaver among the Cree. Bruce Johnsen argues that the salmon fishery fared better before the arrival of the cannery system when there were stream-based tribal rights in the fishery. The modern top-down solutions in the fishery case have failed to account for local culture with the result of "too much land and not enough fish" being allocated to the tribes. With respect to buffalo and salmon it is clear that both the property regime and the sovereign authority will be most effective if they reflect the particular resource and the local population. Benson does stress that property rights were established to agricultural land in the Great Plains river valleys, and that various inputs to and products of agriculture, the hunt, and warfare were owned and traded. Craig Galbraith, Carlos Rodriguez, and Curt Stiles also stress the long tradition of private ownership among Native Americans when the benefits associated with establishing property rights exceed the benefits. Galbraith, Rodriguez and Stiles do much more, however. They explain that the widely held beliefs that Native Americans held communal property rather than private property, that they were environmental stewards, and that they were not entrepreneurial seekers of wealth are all myths that stand in the way of creating better institutions for modern First Nations. Benson's analysis provides further evidence that such beliefs are myths.

Ron Johnson's suggestion that sovereignty among many tribes was really little more than a form of common property confirms that sovereignty exists on a continuum from individual sovereignty in the form of property rights to the plenary powers of a centralized state. Common property is a mechanism for community decision with regard to resource management on a local scale likely to be more responsive to both local interests and local knowledge. Johnson also points out that the regulatory regime for Indian gaming is divided among three sovereignties, resulting in uncertainties that are harmful to economic decision making. A clearer definition of both sovereignty and property rights, with attention paid to where decision-making power is best exercised, would surely benefit economic development in Indian Country.

Finally, Terry Anderson and Dominic Parker suggest that the very local sovereignty of fee-simple property ownership is more important to an agricultural economy than to one based on gaming where tribal ownership may be more effective for cultural reasons. But Anderson and Parker's evidence with respect to state versus tribal court jurisdiction illustrates that local is not always better. Their data suggest that the consistency and objectivity that come from state courts is more supportive of economic activity because it is more likely to provide for the rule of law and less likely to be influenced by one interest or another.

Taken together, the studies reported on in the foregoing chapters underscore that sovereignty could be exercised at many levels in a federal system—from the individual sovereignty of the private property owner to the national sovereignty of the federal government. There are many possibilities in between, including tribal sovereignty and both communal and individual property rights among Indians. Economic development among Indians and on Indian reservations will benefit from a flexible approach to sovereignty in the light of both resource and cultural considerations.

NOTES

1. We are not attempting to identify and address every Indian country property right that could possibly be impacted by state, federal, and tribal laws and regulations. Our goal is to highlight the issue on the main subjects and alert policy makers, tribes, states, and the federal government to the extensive governmental regulation currently present in Indian country.

"Indian country" is defined in federal law, 18 U.S.C. s. 1151, as (a) all lands within the limits of any Indian reservation under the jurisdiction of the United States, notwithstanding the issuance of any deed or rights-of-way, (b) all dependent Indian communities within the borders of the United States, and (c) all Indian allotments, the Indian titles to which have not been extinguished, including rights-of-way.

2. According to Deloria, Jr. (1985):

> Vesting the [federal] agents with a discretionary power to control the flow of trade, which should have been a function of the free market or of the real needs of the Indians, meant that Congress had become a surrogate for Indian decision making in the important area of cultural and economic relations with the settlers. Once this barrier had collapsed, future policy had to be shaped around the proposition that Indians could not or would not make the proper decisions respecting their best interests.

3. See, for example, Treaty with the Cherokee, July 2, 1791, Art. II, 7 Stat. 39; Treaty with the Wyandot, Etc., Aug. 3, 1795, Art. VIII, 7 Stat. 49; Treaty with the Creeks, June 29, 1796, Art. III & IV, 7 Stat. 56.

4. Treaty with the Makah, Jan. 31, 1855, art. XIII, 12 Stat. 939. See also the Treaty with the Sauk and Foxes, Nov. 3, 1804, art. XI, 7 Stat. 84 (the tribes were limited from subjecting traders or other persons "to any toll or extraction").

5. See, for example, Treaty with the Wyandot, Etc., Aug. 3, 1795, Art. VIII, 7 Stat. 49 (eleven tribes agreed to only admit into their territories, and to only trade with, American traders that had federal licenses); Treaty with the Creeks, June 29, 1796, Art. III & IV, 7 Stat. 56; Treaty with the Sauk and Foxes, Nov. 3, 1804, Art. 8 & 9, 7 Stat. 84 (the tribes agreed not to admit unlicensed traders into their territories); Treaty with the Chickasaw, Sept. 20, 1816, Art. 7, 7 Stat. 150 (the chiefs agreed they would not admit traders without federal licenses).

6. See, for example, Treaty with the Cherokee, Oct. 25, 1805, art. IV, 7 Stat. 93; Treaty with the Creeks, Nov. 14, 1805, art. II, 7 Stat. 96; Treaty with the Chippewa, Nov. 25, 1808, art. I, 7 Stat. 112.

7. See 25 U.S.C. ss. 415(a), 4115; *Davis v. Morton* (10th Cir. 1972).

8. U.S. National Water Commission (1973); *Nevada v. United States* (1983). See also The Reclamation Act, Act of June 17, 1902, Pub. L. No. 57–161, 32 Stat. 388 (1902); Amundson (1988, p. 77); McCool (1987, pp. 1, 254); Lawson (1982, pp. xiv and 10).

9. See generally Cohen (1986) regarding dams and tribal fishing rights in the Columbia River; McCool (1987, pp. 1, 254). See also Foreword by Vine Deloria, Jr. in Lawson (1982, p. xiv) stating that the "Pick-Sloan Plan [for 107 dams on the Missouri River] was, without doubt, the single most destructive act ever perpetrated on any tribe by the United States."

10. See *Nevada v. Hicks* (2001) where it was found the tribal court did not have civil jurisdiction over state game officers who allegedly violated a tribal member's civil rights by actions that occurred within a reservation and on tribal trust land. In *Atkinson Trading Company, Inc. v. Shirley* (2001), the tribe could not tax a

non-Indian owned business on non-Indian owned fee-simple land within the reservation. In *Strate v. A-1 Contractors* (1997), the tribal court did not have jurisdiction over an on-reservation car accident between non-Indians that occurred on a state highway. See also *Brendale v. Confederated Tribes & Bands of Yakima Indian Nation* (1989), which dealt with zoning power over non-Indians, and *Montana v. United States* (1981) where it was found the tribe lacked civil legislative jurisdiction over non-Indian activities on non-Indian owned fee-simple lands within the reservation.

11. The case concerns the rights of non-Indians vis-à-vis tribes and mostly discusses non-Indians. However, stray language in the case sometimes refers to non-members. That could be inferred to mean that tribes lack civil authority on a tribe's reservation over nonmember Indians. Some members of the Supreme Court apparently read *Montana* to mean exactly that. See *Atkinson Trading Company, Inc. v. Shirley* (2001) (Souter, J., concurring).

12. Even after the *Montana* case, federal courts used the "direct effect" test and allowed tribes to regulate non-Indians in certain circumstances. See *Cardin v. De La cruz* (9th Cir. 1982) regarding tribal building, health, and safety codes applied to non-Indian store on reservation; *Confederated Salish and Kootenai Tribes v. Namen* (9th Cir. 1982) regarding tribal regulation of rights to use riparian land on reservation; *Knight v. Shoshone & Arapaho Indian Tribes* (10th Cir. 1982) and *Governing Council of Pinoleville Indian Community v. Mendocino County* (1988) regarding zoning of fee lands on a reservation was within tribal inherent sovereignty; *Lummi Indian Tribe v. Hallauer* (1982) regarding tribal sewer hook-up requirements applied to non-Indians. In recent years, the Supreme Court has strengthened and expanded the *Montana* rule and it is difficult to say whether or not the above cases would be decided the same way today.

13. "So long as tribes lack capital, reserved rights will go unused and the tribes' senior priority dates will have little practical effect on non-Indian uses" (Getches 1988, p. 545).

14. See Getches, Wilkinson, and Williams (1998, pp. 844–54) discussing federal statutes that ratified federal, tribal, and state-negotiated settlements regarding tribal water rights and tribal selling and leasing of water rights.

15. See Oregon Revised Statutes ss. 539.300 onwards; Driver (1998).

16. See *New Mexico v. Mescalero Apache Tribe* (1983) where tribal and not state regulation was allowed over reservation elk hunting and fishing on tribally owned trust lands because state control would frustrate federal and tribal efforts and the federal financial investment in developing those activities for tribal economic development; Lacey Act, 16 U.S.C. ss. 3372(a)(1) and 3373(d)(1)(B) where it is unlawful "to import, export, transport, sell, receive, acquire or purchase" any fish or wildlife or plant in violation of a tribal law; *United States v. Big Eagle* (8th Cir. 1989) where a Crow Creek Indian could be federally prosecuted under the Lacey Act for fishing on Lower Brule Tribe's reservation in violation of Lower Brule fishing laws; 18 U.S.C. s. 1165 where it is a federal crime for anyone "without lawful authority or permission

[to go] upon any land that belongs to any Indian or Indian tribe... held by the United States... for the purpose of hunting, trapping, or fishing."

17. States perhaps feel this same way about the exercise of tribal sovereignty within a state's borders. Compare *Worcester v. Georgia* (1832, p. 561) where "The Cherokee nation, then is a distinct community... in which the laws of Georgia can have no force," with *Nevada v. Hicks* (2001, pp. 361–62) where "Ordinarily, it is now clear, 'an Indian reservation is considered part of the territory of the State'."

References

Acemoglu, Daron, Simon Johnson, and James Robinson. 2001. The Colonial Origins of Comparative Development: An Empirical Investigation. *American Economic Review* 91(5): 1369–1401.

Acemoglu, Daron, James Robinson, and Simon Johnson. 2004. Institutions as the Fundamental Cause of Long-Run Growth. *NBER Working Paper No. 10481.* Washington, DC: National Bureau of Economic Research.

Acheson, James. 1988. *The Lobster Gangs of Maine.* Hanover, NH: University Press of New England.

Alcantara, Christopher. 2002. Certificates of Possession: A Solution to the Aboriginal Housing Crisis on Canadian Indian Reserves. Master's Thesis. Calgary: University of Calgary.

———. 2003. Individual Property Rights on Canadian Indian Reserves: The Historical Emergence and Jurisprudence of Certificates of Possession. *Canadian Journal of Native Studies* 23(2): 391–424.

———. 2005. Certificates of Possession and First Nations Housing: A Case Study of the Six Nations Housing Program. *Canadian Journal of Law and Society* 20(2): 183–205.

———. 2006. Indian Women and the Division of Matrimonial Real Property on Canadian Indian Reserves. *Canadian Journal of Women and the Law.* Forthcoming.

Alchian, Armen, and William Allen. 1969. *Exchange and Production: Theory in Use.* Belmont, CA: Wadsworth.

Alchian, Armen, and Harold Demsetz. 1972. Production, Information Costs, and Economic Organization. *American Economic Review* 62(December): 777–92.

Alphonse, Philomena. 2002. Chair of the Land Investigation Committee of Cowichan Tribes. Interview by Christopher Alcantara, British Columbia, Canada, April 15.

Alvarez, Michael, Jose Antonio Cheibub, and Fernando Limongi. 2000. In Adam Przeworski, ed., *Political Institutions and Material Well-Being in the World, 1950–1990.* Cambridge: Cambridge University Press.

American Gaming Association. 2004a. *State of the States: The AGA Survey of Casino Entertainment*. Washington, DC. Online: http://www.americangaming.org/assets/files/uploads/2005_State_of_the_States.pdf. Cited: November 15, 2004.

———. 2004b. *State Information—Statistics*. Washington, DC. Online: http://www.americangaming.org/Industry/state/statistics.cfm. Cited: November 15, 2004.

Amundson, Ann. 1988. *Tribal Water Management Handbook*. Oakland, CA: American Indian Resources Institute.

Anderson, Robert. 2002. Economic Development and Aboriginal Canadians: A Case Study in Economic Development. *Journal of Developmental Entrepreneurship* 7(1): 45–65.

Anderson, Robert, and Robert Giberson. 2004. Aboriginal Entrepreneurship and Economic Development in Canada: Thoughts on Current Theory and Practice. In Curt Stiles and Craig Galbraith eds., *Ethnic Entrepreneurship: Structure and Practice*. Amsterdam: Elsevier Science, Ltd.

Anderson, Terry, ed. 1992. *Property Rights and Indian Economics*. Lanham, MD: Rowman and Littlefield Publishers.

———. 1995. *Sovereign Nations or Indian Reservations? An Economic History of American Indians*. San Francisco, CA: Pacific Research Institute for Public Policy.

———. 1996. Conservation—Native American Style. *PERC Policy Series* No. 6. Bozeman, MT: PERC.

———. 1997a. Conservation—Native American Style. *The Quarterly Review of Economics and Finance* 37(4): 769–85.

———. 1997b. Dances with Myths. *Reason* (February) 45–50.

Anderson, Terry, and P. J. Hill. 1975. The Evolution of Property Rights: A Study of the American West. *Journal of Law and Economics* 18(1): 163–79.

Anderson, Terry, and Dean Lueck. 1992. Land Tenure and Agricultural Productivity on Indian Reservations. *Journal of Law and Economics* 35(2): 427–54.

Anderson, Terry, and Fred McChesney. 1994. Raid or Trade: An Economic Model of Indian-White Relations. *Journal of Law and Economics* 37(1): 39–74.

———, eds. 2003. *Property rights, Cooperation, Conflict, and Law*. Princeton: Princeton University Press.

Anderson, Terry, and Dominic Parker. 2005. Sovereignty, Credible Commitments, and the Wealth of Indian Nations. PERC Working Paper. Bozeman, MT: PERC.

Anderson, Terry, and Randy Simmons, eds. 1993. *The Political Economy of Customs and Culture: Informal Solutions to the Commons Problem*. Lanham, MD: Rowman and Littlefield Publishers.

Archibald, Robert. 1978. Indian Labor at the California Missions: Slavery or Salvation? *Journal of San Diego History* 24(2): 7–15.

Ashcroft, Brian, and James Love. 1995. Employment Change and New Firm Formation in UK Counties, 1981–89. In M. Danson ed., *Small Firm Formation and Regional Economic Development*. London: Routledge.

Ayoungman, Matthew. 2002. Rental Coordinator. Interview by Christopher Alcantara, Siksika First Nation, Alberta, Canada, October 1.

Baden, John, Richard Stroup, and Walter Thurman. 1980. Good Intentions and Self-interest: Lessons from the American Indian. In John Baden ed., *Earth Day Reconsidered*. Washington, DC: The Heritage Foundation.

Bailey, Lynn. 1966. *Native American Slave Trade in the Southwest*. New York: Tower Publications.

Baldwin, Leland, and Robert Kelley. 1965. *The Stream of American History* (3rd ed.) New York: American Book Company.

Bamforth, Douglas. 1994. Indigenous People, Indigenous Violence: Precontact Warfare on the North American Great Plains. *Man* 29(March): 95–115.

Bangs, Jeremy. 2002. *Indian Deeds: Land in Plymouth Colony, 1620–1691*. Boston, MA: New England Historical Society.

Barfield, Chet. 2003a. The Money Tree. *The San Diego Union-Tribune*, May 4.

———. 2003b. Odds Slim Casinos Off Reservation Will be Built: Legal Experts Say Governor, Other Tribes will Block Them. *San Diego Union-Tribune*, June 8.

———. 2003c. Tribe to Pursue Tougher Environmental Review. *San Diego Union-Tribune*, July 24.

———. 2004. Rincon Beset by Suits, Infighting. *San Diego Union-Tribune*, July 8.

Barlett, Donald, and James Steele. 2002. Look Who's Cashing in at Indian Casinos. *Time*, December 16.

Barro, Robert. 1997. *Determinants of Economic Growth: A Cross-Country Empirical Study*. Cambridge, MA: MIT Press.

Barzel, Yoram. 1989. *Economic Analysis of Property Rights*. Cambridge: Cambridge University Press.

———. 1992. Confiscation by the Ruler. *Journal of Law and Economics* 35(1): 1–13.

———. 1997. *Economic Analysis of Property Rights* (2nd ed.) Cambridge: Cambridge University Press.

Barzel, Yoram, Michel Habib, and D. Bruce Johnsen. 2006. Prevention is Better than Cure: Precluding Information Acquisition in IPOs. *Journal of Business* 79(6): Forthcoming.

Bates, Timothy. 1997. Financing Small Business Creation: The Case of Chinese and Korean Immigrant Entrepreneurs. *Journal of Business Venturing* 21(2): 109–124.

Belluck, Pam. 2003. Tribe Loses Suit on Tax-Free Tobacco. *New York Times*, National Section, December 30. Online: http://www.nytimes.com/2003/12/30/national/30TOBA.html?th. Cited: November 15, 2004.

Benedict, Jeff. 2000. *Without Reservation: The Making of America's Most Powerful Indian Tribe and Foxwoods, the World's Largest Casino*. New York: HarperCollins.

Benson, Bruce. 1986. Boom Towns in the West: Is Profit the Culprit? *Review of Regional Economics and Business* 11(1): 27–38.

———. 1992. Customary Indian Law: Two Case Studies. In Terry Anderson ed., *Property Rights and Indian Economies*. Lanham, MD: Rowman and Littlefield Publishers.

———. 1999. To Arbitrate or to Litigate: That is the Question. *European Journal of Law and Economics* 8(2): 91–151.

———. 2000. Arbitration. In Boudewijn Bouckaert and Gerrit De Geest eds., *Encyclopedia of Law and Economics*, vol. 5, 159–193. Cheltenham, UK: Edward Elgar. Online: http://encycl.findlaw.com/7500book.pdf. Cited: November 15, 2004.

———. 2005. Buffalo Wars: An Economic Analysis of Inter-Tribal Relations on the Great Plains. Working Paper. Florida State University, Tallahassee, Florida, December.

Berkes, Fikret. 1986. Common Property Resources and Hunting Territories. *Anthropologica*, New Series 28: 145–62.

Bernardi-Boyle, Dao Lee. 2002. State Corporations for Indian Reservations. *American Indian Law Review* 26(1): 41–65.

Bethell, Tom. 1998. *The Noblest Triumph: Property and Prosperity through the Ages*. New York: St. Martin's Press.

Binkley, Christina, Jon Hisenrath, and Charles Forelle. 2003. States Confronting Budget Deficits Make Long-shot Bets on Gambling. *Wall Street Journal*, March 14.

Binnema, Theodore. 2001. *Common and Contested Ground: A Human and Environmental History of the Northwest Plains*. Norman: University of Oklahoma Press.

Bishop, Charles. 1981. Northeastern Indian Concepts of Conservation and the Fur Trade: A Critique of Calvin Martin's Thesis. In Shepard Krech III ed., *Indians, Animals, and the Fur Trade: A Critique of Keepers of the Game*. Athens, GA: University of Georgia Press.

———. 1986. Territoriality among the Northeastern Algonquians. *Anthropologica*, New Series 28: 37–63.

Bishop, John. 1997. Locke's Theory of Original Appropriation and the Right of Settlement in Iroquois Territory. *Canadian Journal of Philosophy* 27(3): 311–38.

———. 1999. The Lockean Basis of Iroquoian Land Ownership. *Journal of Aboriginal Economic Development* 1(1): 35–43.

Black, Jane, David De Meza, and David Jeffreys. 1996. House Prices, the Supply of Collateral and the Enterprise Economy. *Economic Journal* 106: 60–75.

Blackwell, Sharon. 2001. Deputy Commissioner of Indian Affairs, Bureau of Indian Affairs, Department of the Interior. Statement before the Senate Committee on Indian Affairs. Oversight Hearing on the Indian Gaming Regulatory Act, Washington, DC, July 25.

Boas, Franz. 1966. *Kwakiutl Ethnography*. Chicago: University of Chicago Press.

Böckstiegal, K.-H. 1984. *Arbitration and State Enterprises: A Survey of the National and International State of Law and Practice*. Deventer, Netherlands: Kluwer.

Bolton, Herbert. 1917. The Mission as a Frontier Institution in the Spanish American Colonies. *American Historical Review* 23: 42–61.

Bourie, Steve. 2003. *American Casino Guide—2003 Edition*. Dania, FL: Casino Vacations.

Boyd, Robert. 1999. *The Coming of the Spirit of Pestilence: Introduced Infectious Diseases and Population Decline among Northwest Coast Indians, 1774–1874*. Seattle: University of Washington Press.

Brasser, Ted. 1974. *Riding on the Frontier's Crest: Mahican Indian Culture and Culture Changes*, Paper 13. Ottawa: National Museum of Canada.

Brightman, Robert. 1987. Conservation and Resource Depletion: The Case of the Boreal Forest Algonquians. In Bonnie McCay and James Acheson eds, *The Question of the Commons: The Culture and Ecology of Communal Resources*. Tucson: University of Arizona Press.

British Columbia Treaty Commission. 2004. *Negotiation Update*. Vancouver, BC, Canada. Online: http://www.bctreaty.net/files_3/updates.html. Cited: November 15, 2004.

Brosnan, Dolores. 1996. Indian Policy, Indian Gaming, and the Future of Tribal Economic Development. *American Review of Public Administration* 26(2): 213–30.

Brown, Dee. 1970. *Bury My Heart at Wounded Knee: An Indian History of the American West*. New York: Hold, Rinehart and Winston.

Brubaker, Elizabeth. 1997. Beyond Quotas: Private Property Solutions to Overfishing. In Laura Jones and Michael Walker eds., *Fish or Cut Bait: The Case for Individual Transferable Quotas in the Salmon Fishery of British Columbia*. Vancouver, BC: The Fraser Institute.

Buchanan, James, and Yong J. Yoon. 2000. Symmetric Tragedies: Commons and Anticommons. *Journal of Law & Economics* 43: 1–13.

Burke, Andrew, Felix FitzRoy, and Michael Nolan. 2000. When Less is More: Distinguishing Between Entrepreneurial Choice and Performance. *Oxford Bulletin of Economics and Statistics* 62(5): 565–87.

Butler, B. Robert. 1978. Bison Hunting in the Desert West. *Plains Anthropologist* 23: 106–12.

California Common Cause. 2003. Press Release, February 27, 2003. Online: http://www.commoncause.org/states/california/press-rel/feb27-03. Cited: November 15, 2004.

California Gambling Control Commission. 1999. *Model Tribal-State Compact*. Sacramento, CA. Online: http://www.cgcc.ca.gov/enabling/tsc.pdf. Cited: November 15, 2004.

———. 2003. Bulletin 1 (February 2). Sacramento, CA. Online: http://www.cgcc.ca.gov/bulletin/BulletinFeb03.pdf#search='california%20gambling%20control%20commission%20bulletin'. Cited: November 15, 2004.

California Secretary of State. 1998. *Voter Guide: Proposition 5—Analysis by the Legislative Analyst*. Sacramento, CA. Online: http://vote98.ss.ca.gov/ VoterGuide/Propositions/5analysis.htm. Cited: November 15, 2004.

Calloway, Colin. 1996. *Our Hearts Fell to the Ground: Plains Indian Views of How the West Was Lost*. Boston, MA: Bedford Books of St. Martin's Press.

Canadian Broadcasting Corporation. 2005. *Rent Arrears Prompt First Nation to Take Own Members to Court*. Online: http://www.north.cbc.ca. Cited July 13, 2005.

Canadian Geographic Exploration and Discovery. 2005. *Cartographer's Table*. January/February. Online: http://www.canadiangeographic.ca/magazine/jf05/ indepth/maps.asp. Cited: July 31, 2005.

Carlos, Ann, and Frank Lewis. 1993. Indians, the Beaver and the Bay: The Economics of Depletion in the Lands of the Hudson's Bay Company 1700–1763. *Journal of Economic History* 53: 465–94.

———. 1999a. Property Rights, Competition and Depletion in the Eighteenth-Century Canadian Fur Trade: The Role of the European Market. *Canadian Journal of Economics* 32: 705–28.

———. 1999b. Property Rights and Competition in the Depletion of the Beaver: Native Americans and the Hudson's Bay Company. In Linda Barrington ed., *The Other Side of the Frontier: Economic Explorations in Native American History*. 131–49. New York: Westview Press.

———. 2001. Trade, Consumption and the Native Economy: Lessons from York Factory, Hudson Bay. *The Journal of Economic History* 61: 1037–64.

———. 2002. Marketing in the Land of Hudson Bay: Indian Consumers and the Hudson's Bay Company, 1670–1770. *Enterprise and Society* 3: 285–317.

———. 2004. Survival through Generosity: Property Rights and Hunting Practices of Native Americans in the Sub-Arctic Region. In Stanley Engerman and Jacob Metzer eds., *Land Rights, Ethno-Nationality, and Sovereignty in History*. 319–46. New York: Routledge.

Carlson, Leonard. 1992. Learning to Farm: Indian Land Tenure and Farming Before the Dawes Act. In Terry Anderson ed., *Property Rights and Indian Economics*. Lanham, MD: Rowman and Littlefield Publishers.

Carrico, Richard. 1986. Before the Strangers: American Indians in San Diego at the Dawn of Contact. In *The Impact of European Exploration and Settlement in Local Native Americans*, 5–12. San Diego, CA: Cabrillo Historical Association.

Center for Responsive Politics. 2002. *Casinos/Gambling: Long-Term Contribution Trends*. Washington, DC. Online: http://opensecrets.org/industries/indus.asp? Ind=N07. Cited: November 15, 2004.

Chandler, Alfred. 1945. *Land Title Origins*. New York: Robert Schalkenback Foundation.

Cheung, Steven. 1969. *A Theory of Share Tenancy*. Chicago: University of Chicago Press.

———. 1970. The Structure of a Contract and the Theory of a Non-Exclusive Resource. *Journal of Law and Economics* 13(1): 49–70.

Christian Capital Advisors LLC. 2004. *The 2003 Gross Annual Wager-Revenue By Industry, Dollar and Percentage Changes from 2002*. Online: http://www.cca-i.com/Primary%20Navigation/Online%20Data%20Store/Free%20Research/2003%20Revenue%20by%20Industry.pdf. Cited: November 15, 2004.

Christmas, Bernd. 2003. Membertou CEO. Interview by Jacqueline Thayer Scott, April 14.

Churchill, Ward. 1996. *From A Native Son: Selected Essays on Indigenism, 1985–1995*. Boston, MA: South End Press.

————. 2003. *Acts of Rebellion: The Ward Churchill Reader*. New York: Routledge.

Clague, Christopher, Philip Keefer, Stephen Knack, and Mancur Olson. 1997. Democracy, Autocracy and the Institutions Supportive of Economic Growth. In Christopher Clague ed., *Institutions and Economic Development: Growth and Governance in Less-Developed and Post-Socialist Countries*, 91–119. Baltimore, MD: John Hopkins University Press.

Coase, Ronald. 1937. The Nature of the Firm. *Economica* 4(16): 386–405.

Codere, Helen. 1950. Fighting with Property: A Study of Kwakiutl Potlatching and Warfare, 1792–1930. *American Ethnological Society Monographs* 18.

Cohen, Fay. 1986. *Treaties on Trial: The Continuing Controversy Over Northwest Indian Fishing Rights*. Seattle: University of Washington Press.

Cohen, Morris. 1927. Property and Sovereignty. *Cornell Law Quarterly* 13(1): 8–30.

Cole, Douglas, and Ira Chaikin. 1990. *Iron Hand Upon the People: The Law Against the Potlatch on the Northwest Coast*. Seattle: University of Washington Press.

Collings, Peter. 1997. The Cultural Context of Wildlife Management on the Canadian North. In Eric Alden Smith and Joan McCarter eds., *Contested Arctic: Indigenous Peoples, Industrial States, and the Circumpolar Environment*, 13–40. Seattle: University of Washington Press.

Coplin, William, Michael O'Leary, and Tom Sealy. 1996. *A Business Guide to Political Risk for International Decisions*. Syracuse, NY: Political Risk Services.

Copper, John. 1949. Indian Land Tenure Systems. In *Indians of the United States*. Cuzco, Peru: Policy Board of the National Indian Institute.

Cordeiro, Eduardo. 1989. The Economics of Bingo: Factors Influencing the Success of Bingo Operations on American Indian Reservations. Harvard Project on American Indian Economic Development, John F. Kennedy School of Government, PRS89-11, March. Cambridge, MA.

Cornell, Stephen. 1999. *Keys to Nation-Building in Indian Country*. Udall Center for Studies in Public Policy, University of Arizona. Online: http://12.39.209.165/ImageCache/EDAPublic/documents/pdfdocs/keystonatbuild_2epdf/v1/keystonatbuild.pdf. Cited: October 31, 2003.

Cornell, Stephen, and Joseph Kalt, eds. 1992. *What Can Tribes Do? Strategies and Institutions in American Indian Economic Development*. Los Angeles, CA: UCLA American Indian Studies Center.

————. 1998. Sovereignty and Nation-Building: The Development Challenge in Indian Country Today. *American Indian Culture and Research Journal* 22(3): 187–214.

————. 2000. Where's the Glue? Institutional and Cultural Foundations of American Indian Economic Development. *Journal of Socio-Economics* 29(5): 443–70.

Cox, Ross. 1832. *The Columbia River*, 2 vols. London: J & J Harper.

Cronon, William. 1983. *Changes in the Land: Indians, Colonists, and the Ecology of New England*. New York: Hill & Wang.

Cross Child, Calvin. 2002. Technical Advisor to Blood Tribe. Interview by Christopher Alcantara, Alberta, Canada, October 16.

Crow Shoe, Darrel. 2002. Housing Manager at Piikani First Nation. Interview by Christopher Alcantara, Alberta, Canada, October 16.

————. 2003. Housing Manager at Piikani First Nation. Telephone Interview by Christopher Alcantara, Alberta, Canada, January 16.

Crowley, Brian Lee. 1995. Property, Culture and Aboriginal Self-Government. In Helmar Drost, Brian Lee Crowley, and Richard Schwindt eds., *Market Solutions for Native Poverty: Social Policy for the Third Solitude*. Toronto: C.D. Howe Institute.

Cummins, Bryan. 2003. *Aboriginal Policing: A Canadian Perspective*. Toronto: Prentice-Hall.

Day Chief, Jr., Winston. 2002. Director of Housing at Blood Tribe. Interview by Christopher Alcantara, Alberta, Canada, October 16.

De Alessi, Louis. 1980. The Economics of Property rights: A Review of the Evidence. *Research in Law and Economics* 2: 1–47.

De Soto, Hernando. 1989. *The Other Path*. New York: Basic Books.

————. 2000. *The Mystery of Capital: Why Capitalism Triumphs in the West and Fails Everywhere Else*. New York: Basic Books.

De Vries, Jan. 1993. Between Purchasing Power and the World of Goods: Understanding the Household Economy in Early Modern Europe. In John Brewer and Roy Porter eds., *Consumption and the World of Goods*. London: Routledge, 85–132.

Debo, Angie. 1970. *A History of the Indians of the United States*. Norman: University of Oklahoma Press.

DeLong, J. Bradford, and Andrei Shleifer. 1993. Princes and Merchants: City Growth Before the Industrial Revolution. *Journal of Law and Economics* 36(2): 671–702.

Deloria, Vine, Jr. 1970. *We Talk, You Listen: New Tribes, New Turf*. New York: Delta.

————., ed. 1985. *The Evolution of Federal Indian Policy Making, in American Indian Policy in the Twentieth Century*. Norman: University of Oklahoma Press.

————. 1988. *Custer Died for Your Sins: An Indian Manifesto*. Norman: University of Oklahoma Press.

————. 1995. *Red Earth, White Lies: Native Americans and the Myth of Scientific Fact*. New York: Scribner.

————. 2004. Native Wisdom: A New Respect for Old Ways. *National Museum of the American Indian* (Fall): 30–37.

Demsetz, Harold. 1967. Toward a Theory of Property Rights. *American Economic Review* 57(2): 347–59.

Densmore, Frances. 1939. *Nootka and Quileute Music*. Washington, DC: Bureau of American Ethnology, Bulletin 124.

Dickson-Gilmore, Jane. 2005. *'Will the Circle Be Unbroken?' Aboriginal Communities, Restorative Justice, and the Challenges of Conflict and Change*. Toronto: University of Toronto Press.

Djankov, Simeon, Edward Glaeser, Rafael La Porta, Florencio Lopez De Silanes, and Andrei Shleifer. 2003. The New Comparative Economics. *Journal of Comparative Economics* 31(4): 595–619.

Donald, Leland. 1997. *Aboriginal Slavery on the Northwest Coast of North America*. Berkeley: University of California Press.

Donald, Leland, and Donald Mitchell. 1975. Some Correlates of Local Group Rank Among the Southern Kwakiutl. *Ethnology* 14: 325–46.

Downs, James. 1966. *The Two Worlds of the Washo: An Indian Tribe of California and Nevada*. New York: Holt, Rinehard and Winston.

Driver, Susan. 1988. Confederated Tribes of the Warm Springs Reservation Reach Historic Water Settlement Agreement. *Big River News* 4(2): 1, 3.

Drucker, Philip. 1955. *Indians of the Northwest Coast*. New York: Published for the American Museum of Natural History [by] McGraw-Hill.

————. 1965. *Cultures of the North Pacific Coast*. Scranton: Chandler Publishing Company.

Drucker, Philip, and Robert Heizer. 1967. *To Make My Name Good*. Berkeley: University of California Press.

Eadington, William. 1999. The Economics of Casino Gambling. *Journal of Economic Perspectives* 13(3): 173–92.

Eggertsson, Thráinn. 1990. *Economic Behavior and Institutions*. Cambridge: Cambridge University Press.

————. 2003. Open Access versus Common Property. In Terry Anderson and Fred McChesney eds., *Property Rights: Cooperation, Conflict, and Law*, 73–89. Princeton: Princeton University Press.

Egleston, Melville. 1886. *The Land System of the New England Colonies*, 4th ser., vols. 11–12. Baltimore: Johns Hopkins University Studies in Historical and Political Science.

Eisler, Kim Isaac. 2001. *Revenge of the Pequots*. New York: Simon and Schuster.

Ellickson, Robert. 1993. Property in Land. *Yale Law Journal* 102: 1315–1400.

Evans, David. and Linda Leighton. 1989. Some Empirical Aspects of Entrepreneurship. *American Economic Review* 79(3): 519–35.

Evans, William, and Julie Topoleski. 2002. The Social and Economic Impact of Native American Casinos. *NBER Working Paper No. 9198*. Cambridge, MA: National Bureau of Economic Research.

Ewers, John. 1968. *Indian Life on the Upper Missouri*. Norman: University of Oklahoma Press.

———. 1969. *The Horse in Blackfoot Indian Culture*. Washington, DC: Smithsonian Institution Press.

———. 1992. Introduction. In Frank R. Secoy's reprint of *Changing Military Patterns of the Great Plains Indians (Seventeenth Century through Early 19th Century)*. Lincoln: University of Nebraska Press.

———. 1997. *Plains Indian History and Culture: Essays on Continuity and Change*. Norman: University of Oklahoma Press.

Feeny, David, Fikret Berkes, Bonnie McCay, and James Acheson. 1990. The Tragedy of the Commons: Twenty-Two Years Later. *Human Ecology* 18: 1–19.

Ferguson, Brian. 1979. Ecology and Political Organization on the Northwest Coast of America. In Elisabeth Tooker and Morton Fried eds., *The Development of Political Organizations in Native North America*. Washington, DC: *Proceedings of the American Ethnological Society*.

Flanagan, Tom. 2000. *First Nations? Second Thoughts*. Montreal: McGill-Queen's University Press.

Flanagan, Tom, and Christopher Alcantara. 2004. Individual Property Rights on Canadian Indian Reserves. *Queen's Law Journal* 29: 489–532.

———. 2005. Individual Property Rights on Canadian Indian Reserves: A Review of the Jurisprudence. *Alberta Law Review* 42(4): 1019–46.

Flores, Dan. 1991. Bison Ecology and Bison Diplomacy: The Southern Plains from 1800 to 1850. *Journal of American History* 78(September): 465–85.

Fogel, Robert. 1964. *Railroads and American Economic Growth: Essays in Econometric History*. Baltimore: Johns Hopkins Press.

Foreman, Grant. 1934. *The Five Civilized Tribes*. Norman: University of Oklahoma Press.

Fox, Elliot. 2002. Director of Land Management with Blood Tribe. Interview by Christopher Alcantara, Alberta, Canada, October 16.

Fraser of Allander Institute. 2001. *Promoting Business Start-ups: A New Strategic Formula*. Final Report to the Fraser of Allander Institute for Research on the Scottish Economy. Glasgow: University of Strathclyde.

Frederick, Howard, and Ella Henry. 2004. Innovation and Entrepreneurship Amongst Pakeha and Maori in New Zealand. In Curt Stiles and Craig Galbraith eds., *Ehtnic Entrepreneurship: Structure and Practice*. Amsterdam: Elsevier Science, Ltd.

Friedman, David. 2000. *Law's Order: What Economics Has to Do with Law and Why It Matters*. Princeton: Princeton University Press.

Friedman, Milton. 1953. The Methodology of Positive Economics. In *Essays in Positive Economics*. Chicago: University of Chicago Press.

Galbraith, Craig, and Neil Kay. 1986. Towards a Theory of Multinational Enterprise. *Journal of Economic Behavior and Organization* 7: 3–19.

Galbraith, Craig, and Curt Stiles. 2003. Expectations of Indian Reservation Gaming: Entrepreneurial Activity Within a Context of Traditional Land Tenure and Wealth Acquisition. *Journal of Developmental Entrepreneurship* 8(2): 93–111.

Gambling Answers. 2003. *States in United States with Casinos*. Online: http://www.gamblinganswers.com/casinos/country/US/. Cited: November 12, 2003.

Garfield, Seth. 2001. *Indigenous Struggle in the Heart of Brazil*. Durham, NC: Duke University Press.

———. 2004. A Nationalist Environment: Indians, Nature, and the Construction of the Xingu National Park in Brazil. *Luso-Brazilian Review* 41(1): 139–67.

Garfield, Viola. 1945. A Research Problem in Northwest Indian Economies. *American Anthropologist* 47: 626–30.

General Accounting Office (GAO). 1997. *Tax Policy: A Profile of the Indian Gaming Industry*. GAO/GGD-97-91. Washington, DC: GAO.

———. 2001. *Indian Issues: Improvements Needed in Tribal Recognition Process*. GAO-02-49. Washington, DC: GAO.

George, Larry. 2002. Land and Governance Manager with Cowichan Tribes. Interview by Christopher Alcantara, British Columbia, Canada, April 17.

Getches, David. 1988. Management and Marketing of Indian Water: From Conflict to Pragmatism. *University of Colorado Law Review* 58: 515–549.

Getches, David, Charles Wilkinson, and Robert Williams, Jr. 1993. *Cases and Materials on Federal Indian Law* (3rd ed.). St. Paul, MN: West Group.

———. 1998. *Cases and Materials on Federal Indian Law* (4th ed.). St. Paul, MN: West Publishing Company.

Glaeser, Edward, Rafael La Porta, Florencio Lopez-de-Silanes, and Andrei Shleifer. 2004. Do Institutions Cause Growth? *NBER Working Paper No. 10568*. National Bureau of Economic Research, Washington, DC.

Goldberg-Ambrose, Carole. 1997. *Planting Tail Feathers: Tribal Survival and Public Law 280*. Los Angeles, CA: University of California.

Greaves, Thomas. 1996. Tribal Rights. In Stephen Brush and Doreen Stabinski eds., *Valuing Local Knowledge: Indigenous People and Intellectual Property rights*. Washington, DC: Island Press.

Grinnell, George. 1923. *Cheyenne Indians, Their History and Ways of Life*, 2 vols. New Haven, CT: Yale University Press.

Grumet, Robert. 1979. Managing the Fur Trade: The Coast Tsimshian to 1862. In Stephen Brush and Doreen Stabinski eds., *The Development of Political Organizations in Native North America*. Washington, DC: *Proceedings of the American Ethnological Society*.

Gruszecki, Debra. 2003. Casinos Tell Lawmakers of Tax Impact. *The Times*, September 3.

Gwartney, James, Robert Lawson, and Randall Holcombe. 1999. Economic
    Freedom and the Environment for Economic Growth. *Journal of Institutional
    and Theoretical Economics* 155(4): 643–63.

Gwartney, James, Robert Lawson, with Neil Emerick. 2003. *Economic Freedom of
    the World: 2003 Annual Report.* Vancouver, BC: Fraser Institute.

Habib, Michel A., and D. Bruce Johnsen, 1999. The Financing and Deployment
    of Specific Assets. *Journal of Finance* 54(2): 693–720.

————.2000. The Private Placement of Debt and Outside Equity as an
    Information Revelation Mechanism. *Review of Financial Studies* 13(4): 1017–55.

Haddock, David. 1994. Foreseeing Confiscation by the Sovereign: Lessons from
    the American West. In Terry Anderson and Peter Hill eds., *The Political
    Economy of the American West.* Lanham, MD: Rowan and Littlefield
    Publishers.

————. 1998. Sizing Up Sovereigns. In Terry Anderson and Peter Hill eds.,
    Environmental Federalism. Lanham, MD: Rowman and Littlefield Publishers.

————. 2003. Force, Threat, Negotiation: The Private Enforcement of Rights. In
    Terry Anderson and Fred McChesney eds., *Property Rights: Cooperation,
    Conflict, and Law.* Princeton, NJ: Princeton University Press.

————. 2005. To Tax Indians or Not to Tax Indians? That is the Question.
    Working Paper. Northwestern University School of Law, Evanston, Illinois.

Haddock, David, and Thomas Hall. 1983. The Impact of Making Rights
    Inalienable. *Supreme Court Economic Review* 2(1): 1–41.

Haddock, David, and Robert Miller. 2004. Can a Sovereign Protect Investors
    From Itself? Tribal Institutions to Spur Reservation Investment. *Journal of
    Small and Emerging Business Law* 8(2): 173–228.

Haines, Francis. 1970. *The Buffalo.* New York: Thomas Y. Crowell.

Hall, Robert, and Charles Jones. 1999. Why do Some Countries Produce so Much
    More Output per Worker than Others? *Quarterly Journal of Economics* 114(1):
    83–116.

Hansen, Robert, and John Lott, Jr. 1996. Externalities and Corporate Objectives in
    a World with Diversified Shareholders/Consumers. *Journal of Financial and
    Quantitative Analysis* 31(1): 43–68.

Hardin, Garrett. 1968. The Tragedy of the Commons. *Science* 162(December):
    1243–48.

Harris, Cole. 2002. *Making Native Space: Colonialism, Resistance, and Reserves in
    British Columbia.* Vancouver: UBC Press.

Harris, Douglas. 2001. *Fish, Law, and Colonialism: The Legal Capture of Salmon in
    British Columbia.* Toronto: University of Toronto Press.

Harris, R. Cole, ed. 1987. *Historical Atlas of Canada* 1. Toronto: University of
    Toronto Press.

Harvey, Sioux. 1996. Two Models to Sovereignty: A Comparative History of the
    Nashantucket Pequot Tribal Nation and the Navajo Nation. *Native American
    Culture and Research Journal* 20: 147–95.

Hearne, Samuel. 1969. *A Journey from Prince of Wales's Fort in Hudson's Bay to the Northern Ocean in the Years 1769, 1770, 1771, and 1772*. Westport, CT: Greenwood Press.

Heidenreich, Conrad, and Arthur Ray. 1976. *The Early Fur Trade: A Study in Cultural Interaction*. Toronto: McClelland and Stewart.

Helm, Jane, ed. 1981. *Handbook of North American Indians—Subarctic 6*. Washington, DC: Smithsonian Institution Press.

Herskovits, Melville. 1940. *The Economic Life of Primitive Peoples*. London: Knopf.

Hickerson, Harold. 1967. *Land Tenure of the Rainy Lake Chippewa at the Beginning of the 19th Century*. Washington, DC: Smithsonian Press.

Higgs, Robert. 1982. Legally Induced Technical Regress in the Washington Salmon Fishery. *Research in Economic History* 7: 55–86.

Hodge, Frederick. 1910. *Handbook of American Indians North of Mexico*. Washington, DC: Government Printing Office.

Hoffman, Elizabeth, Kevin McCabe, and Vernon Smith. 1998. Behavioral Foundations of Reciprocity: Experimental Economics and Evolutionary Psychology. *Economic Inquiry* 36: 335–52.

Hoig, Stan. 1993. *Tribal Wars of the Southern Plains*. Norman: University of Oklahoma Press.

Holder, Preston. 1970. *The Hoe and the Horse on the Plains: A Study of Cultural Development among North American Indians*. Lincoln: University of Nebraska Press.

Hosley, Edward. 1981. Kolchan. In June Helm ed., *Handbook of North American Indians–Subarctic 6*. Washington, DC: Smithsonian Institution Press.

Hudson, William. 1901. *The Famous Missions of California*. New York: Dodge Publishing.

Huffman, James. 1992. An Exploratory Essay on Native Americans and Environmentalism. *University of Colorado Law Review* 63(4): 901–20.

Hurt, F. Douglas. 1987. *Indian Agriculture in America: Prehistory to the Present*. Lawrence: University of Kansas Press.

Innis, Harold. 1956. *The Fur Trade in Canada*. Toronto: University of Toronto Press.

Isenberg, Andrew. 2000. *The Destruction of the Bison: An Environmental History, 1750–1920*. Cambridge: Cambridge University Press.

Jackson, Robert, and Edward Castillo 1996. *Indians, Franciscans, and Spanish Colonization: The Impact of the Mission System on California Indians*. Albuquerque: University of New Mexico Press.

Jacobs, Wilbur. 1972. *Dispossessing the American Indian: Indians and Whites on the Colonial Frontier*. New York: Charles Scribner's Sons.

Jensen, Michael, and William Meckling. 1976. Theory of the Firm: Managerial Behavior, Agency Costs and Ownership Structure. *Journal of Financial Economics* 3(4): 305–60.

Jimenez, Vanessa, and Soo C. Song. 1998. Concurrent Tribal and State Jurisdiction Under Public Law 280. *American University Law Review* 47(August): 1627–1707.

Joe, Abraham, and Angus. 2002. Elders and Members of the Cowichan Tribes Lands Investigation Committee. Interview by Christopher Alcantara, British Columbia, Canada, April 17.

Johansen, Bruce, ed. 1999. *The Encyclopedia of Native American Economic History*. Westport, CT: Greenwood Press.

Johnsen, D. Bruce. 1986a. The Formation and Protection of Property Rights among the Southern Kwakiutl Indians. *Journal of Legal Studies* 15(1): 41–67.

———. 1986b. Wealth is Value. *Journal of Legal Studies* 15: 263–88.

———. 1995. The Quasi-Rent Structure of Corporate Enterprise: A Transaction Cost Theory. *Emory Law Journal* 44: 1277–1356.

———. 2001. Customary Law, Scientific Knowledge, and Fisheries Management Among Northwest Coast Tribes. *New York University Environmental Law Journal* 10(1): 1–69.

———. 2003. A Critical Look at Socially Responsible Investing. *Journal of Business Ethics* 43(3): 219–22.

Johnson, Ronald, and Gary Libecap. 1982. Contracting Problems and Regulation: The Case of the Fishery. *American Economic Review* 72(5): 1005–22.

Jones, Laura. 1997. Introduction. In Laura Jones and Michael Walker eds., *Fish or Cut Bait: The Case for Individual Transferable Quotas in the Salmon Fishery of British Columbia*. Vancouver, BC: The Fraser Institute.

Jorgensen, Miriam. 2000. Bringing the Background Forward: Evidence from Indian Country on the Social and Cultural Determinants of Economic Development. Ph.D. dissertation, John F. Kennedy School of Government, Harvard University, Cambridge, MA.

Jorgensen, Miriam, and Jonathan Taylor. 2000. *What Determines Indian Economic Success? Evidence from Tribal and Individual Indian Enterprises*. Cambridge: Harvard Project on American Indian Economic Development, JFK School of Government, Harvard University.

———. 2000a. *Patters of Indian Enterprise Success: A Statistical Analysis of Tribal and Individual Indian Enterprise Performance*. Report to the National Congress of American Indians. Cambridge: Harvard Project on American Indian Economic Development, JFK School, Harvard University.

Kay, Neil. 1997. *Patterns in Corporate Evolution*. London: Oxford University Press.

Keefer, Philip, and Stephen Knack. 1997. Why Don't Poor Countries Catch Up? A Cross-national Test of An Institutional Explanation. *Economic Inquiry* 35(3): 590–602.

Kehoe, Thomas. 1978. Paleo-Indian Drives. *Plains Anthropologist* 23: 79–83.

Kennard, Edwards. 1979. Hopi Economy and Subsistence. In *Handbook of North American Indians* 9. Washington, DC: Smithsonian Institution.

Khanna, Tarun, and Krishna Palepu. 1997. Why Focused Strategies May be Wrong for Emerging Markets. *Harvard Business Review* 75(4): 41–51.

Klein, Benjamin, Robert Crawford, and Armen Alchian. 1978. Vertical Integration, Appropriable Rents, and the Competitive Contracting Process. *Journal of Law and Economics* 21(3): 297–326.

Knack, Steven, and Philip Keefer. 1995. Institutions and Economic Performance: Cross-Country Tests Using Alternative Measures. *Economics and Politics* 7(3): 207–27.

Krauss, Michael. 1998. The Condition of Native North American Languages: The Need for Realistic Assessment and Action. *International Journal of the Sociology of Language* 132: 9–21.

Krech III, Shepard. 1999. *The Ecological Indian: Myth and History.* New York: Norton.

LaDuke, Winona. 1999. Native Struggles for Land and Life. *Multinational Monitor* 20(21): 1–6.

Laird, Carobeth. 1976. *The Chemehuevis.* Banning, CA: Malki Museum Press.

Lands Committee. 2002. Piikani Land Management Department. Interview by Christopher Alcantara, Alberta, Canada, September 26.

Lawson, Michael. 1982. *Dammed Indians: The Pick-Sloan Plan and the Missouri River Sioux, 1944–1980.* Norman: University of Oklahoma Press.

Leacock, Eleanor. 1954. *The Montagnais 'Hunting Territory' and the Fur Trade,* Memoir No. 78. Menasha, WI: American Anthropological Association.

Lehman, Dina. 1997. The Buffalo Harvest. *ICE Case Studies.* Washington, DC: The Inventory of Conflict and Environment, American University, December 18. Online: http://www.american.edu/ted/ice/buffalo.htm. Cited: July 31, 2005.

Lekson, Stephen. 2002. *Salado Archaeology of the Upper Gila, New Mexico.* Tucson: University of Arizona Press.

Levie, Jonathan, and Laura Steele. 2000. *Global Entrepreneurship Monitor.* Glasgow: University of Strathclyde.

Libecap, Gary, and Ronald Johnson. 1980. Legislating Commons: The Navajo Tribal Council and the Navaho Range. *Economic Inquiry* 18(1): 69–86.

Linton, Ralph. 1942. Land Tenure in Aboriginal America. In Oliver LaFarge ed., *The Changing Indians.* Norman: University of Oklahoma Press.

Lippert, Owen. 1998. Death by a Thousand Courts. In *Fraser Forum.* Vancouver, BC: The Fraser Institute, January. Online: http://oldfraser.lexi.net/publications/forum/1998/january/land_claims.html. Cited: November 15, 2004.

Lips, Julius. 1947. Notes on Montagnais-Naskapi Economy. *Ethnos* 12: 1–78.

Lipset, Seymour Martin. 1960. *Political Man: The Social Basis of Modern Politics.* New York: Doubleday.

Little Chief, Marilyn. 2002. Financial Adjuster at Siksika First Nation. Interview by Christopher Alcantara, Alberta, Canada, October 1.

Llewellyn, Karl, and E. Adamson Hoebel, eds. 1973. *The Cheyenne Way: Conflict and Case Law in Primitive Jurisprudence.* Norman: University of Oklahoma Press.

Lowie, Robert. 1927. *Primitive Society*. New York: Boni and Liveright.

———. 1954. *Indians of the Plain*. New York: McGraw-Hill Book Company.

Macdonald, Tania Collier. 2003. Membertou Says Toxic Waste Hurt Fishing, Wants Compensation. *Cape Breton Post*, June 17.

Machlup, Fritz, and Martha Taber. 1960. Bilateral Monopoly, Successive Monopoly, and Vertical Integration. *Economica* 27(1): 101–19.

MacLeod, Kevin. 2005. Member of Lac La Ronge Indian Band. Interview by Christopher Alcantara, Saskatchewan, Canada, July 15.

Manne, Henry. 1965. Mergers and the Market for Corporate Control. *Journal of Political Economy* 73(2): 110–20.

Margolin, Malcolm. 1978. *The Ohlone Way: Indian Life in the San Francisco-Monterey Bay Area*. Berkeley, CA: Heyday Books.

Marsh, George. 1874. *The Earth as Modified by Human Action*. New York: Scribner, Armstrong & Co.

Martin, Aurene. 2003. Acting Assistant Secretary of Indian Affairs, Department of the Interior. *Statement before the Committee on Indian Affairs United States Senate on the Indian Gaming Regulatory Act*. Washington, DC, July 9.

Martin, Paul, and Richard Klein, eds. 1984. *Quaternary Extinctions: A Prehistoric Revolution*. Tucson: University of Arizona Press.

Martin, Paul, and Christine Szuter. 1999. War Zones and Game Sinks in Lewis and Clark's West. *Conservation Biology* 13(February): 36–45.

Mason, Dale. 2000. *Indian Gaming: Tribal Sovereignty and American Politics*. Norman: University of Oklahoma Press.

McChesney, Fred. 1987. Rent Extraction and Rent Creation in the Economic Theory of Regulation. *Journal of Legal Studies* 16(January): 101–18.

McClung, Tom. 1997. Bureaucratic Management versus Private Property: ITQs in New Zealand after 10 Years. In Laura Jones and Michael Walker eds., *Fish or Cut Bait: The Case for Individual Transferable Quotas in the Salmon Fishery of British Columbia*. Vancouver, BC: The Fraser Institute.

McCool, Daniel. 1987. *Command of the Waters: Iron Triangles, Federal Water Development, and Indian Water*. Berkeley: University of California Press.

McLish, Thomas. 1988. Tribal Sovereign Immunity: Searching for Sensible Limits. *Columbia Law Review* (January): 173–93.

McManus, John. 1972. An Economic Analysis of Indian Behavior in the North American Fur Trade. *Journal of Economic History* 32: 36–53.

McMillan, Alan. 1999. *Since the Time of the Transformers: The Ancient Heritage of the Nuu-Chah-Nulth, Ditidaht and Makah*. Vancouver: UBC Press.

Membertou First Nation. 2003. Auditor General Presentation, March 31.

Mika, Karin. 1995. Private Dollars on the Reservation: Will Recent Native American Economic Development Amount to Cultural Assimilation. *New Mexico Law Review* 25(Winter): 23–34.

Miklas, Christine, and Charles Wilkinson. 1988. *Indian Tribes as Sovereign Governments : A Sourcebook on Federal-tribal History, Law, and Policy*. Oakland, CA : American Indian Resources Institute.

Miller, Char, ed. 2001. *Fluid Arguments: Five Centuries of Western Water Conflict.* Tucson: University of Arizona Press.

Miller, Christopher, and George Hamell. 1986. New Perspective on Indian-White Contact: Cultural Symbols and Colonial Trade. *Journal of American History* 73: 311–28.

Miller, Robert. 2001. Economic Development in Indian Country: Will Capitalism or Socialism Succeed? *Oregon Law Review* 80(3): 757–859.

Milloy, John. 1991. "Our Country": The Significance of the Buffalo Resource for a Plains Cree Sense of Territory. In Kerry Abel and Jean Friesen eds., *Aboriginal Resource Use in Canada: Historical and Legal Aspects,* 51–70. Manitoba Studies in Native History: University of Manitoba Press.

Mishkin, Bernard. 1940. *Rank and Warfare Among the Plains Indians.* Monographs of the American Ethnological Society III. New York: J.J. Augustin Publisher.

Mithun, Marianne. 1999. *The Languages of Native North America.* Cambridge: Cambridge University Press.

Morantz, Toby. 1986. Historical Perspectives on Family Hunting Territories in Eastern James Bay. *Anthropologica.* New Series 28: 64–91.

Morriss, Andrew. 1998. Miners, Vigilantes & Cattlemen: Overcoming Free Rider Problems in the Private Provision of Law. *Land and Water Law Review* 33(2): 581–696.

———. 2001. Lessons from the Development of Western Water Law for Emerging Water Markets: Common Law vs. Central Planning. *Oregon Law Review* 80(3): 861–946.

Murphy, Robert. 1957. Intergroup Hostility and Social Cohesion. *American Anthropologist* 59: 1018–35.

Myers, Stewart. 1977. Determinants of Corporate Borrowing. *Journal of Financial Economics* 5(2): 147–76.

National Gambling Impact Study Commission. 1999. *National Gambling Impact Study Commission Report.* Washington, DC: U.S. Government Printing Office. Online: http://govinfo.library.unt.edu/ngisc/reports/2.pdf. Cited: November 15, 2004.

National Indian Gaming Association. 2003. *Indian Gaming Facts.* Online: http://www.indiangaming.org/library/indian-gaming-facts/index.shtml. Cited: November 12, 2003.

National Indian Gaming Commission (NIGC). 2002. *Tribal Gaming Commission Survey.* Washington, DC.

———. 2004a. *Gaming Revenues by Region 2003 vs. 2002.* Washington, DC. Online: http://www.nigc.gov/nigc/tribes/Gaming_Rev_2003_2002.jsp. Cited: November 15, 2004.

———. 2004b. *Gaming Revenues 2004–2002.* Washington, DC. Online: http://www.nigc.gov/nigc/tribes/trigamrev2004to2003.jsp. Cited: November 15, 2004.

———. 2004c. *Growth in Indian Gaming 1995–2003.* Washington, DC. Online: http://www.nigc.gov/nigc/tribes/pr_revenue_2003.jsp. Cited: November 15, 2004.

National Water Commission. 1973. *Water Policies for the Future—Final Report to the President and to the Congress of the United States.* Washington, DC: National Water Commission.

Nelson, Richard. 1973. *Hunters of the Northern Forest.* Chicago: University of Chicago Press.

Nemoto, Akihiko. 2002. Dynamics of Aboriginal Land Use Institutions: The Rise and Fall of Community Control over Reserve Systems in the Lil'Wat Nation, Canada. *Canadian Journal of Native Studies* 22: 207–37.

Netboy, Anthony. 1958. *Salmon of the Pacific Northwest: Fish vs. Dams.* Portland, OR: Binfords and Mort.

Newsday.com. 2003. *Mohawks Settle Tribal Tax Dispute*, August 6. Online: http://www.newsday.com/news/local/wire/. . . -mohawk-tobacco806aug06, 0,2283565.sto. (Hard copy on file with authors).

North, Douglass. 1990. *Institutions, Institutional Change and Economic Performance.* Cambridge: Cambridge University Press.

North, Douglass, and Robert Paul Thomas. 1977. The First Economic Revolution. *Economic History Review (Second Series)* 30(2): 229–41.

Notzke, Claudia. 1985. *Indian Reserves in Canada: Development Programs of the Stoney and Peigan Reserves in Alberta.* Marburg/Lahn: Im Selbstverlag des Geographischen Instituts der Universität Marburg.

Oberg, Kalervo. 1934. Crime and Punishment in Tlingit Society. *American Anthropologist* 36(2): 145–55.

———. 1973. *The Social Economy of the Tlingit Indians.* Seattle: University of Washington Press.

Ostrom, Elinor. 2000. Private and Common Property Rights. In Boudewijn Bouckaret and Gerrit De Geest eds., *Encyclopedia of Law and Economics II.* Cheltenham: Edward Elgar.

Otis, Delos Sacket. 1973. *The Dawes Act and the Allotment of Indian Lands.* Edited and with Introduction by Francis Paul Prucha. Norman: Oklahoma University Press.

Owlchild, Emil. 2002. Land Manager at Siksika First Nation. Interview by Christopher Alcantara, Alberta, Canada, October 1.

Parkman, Francis. 1910. *La Salle and the Discovery of the Great West.* Boston, MA: Little Brown and Co.

Payne, Brenda. 2002. Acting Deputy Registrar with the Indian Affairs and Northern Development. Interview by Christopher Alcantara, Hull, Quebec, Canada, July 15.

Peltzman, Sam. 1976. Toward a More General Theory of Regulation. *Journal of Law and Economics* 19(2): 211–40.

Peredo, Ana Maria, Robert Anderson, Craig Galbraith, Benson Honig, and Leo Paul Dana. 2004. Towards a Theory of Indigenous Entrepreneurship. *International Journal of Entrepreneurship and Small Business* 1(1/2): 1–20.

Piddocke, Stuart. 1968. The Potlatch System of the Southern Kwakiutl: A New Perspective. In Edward LeClair, Jr. and Harold Schneider eds., *Economic*

Anthropology: Readings in Theory and Analysis. New York, Holt, Rinehart and Winston.

Pipes, Richard. 1999. *Property and Freedom.* New York: Alfred A. Knopf.

Posner, Richard. 1980. A Theory of Primitive Society, with Special Reference to Law. *Journal of Law and Economics* 23: 1–53.

Ray, Alan. 2002. Treaty and Lands Manager at Sandy Lake First Nation. Telephone conversation with Christopher Alcantara, June 10.

Ray, Arthur. 1974. *Indians in the Fur Trade: Their Role as Hunters, Trappers and Middlemen in the Lands Southwest of Hudson Bay, 1660–1870.* Toronto: University of Toronto Press.

———. 1987. Bayside Trade, 1720–1780. In R. Cole Harris ed., *Historical Atlas of Canada* 1, Plate 60. Toronto: University of Toronto Press.

Ray, Arthur, and Donald Freeman. 1978. *"Give Us Good Measure": An Economic Analysis of Relations Between the Indians and the Hudson's Bay Company Before 1763.* Toronto: University of Toronto Press.

Rea, K. J. 1991. *A Guide to Canadian Economic History.* Toronto: Canadian Scholars' Press.

Reeves, Brian. 1990. Communal Bison Hunters. In Leslie Davis and Michael Wilson eds., *Hunters of the Recent Past.* London: Unwin Hyman.

Rich, E. E. 1958. *The Hudson's Bay Company 1670–1870*, 2 vols. London: Hudson's Bay Record Society.

———. 1960. Trade Habits and Economic Motivation among the Indians of North America. *Canadian Journal of Economics and Political Science* 26: 35–53.

Richards, John. 2003. A New Agenda for Strengthening Canada's Aboriginal Population: Individual Treaty Benefits, Reduced Transfers to Bands and Own-Source Taxation. *C.D. Howe Institute Backgrounder* 66, February.

Richter, Daniel. 2001. *Facing East From Indian Country: A Native History of Early America.* Cambridge: Harvard University Press.

Rider, Robert. 1993. War Pillage, and Markets. *Public Choice* 75(2): 149–56.

Robbins, K. 2000. Reflecting on the Numbers: Media Hype Breeds Misperception. *American Indian Report*, September 22.

Robson, Joseph. 1752. *An Account of Six Years Residence in Hudson Bay, From 1733 to 1736, and 1744 to 1747.* London: Printed for J. Payne and J. Bouquet in Pater-Noster-Row.

Roe, Frank. 1955. *The Indian and the Horse.* Norman: University of Oklahoma Press.

Rogers, Edward, and J. Garth Taylor. 1981. Northern Ojibwa. In *Handbook of North American Indians—Subarctic* 6. Washington D.C: Smithsonian Institution.

Royal, Darcie. 2002. Housing Administrator at Siksika First Nation. Interview by Christopher Alcantara, Alberta, Canada, October 1.

Rubin, Rick. 1999. *Naked Against the Rain: The People of Lower Columbia River 1770–1830.* Portland, OR: Far Shore Press.

Salisbury, Neal. 1996. The Indians' Old World: Native Americans and the Coming of Europeans. *William and Mary Quarterly* 53: 435–58.

Sauer, Raymond. 2001. The Political Economy of Gambling Regulation. *Managerial and Decision Economics* 22: 5–15.

Schumpeter, Joseph. 1934. *The Theory of Economic Development.* New Brunswick, NJ: Transaction Publishers.

Scott, Anthony. 1989. Conceptual Origins of Rights Based Fishing. In P. Neher, R. Arnason, and N. Mollett eds., *Rights Based Fishing: Proceedings of a Workshop on the Scientific Foundations for Rights Based Fishing.* Reykjavik, Iceland, June 27–July 1, 1988. Netherlands: Kluwer Academic Publishers.

Scott, James. 1998. *Seeing Like a State: How Certain Schemes to Improve the Human Condition Have Failed.* New Haven, CT: Yale University Press.

Secoy, Frank. 1953. *Changing Military Patterns of the Great Plains.* Monographs of the American Ethnological Society 21.

Secoy, Frank. 1971 [1953]. *Changing Military Patterns of the Great Plains Indians (Seventeenth Century through Early 19th Century).* Lincoln: University of Nebraska Press.

Secoy, Frank. 1992 [1953]. *Changing Military Patterns of the Great Plains Indians (Seventeenth Century through Early 19th Century).* Lincoln: University of Nebraska Press.

Selden, Ron. 2001. Economic Attitudes Must Change. *Indian Country Monitor,* June 13.

Shanks, Gordon. 2003. Interview by Jacqueline Thayer Scott. Ottawa, Canada, June 24.

Shipek, Florence. 1982. Kumeyaay Socio-political Structure. *Journal of California and Great Basin Anthropology* 4: 293–303.

———. 1986. The Impact of Europeans Upon Kumeyaay Culture. In *The Impact of European Exploration and Settlement in Local Native Americans,* 13–25. San Diego, CA: Cabrillo Historical Association.

———. 1987. *Pushed Into the Rocks.* Lincoln: University of Nebraska Press.

Siksika Chief and Council. 2002. *Siksika Housing Policy Manual.* Gleichen, AB: Siksika Chief and Council, November.

Simmel, George. 1955. *Conflict and the Group of Web Affiliations.* Trans. Kurt Wolf and Reinhard Bendix. Glencoe, NY: The Free Press.

Skaperdas, Stergios. 1992. Cooperation, Conflict, and Power in the Absence of Property Rights. *American Economic Review* 82(4): 720–39.

Skari, Andrea. 1992. The Tribal Judiciary: A Primer for Policy Development. In Stephen Cornell and Joseph Kalt eds., *What Can Tribes Do? Strategies in American Indian Economic Development.* Los Angeles, CA: UCLA American Indian Studies Center.

Smith, Ferris. 2002. Service Manager at Siksika First Nation. Interview by Christopher Alcantara, Alberta, Canada, October 1.

Smith, Marian. 1938. The War Complex of the Plains Indians. *Proceedings of the American Philosophical Society* 78(3): 425–64.

Smith, Vernon. 1975. The Primitive Hunter Culture, Pleistocene Extinction, and the Rise of Agriculture. *Journal of Political Economy* 83(4): 727–55.

Snow, Alpheus. 1921. *The Question of Aborigines in the Law and Practice of Nations.* New York: G. P. Putnam's Sons.

Soto, Onell. 2003. Agents Say Indian Casinos Probes Stymied. *San Diego Union-Tribune*, September 26.

Speck, Frank. 1915. The Basis of American Indian Ownership of Land. *Old Penn Weekly Review* (January 16): 491–95.

———. 1939. Aboriginal Conservators. *Bird Lore* 40: 258–61.

Speck, Frank, and Loren Eisley. 1942. Montagnais-Naskapi Bands and Family Hunting Districts of the Central and Southeastern Labrador Peninsula. *American Philosophical Society Proceedings* 85: 215–42.

Sproat, Gilbert Malcolm. 1868. *Scenes and Studies of Savage Life.* London: Smith, Elder and Co.

Starna, William. 1982. Review of American Indian Environments, by Christopher Vecsey and Robert Venables. *American Anthropologist* 84(182): 468.

State of Connecticut, Division of Special Revenue. 2004. *Gaming Revenue and Statistics: Statistics for Tribal Casinos.* Newington, CT. Online: http://www.ct.gov/dosr/cwp/view.asp?a=3&q=290840&dosrNav=|. Cited: November 15, 2004.

Steckel, Richard, and Joseph Prince. 2001. Tallest in the World: Native Americans of the Great Plains in the Nineteenth Century. *American Economic Review* 91(March): 287–94.

Stevens, Ernest. 2001. Chairman, National Indian Gaming Association. Testimony before the US Senate Committee on Indian Affairs. Oversight Hearing of the National Gaming Commission, Washington, DC, July 25.

———. 2003. Chairman, U.S. Senate, Committee on Indian Affairs. Statement before the Indian Gaming Oversight Hearings. Washington, DC, May 14.

Steward, Julian. 1938. *Basin-plateau Aboriginal Sociopolitical Groups.* Washington, DC: Bureau of American Ethnology, Bulletin 120, 253.

Strickland, Rennard, and Charles Wilkinson, eds. 1982. *Felix S. Cohen's Handbook of Federal Indian Law.* Charlottesville, VA: The Michie Company.

Sullivan, Rhonda. 2002. Land Administrator at Cowichan Tribes. Interview by Christopher Alcantara, British Columbia, Canada, April 16.

Suttles, Wayne. 1960. Affinal Ties, Subsistence, and Prestige among the Coast Salish. *American Anthropologist* 62: 296–305.

———. 1968. Coping with Abundance: Subsistence on the Northwest Coast. In Richard Lee and Irvin DeVore eds., *Man the Hunter.* Chicago: Aldine, 56–68.

———, ed. 1990. History of Research in Ethnology. In *Handbook of North American Indians* 7. Washington, DC: Smithsonian Institution.

Tanner, Adrian. 1979. *Bringing Animals Home: Religious Ideology and Mode of Production of the Mistassini Cree Hunters.* Social and Economics Studies 23.

St. John's, Newfoundland: Institute of Social and Economic Research, Memorial University of Newfoundland.

Teece, David. 1982. Towards a Theory of the Multiproduct Firm. *Journal of Economic Behavior and Organization* 3: 39–63.

Testerman, Jeff. 2004. Government Tells Tribe to Toe the Line on Casinos. *St. Petersburg Times*, February 25.

Thompson, William, and Robert Schmidt. 2002. Not Exactly 'A Fair Share:' Revenue Sharing and Native American Casinos in Wisconsin. *Wisconsin Policy Research Institute Report* 15(1). Thiensville, WI: Wisconsin Policy Research Institute, February.

Thwaites, Reuben, ed. 1896–1901. *The Jesuit Relations and Allied Documents, 1610–1791*, 73 vols. Cleveland, OH. The Burrows Brothers Company.

Tollison, Robert. 1997. Rent Seeking. In Dennis Mueller ed., *Perspectives on Public Choice: A Handbook*. Cambridge: Cambridge University Press.

Trigger, Bruce, ed. 1978. *Handbook of North American Indians (Northeast)*. Washington, DC: Smithsonian Institution.

———. 1990. *The Huron Farmers of the North*. Fort Worth, TX: Holt, Rinehart, and Winston.

Trosper, Ronald. 1978. American Indian Relative Ranching Efficiency. *American Economic Review* 68(4): 503–16.

Tullock, Gordon. 1967. The Welfare Costs of Tariffs, Monopolies, and Theft. *Western Economic Journal* 5: 224–32.

———. 1993. *Rent Seeking*. Hants, England: Edward Elgar.

Tully, James. 1994. Rediscovering America: The Two Treatises and Aboriginal Rights. In G. A. J. Rogers ed., *Locke's Philosophy: Content and Context*. Oxford: Clarendon Press.

———. 1995. Property, Self-Government and Consent. *Canadian Journal of Political Science* 23(1): 105–33.

Turney-High, Harry H. 1971 [1949]. *Primitive Warfare: Its Practice and Concepts*. Columbia, SC: University of South Carolina Press.

Twain, Mark. 1897. Pudd'nhead Wilson's New Calendar. In *Following the Equator*. Hartford: CT: American Publishing Company.

U.S. Census Bureau. 1990. *United States Census 1990*. Washington, DC.

———. 2000. *United States Census 2000*. Washington, DC.

U.S. Commission on Civil Rights. 2003. *A Quiet Crisis: Federal Funding and Unmet Needs in Indian Country*, July. Washington, DC: U.S. Commission on Civil Rights. Online: http://www.usccr.gov/pubs/na0703/na0204.pdf. Cited: November 11, 2004.

U.S. Congress. Senate Report No. 699, July 29, 1953. Washington, DC.

U.S. Department of the Interior. 1997. *Statement of Secretary of the Interior Bruce Babbitt on the New Mexico Gaming Compacts*. Press release, August 23. Washington, DC. Online: http://www.doi.gov/news/archives/indnmcom.html. Cited: November 15, 2004.

U.S. Department of the Interior, Bureau of Indian Affairs. 1999. *Indian Labor Force Report*. Washington, DC.

U.S. National Water Commission. 1973. *Water Policies for the Future—Final Report to the President and to the Congress of the United States*. Washington, DC: U.S. National Water Commission.

Umbeck, John. 1981a. Might Makes Right: A Theory of the Foundation and Initial Distribution of Property Rights. *Economic Inquiry* 19(1): 38–59.

———. 1981b. *A Theory of Property Rights with Applications to the California Gold Rush*. Ames: Iowa State University Press.

UNESCO Institute for Statistics. 2003. *Financing Education—Investments and Returns, Analysis of the World Education Indicators, 2002 Edition*. Paris, France: UNESCO/OECD.

Usher, Peter. 1992. Property as the Basis of Inuit Hunting Rights. In Terry Anderson ed., *Property Rights and Indian Economies*. Lanham, MD: Rowman and Littlefield Publishers.

Vinje, David. 1996. Native American Economic Development on Selected Reservations: A Comparative Study. *The American Journal of Economics and Sociology* 55: 427–43.

Walke, Roger. 2000. Indian-Related Federal Spending Trends, FY 1975–2001. U.S. Congressional Research Service Memorandum, March 1, 2000. In *Report of the Committee on the Budget, United States Senate, S. Con. Res 101*, together with Additional and Minority Views. Senate Report 106–251, 199–251.

Walker, Ruth. 2001. Indian Land Claims Flood Ottawa, *Christian Science Monitor*, March 20.

Walter, Emily, R. Michael M'Gonigle, and Celeste McKay. 2000. Fishing Around the Law: The Pacific Salmon Management System as a "Structural Infringement" of Aboriginal Rights. *McGill Law Journal* 45(1): 263–313.

WCCO-TV. 2003. I-team Investigates Federal Subsidies for Local Tribe. February 12. Online: http://wcco.com/iteam/local_story_043282036.html. Cited: November 15, 2004.

White, Richard. 1978. The Winning of the West: The Expansion of the Western Sioux in the Eighteenth and Nineteenth Centuries. *Journal of American History* 65(September): 319–43.

Wilgress, Fran. 2002. Land Manager and Chair of the Land Management Committee at Cowichan Tribes. Interview by Christopher Alcantara, British Columbia, Canada, April 16.

Wilkinson, Charles, and John Volkman. 1975. Judicial Review of Indian Treaty Abrogation. *California Law Review* 63(3): 601–61.

Williams, Glyndwr, ed. 1969. *Andrew Graham's Observations on Hudson's Bay, 1767–1791*. London: Hudson's Bay Record Society.

Williams, Robert, Jr. 1990. *The American Indian in Western Legal Thought: The Discourses of Conquest*. New York: Oxford University Press.

Williamson, Oliver. 1975. *Markets and Hierarchies*. New York: Free Press.

————. 1983. Credible Commitments: Using Hostages to Support Exchange. *American Economic Review* 73(3): 519–40.

————. 1984. Credible Commitments: Further Results. *American Economic Review* 74(2): 488–90.

Wilson, Paul. 1992. What Chief Seattle Said. *Environmental Law* 22: 1451–68.

Wilson, Samuel. 1992. That Unmanned Wild Country: Native Americans both Conserved and Transformed New World Environments. *Natural History* (May): 16–17.

Wollenberg, Charles. 2002. *Berkeley, A City in History*. Berkeley: CA: Berkeley Public Library. Online: http://berkeleypubliclibrary.org/system/Chapter1.html. Cited: September 1, 2005.

World Bank. 2005. A Better Investment Climate for Everyone. *World Development Report*. Washington, DC, and Oxford, UK: A Co-Publication of the World Bank and Oxford University Press.

Wright, Harry. 1906. *Indian Deeds of Hampden County, Being Copies of All Land Transfers from the Indians Recorded in the Co. of Hampden*. Boston: New England Historical Society.

Yandle, Bruce. 1983. Bootleggers and Baptists: The Education of a Regulatory Economists. *Regulation* 7(May/June): 12–16.

Zoellner, Tom. 2003. Montana: The Last, Worst Place for Indian Gaming. *Indian Country Today*, August 11.

Cases Cited

Iowa Mutual Insurance Co. V. LaPlante, 480 U.S. 9 (1987).

Joe v. Findlay, 2 C.N.L.R. 58 (1981).

Joe v. Findlay, 2 C.N.L.R. 75 (1987).

Johnstone v. Mistawasis, S.K.Q.B. 240 (2003).

Kennerly v. Montana District Court, 400 U.S. 423 (1971).

Kiowa Tribe v. Manufacturing Technologies, Inc., 523 U.S. 751 (1998).

Knight v. Shoshone & Arapaho Indian Tribes, 670 F.2d 900 (10th Cir. 1982).

Leonard v. Gottfriedson, 1 C.N.L.R. 60 (1982).

Lone Wolf v. Hitchcock, 187 U.S. 553 (1903).

Lummi Indian Tribe v. Hallauer, 9 Indian L. Rep. 3025 (W.D. Wa. 1982).

Menominee v. United States, 391 U.S. 404 (1968).

Merrion v. Jicarilla Apache Tribe, 455. U.S. 130 (1982).

Montana v. Blackfeet Tribe of Indians, 471 U.S. 759 (1985).

Montana v. Shook, 67 P.3d 863 (Mont. 2002), *cert. denied*, 540 U.S. 815 (2003).

Montana v. United States, 450 U.S. 544 (1981).

National Mutual Farmers Union Ins. Companies v. Crow Tribe of Indians, 471 U.S. 845 (1985).

Nevada v. Hicks, 533 U.S. 353 (2001).

Nevada v. United States, 463 U.S. 110 (1983).

New Mexico v. Mescalero Apache Tribe, 462 U.S. 324 (1983).

Nicola Band et al. v. Trans-Can Displays et al., B.C.S.C. 1209 (2000).

Oliphant v. Suquamish Indian Tribe, 435 U.S. 191 (1978).

Paul v. Paul, 2 C.N.L.R. 74 (S.C.C.) (1986).

R. v. Gladstone, 2 S.C.R. 723 (1996).

R. v. N.T.C. Smokehouse Ltd., 2 S.C.R. 672 (1996).

R. v. Sparrow, 70 D.L.R. (4th) (1990).

R. v. Van der Peet, 2 S.C.R. 507 (1996).

Roberts v. Canada, 1 S.C.R. 322 (1989).

Rosebud Sioux Tribe v. McDivitt, 286 F.3d. 1031 (8th Cir. 2002), *cert. denied sub nom Sun Prairie v. McCaleb*, 123 S.Ct. 1255 (2003).

Sandy v. Sandy, 100 D.L.R. (3d) (1978).

Santa Rosa Band of Indians v. Kings County, 532 F.2d 655 (9th Cir. 1975).

Seminole Tribe v. Butterworth, 658 F.2d 310 (1981).

Seminole Tribe of Florida v. Florida, 517 U.S. 44 (1996).

Strate v. A-1 Contractors, 520 U.S. 438 (1997).

Tamiami Partners, Limited v. Miccosukee Tribe of Indians of Florida, 999 F.2d 503 (11th Cir. 1993); 63 F.3d 1030 (11th Cir. 1995).

Tamiami Partners, Ltd. v. Miccosukee Tribe of Indians of Fla; Dexter Lehtinen et al., 177 F.3d 1212 (11th Cir. 1999), *cert. denied*, 529 U.S. 1018 (2000).

United States v. Big Eagle, 881 F.2d 539 (8th Cir. 1989), *cert. denied*, 493 U.S. 1084 (1990).

United States v. Kagama, 118 U.S. 375 (1886).

Washington v. Confederated Bands of Yakima Indian Nation, 439 U.S. 463 (1979).
Washington v. Confederated Tribes of Colville Indian Reservations, 447
    U.S. 134 (1980).
Williams v. Lee, 358 U.S. 217 (1959).
Williams et al. v. Briggs, B.C.S.C. 78 (2001).
Winters v. United States, 207 U.S. 564 (1908).
Worcester v. Georgia, 31 U.S. 515 (1832).

Index